self-injurious behavior

self-injurious behavior

gene–brain–behavior relationships

edited by

stephen r. schroeder

mary lou oster-granite

travis thompson

American Psychological Association   Washington, DC

First Printing February 2002
Second Printing June 2006

Published by
American Psychological Association
750 First Street, NE
Washington, DC 20002
www.apa.org

To order
APA Order Department
P.O. Box 92984
Washington, DC 20090-2984

Tel: (800) 374-2721, Direct: (202) 336-5510
Fax: (202) 336-5502, TDD/TTY: (202) 336-6123
Online: www.apa.org/books/
Email: order@apa.org

In the U.K., Europe, Africa, and the Middle East, copies may be ordered from
American Psychological Association
3 Henrietta Street
Covent Garden, London
WC2E 8LU England

Cover designed by: Anne Masters, Washington, DC
Typeset by: Nova Graphic Services, Inc., Ft. Washington, PA
Printed by: United Book Press, Inc., Baltimore, MD
Technical/Production Editor: Catherine Hudson

The opinions and statements published are the responsibility of the authors, and such opinions and statements do not necessarily represent the policies of the American Psychological Association.

Library of Congress Cataloging-in-Publication Data
Self-injurious behavior: gene–brain–behavior relationships / edited by Stephen R. Schroeder, Mary Lou Oster-Granite, and Travis Thompson.
    p. cm.
Includes bibliographical references and index.
ISBN 10: 1-55798-885-4
ISBN 13: 978-1-55798-885-0
1. Self-injurious behavior—Etiology.   2. Self-injurious behavior—Treatment.   I. Schroeder, Stephen R.   II. Oster-Granite, Mary Lou.   III. Thompson, Travis.

RC569.5.S48 S4525 2002
616.85'82—dc21

2001053268

British Library Cataloguing-in-Publication Data
A CIP record is available from the British Library.

Printed in the United States of America

To Jeff

CONTENTS

CONTRIBUTORS

P. Barker, Johns Hopkins University, Baltimore, MD

Gershon Berkson, University of Illinois at Chicago

James W. Bodfish, Western Carolina Center, Morganton, NC

George R. Breese, University of North Carolina School of Medicine, Chapel Hill

Mary Caruso, University of Kansas Medical Center, Kansas City

Michael F. Cataldo, Johns Hopkins University, Baltimore, MD

Carolyn M. Crockett, University of Washington, Seattle

Iser G. DeLeon, Johns Hopkins University, Baltimore, MD

Anna J. Esbensen, Ohio State University, Columbus

Wayne W. Fisher, Marcus Behavioral Center, Atlanta, GA

Rachel L. Freeman, University of Kansas, Lawrence

James C. Harris, Johns Hopkins University, Baltimore, MD

Robert H. Horner, University of Oregon, Eugene

Brian A. Iwata, University of Florida, Gainesville

Hyder A. Jinnah, Johns Hopkins University, Baltimore, MD

Sung Woo Kahng, Johns Hopkins University, Baltimore, MD

Suhail Kasim, Johns Hopkins University, Baltimore, MD

Craig H. Kennedy, Vanderbilt University, Nashville, TN

Zubair Khan, Johns Hopkins University, Baltimore, MD

Bryan H. King, Dartmouth Medical School, Hanover, NH

Adam B. Lewin, Johns Hopkins University, Baltimore, MD

Mark H. Lewis, University of Florida, Gainesville

Pippa S. Loupe, University of Kansas, Lawrence

Karl M. Newell, Pennsylvania State University, College Park

Melinda A. Novak, University of Massachusetts, Amherst

William L. Nyhan, University of California–San Diego, La Jolla

Mary Lou Oster-Granite, National Institute of Child Health and Human Development, Bethesda, MD

Cathleen C. Piazza, Marcus Behavioral Center, Atlanta, GA

Joe Reichle, University of Minnesota, Minneapolis
David M. Richman, University of Kansas, Lawrence
Henry S. Roane, Marcus Behavioral Center, Atlanta, GA
Vanessa Rodriguez-Catter, Johns Hopkins University, Baltimore, MD
Johannes Rojahn, Ohio State University, Columbus
Eileen M. Roscoe, University of Florida, Gainesville
Gene P. Sackett, University of Washington, Seattle
Curt A. Sandman, University of California at Irvine, Orange
D. Schretlen, Johns Hopkins University, Baltimore, MD
Stephen R. Schroeder, University of Kansas, Lawrence
Frank J. Symons, University of Minnesota, Minneapolis
Richard E. Tessel, University of Kansas, Lawrence
Travis Thompson, University of Kansas Medical Center, Kansas City
Paul Touchette, University of California at Irvine, Orange
Megan Tupa, University of Illinois at Chicago
Cortney A. Turner, University of Florida, Gainesville
Dean F. Wong, Johns Hopkins University, Baltimore, MD
Jennifer R. Zarcone, University of Kansas Medical Center, Kansas City

PREFACE

This volume is the distillation of two important recent multidisciplinary conferences that integrated 40 years of research on self-injurious behavior (SIB). The first conference, which focused on SIB, was cosponsored by the National Institute for Child Health and Human Development (NICHD) and the Merrill Advanced Study Center of the University of Kansas. For the first time, 25 leading researchers assembled in Rockville, Maryland, for two days to discuss the relationships among the genetic, neurobiological, and behavioral causes and treatments for SIB. The second conference was part of the Gatlinburg Conference for Research and Theory in Mental Retardation and Developmental Disabilities. It also was sponsored by NICHD and was held in San Diego, California, in March 2000. This conference was held in honor of Gershon Berkson, a long-time distinguished researcher of stereotyped behavior and its related self-injurious counterparts. Together, these two conferences are a rich resource of some of the old and many new findings from the perspective of gene–brain–behavior relationships.

In his 1937–1938 Gifford Lectures, C. S. Sherrington (1951) stated that it was "Reflex action . . . and not mind which primarily integrated the motor individual. The simpler motor acts were there before the mind. . . . As motor integration proceeds mind proceeds with it, the servant of an 'urge' seeking satisfaction" (p. 161). Sherrington's analysis suggested that reflex actions were integrated into more complex movements, which create the motivation to respond in specific ways.

Throughout his career, Berkson has systematically attempted to understand the integration of simple and more complex repetitive motor movements of nonhuman primates and people with disabilities. In the early 1960s, when Berkson began his work on motor stereotypies, few others shared his commitment. In the words of Robert Frost, Berkson has taken the road less traveled, and that has made all the difference. While others pursued their one major breakthrough, Berkson embarked on a program of research of both theoretical and practical importance, layering finding on finding to create a cumulative corpus of knowledge. Drawing on concepts from ethology, Berkson proposed that stereotyped motor movements serve self-regulatory homeostatic functions used by the individual to modulate excessive or insufficient extrinsic stimulation. Through an ingenious series of studies, Berkson parsed out the variables that contributed to repetitive rocking, hand flapping, and other stereotypies of monkeys raised in under-stimulating environments, as well as to people with severe intellectual disabilities in institutions. His work on stereotypies continues to be among the most widely cited in the field.

Berkson and his colleagues currently are conducting one of the few longitudinal studies of the ontogeny of self-injury of children with developmental disabilities in an effort to identify the precursors to this disturbing behavior problem, as well as to examine the course of the emergence of various forms of self-injury. Is self-injury a stereotyped response that grows more intense, or is it a qualitatively different type of behavior? How is the emerging self-injury nested in its social environment? Answers to these questions will be of immense theoretical as well as practical significance.

Berkson is widely recognized as a behavioral scientist of the first order who has distinguished himself by his steadfast insistence on clarity of thinking and the quality and integrity of his work. If Berkson says it, you can take it to the bank. Before few researchers spoke of *relevance*, Berkson and several of his colleagues (notably Al Baumeister, Norman Ellis, and several others) created a national research agenda in mental retardation and developmental disabilities. John F. Kennedy announced, "For the first time, there will be research centers capable of putting together teams of experts working in many different fields." Berkson and his colleagues helped translate into reality Kennedy's vision of a national program of basic mental retardation research. Berkson, who has served on research review committees of the NICHD and the National Institutes of Health for three decades, has consistently advocated for the highest quality behavioral and biomedical research on the causes of, prevention of, and intervention for the adverse outcomes associated with developmental disabilities. He has been a tireless advocate for the importance of both basic and applied research on mental retardation and has been a long-time friend of the Mental Retardation and Developmental Disabilities Branch of the NICHD.

It was fitting, therefore, that at the 2000 Gatlinburg Conference for Research and Theory on Mental Retardation and Developmental Disabilities in San Diego (which was sponsored by the NICHD) a special symposium was convened in honor of Gershon Berkson's 65th birthday. Several of the chapters in this book were developed from that symposium, and they have since been revised and updated. If we are nearer to understanding the causes, course of development, and treatment of self injury and related stereotyped movements of people with intellectual disabilities today than we were four decades ago, it is in no small measure due to the contributions of Berkson.

Forty years ago, SIB was an inexplicable and untreatable behavior. Since that time, a great deal has been learned about its causes, prevalence, and treatment. There are now a host of animal models for different genetic and neurobiological systems that affect susceptibility to SIB. Interest in this work from a variety of fields has been increasing at an exponential rate during the past two decades. Although no biomedical cure is yet known, it is likely that a cure for some forms of SIB will be found in the near future. Many effective behavioral interventions have been found, but they are difficult to maintain in the long term. For lasting cures to be found, the collaboration of individuals from a broad array of relevant disciplines, such as those represented at those two conferences, is required.

Many new findings and new tools have developed during the past 40 years, allowing excellent research on SIB, yet sufficient integration of the knowledge has not occurred. Researchers are now in an excellent position to take advantage of these validated assessment tools, animal models, psychotropic drugs, and behavioral interventions by cross-validating their theories across domains. The research should be consistent in all levels—from the genes to the brain to the behavior. If these relationships do not agree, they should be reconciled by further research. The next decade holds promise for a more comprehensive, theoretically driven approach to SIB.

We are grateful to the NICHD and the Merrill Advanced Study Center of the University of Kansas for their vision in making these conferences possible. We particularly wish to acknowledge Virginia Merrill and Melinda Merrill, board members; Mabel Rice, director; and Joy Simpson, administrative assistant, for their help and encouragement.

Travis Thompson

Stephen R. Schroeder

REFERENCES

Frost, R. (1916). The road not taken. In E.C. Lathem (Ed.), *The poetry of Robert Frost by Robert Frost*. New York: Holt, Rinehart, & Winston.

Kennedy, J. F. (1963, October 31). *At the signing of the mental retardation facilities bill.*

Sherrington, C. S. (1951). *Man on his nature: The Gifford Lectures (1937-8)*. Cambridge, England: Cambridge University Press.

I

OVERVIEW OF SELF-INJURIOUS BEHAVIOR

Self-injurious behavior (SIB) refers to acts people direct toward themselves that result in tissue damage (Tate & Baroff, 1966). SIB is a heterogeneous class of responses that have multiple topographies with numerous causes and effects (Schroeder, Mulick, & Rojahn, 1980). Of the many topographies in which it manifests, the most frequent are head-banging, self-biting, and self-scratching (Rojahn, 1994). SIB occurs among a significant proportion of people with autism and mental retardation. Estimates vary according to the population studied and the definition of the case (see chapter 3). The type of definition used, characterization of the behavior, and the behavior's prevalence and comorbidity are very important to the understanding of SIB and what it has come to mean during the past 40 years.

Part I of this book contains an overview of SIB mechanisms, epidemiology, and comorbidity and their relationship to treatment. In chapter 1, Travis Thompson and Mary Caruso review a variety of hypotheses that researchers have developed over the years to understand SIB. Initial hypotheses focused on underlying causes related to psychopathology, social deprivation, homeostasis, and arousal. Researchers have more recently focused on learning, social communicative functions of SIB, and specific neurochemical pathological conditions or behavioral phenotypes and their relationship to certain genetic syndromes such as Lesch–Nyhan syndrome and Prader–Willi syndrome. No single factor causes SIB. A comprehensive approach to treatment based on the etiology, underlying social and neurochemical mechanisms, and exacerbating medical conditions is required to treat SIB and obtain lasting results.

In chapter 2, James W. Bodfish and Mark H. Lewis search for common etiologies of SIB by exploring comorbidities of SIB in various developmental, neurological, psychiatric, and genetic disorders. They explain that in people with various disorders SIB is associated with (a) decreased cognitive skills, (b) abnormal repetitive behaviors, (c) movement disorders, and (d) sleep disorders. In chapter 3, Johannes Rojahn and Anna J. Esbensen review

1

all the prevalence studies of SIB that have been conducted from 1971–1999 and describe many severe methodological shortcomings. Prevalence varied greatly depending on the population studied, the survey methods used, and the measurement instruments used. In the largest studies, which were done in New York and California, SIB prevalence was about 8% of the population with retardation for all ages and levels of retardation.

1

SELF-INJURY: KNOWING WHAT WE'RE LOOKING FOR

TRAVIS THOMPSON AND MARY CARUSO

Self-injury behavior (SIB) is one of the most excruciating and costly behaviors of people with developmental disabilities. According to needs assessments by professionals, parents, and caregivers, SIB is near the top of the priority list (National Institutes of Health, 1991). Historically, family members, doctors, psychologists, teachers, and others who are responsible for providing care and services for people with developmental disabilities have been stymied in their attempts to understand the causes and to develop treatments for this refractory behavior problem. The notion that people could intentionally injure their bodies day after day for years at a time—and sometimes even cause life-threatening damage—defies common sense.

For centuries, self-injury has been recognized as an integral part of the human condition, including the condition of people with mental disabilities. From the 13th to the 16th centuries, a fanatical sect of people known as *Flagellants* flourished in Italy and then spread beyond the Alps to Alsace, Bavaria, Bohemia, Poland, and Germany (Toke, 1909/1999). Despite condemnation by the official Catholic Church, Flagellants proceeded through the streets of towns throughout central Europe as the church bells sounded at 6 a.m. and 6 p.m., beating their backs with bundles of twigs until they bled. Although their purpose was religious mortification, other psychological, physiological, and neurochemical factors may have played a role in sustaining this practice as well. In his *Rake's Progress* paintings (1732–1733), which depicted the deplorable conditions in the Bethlehem Hospital at Bishopsgate, William Hogarth painted the figure of Thomas Rakewell. Rakewell wore a bandage where he had injured himself, suggesting that self-

Supported in part by P01HD30329 from the National Institute of Child Health and Human Development to Vanderbilt University and P30HD02528 and RO1HD3029 to the University of Kansas. Thanks to Frank Symons, Craig Kennedy, and Rachel Freeman for their helpful suggestions during the preparation of this chapter.

injury may have been commonplace at "Bedlam" (O'Donoghue, 1915). Jean Itard (Lane, 1976) described the temper outbursts of Victor, a 12-year-old boy with autism. This so-called "wild child" was found in the forest in southern France, and he struck himself during his outbursts. In her famous lecture, *Memorial to the Legislature of Massachusetts*, Dorothea Dix (1843) described the agonizing self-inflicted injuries sustained by some of the people she found incarcerated in rural Massachusetts almshouses and sheds, which were used to house people with mental illness and intellectual disabilities. In short, combating self-injury is not a new challenge.

CHARACTERISTICS AND PREVALENCE OF SELF-INJURY IN PEOPLE WITH DEVELOPMENTAL DISABILITIES

A wide array of behaviors can cause self-inflicted bodily harm, but the various actions clearly are not all the same. Carl Menninger (1935, 1938) devised a classification scheme for self-mutilation, which ranged from nail biting and beard trimming among members of the general population to enucleation and genital removal by people with florid psychoses. Among people with developmental disabilities, especially those with intellectual functioning in the moderate to profound range of intellectual disability, self-injury has common characteristics that distinguish it from self-injury exhibited by most psychiatric patients with typical intellectual abilities.

Common characteristics of self-injury by people with intellectual disabilities include the following:

- Repetitive movements of the limbs, the head, the trunk, or other body parts produce physical damage or potential damage if repeated frequently.
- Episodes occur in discrete bouts, often many times per day, with the same or very similar movements being repeated on most occasions.
- The two relatively distinct patterns of self-injury that exist may be related to their causes and maintaining conditions:

  1. One pattern involves punctuate bouts that last for seconds (not minutes) and are followed by a cessation of activity. Often these episodes are environmentally maintained.
  2. Another pattern involves protracted episodes, which may occur more or less continuously for hours with only brief pauses. During these episodes the person may not eat or sleep. Once initiated, these episodes seem to be neurochemically driven and independent of environmental events.

- Self-injurious behavior may be initiated by an aversive environmental event (e.g., a parental or teacher request) but may continue autonomously once it has begun.
- People may injure themselves at particular bodily locations. These locations seem to vary with etiology of the disability and may also vary with the reasons for the self-injury.

Overall prevalence rates of self-injury among people with developmental disabilities ranges from 5% to 16% in various studies (Schroeder, Rojahn, & Oldenquist, 1991). Prevalence varies with intellectual ability (Borthwick, Meyers, & Eyman, 1981; Sherman, 1988), setting (Borthwick-Duffy, Eyman, & White, 1987), and etiology (Myrianthopoulos, 1981; Singh & Pullman, 1979; Nyhan, 1967). Self-injury is universal in people with certain disabilities (e.g., Lesch–Nyhan syndrome). In people with other disabilities it is very common (e.g., autism), and in still others it is uncommon except in those with a severe or profound intellectual disability (e.g., Down's syndrome).

APPROACHES TO UNDERSTANDING SELF-INJURY

Schroeder, Reese, Hellings, Loupe, and Tessel (1999) recently provided an excellent review of hypotheses concerning the causes of SIB by people with intellectual disabilities. The present overview supplements the Schroeder et al. review by emphasizing recent progress and trends in understanding the multiplicity of causes and various treatment strategies for overcoming this intractable behavior problem.

Early Efforts

The first theorists who attempted to understand self-injury used psychoanalytic theory to hypothesize that self-injury had psychopathological causes (e.g., Menninger, 1935). These early theorists speculated that self-injury was symbolic behavior driven by thwarted infantile motives (e.g., Bettleheim, 1973; Sandler, 1964). Kanner (1943) noted that children with autism usually displayed stereotypic movements that included self-injury. He observed that family members of the children with autism displayed some of the same ritualistic tendencies as their children, although they did not physically harm themselves. Instead, they were often inflexible, displaying compulsive tendencies. He speculated that autism is an inherited or congenital brain disorder, which he thought accounted for tantrums, stereotypies, and self-injury. Later, Harlow and Harlow (1979) studied social-isolation–induced self-biting by monkeys, which they attributed to psychopathology resulting from failure of maternal attachment during a critical developmental period.

Homeostatic and Neural Oscillator Approaches

Lourie (1949), Berkson (1967), and Baumeister and Forehand (1973) applied concepts from ethology and physiological psychology in an effort to improve understanding of self-injury. They noted that people with developmental disabilities often appear either overstimulated or understimulated and hypothesized that self-injury may be used to regulate arousal levels. They argued that self-injury and other stereotyped movements block out excessive stimulation (e.g., noise in an overcrowded classroom) or increase arousal during prolonged periods of isolation or understimulation (e.g., in an institutional setting or among people who are blind). Baumeister and Rollings (1976) pointed out that these homeostatic hypotheses are difficult to test because the parameters of "low" and "high" stimulation are unspecified. Moreover, many of the situations that are associated with what seem to be higher levels of stimulation (e.g., noise in an institutional ward) are also associated with higher levels of self-injury; situations that are quiet and understimulating often are not associated with self-injury, raising questions about the validity of the homeostatic theory of self-injury. Lewis and Baumeister (1982) proposed that an intrinsic neural timing mechanism may be responsible for rhythmic patterns of behavior, including stereotypies and self-injury. This has been a very difficult hypothesis to test.

Operant Learning Approaches

Lovaas and Simmons (1969) argued that self-injury is a learned behavior and, like any other learned behavior, can be increased or reduced by positive reinforcement, negative reinforcement, extinction, or aversive consequences. They taught elementary school-age children with autism basic speaking skills and compliance with social requests, as well as everyday functional skills. In addition, they punished self-injury with faradic skin shocks. The children showed dramatic reductions in self-injury and substantial increases in adaptive skills. This was the first demonstration that self-injury could be reduced by using environmental learning principles. Regrettably, the gains made were not well maintained. Many adaptive skills taught were eventually lost, and self-injury resumed. Lovaas (1987) has subsequently shown that the age at which intervention is initiated and the intervention's intensity account for much of the magnitude and durability of its effects. By the time they entered first grade, as many as half of the children with autism who received intensive early intervention no longer displayed many of their behavior problems, including self-injury.

Approaches Based on Functions of Self-Injury

In 1977, Carr published a paper titled "The Motivation of Self-Injurious Behavior: A Review of Some Hypotheses." This paper set the stage for a new approach to understanding and treating self-injury. Carr proposed that self-injury is sometimes an attention- or commodity-seeking behavior (i.e., maintained by positive reinforcement), helps people avoid or escape disliked activities or situations (negative reinforcement), or is a form of automatically reinforced self-stimulation. His analysis is similar to one previously suggested by Bachman (1972). In the intervening years, other researchers pursued this line of investigation, most notably Rincover, Cook, Peoples, and Packard (1979); Iwata, Dorsey, Slifer, Bauman, and Richman (1982); Durand (1990); Wacker, Berg, Harding, and Asmus (1996); and Koegel, Koegel, and Dunlap (1996). Using functional analysis (e.g., Iwata et al., 1982) or functional assessment (e.g., Horner, 1994) behavioral observational methods, which are discussed in detail in a later section of this chapter, researchers are able to identify the putative social functions served by the SIB and the circumstances under which they are likely to occur. Numerous studies have shown that many people who exhibit SIB and have developmental disabilities can be successfully treated by learning an alternative form of communication (e.g., gestural or iconic communication) and additional adaptive skills that serve the same social function as the self-injury [see Horner and Carr (1997) for a review] combined with additional adaptive skills that serve the same social function as the self-injury. However, despite many successes, a substantial number of individuals display SIB that is either not responsive to or is only partially and temporarily reduced by such environmental interventions. Until recently, these unresponsive individuals remained a mystery to researchers and clinicians.

Neurochemical Approaches

Dopamine

Lloyd et al. (1981) conducted a postmortem study of brain tissue from individuals with Lesch–Nyhan syndrome, which is associated with severe and unremitting self-biting. In the three patients studied, the researchers found a 65% to 90% depletion of dopamine from the basal ganglia. Breese et al. (1984a) demonstrated that destroying dopamine neurons in the ventral tegmentum of neonatal rats leads to dopamine supersensitivity. Subsequent administration of dopamine agonists elicits severe self-mutilation. In addition, chronic high doses of amphetamine, cocaine, and other dopamine agonists can lead to self-mutilation in rats (Goldstein et al., 1986) as well as in people (Grabowski, 1984). If binding of dopamine agonists to their receptors causes self-injury, it follows that blocking dopamine receptors should reduce self-injury. Conventional neuroleptics produce their antipsychotic effects by blocking the brain's dopamine receptors (D1, D2, and D5). Thompson, Hackenberg, and Schaal (1991) reviewed 20 years of research literature concerning the effects of psychotropic medications, including conventional neuroleptics, on problem behavior of people with developmental disabilities. There was little evidence that typical neuroleptics selectively reduce self-injury apart from general sedation, which affects all behavior. Because movement disorders are frequently associated with medications that block the D2 receptor, atypical neuroleptics were developed that had little or no D2 affinity (e.g., clozapine, risperidone) but substantial affinity for D1 and D5. Gualtieri and Schroeder (1989) proposed that self-injury is specifically regulated by the D1 receptor and suggested that the reason conventional neuroleptics have not proven effective is that they have higher affinity for the D2 receptor and relatively lower affinity for the D1 receptor. Researchers demonstrated that clozapine (Schroeder et al., 1995) and risperidone (Hellings et al., 1999; Zarcone et al., 2001), which are selective D1 receptor agonists, can both be effective in reducing self-injury, lending credence to the D1 receptor hypothesis of SIB.

Endogenous Opiates

Cataldo and Harris (1982) proposed that some self-injurious behavior may be maintained by release of the brain's endogenous opioids, which then bind to the opioid receptors, producing analgesia and the other psychological effects associated with opiate self-administration. Sandman et al. (1983) reported significant reductions in self-injury when adults with severe intellectual disabilities were treated with naloxone. Herman et al. (1987) built on this hypothesis by treating children with autism who were self-injurious with the opiate antagonist naltrexone, which resulted in significant reductions in self-injury. The finding was replicated by Thompson et al. (1994), who found the greatest decreases in self-injury were seen among individuals who bit their hands and struck their heads with their hands or against hard surfaces.

Implications of Form and Location

The locations on the body where people self-injure are not random; certain sites are selected instead of others. However, the implications of the form and site of self-injury have received relatively little attention. Maurice and Trudel (1982) studied the form and location of SIB in a large institutional population in Canada and found the most frequent self-injury topographies were head banging, hitting the body, biting, and scratching. In a survey study, Rojahn (1994) found that people with severe intellectual disability displayed 38 forms of self-injury, most often involving head banging, biting, scratching, and hitting the body with objects.

Symons and Thompson (1997) studied 29 children and adolescents with severe intellectual disabilities and self-injury, approximately half of whom were also diagnosed as having autism. Approximately 80% of the injuries occurred on 5% of the body's surface area—primarily the forehead, temples, the area between the thumb and wrist on the hand, the back of the hand, and the mediolateral surface of the first finger. The head areas are typically struck with the hand or fist or banged against hard surfaces. The hand areas are usually bitten. Independent studies have shown that when the same areas are electrically stimulated with needles inserted into the skin, analgesia is produced and blood levels of the endogenous opioid beta-endorphin increase (Pomeranz, 1987).

This topographical pattern and form of self-injury (biting or striking with the hand) are distinctively different from the self-injury pattern in people with Prader–Willi syndrome, who usually pick the skin (Cassidy, 1984; Dykens et al., 1997; Greenswag, 1987). Figure 1.1 compares the body areas where people with Prader–Willi syndrome most frequently pick their skin with the findings in the Symons and Thompson (1997) study of people with severe intellectual disabilities, autism, or both. Overlap in the location of the self-injury sites by the two groups of people is limited. We (Thompson

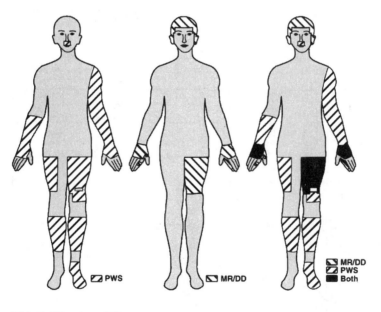

☑ PWS   ☒ MR/DD   ☒ MR/DD ☑ PWS ■ Both

☑ Prader-Willi syndrome (PWS)

☒ Mental Retardation/Developmental Disabilities (MR/DD)

Figure 1.1. Comparison of self-injury body sites among people with Prader–Willi syndrome who pick their skin and people with severe intellectual disabilities, autism, or both who strike with their hand or bite.

Note. From "Self-Injurious Behavior and Body Site Preference," by F. J. Symons and T. Thompson, 1997, *Journal of Intellectual Disability Research*, 6, p. 8. Copyright 1997 by Blackwell Science Ltd. Adapted with permission.

et al., 1994) had previously found a relation between body location of self-injury and the degree of reduction in SIB when treated with the opioid antagonist naltrexone. People who directed blows to the head or bit their hands were most responsive to naltrexone. Sandman et al. (1990, 1997) have shown a significant positive correlation between the amount of increase in plasma beta-endorphin following SIB and the degree to which naltrexone reduces self-injury ($r = .67$). On the other hand, skin picking by people with Prader–Willi syndrome does not appear to be affected by naltrexone; however, researchers report that selective serotonin reuptake inhibitor antidepressants reduced skin picking in people with obsessive–compulsive disorder (Hellings & Warnock, 1994). People with Prader–Willi syndrome who have a deletion of the 15q 11-13 region of chromosome 15, rather than those who have two maternal copies of chromosome 15 (and no paternal copy), show differences in their skin-picking patterns. This suggests that the absence of one or more genes in the chromosome region may contribute to this unique pattern of self-injury (Figure 1.2).

Self-injury forms and locations differ among other diagnostic groups. People with Cornelia de Lange syndrome usually insert the tips of their fingers in their mouth and bite their fingers (Berney, Ireland, & Burn, 1999) and engage in other forms of self-injury. Females with Rett syndrome display two distinctive forms of self-injury. They wring their hands, often digging

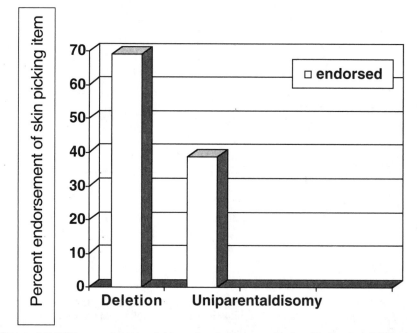

Figure 1.2. Difference in skin-picking sites between people with Prader–Willi syndrome who have a deletion of the 15q 11-13 region of chromosome 15 and those who have two maternal copies of chromosome 15.

the fingernails of one hand into the skin of the other hand to the point of causing lesions. In addition, they continually mouth their hands, eventually causing maceration and tissue damage (Nomura & Segawa, 1990).

These differences in the manner in which self-injury is executed (e.g., biting, or head blows) and the body locations involved may have implications for underlying neurochemical mechanisms. This does not mean that hand biting, for example, could not be maintained by attention from parents and staff gained after hand biting, as well as release and binding of beta-endorphin to the mu opioid receptor. We (Symons & Thompson, 1998) have evidence suggesting that both neurochemical and environmental factors may be involved. Figure 1.3 shows findings from a case study in which a 14-year-old boy with severe intellectual disability and autism was treated in a blind, placebo-controlled study with naltrexone alone, functional communication training (FCT) alone, and a combination of naltrexone and functional communication. Naltrexone alone produced a 50% decrease in

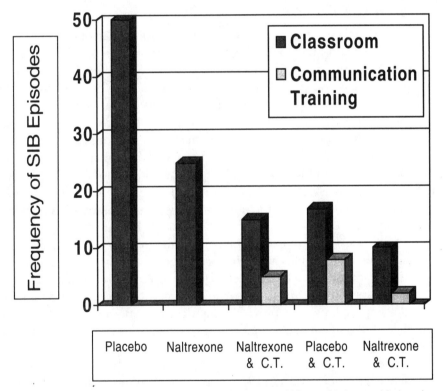

Figure 1.3. Comparison of treatments for a 14-year-old boy who bangs his head and bites his hand: naltrexone only, functional communication training only, and a naltrexone and functional communication training combination.

Note. From "Functional Communication Training and Naltrexone Treatment of Self-Injurious Behavior: An Experimental Case Report," by F. J. Symons, N. D. Fox, and T. Thompson, 1998, *Journal of Applied Research and Intellectual Disabilities*, 3, p. 10. Copyright 1997 by BILD Publication. Reprinted with permission of the publishers, the British Institute of Learning Disabilities, Kidderminster, UK.

self-injury (head banging and hand biting primarily). The addition of FCT (icons) reduced self-injury to near zero during instructional sessions and by 90% to 95% during classroom generalization sessions. In this case, it seems the self-injury served a social function but was also being maintained by beta-endorphin binding to the opiate receptor.

Current and Emerging Approaches to Treatment

Self-injury by people with developmental disabilities clearly does not involve only a single mechanism. SIB takes different forms, by people with disabilities of different etiologies, and likely involves different underlying neurochemical mechanisms caused by varied learning histories and current environmental conditions. Accordingly, it is rational to focus attention on subpopulations thought to share common mechanisms underlying their self-injury patterns.

Social Communicative Functions

From the late 1960s to the 1980s, interventions based on learning theory for SIB were commonly used but often with mixed results. For practical reasons, behavior-analytic research focused on reducing this disturbing behavior rather than discovering its causes (Wacker, Berg, Harding, & Asmus, 1996). Two seminal publications changed the focus of research on self-injury and provided new direction to the field. As noted previously, Carr (1977) discussed current research on the motives for SIB and suggested that self-injury had multiple functions. He proposed that intervention should match the social function of self-injury (e.g., avoidance or escape, positive reinforcement such as attention, self-stimulation). Later, Iwata et al. (1982) introduced the concept of functional analysis of self-injury, a method for experimentally testing three of the motivational hypotheses discussed by Carr. They assessed the SIB of nine participants when play materials were present or absent; demands were high or low; and attention was provided for SIB or for the absence of SIB. Differentiated patterns of self-injury response emerged for six of the nine participants, suggesting specific functions for their self-injury. This study provided empirical support for Carr's hypotheses and suggested that treatment outcome might be linked to a match between function and intervention.

Functional Assessment and Functional Analysis. Two related areas of research emerged from Carr's (1977) hypotheses and the findings of Iwata et al. (1982). One was the further development of functional assessment technology. The second was the development of treatment that matched intervention to function. Attempts to explore the parameters of the functional analysis resulted in the technology of functional assessment, which includes indirect, observational, and experimental methods of identifying the antecedents and consequences that maintain self-injury (Carr et al., 1994; Horner, 1994; Mace, 1994). Indirect methods include interviews (Carr et al., 1994) and rating scales such as the Motivational Assessment Scale (Durand & Crimmins, 1988). Direct observational methods of functional assessment involve observing the subject's behavior and natural environmental events surrounding self-injury. Methods such as the antecedent-behavior-consequence analysis (Bijou, Peterson, & Ault, 1968) and the observational process described by Carr et al. (1994) provide information on the interpersonal and environmental context and baseline rates of self-injury. They also provide an objective description and reaction to the behavior as well as the natural schedule of consequences for self-injury and adaptive behavior (Lalli & Goh, 1993).

In addition to indirect and observational methods, experimental approaches such as structural and functional analyses are included in functional assessment methodology. Structural analysis involves the manipulation of antecedent events that set the occasion for SIB (Wacker, Berg, Harding, & Asmus, 1996). If a person may be using self-injury as a means of escape, levels of demand are manipulated to determine whether high rates of SIB occur in high-demand situations but not low-demand situations. Conversely, the functional analysis involves direct manipulation of consequences to determine the function of the behavior under four conditions. The first condition tests the positive reinforcement hypothesis. The participant receives attention in the form of social disapproval (e.g., "No, don't hit yourself") contingent on the display of SIB to determine whether he or she engages in self-injury to gain attention. During the negative reinforcement condition, demands are discontinued following a display of SIB. The unstructured-play condition serves as a control condition during which a variety of age-appropriate activities are available. The clinician provides social praise in the absence of self-injury and ignores any SIB. The alone condition tests the self-stimulation hypothesis and consists of placing the participant alone in an impoverished environment such as an empty therapy room (Iwata et al., 1982).

Because each assessment method has distinct advantages and disadvantages, clinicians often combine techniques when assessing self-injury. Indirect methods are a convenient way to attempt to assess the function of aberrant behavior; however, the results are often less reliable and predict treatment outcome less effectively than direct observation or functional analysis (Iwata, 1994; Mace, 1994). Direct observational methods provide more reliable hypotheses regarding the operant function of self-injury; however, the variables believed to be responsible for maintaining the problem behavior are not systematically manipulated. In addition, the process can be time-consuming and costly because observations are conducted for 1 to 2 weeks during all waking hours using a time sampling method (Sandman et al., 2000; Symons & MacLean, 2000). Using the scatter plot observational method (Touchette, McDonald, & Langer, 1985) to identify times when and circumstances under which most self-injury occurs (e.g., mealtimes, bathing, getting ready for bed) and then conducting observations only during those intervals is more efficient. Finally, the observational method reflects only current circumstances in the natural environment (Carr et al., 1994). For example, the relationship between SIB and level of demands will not be revealed if staff members rarely make demands on an individual because it results in self-injury. As a result, functional assessment in clinical practice generally is followed by probe interventions, during which clinicians make periodic demands and collect data to reveal the social function of self-injury.

Clinicians using functional or experimental analysis may overlook important variables affecting the individual's natural setting (Carr, Yarborough, & Langdon 1997; Mace, 1994). Moreover, the conditions that prevail during the functional analysis sessions (e.g., repeated demands to engage in an activity the individual dislikes) may rarely be encountered in the natural environment. Thus, the analysis demonstrates what could happen under a set of circumstances that seldom actually occurs. In addition, repeatedly exposing individuals with developmental disabilities to conditions that provoke self-injury for purely diagnostic purposes could pose ethical problems. In practice, one rarely implements an intervention that provokes self-injury. Instead, the clinician introduces a series of gradually graded demands to minimize the likelihood of self-injury while simultaneously teaching a more adaptive way of obtaining attention or escaping an aversive situation.

Functional Communication Training (FCT). Durand and Carr (1985) suggested that self-injury is often a form of communication. They proposed that children displaying SIB are actually indicating that they want something and therefore should be taught to communicate what they want (whether it is attention, a tangible object, or the removal of an unpleasant task or activity). Durand and Carr emphasized the importance of matching the consequence of the replacement behavior to the consequence of self-injury. Accordingly, the first step of FCT involves conducting a functional assessment to determine the consequences maintaining SIB. The person learns a verbal or gestural request that produces the same results (e.g., attainment of a needed item, cessation of an unpleasant activity) as self-injury; at the same time, they receive little or no reinforcement for self-injury (extinction). Durand and Carr (1982) reduced the SIB of three children almost completely by teaching them appropriate attention- and assistance-seeking phrases. In a follow-up study, two of the three children had maintained their treatment gains 18 months after training (Durand & Carr, 1983). Functional communication skills can be effective in reducing self-injury and are well maintained over time (Derby et al., 1997; Durand & Carr, 1992). They generalize to environments in which training has not occurred (Durand & Carr, 1991) and have been successfully implemented in employment settings (Kemp & Carr, 1995), the homes of young children (Derby et al., 1997), schools (Durand & Carr, 1985), and community locations such as the grocery store (Carr & Carlson, 1993). In addition, FCT reduces self-injury that is multiply determined (e.g., to gain attention, to escape demands) as long as the person learns requests for each function (Day, Horner, & O'Neill, 1994; Sigafoos & Meikle, 1996).

Other Functionally Based Treatments. Practitioners and caregivers generally prefer nonaversive, positive behavioral interventions. In light of the recognition that self-injury is a complex, multifaceted problem behavior, many clinicians now combine interventions to meet individual needs. Research has focused on expanding use of nonaversive, positive behavioral interventions. Interventions such as curricular or environmental revision, antecedent manipulation, and choice making can be used individually or in combination (Horner & Carr, 1997). These interventions involve arranging the person's environment to minimize SIB and maximize skill development. For example, a classroom teacher working with a student who engages in self-injury to escape unpleasant activities or situations could make the introduction of a new task less likely to result in SIB by removing distracting items from the work area (antecedent environmental manipulation), by preceding the new task with an already mastered task (antecedent manipulation that builds behavioral momentum), by allowing the child to choose from task materials (choice making), and by prompting the child to ask for a break when needed (FCT). The combined use of FCT, reinforcer delay, and response chaining increases tolerance for delayed reinforcement (Fisher, Thompson, Hagopian, Bowman, & Krug, 2000; Lalli, Casey, & Kates, 1995). In the example, during the initial phase of FCT the student would be immediately reinforced by receiving a break for each appropriate verbal or gestural request. As self-injury episodes decreased, breaks would be provided only after an appropriate request was made and a specified number of steps in the task were completed. The amount of work would be increased until the task was completed. Finally, pharmacotherapy and behavioral interventions are indicated when self-injury is behaviorally and neurochemically driven (Symons, Fox, & Thompson, 1998).

NEUROCHEMICAL AND PSYCHOPATHOLOGICAL CONTRIBUTIONS TO SELF-INJURY: ANXIETY AND COMPULSIVITY

Several lines of evidence suggest a relationship exists among compulsivity, anxiety, neurochemical dysregulation, and self-injury by people with developmental disabilities. King (1993) proposed a theory of self-injury based on the notion that it was a form of obsessive–compulsive behavior. It is well established that medications that block serotonin reuptake reduce ritualistic symptoms of obsessive–compulsive disorder (OCD) and reduce anxiety symptoms in psychiatric patients with typical intellectual ability (Todorov, Freeston, & Borgeat, 2000). Lewis et al. (1995) and Garber et al. (1992) have published several papers indicating that clomipramine, a tricyclic antidepressant with serotonin-reuptake-blocking properties (Thoren et al., 1980), reduced self-injury significantly among individuals with severe to profound intellectual disabilities in various settings. Clomipramine is also a dopamine receptor antagonist (Delini-Stula & Vassout, 1979). MacLean et al. (1985) and Bodfish et al. (1995) also found a correlation between eye-blink rates and amount of stereotypic activity and SIB. Eye-blink rates negatively correlate with dopamine levels in the substantia nigra, in both animal models and humans with disabilities such as Parkinson's disease (Karson, 1984). Dopamine levels also mediate Tourette's syndrome, which involves tics and compulsive rituals such as throwing objects, emitting guttural sounds, and cursing (Wong et al., 1997). Robertson, Trimble, and Lees (1989) found that one third of the patients with Tourette's syndrome who were treated in an outpatient clinic displayed SIB—most often head banging, hand-to-object hitting, biting and scratching, hair pulling, and poking objects into bodily orifices. Dopamine antagonists often reduce tics and compulsive behavior in people with Tourette's syndrome (Leckman et al., 1987).

GABA is an important inhibitory neurotransmitter that plays a major role in regulating activity of dopaminergic and serotonergic neurons in the brain, including those in the orbitofrontal cortex (Feifel, 1999). People with the deletion form of Prader–Willi syndrome (PWS) are missing genes that provide instructions for components of the γ-aminobutyric acid A or GABA (A) receptor (Wagstaff et al., 1991). Individuals with PWS also demonstrate significant increases in GABA blood levels compared with matched controls, which is consistent with GABA up-regulation in response to defective binding of the GABA (A) receptor (Ebert et al., 1997). In addition, people with lesions in the orbitofrontal cortex frequently display impulsive and repetitive compulsive behavior. Brain imaging studies implicate involvement of the orbitofrontal cortex in people with OCD (Garber et al., 1989). Thus inadequate GABAergic inhibition of oribitofrontal cortical neurons may be responsible for the obsessive and compulsive symptoms commonly seen in people with Prader–Willi syndrome (Dykens, Leckman, & Cassidy, 1996), again implicating the involvement of dopaminergic pathways in people with self-injury.

Cook et al. (1997) reported that people with autism, among whom self-injury is very common, have a genetically programmed defect in the serotonin transporter, which interferes with the ability of presynaptic serotonergic neurons to regulate intracellular and extracellular serotonin concentrations. However, researchers in another study (Maestrini et al., 1999) did not find such an association. Interestingly, the first-degree relatives of as well (Kennedy & Thompson, 2000). A correlation between self-injury to the head and otitis media has been demonstrated in mice (Harkness & Wagner, 1975) and children with developmental disabilities (O'Reilly, 1997). A child with William's syndrome who had otitis media intermittently self-injured to escape from loud noise. He banged his back and poked his ear when his ear infection flared up and someone played a radio loudly. The boy did not injure himself when the radio was played loudly and he had no ear infection (O'Reilly, 1997), indicating that otitis media was an establishing operation that made loud sounds more aversive.

Gastroesophageal Reflux Disease

Another example of escape-motivated self-injury is shown by individuals with gastrointestinal disorders. Gastroesophageal reflux disease and other gastrointestinal disorders have been associated with self-injurious episodes occurring in bouts around mealtimes (Kennedy & Thompson, 2000). Bohmer (1996) found that 10% to 25% of institutionalized people experience vomiting, regurgitation, or rumination, whereas up to 75% of this group experience pathological reflux. In addition, although behavior problems occur in 45% to 56% of people with developmental disabilities, challenging behaviors (including self-injury) are shown by 86% of those diagnosed with gastrointestinal disorders (Bohmer, 1996).

Sleep Deprivation

Sleep irregularities are common among people with developmental disabilities (Bartlett et al., 1985; Clements et al., 1986; Stores, 1992). Sleep deprivation is associated with self-injury (Griffin, 1986) and has an array of behavioral effects, including reducing the value of positive reinforcers and increasing the aversive value of negative reinforcers (Kennedy & Thompson, 2000). Consequently, sleep-deprived people may be less likely to engage in a behavior so that they can interact with a caregiver (positive reinforcement) and may be more likely to injure themselves to avoid an aversive event (negative reinforcement).

Symons, Davis, and Thompson (2000) studied sleep patterns of 30 people who injured themselves and 30 people who did not, all of whom were in an institutional setting. People who injured themselves slept significantly less and varied more in the number of hours they slept from night to night. O'Reilly (1995) demonstrated that escape-motivated aggression increased when an adult man with severe mental retardation was sleep deprived, and Kennedy and Meyer (1996) found that escape-motivated SIB increased in the presence of sleep deprivation or allergy symptoms. Thus, sleep deprivation serves as an establishing operation that increases escape-motivated behavior problems.

people with autism also have a higher incidence of the same gene defect. Folstein and Rutter (1977), Piven et al. (1991), and Smalley (1995) have reported that relatives of individuals with autism have higher incidences of anxiety disorder and depression than matched controls. People with autism who have good verbal skills commonly report severe anxiety, including participating in obsessive–compulsive rituals and having feelings of agoraphobia (e.g., Grandin, 1996). People with autism experience significant anxiety when attempting to avoid an anxiety-provoking situation. Not surprisingly, people with autism who have poor verbal skills resort to self-injury as a form of avoidance behavior. Reductions in self-injury produced by selective serotonin reuptake inhibitors (SSRIs) and clomipramine may be in part caused by a reduction in anxiety and decreased need to avoid situations that produce anxiety.

HEALTH CONDITIONS CONTRIBUTING TO SELF-INJURY

Although behavioral and pharmacological treatments alone or in combination are often effective in reducing self-injury, self-destructive behavior may still persist and is highly variable for reasons that are not apparent. Practitioners often conclude that treatment has lost its effectiveness and abandon appropriate treatments. Such variations may be attributable to the effect of unrecognized health conditions that increase the likelihood of self-injury. For example, having constipation or a sleepless night may lower the value of a favorite food or increase the aversiveness of a task. Otitis media, gastrointestinal disorders, sleep deprivation, and menses are only a few of the health conditions that may increase the probability of self-injury. Under these conditions, demands that would otherwise be tolerated become more aversive; self-injury may terminate demands or attenuate pain (Bailey & Pyles, 1989). Horner, Vaughn, Day, and Ard (1996) found that baseline levels of escape-motivated behavior problems ranged from 11% to 26.5% of intervals in 15 adolescents and adults with developmental disabilities. When individuals had physical discomfort (e.g., illness, painful menses, constipation, fatigue), problem behaviors increased to 32% to 65.5% of intervals. The effects of physical discomfort or other biological state changes on behavior have been described as *setting events* (Horner et al., 1996), *establishing operations* (Kennedy & Meyer, 1998), or *biological contexts* (Carr, Reeve, & Magito-McLaughlin, 1996).

Otitis Media

It has been hypothesized that head banging associated with otitis media may initially reduce pain because of the release of endogenous opiates, which are analgesics, but is eventually controlled by social functions employment settings (Kemp & Carr, 1995), the homes of young children (Derby et al., 1997), schools (Durand & Carr, 1985), and community locations such as the grocery store (Carr & Carlson, 1993). In addition, FCT reduces self-injury that is multiply determined (e.g., to gain attention, to escape demands) as long as the person learns requests for each function (Day, Horner, & O'Neill, 1994; Sigafoos & Meikle, 1996).

Other Functionally Based Treatments. Practitioners and caregivers generally prefer nonaversive, positive behavioral interventions. In light of the recognition that self-injury is a complex, multifaceted problem behavior, many clinicians now combine interventions to meet individual needs. Research has focused on expanding use of nonaversive, positive behavioral interventions. Interventions such as curricular or environmental revision, antecedent manipulation, and choice making can be used individually or in combination (Horner & Carr, 1997). These interventions involve arranging the person's environment to minimize SIB and maximize skill development. For example, a classroom teacher working with a student who engages in self-injury to escape unpleasant activities or situations could make the introduction of a new task less likely to result in SIB by removing distracting items from the work area (antecedent environmental manipulation), by preceding the new task with an already mastered task (antecedent manipulation that builds behavioral momentum), by allowing the child to choose from task materials (choice making), and by prompting the child to ask for a break when needed (FCT). The combined use of FCT, reinforcer delay, and response chaining increases tolerance for delayed reinforcement (Fisher, Thompson, Hagopian, Bowman, & Krug, 2000; Lalli, Casey, & Kates, 1995). In the example, during the initial phase of FCT the student would be immediately reinforced by receiving a break for each appropriate verbal or gestural request. As self-injury episodes decreased, breaks would be provided only after an appropriate request was made and a specified number of steps in the task were completed. The amount of work would be increased until the task was completed. Finally, pharmacotherapy and behavioral interventions are indicated when self-injury is behaviorally and neurochemically driven (Symons, Fox, & Thompson, 1998).

NEUROCHEMICAL AND PSYCHOPATHOLOGICAL CONTRIBUTIONS TO SELF-INJURY: ANXIETY AND COMPULSIVITY

Several lines of evidence suggest a relationship exists among compulsivity, anxiety, neurochemical dysregulation, and self-injury by people with developmental disabilities. King (1993) proposed a theory of self-injury based on the notion that it was a form of obsessive–compulsive behavior. It is well established that medications that block serotonin reuptake reduce ritualistic symptoms of obsessive–compulsive disorder (OCD) and reduce anxiety symptoms in psychiatric patients with typical intellectual ability (Todorov, Freeston, & Borgeat, 2000). Lewis et al. (1995) and Garber et al. (1992) have published several papers indicating that clomipramine, a tricyclic antidepressant with serotonin-reuptake-blocking properties (Thoren et al., 1980), reduced self-injury significantly among individuals with severe to profound intellectual disabilities in various settings. Clomipramine is also a dopamine receptor antagonist (Delini-Stula & Vassout, 1979). MacLean et al. (1985) and Bodfish et al. (1995) also found a correlation between eye-blink rates and amount of stereotypic activity and SIB. Eye-blink rates negatively correlate with dopamine levels in the substantia nigra, in both animal models and humans with disabilities such as Parkinson's disease (Karson, 1984). Dopamine levels also mediate Tourette's syndrome, which involves tics and compulsive rituals such as throwing objects, emitting guttural sounds, and cursing (Wong et al., 1997). Robertson, Trimble, and Lees (1989) found that one third of the patients with Tourette's syndrome who were treated in an outpatient clinic displayed SIB—most often head banging, hand-to-object hitting, biting and scratching, hair pulling, and poking objects into bodily orifices. Dopamine antagonists often reduce tics and compulsive behavior in people with Tourette's syndrome (Leckman et al., 1987).

GABA is an important inhibitory neurotransmitter that plays a major role in regulating activity of dopaminergic and serotonergic neurons in the brain, including those in the orbitofrontal cortex (Feifel, 1999). People with the deletion form of Prader–Willi syndrome (PWS) are missing genes that provide instructions for components of the γ-aminobutyric acid A or GABA (A) receptor (Wagstaff et al., 1991). Individuals with PWS also demonstrate significant increases in GABA blood levels compared with matched controls, which is consistent with GABA up-regulation in response to defective binding of the GABA (A) receptor (Ebert et al., 1997). In addition, people with lesions in the orbitofrontal cortex frequently display impulsive and repetitive compulsive behavior. Brain imaging studies implicate involvement of the orbitofrontal cortex in people with OCD (Garber et al., 1989). Thus inadequate GABAergic inhibition of oribitofrontal cortical neurons may be responsible for the obsessive and compulsive symptoms commonly seen in people with Prader–Willi syndrome (Dykens, Leckman, & Cassidy, 1996), again implicating the involvement of dopaminergic pathways in people with self-injury.

Cook et al. (1997) reported that people with autism, among whom self-injury is very common, have a genetically programmed defect in the serotonin transporter, which interferes with the ability of presynaptic serotonergic neurons to regulate intracellular and extracellular serotonin concentrations. However, researchers in another study (Maestrini et al., 1999) did not find such an association. Interestingly, the first-degree relatives of

Menses

Menstrual pain has also been implicated as an establishing operation that results in increased rates of escape-motivated self-injury. Carr et al. (1996) examined the role of menses in problem behavior maintained by social consequences. During a functional analysis the combined effect of menses and demands increased problem behavior, whereas combinations involving only demands or menses did not. Their findings suggest that menses functions as an establishing operation for self-injury. As a result, the researchers decreased the aversiveness of demands by teaching choice-making and communication skills. They addressed the menstrual discomfort through exercise, medication, diet, massage, and hot water bottles. One and a half years after intervention, behavior problems remained at low levels during menses, and the woman continued to participate in tasks that had previously led to SIB. In addition, Taylor, Rush, Hetrick, and Sandman (1993) explored neurochemical mechanisms that serve as an establishing operation for increased SIB by menstruating women. Self-injury increased during the early and late follicular phases (14 days starting with onset of menses), and seven of the nine women had high correlations between menstrual phase and level of self-injury.

Health Conditions and Assessment

No matter how potent a behavioral or pharmacological intervention may be in reducing self-injury, when the patient is in pain because of an earache or gastric reflux flare-up, the same treatments may lose their effectiveness. Health factors must be assessed during the functional analysis/assessment and the diagnostic process. Familiarity with health problems commonly associated with specific syndromes can be valuable in planning adjunctive treatments (e.g., cisapride for esophageal reflux in people with Cornelia deLange syndrome). Self-injury that varies in similar environmental conditions over time may indicate intermittent health conditions that make self-injury more likely. Finally, cyclical fluctuations in self-injury episodes, such as monthly increases from menstrual distress or daily fluctuations around mealtimes from gastrointestinal distress, may indicate a source of physical discomfort associated with self-injury.

AROUSAL AND STRESS REVISITED

Various writers have hypothesized a relation between arousal and self-injury (Davenport & Menzel, 1963; Gluck & Sackett, 1974; Romanczyk & Goren, 1975). Skinner (1953) pointed out that stimuli associated with aversive events can develop conditioned aversive and discriminative properties.

Bachman (1972), Bucher and Lovaas (1968), and Lovaas and Simmons (1969) speculated that the painful consequences of self-injury developed conditioned reinforcing properties and also served as a discriminative stimulus for further self-injury. We previously suggested that self-injury may be maintained by the release and binding of dopamine, endogenous opioids, or both to receptors in the ventral tegmentum and nucleus accumbens, comparing self-injury with stimulant or opiate self-administration (Thompson et al., 1995). In drug self-administration paradigms, when self-administration has ceased for a period of time, a single "priming" injection of the previously self-administered drug sets the occasion for a burst of further self-administration (Stewart, 1984; Stewart & Wise, 1992). Subjecting laboratory animals to physically painful or psychologically stressful events (such as hearing another animal being shocked) causes the release of dopamine and endogenous opiates. Human subjects also release dopamine during stressful situations (Adler et al., 2000; Breier, 1989). Other research has shown that when dopamine receptors are bound by agonists, characteristic discriminative stimulus properties develop (Colpaert & Balster, 1988). Hence an initial bout of self-injury could not only cause pain with its own conditioned reinforcing and discriminative properties, but also could release dopamine and endogenous opiates that bind to their respective receptors and serve as cues for sustained self-injury.

Self-injury that seems to be independent of current external environmental circumstances may resemble processes in people with panic attack disorder. A panic attack may be initiated by a brief, anxiety-provoking event but then run its course autonomously. Internal cues associated with anxiety elicit further physiological changes (e.g., hyperventilation, tachycardia, perspiration) that serve as conditioned stimuli for further physiological responses, which intensify the feelings of anxiety. Administration of medications that reduce these autonomically mediated physiological changes (e.g., beta blockers or clonidine) can reduce panic attacks and have also been implicated in reducing self-injury by people with autism (Ratey et al., 1992). Romanczyk and Mathews (1998) have proposed a similar model involving an interaction of classically conditioned and operantly maintained self-injury. Based on similar reasoning, Freeman, Horner, and Reichle (1999) have shown that bouts of self-injury are often preceded by several seconds of an increased heart rate. Not surprisingly, heart rates also increased following self-injury. Presumably the anticipatory heart rate increase is adrenergically mediated, which is consistent with this interpretation. In short, arousal may be relevant as an antecedent to self-injury when it is associated with autonomically mediated physiological and neurochemical changes that have eliciting and discriminative stimulus properties. Medications reducing aversiveness of anxiety producing events (e.g., clomipramine, fluvoxamine) or that reduce the physiological response to such stressful events (e.g., propranolol, nadolol) are therefore effective in reducing some forms of self-injury (Lewis, Bodfish, Powell, & Parker, 1996; Ratey et al., 1992).

CONCLUSION

The father of experimental physiology, Claude Bernard, wrote, "The experimenter who does not know what he is looking for will never understand what he finds." After decades of trying to make scientific sense of the self-destructive behavior of people with developmental disabilities, we are finally beginning to learn what we are looking for. During the past decade a great deal of progress has been made in understanding self-injury. Many people who display SIB can now be treated successfully with communication training, adaptive skills acquisition, pharmacotherapy matched to social functions and underlying neurochemical mechanisms, or a combination of the three. People with developmental disabilities injure themselves for several reasons and, accordingly, they require different treatments. Just as a bad cough may be a signal of pneumonia, an asthma attack, or a common cold, self-injury may indicate a maladaptive coping mechanism caused by an inability to communicate, thwarting of a ritual involved in OCD, or a self-administration of beta-endorphin—maintaining a vicious circle of self-injury, as the endogenous opiate binds to the brain's opiate receptors.

In other studies, we have suggested the possible benefits of approaching behavioral and pharmacological treatment of self-injury via an understanding of the underlying behavioral mechanisms that create the occasion for or maintain the problem behavior (Thompson & Symons, 1999). Clinicians no longer question whether they should use only behavioral treatments or only pharmacological treatments. Such strategies ignore the fundamental interactive nature of the variables regulating self-injury. In autism, for example, genes may set the parameter values that determine whether social stimuli are more or less aversive. They do so in part via effects on the serotonin transporter of the surface of brain cells, which may lead to self-injury as a means of escape from a frightening situation. Treating such an individual with a medication that raises the threshold for social anxiety, such as a selective serotonin reuptake inhibitor, may reduce self-injury episodes. In addition, the combination of medication intervention with behavioral intervention, such as teaching people appropriate means of communication so that they can leave a socially alarming situation, could eliminate self-injury. The major hurdle in understanding and overcoming self-injury is devising better methods for diagnosing and identifying underlying mechanisms in individual cases. Unraveling such intricately choreographed interplay between neurochemical and learned environmental mechanisms is at the heart of the task before researchers and will become a focal strategy in the future research agenda.

2

SELF-INJURY AND COMORBID BEHAVIORS IN DEVELOPMENTAL, NEUROLOGICAL, PSYCHIATRIC, AND GENETIC DISORDERS

JAMES W. BODFISH AND MARK H. LEWIS

Self-injurious behavior (SIB) has typically been studied as a discrete form of behavior disorder independent of other forms of aberrant behavior. For example, in treatment studies, researchers select participants on the basis of the presence of SIB, but they rarely report or analyze other forms of co-occurring aberrant behaviors. The clinical reality, in contrast to the research reporting, is that people with SIB typically exhibit various other forms of aberrant behavior. In addition, SIB has been studied primarily in people with mental retardation. Regardless, clinicians know that SIB is associated with a wide variety of developmental, neurological, psychiatric, and genetic conditions (see Table 2.1). Researchers have published reports detailing the occurrence of SIB in people with various neurological and psychiatric disorders other than mental retardation, and the pattern of symptom comorbidity in people with these disorders seems to mirror the pattern of SIB in people with mental retardation. In this chapter, we review these parallels and in particular examine the following questions: (a) Which neurological, psychiatric, and genetic disorders have a significantly increased prevalence of SIB? (b) Which patterns of comorbidity occur in association with SIB in these disorders? (c) Is the pattern of SIB comorbidity in people with developmental disabilities similar to that in people with neurological, psychiatric, and genetic disorders? and (d) Does the prevailing pattern of SIB comorbidity suggest certain models for the etiology, maintenance, and treatment of SIB?

TABLE 2.1
Developmental, Neurological, Psychiatric,
and Genetic Disorders Associated With SIB

Developmental disorders	Neurological disorders	Psychiatric disorders	Genetic disorders
Mental retardation	Tourette's syndrome	Personality disorders	Lesch–Nyhan syndrome
Autism	Neuroacanthocytosis	Eating disorders	Prader–Willi syndrome
	Frontal-lobe epilepsy	Schizophrenia	Rett syndrome
		Trichotillomania	de Lange syndrome
		Onychophagia	Smith–Magenis syndrome
			Fragile X syndrome

ISSUES IN DEFINITION, MEASUREMENT, AND CLASSIFICATION

A major source of difficulty in examining comorbid behavioral, neurological, and psychiatric symptoms is the plethora of poorly operationalized terms used to refer to the various symptoms, behaviors, or movements that are seen in a clinical setting. For example, a given action such as skin picking or head hitting may be called *self-injury*, a *habit*, *self-stimulation*, *stereotypy*, a *mannerism*, a *tic*, a *compulsion*, or a *ritual*. Often, the choice of terms (and thus of measurement strategies) is dictated by clinical discipline. A behavioral psychologist who observed skin picking by a person with mental retardation would call it a *self-injurious behavior*, a neurologist who observed skin picking by a person with Tourette's syndrome would call it a *tic*, a psychiatrist who observed skin picking by a person with obsessive–compulsive disorder (OCD) would call it a *compulsion*, and a casual observer who observed skin picking by a member of the general population would call it a *habit*. Discipline-specific terminology has given rise to various taxonomies of aberrant behavior and movement. Complicating the matter is the fact that choice of a behavioral label and the discipline from which it derives are often taken as suggestive evidence for the etiology or maintaining factors for the behavior in question. For example, actions labeled *tics* are presumed to be involuntary, actions labeled *dyskinesias* are presumed to be drug induced, actions labeled *self-stimulatory* are presumed to be maintained by the sensory consequences they generate, and actions labeled *stereotypies* or *habits* may be deemed not significant enough to warrant treatment and may even be labeled *normal*. In addition, the choice of terms can lead to adherence to a theoretical dichotomy of structure versus function, as opposed to the recognition that behavior can be simultaneously brain based and environmentally mediated. Although a considerable amount of research on the behavioral, motor, and psychiatric symptoms of humans exists, one has to wonder to what extent the validity of the findings rests precariously upon arbitrary decisions regarding the labels for the symptoms that were studied.

How then does one proceed to examine something like co-occurring stereotypies, compulsions, and tics in people who engage in SIB? Avoiding this thorny issue by simply operationally defining the action based on the movements involved negates the possibility that insights into the behavior's etiology, pathophysiology, and response to treatment can be gained on the basis of its similarity to other symptoms of established disorders. For example, a link between forms of SIB in people with mental retardation and forms of repetitive behavior in people with OCD would suggest a finite set of empirically derived OCD treatments that could be applied to the treatment of SIB in the context of mental retardation. In the absence of clinical markers of behavioral disorders (e.g., a specific gene defect, a biochemical abnormality, a biobehavioral marker, an instrumental measure), identification of such a link would require evidence of some form of phenomenological similarity between, in this case, behaviors of people with SIB and behaviors of people with OCD. The similarity could be investigated by jointly administering a rating scale that measures SIB without reference to common compulsions associated with OCD and a rating scale that measures compulsions without reference to common forms of SIB. This strategy requires the use of orthogonal, or item-independent, rating scales to measure the varieties of the phenomena in question. Such an orthogonal assessment strategy provides a more objective means to catalogue and discriminate the various comorbid behaviors that may occur in conjunction with SIB.

Unfortunately, many of the existing instruments used to measure abnormal behavior and movement were not designed with the issues of potential comorbidity in mind. As a result, a single discrete behavior such as skin picking might be a test item on multiple rating scales, each purporting to measure separate clinical phenomena (see Lewis & Bodfish, 1998). For this reason, and because clinicians have recognized that people with SIB often display various other abnormal behaviors and movements, we developed a series of standardized rating scales that are item independent and thus can be used to examine issues of comorbidity in people displaying SIB. We have found these instruments to have acceptable levels of reliability, stability, and validity for people with developmental disabilities (Bodfish, Crawford, Powell, Golden, & Lewis, 1995; Lewis & Bodfish, 1998), and recently these psychometric findings have been independently replicated (Johnson, 1999). In the next section, we review the results of our comorbidity studies with respect to SIB in people with developmental disabilities. In the following sections, we examine the literature on SIB and comorbid symptoms in people with neurological, psychiatric, and genetic disorders. Recognize, however, that SIB in people with these disorders has not been studied using standard and orthogonal assessment methods, so the available information in these areas is necessarily limited.

SELF-INJURY IN DEVELOPMENTAL DISORDERS

In a series of studies, we examined the associated clinical features in people with SIB secondary to developmental disabilities. For several reasons, one focus of this work has been the relationship between SIB and abnormal repetitive behaviors such as stereotypy, compulsions, and tics. First, clinical observations confirm that many forms of SIB appear repetitive or stereotypic. For example, head hitting often involves highly similar arm motions and a fixed point of hand-to-head contact (see chapter 16, in this volume). Second, individuals who display SIB also frequently engage in common forms of stereotypic behavior such as body rocking, hand waving, or arm waving (Rojahn, 1986). Third, in addition to mental retardation, various forms of SIB are associated with various obsessive–compulsive spectrum disorders (Simeon, Stein, & Hollander, 1995). In people with these conditions, such as *trichotillomania* (hair twirling and pulling) and *onychophagia* (fingernail biting), discrete forms of obsessive or compulsive behaviors tend to co-occur with SIB. Finally, SIB is frequently a comorbid symptom in people with Tourette's syndrome (Robertson, Trimble, & Lees, 1989; Trimble, 1989). Using standardized and item-independent rating scales to measure the varieties of abnormal repetitive behavior in people with mental retardation, we found that in relation to non-SIB cases, people exhibiting SIB have a significantly increased prevalence of stereotypy (Bodfish et al., 1995), compulsions (Powell, Bodfish, Parker, Crawford, & Lewis, 1996), and tics (Bodfish & Lewis, 1997; Rosenquist, Bodfish, & Thompson, 1997; see Figure 2.1). We have replicated this finding for people with autism (Bodfish, Symons, Parker, & Lewis, 2000). Other researchers have also shown an association between SIB and ritualistic behaviors in people with mental retardation (Collacott, Cooper, Branford, & McGrother, 1998), and many previous researchers have noted the co-occurrence of SIB and stereotypy (Berkson & Davenport, 1962; Rojahn, 1986). This pattern of comorbid abnormal repetitive behaviors appears to be independent of age and gender. These findings support the notion that in people with developmental disabilities, at least some forms of SIB may be part of a larger spectrum or dimension of abnormal repetitive behavior.

Researchers have also begun examining the extent to which people with SIB also display forms of abnormal movements such as dyskinesia.

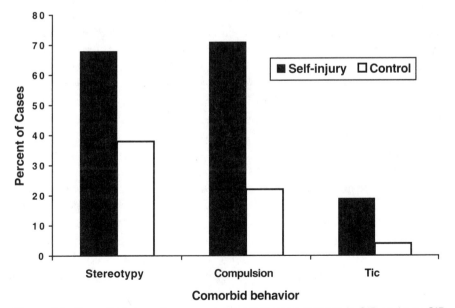

Figure 2.1. Comorbid stereotypy, compulsive behavior, and tics in SIB and non-SIB control cases in a sample of adults with mental retardation (n = 298).

Interestingly, this kind of research question would not arise from the traditional view of SIB as an isolated form of functional behavior disorder. In addition, traditional neurological models of movement disorder would not lead to consideration of an apparently "behavioral" phenomenon such as SIB. However, there are several reasons for hypothesizing a relationship between SIB and motor disorder. First, studies of motor disorder in people with psychiatric and behavioral disorders have revealed a significant association between the two in both psychiatric (e.g., schizophrenia) and mental retardation populations (Rogers, 1992). Second, in Lesch–Nyhan syndrome, SIB co-occurs with a variety of clinically significant abnormal movements (Visser, Bar, & Jinnah, 2000). Third, in animal models of SIB, such as the neonatal 6-hydroxydopamine (6-OHDA) rat model, various forms of impaired mobility and abnormal motor actions are seen as dose-dependent precursors of a chain of movement and behavior that later culminates in SIB (Breese et al., 1984). In addition, previous studies showed an increased prevalence of movement disorders in people with stereotypy (Bodfish, Newell, Sprague, Harper, & Lewis, 1996, 1997). The established link between stereotypy and SIB in people with mental retardation suggests that a risk for movement disorders may also exist for people with SIB. Using standardized and item-independent rating scales to measure motor disorder (e.g., dyskinesia, akathisia) in people with mental retardation, we have found that in relation to non-SIB cases, people with SIB have a significantly increased prevalence of abnormal involuntary movements such as dyskinesia and akathisia. Further, this association appears to hold in samples of adults who have been previously exposed to neuroleptic medication (i.e., dopamine-blocking agents) and samples of adults who were neuroleptic-free at the time of testing. To our knowledge, this relationship has not been examined to date in other studies, so more definitive information about a potential link between SIB and motor disorders must await further studies of this phenomenon. If this is a robust finding, however, then it could present a troubling clinical dilemma. A significant minority of people with SIB are unresponsive to many routinely applied treatments and are therefore treated by default with neuroleptic medications.

Another robust finding with respect to the phenomenology of SIB in developmental disabilities is the strong negative relationship between IQ and SIB. The relationship has been found repeatedly in people with mental retardation (Rojahn, 1986) and also has been shown to exist in people with autism (Bartak & Rutter, 1976). In our studies of adults with mental retardation, we have found that this association with cognitive dysfunction exists not only for SIB, but also for stereotypy and compulsions (Bodfish et al., 1995). In studies of dyskinesia, we have also found that both the prevalence of dyskinesia and the co-occurrence of dyskinesia and other motor disorders (e.g., akathisia) are related negatively to IQ (Bodfish et al., 1996). Thus, the association with IQ provides another link among SIB and the various abnormal repetitive behaviors and movements. The association also provides indirect evidence that the presence of abnormal repetitive behavior and movement indicates the underlying level of neuropathology in people with developmental disabilities.

On the basis of this work on the phenomenology of SIB, we have identified three features that appear to be strongly associated with the occurrence of SIB in persons with developmental disabilities: (a) abnormal repetitive behaviors such as stereotypy and compulsions, (b) abnormal repetitive movements such as dyskinesia and tics, and (c) cognitive disability. In the next sections, we review the existing literature on SIB in neurological, psychiatric, and genetic conditions, with an emphasis on potentially similar patterns of comorbidity in these conditions.

SELF-INJURY IN NEUROLOGICAL DISORDERS

Tourette's syndrome is an important clinical example of the potential association between SIB and movement disorder. *Tourette's syndrome* is a complex neurological disorder characterized by multiple involuntary motor and vocal tics that begin during childhood and then wax and wane over time. In his original paper in 1885, Gilles de la Tourette described two patients with tics who also displayed SIB. Multiple studies of the occurrence of SIB in people with Tourette's syndrome have shown the prevalence of SIB to be in the range of one third to one half of all cases (Robertson, Trimble, & Lees, 1989; Trimble, 1989). Various forms of SIB occur in people with Tourette's syndrome, including head banging, punching, lip biting, tongue biting, eye poking, and skin picking. With respect to comorbid symptoms, people with Tourette's syndrome display a wide variety of repetitive stereotypies and mannerisms in addition to their tics (Miguel et al., 1995). In addition, a strong association exists between Tourette's syndrome and obsessive–compulsive disorder (OCD), with approximately 50% of people with Tourette's syndrome displaying OCD symptoms and as many as 25% of people with OCD displaying tics (George, Trimble, Ring, Sallee, & Robertson, 1993; Leonard et al., 1992; Zohar et al., 1997). SIB in people with Tourette's syndrome has been found to correlate with both increased tic severity and increased severity of obsessive–compulsive symptoms (Robertson, Trimble, & Lees, 1989; Trimble, 1989). Although on average, people with Tourette's syndrome score in the average or above-average range on intellectual tests, specific patterns of neuropsychological deficits have been found in people with Tourette's syndrome, and as many as 50% of people with Tourette's syndrome meet criteria for a specific learning disability (Burd, Kauffman, & Kerbeshian, 1992; Ferrari, Mathews, & Barabas, 1984).

Acanthocytosis is a blood disorder that is associated with various neurological symptoms including dyskinesia, tics, dystonia, peripheral neuropathy, parkinsonism, and dementia (Levine, Estes, & Looney, 1968). *Neuroacanthocytosis* is a progressive neurological disorder characterized by a host of behavioral and movement disorders. The primary clinical hallmark of neuroacanthocytosis, however, is the presence of tongue and lip biting (Jankovic, 1988). Various other stereotypies and mannerisms can occur in people with neuroacanthocytosis in conjunction with a range of movement disorders, including tics, dyskinesias (typically orobuccolingual movements), parkinsonism, rigidity, and bradykinesia. Progressive and marked cognitive impairment also occurs, with the majority of patients exhibiting a global dysfunction characteristic of frontosubcortical dementia (Spitz, Jankovic, & Killian, 1985).

SIB has also been reported to occur during frontal-lobe seizures (Gedye, 1992; Paul, 1997; Williamson, 1995; Williamson, Spencer, Spencer, Novelly, & Mattson, 1985). The behaviors include head hitting, skin picking, tongue biting, hand biting, and scratching (Gedye, 1989). Frontal-lobe seizures are typically brief, with rapid recovery and no loss of consciousness. Further, frontal-lobe seizures associated with SIB are nonconvulsive (i.e., are partial-complex and not generalized). The origin of abnormal electrical activity during frontal-lobe seizures is typically at sites that are deeper in the brain than can be detected by routine, scalp-electrode electroencephalogram (EEG) recordings, and often more invasive EEG recordings are required for identification. Frontal-lobe seizures typically cluster together in bouts or episodes—a clinical pattern often seen in treatment of refractory SIB cases. Patients with frontal-lobe seizures show various stereotyped motor movements in addition to SIB movements (Williamson et al., 1995).

Tourette's syndrome, neuroacanthocytosis, and frontal-lobe epilepsy are neurological disorders that can develop in people of normal intelligence and are associated with the occurrence of clinically significant SIB. It is interesting to note the similarity of the forms of SIB in people with these neurological disorders to those seen typically in people with developmental disabilities. One feature of SIB in these neurological disorders is that it is involuntary or at best can only be temporarily suppressed (i.e., is "partially voluntary") in affected people. The possibility that some form of SIB in people with mental retardation or autism is involuntary has received very little consideration in the research literature or clinical practice (but see Gedye, 1989, 1992). In addition, each type of neurological disorder is associated with a pattern of comorbidity similar to that of SIB in people with developmental disabilities, including evidence of comorbid abnormal repetitive behavior, movement disorders, and cognitive dysfunction.

SELF-INJURY IN PSYCHIATRIC DISORDERS

A wide variety of forms of self-injury are associated with psychiatric disorders, although no consistent taxonomy for their classification exists.

Favazza (1998) has proposed a classification according to differences in observed frequency and resulting level of tissue damage: (a) major SIB, consisting of infrequent acts such as enucleation or autocastration; (b) moderate, or superficial, SIB that occurs more frequently but with only moderate levels of tissue damage and includes such forms as hair pulling, nail biting, skin picking, skin cutting, and skin burning; and (c) minor or stereotypic SIB that occurs frequently but does not manifest with observable skin damage after each episode and includes such forms as head hitting, eye poking, orifice digging, and biting. Others have proposed that SIB that occurs in association with psychiatric disorders be conceptualized as being either *impulsive* or *compulsive* (Simeon, Stein, & Hollander, 1995). This distinction is supported by factor analytical studies of SIB types. For example, Favaro and Satonastoso (1998) examined the variety of SIB in patients with bulimia and found evidence of two separate factors—one including nail biting, hair pulling, and skin picking (compulsive SIB) and the second including skin cutting, skin burning, laxative abuse, and suicide attempts (impulsive SIB).

The quintessential forms of impulsive SIB seem to be skin cutting or skin burning, which are sometimes termed *self-mutilation*. These forms of SIB are frequently encountered in association with more severe forms of personality disorders (Shearer, 1994). Phenomenological studies have demonstrated that the frequency of these forms of SIB is significantly correlated with independent indices of impulsivity. Favazza and Conterio (1989) reported that 78% of patients who self-mutilate decided to do so on the spur of the moment (i.e., with no resistance or delay between the impulse and the behavior). Impulsive SIB has been shown to occur in up to 80% of patients with borderline personality disorder, 75% of patients with intermittent explosive disorder, 60% of patients with posttraumatic stress disorder, 50% of patients with substance abuse disorders, and 48% of patients with eating disorders (Favazza & Rosenthal, 1990; Zlotnick, Mattia, & Zimmerman, 1999). Although the performance of self-mutilation in these disorders seems to be impulsive, it is interesting to note that studies have also indicated that patients who engage in impulsive self-mutilation tend to have comorbid obsessive–compulsive symptoms (Gardner & Gardner, 1975; McKerracher, Loughnane, & Watson, 1968). This suggests two possibilities for the phenomenon of SIB in some psychiatric disorders: First, perhaps a combination of impulsive and compulsive traits facilitates the expression of SIB, and second, individuals who have compulsive tendencies may be more prone to become fixated on initially episodic or impulsive behaviors and thereby develop a pattern of increasingly repetitive, compulsive SIB over time.

People with psychiatric disorders who have forms of SIB that are repetitive, ego-dystonic, and associated with anxiety release can be more readily viewed as compulsive. The SIB forms include hair pulling (trichotillomania), nail biting (onychophagia), and skin picking. By historical convention, these forms have been variously categorized as a form of psychosis, a habit disorder, an impulse control disorder, or a stereotyped movement disorder depending on the issue of the *Diagnostic and Statistical Manual of Mental Diseases* in use. More recently, however, results of research in this area support the conceptualization of these forms of SIB as variants of obsessive–compulsive spectrum disorder. People with compulsive SIB in the forms of trichotillomania, onychophagia, and skin picking share several clinical features with patients with OCD, including a comparable pattern of neuropsychological or specific cognitive deficits, related family histories, and similar response to drug treatment (Rapoport, 1991; Simeon, Stein, & Hollander, 1995). In the case of both compulsive SIB and OCD, excessive grooming behaviors are performed in a repetitive or ritualistic manner, and the patients acknowledge the irrationality of the behavior and resist performing them. Although the symptoms of compulsive SIB in people with psychiatric disorders usually involve a primary form of SIB (e.g., hair pulling in trichotillomania), patients tend to display multiple co-occurring types of SIB. In a study of comorbid SIB in adults with trichotillomania, 54% of participants engaged in multiple other forms of SIB (Simeon et al., 1997). The comorbidity pattern for psychiatric patients with SIB also appears to frequently involve co-occurring compulsions and motor stereotypies. In a study of comorbid behaviors in adults who engaged in severe skin picking, 48% manifested obsessive–compulsive symptoms, and 65% reported current or past body rocking (Wilhelm et al., 1999).

On the basis of the apparent association between SIB and movement disorders in people with developmental disabilities and people with neurological disorders, it would be interesting to know whether a similar pattern of comorbid movement disorders exists for SIB secondary to psychiatric disorders. One can hypothesize that relative to non-SIB psychiatric cases, SIB cases might manifest more spontaneous or drug-induced abnormal movements. Unfortunately, this question has not been the subject of research for SIB in psychiatric disorders. One can speculate that this is related to the overall dearth of research on movement variables in psychiatric disorders (Rogers, 1992) or to the more general schism between neurology and psychiatry.

Another facet of the comorbidity pattern for SIB in people with psychiatric disorders that has not been studied directly is the possible association with cognitive deficits. This comorbidity pattern seems to apply to SIB in the context of both developmental and neurological disorders. Although no studies have been done in this area, it is interesting to note the specific cognitive deficits that have been found in people with OCD given the apparent association between SIB and obsessive–compulsive spectrum disorders. Multiple studies have documented a relatively specific pattern of deficit in neuropsychological performance associated with OCD that includes marked deficits in frontal-lobe functions (Bornstein, 1991; Purcell, Maruff, Kyrios, & Pantelis, 1998). This is interesting in light of the role that frontal-lobe deficits play in the pathophysiology of perseverative, repetitive, and compulsive behavioral phenomenon in various neurological disorders (Ames, Cummings, Wirshing, Quinn, & Mahler, 1994; Ridley, 1994), including the neurological disorders such as Tourette's syndrome and frontal-lobe epilepsy that are associated with SIB.

SELF-INJURY IN GENETIC DISORDERS

Various specific genetic disorders cause developmental brain damage, mental retardation, and SIB. These disorders include Lesch–Nyhan syndrome, Prader–Willi syndrome, Rett syndrome, Cornelia de Lange syndrome, Smith–Magenis syndrome, and fragile X syndrome. The prevalence and form of SIB vary considerably in all these disorders. At one extreme is Lesch–Nyhan syndrome, in which 100% of affected individuals display SIB (Anderson & Ernst, 1994) that typically involves lip biting or other forms of biting but can also involve head hitting, eye poking, and other forms of SIB in a minority of people (e.g., catching limbs in doorways, placing feet under wheelchairs, placing fingers in wheelchair spokes). SIB is prevalent in people with other genetic disorders but is not an invariant part of the phenotype. Other disorders include Prader–Willi syndrome (60% to 80% of people pick their skin; Symons, Butler, Sanders, Feurer, & Thompson, 1999; Whitman & Accardo, 1987), Smith–Magenis syndrome (50% to 70% of people have various forms of SIB; Smith, Dykens, & Greenberg, 1998), and Rett syndrome (30% to 40% of people have various forms of SIB; Sansom et al., 1993). Various forms of SIB have also been reported in association with fragile X syndrome, although more recent studies have found this to be a relatively infrequent part of the phenotype (Symons, Clark, Roberts, & Bailey, in press).

Lesch–Nyhan syndrome is perhaps the prototypical disorder for self-injury. The most prominent feature of the phenotype, however, is movement disability. Motor disorders include choreoathetosis, dyskinesia, dystonia, ataxia, dysarthria, and other involuntary movements (Visser, Bar, & Jinnah, 2000). These movement disorders occur with great frequency and are extremely severe in all affected people. SIB is also a hallmark feature of the Lesch–Nyhan phenotype, emerging in nearly all cases within the first few years of life. It is interesting to note the typical temporal course of SIB episodes in Lesch–Nyhan syndrome. SIB tends to be episodic, waxing and waning over time, which is similar to the pattern of SIB in people with involuntary movement disorders, such as tics in Tourette's syndrome. All reports of the phenomenology of SIB in Lesch–Nyhan syndrome have stressed the apparent compulsive nature of the self-injury (Christie et al.,

1982). Children and adults with Lesch–Nyhan syndrome try to avoid engaging in SIB. For example, some sit on their hands (engage in self-restraint), whereas others request help or mechanical restraints to prevent the SIB (Anderson & Ernst, 1994). One of the main arguments against classifying SIB in Lesch–Nyhan syndrome as compulsive is that affected individuals cannot explicitly verbalize a motivating force (e.g., to lessen anxiety), and currently no evidence supports a generalized tendency for obsessive–compulsive behaviors. However, other recognized forms of obsessive–compulsive spectrum disorders such as trichotillomania and onychophagia also involve a single repetitive behavior without other features of OCD. Finally, all people with Lesch–Nyhan syndrome have cognitive deficits, usually in the form of moderate to severe mental retardation. Thus Lesch–Nyhan syndrome involves SIB and the kinds of motor, behavioral, and cognitive features associated with SIB in people with other developmental, neurological, and psychiatric disorders.

Prader–Willi syndrome and Rett syndrome also provide strong evidence in support of a common motor and behavioral comorbidity pattern for SIB. In both disorders, SIB is a prominent part of the phenotype. Co-occurring abnormal repetitive behaviors are also key features of each disorder. In Prader–Willi syndrome, multiple forms of compulsive behaviors are known to occur in a majority of affected individuals (Dykens, Leckman, & Cassidy, 1996; Feurer et al., 1998). In Rett syndrome, progressively increasing stereotyped hand movements are a hallmark feature (Sansom et al., 1993). Rett syndrome is also characterized by a host of parkinsonism-like movement disorders, such as bradykinesia or tremors (Jankovic, 1988). Finally, both Prader–Willi and Rett syndromes are characterized by marked cognitive disorder in the form of mental retardation.

Existing studies of the other genetic disorders associated with SIB show less evidence for a common behavioral and motor comorbidity pattern. Interestingly, these genetic disorders are the ones with the lower prevalence rates of SIB relative to Lesch–Nyhan syndrome, Prader–Willi syndrome, and Rett syndrome, thus SIB plays a lesser role in these phenotypes. However, evidence for some of the comorbidity features does exist in people with these disorders. Motor disorders occur in Cornelia de Lange and fragile X syndromes, and both stereotyped behaviors and cognitive disabilities occur in association with SIB in Cornelia de Lange, fragile X, and Smith–Magenis syndromes.

SELF-INJURY, COMORBID BEHAVIORS, AND BASAL GANGLIA CIRCUITRY

This chapter's review of existing data on the clinical phenomenology of SIB has demonstrated that SIB occurs in various developmental, neurological, psychiatric, and genetic disorders. Evidence shows that in people with disorders involving SIB, comorbid repetitive behavior, movement disorders, and cognitive deficits also occur (see Table 2.2). Although SIB is most frequently studied in isolation and with respect to mental retardation, clearly similarities exist with respect to comorbidity patterns for SIB in people with mental retardation compared with the other neurological, psychiatric, and genetic conditions with which SIB is associated. The consistency with which this comorbidity pattern occurs suggests that various etiologies may converge on a common brain circuit in at least a subgroup of SIB cases. Elements of this comorbidity pattern (i.e., repetitive behaviors, abnormal movements, cognitive deficits) are consequences of a wide variety of disorders of the basal ganglia, and thus basal ganglia circuitry is a logical candidate for examination in the search for pathophysiological mechanisms for SIB.

The term *basal ganglia* is used to refer to the striatum (caudate, putamen, accumbens, and olfactory tubercle) and the globus pallidus. Historically, examinations of the functions of the basal ganglia have been limited to its role in motor control and movement disorders. More recent research has revealed that the basal ganglia play a major role in nonmotor functions as well. Currently, the functions of the basal ganglia are grouped into five circuits and include motor, ocular motor, cognitive, behavioral/personality,

Table 2.2
Comorbidity Pattern in Disorders Associated with SIB

Disorder	Stereotypy[a]	Compulsion[a]	Tics[a]	Motor Disorder[a]	Cognitive Deficit[a,b]
Mental retardation	Yes	Yes	Yes	Yes	Yes (general)
Autism	Yes	Yes	Yes	Yes	Yes (general)
Tourette's syndrome	Yes	Yes	Yes	Yes	Yes (specific)
Neuroacanthocytosis	Yes	Yes	Yes	Yes	Yes (general)
Frontal-lobe epilepsy	Yes	No	Yes	Yes	Yes (specific)
Personality disorders	No	Yes	No	?	Yes (specific)
Eating disorders	No	Yes	No	?	Yes (specific)
Lesch–Nyhan syndrome	Yes	Yes	Yes	Yes	Yes (general)
Prader–Willi syndrome	No	Yes	No	No	Yes (general)
Rett syndrome	Yes	No	No	Yes	Yes (general)
de Lange syndromes	Yes	?	?	Yes	Yes (general)
Smith–Magenis syndrome	Yes	?	?	Yes	Yes (general)
Fragile X syndrome	Yes	Yes	?	Yes	Yes (general)

[a] presence or absence of comorbid feature: Yes = feature present in typical SIB case, No = feature not present in typical case, ? = unknown, no existing studies.

[b] presence and type of cognitive deficit: Yes = cognitive deficit present in typical SIB case, general = generalized cognitive deficit such as mental retardation or dementia, specific = specific cognitive deficit such as specific learning disability or specific pattern or deficit on neuropsychological testing, ? = unknown, no existing studies.

and limbic divisions (Alexander, Delong, & Strick, 1986; Visser, Bar, & Jinnah, 2000). These circuits each have their origin in distinct cortical areas, are processed through distinct structures within the basal ganglia, and then return through the thalamus to the frontal cortex. Given the functionally integrated nature of the system, lesions to distinct portions of these corticostriatal–thalamic circuits produce circuit-specific symptoms. Of interest is the fact that lesions to these basal ganglia circuits produce the kinds of behavioral, movement, and cognitive symptoms that are part of the comorbidity pattern in the variety of disorders in which SIB occurs (Bhatia & Marsden, 1994). In addition to focal lesions, a set of degenerative and developmental diseases selectively target basal ganglia circuits, and considerable overlap exists among the symptom patterns in these disorders and the behavioral, movement, and cognitive symptoms that tend to occur in association with SIB.

Huntington's disease and Parkinson's disease are adult-onset degenerative diseases of the basal ganglia (Marsden, 1994; Marshall & Shoulson, 1997). Tourette's syndrome is a childhood-onset neurological disorder of the basal ganglia. Motor disorders and abnormal movements are a prominent feature of each condition, and in each condition these features have been linked to specific deficits in basal ganglia motor circuits and supporting neurochemical processes. Abnormal repetitive behaviors in the form of motor stereotypies, obsessive–compulsive symptoms, and perseveration or behavioral rigidity are also prominent features of each of these conditions. Cognitive deficits in the form of dementia are present in severe cases of Huntington's and Parkinson's diseases. People with Tourette's syndrome have cognitive deficits also but they are milder, generally taking the form of specific learning disabilities.

Although a tremendous overlap exists among the motor, behavioral, and cognitive disorders of these three basal ganglia diseases, it is important to note that SIB occurs only in people with Tourette's syndrome. This apparent disparity may be taken as evidence against the role of basal ganglia circuitry in SIB. On the other hand, the developmental nature of Tourette's syndrome distinguishes it from the adult-onset degenerative diseases like Huntington's and Parkinson's. The developing brain responds differently to insults than does the adult brain. Thus, the sequelae of basal ganglia dysfunction that manifest in childhood would be expected to differ from the sequelae of later basal ganglia dysfunction. In this light, it appears that a developmental insult to the basal ganglia circuits is necessary for the manifestation of SIB. This is consistent with existing preclinical models of SIB that have shown that cytochemical lesions in striatal dopamine systems produce SIB in neonatal animals with lesions but not in adult animals with lesions (Breese et al., 1984). This is also consistent with the fact that typical cases of the neurological and psychiatric disorders associated with SIB are childhood- or adolescent-onset disorders. In addition, the highest prevalence of SIB occurs in people with developmental disorders (e.g., mental retardation, autism) and the specific genetic disorders that affect early brain development. Therefore, one reasonable model for the pathogenesis of SIB involves selective insult to the basal ganglia and its functionally integrated structures during early development. Aside from SIB, clinical signs that support this model include comorbid abnormal repetitive behaviors, abnormal involuntary movements, and cognitive deficits.

One critical missing piece of information pertaining to the neural basis for SIB must be found in future neuroimaging studies. As has been the case for imaging studies involving other neurodevelopmental disorders with complex behavioral phenotypes in neurology and psychiatry, perhaps once data from multiple imaging studies are gathered, a confusing picture may emerge, with multiple and even independent brain areas implicated. One way to avoid such confusion may involve careful phenotyping of the presence or absence of key behavioral, motor, and cognitive features that are known to co-occur with SIB in people with various disorders. Given that SIB has multiple etiologies and pathophysiological features, it will be important to identify reliable phenotypic features that are most strongly associated with the various pathophysiological symptoms. For this reason, careful subgrouping based on comorbid features may help shed light on possible areas of neural disorder and thereby potential targets for treatment. For example, on the basis of the present review, it could be hypothesized that SIB in people with autism or mental retardation associated with significant comorbid repetitive behaviors and involuntary movements would be more likely to be related to basal ganglia dysfunction than would SIB that does not occur as a part of this comorbidity pattern.

One potential criticism of the present basal ganglia model is that it does not take into account established environmental influences on SIB. However, this may relate more to the historical split between structural and functional conceptualizations of behavior than to clinical reality in the case of SIB. It is important to note that accounts of the phenomenology of SIB in Lesch–Nyhan syndrome have indicated that the SIB is commonly responsive to changes to ambient social environment (Anderson & Ernst, 1994), despite the genetic and neurobiological factors involved. Thus the relationship among etiology, maintaining factors, and treatment is not always straightforward. Underlying basal ganglia dysfunction may predispose one to unique patterns of environmental sensitivity that are associated with the frequent expression of SIB in certain environmental contexts. The basal ganglia model of SIB and associated behaviors also fails to account for the behavioral specificity of SIB in various cases and conditions (i.e., the reason SIB manifests in distinct forms, such as lip biting or head hitting, in different cases). One possibility, in light of the association between SIB and obsessive–compulsive spectrum disorders, is that SIB, SIB-like compulsions (e.g., hair pulling, nail biting, skin picking), and other non-SIB compulsive behaviors (e.g., washing, ordering) all represent variants of excessive species-specific grooming behaviors (Rapoport, 1991; Stein, Shoulberg, Helton, & Hollander, 1992). Alternatively, the neural basis for SIB and associated repetitive behaviors may overlap with the basal ganglia circuitry that produces species-typical grooming behaviors. A third possibility is that SIB of any form that is initially displayed impulsively (e.g., as part of a tantrum) may be co-opted as a form of compulsive behavior in people predisposed to abnormal repetitive behavior caused by underlying basal ganglia dysfunction.

The proposed comorbidity model of SIB has clinical implications with respect to assessment and treatment protocols. Traditionally, SIB has been assessed as a singular behavioral disorder. The present model suggests that people who engage in SIB should be assessed for co-occurring abnormal repetitive behaviors (e.g., stereotypy, compulsions), motor control deficits, and movement disorders (e.g., tics, dyskinesia, dystonias). The possible association between SIB and OCD, SIB and Tourette's syndrome, and SIB and movement disorders suggests that established treatments for these disorders might prove useful as empirical forms of treatment for refractory SIB in people with mental retardation or autism. Given the established role for dopamine and serotonin in OCD, Tourette's syndrome, and other basal ganglia disorders, this model is consistent with the available data from controlled psychopharmacological studies that have demonstrated the efficacy of serotonin reuptake inhibitors (Rascusin, Klover-Kline, & King, 1999) and dopamine antagonists (Aman & Madrid, 1999) in the treatment of SIB.

In light of the existing phenomenological data on SIB in neurological and psychiatric disorders, it is also interesting to speculate on the degree of voluntary control that is present in people with cognitive disabilities who display SIB. SIB that occurs in association with Tourette's syndrome, frontal-lobe epilepsy, or obsessive–compulsive spectrum disorders (e.g., trichotillomania) occurs in people who can describe their ability to suppress it. Such people report only a partial ability to suppress SIB, similar to the partial voluntary control that exists for tics or compulsions. The partial control is in marked contrast to the assumed degree of voluntary control of SIB in people with mental retardation and autism—despite the necessarily greater degree of generalized cognitive deficit associated with mental retardation. Objective measurement of conscious control in primarily nonverbal people is difficult at best. In the absence of an objective test of conscious control, the presence of observable signs of other involuntary or partially voluntary phenomena such as tics, dyskinesia, or compulsions provides at least indirect support that SIB in such people is not under complete voluntary control in at least some instances.

The model presented here suggests a specific neurobiological system underlying the pattern of behavioral and movement disorders that are seen in association with SIB in a wide variety of clinical conditions. Further, the occurrence of SIB in this pattern of symptoms may be exclusively associated with those conditions that involve insult to the system during the early developmental period. The evidence in support of this model indicates that self-injury can be viewed as part of a set of co-occurring repetitive behaviors and movements in at least a significant subset of people with SIB.

CONCLUSION

The co-occurrence of self-injury with abnormal repetitive behaviors, movement disorders, and cognitive deficits appears to be a pattern of comorbidity that is consistent in various different developmental, neurological, psychiatric, and genetic disorders. This comorbidity pattern appears to hold for a variety of discrete self-injurious actions including the common behavioral topographies of head hitting and hand biting in people with mental retardation, compulsive forms of self-injury such as hair pulling and skin picking in people with certain psychiatric disorders, and such phenotype-specific forms of self-injury as lip biting in people with Lesch–Nyhan syndrome. This comorbidity model of self-injury can be used to guide the search for both mechanisms and treatments of self-injury. The combined motor, behavioral, and cognitive functions of the basal ganglia are a plausible model for the pathophysiology of self-injury that is consistent with the evidence in favor of a common motor, behavioral, and cognitive symptom comorbidity pattern for self-injury. Further, basal ganglia dysfunction is an established part of the pathophysiology of several of the neurological and psychiatric conditions associated with self-injury. The clinical implication of the basal ganglia dysfunction model is that if the treatment focus expands from self-injury as a discrete symptom to self-injury in the context of comorbid neurological and psychiatric features, then a corresponding range of potential treatments and treatment targets can be considered.

3

EPIDEMIOLOGY OF SELF-INJURIOUS BEHAVIOR IN MENTAL RETARDATION: A REVIEW

JOHANNES ROJAHN AND ANNA J. ESBENSEN

They came to Gerasene territory on the other side of the lake. As he [Jesus] got out of the boat, he was immediately met by a man . . . who had an unclean spirit. The man . . . could no longer be restrained even with a chain. In fact, he had frequently been secured with handcuffs and chains, but had pulled the chains apart and smashed the fetters. No one had proved strong enough to tame him. Uninterruptedly night and day . . . he screamed and gashed himself with stones. (*The Bible*, Mark 5:1–5)

As cultural anthropologists have documented (Favazza, 1987), an abundance of socially accepted forms of self-mutilation have been around for centuries, and by no means has self-mutilation been found only in primitive societies. However, few have debated the acceptability of certain forms of self-mutilation that are associated with recognized pathological conditions, such as those in people with mental illness or mental retardation. Whether the man in the opening quote has a form of mental illness or perhaps mental retardation cannot be discerned from the description—and it is not even relevant. This biblical anecdote is a remarkable early example of the menacing nature that severe, pathological self-mutilation can represent, as well as the fear and consternation it can evoke in people who are confronted with it.

People with mental retardation are particularly susceptible to developing serious problem behaviors, particularly self-injurious behavior (SIB; Schroeder, Rojahn, & Oldenquist, 1991). Besides the potential harm and actual physical injury engendered by it, SIB is most troublesome because it can seriously diminish psychological and social development, lead to isolation, and generally worsen a person's quality of life. To develop a better sense of the extent of the

SIB problem within the population of people with mental retardation, we have carried out an exhaustive review of the relevant epidemiological literature.

REVIEW OF METHODOLOGY

This review is modeled in part on previous reviews, particularly those by Johnson and Day (1992) and Rojahn (1994). All studies reported in those reviews were re-examined, and most of them were included in this chapter. In addition, we identified several studies that have appeared since that time. Unlike Johnson and Day, we also reviewed epidemiological reports that were presented at scientific conferences but never published. To identify new or previously unpublished studies, manual and computerized (PsycInfo) searches were conducted, supplemented by personal contacts with colleagues. Two studies from Johnson and Day (1992) are missing in this review. The first one—a study by Kravitz and Boehm (1971)—was omitted because it included only normally developing infants. The paper by Ressman and Butterworth (1952) was excluded because the journal in which the study was published was unavailable, and the information provided by Day and Johnson was not sufficient for the purpose of this review. In total, we reviewed and analyzed 38 individual publications or reports of epidemiological studies and administrative database reports.

To systematize our effort, we followed the example of Johnson and Day (1992) by creating a table that allowed us to perform a qualitative meta-analysis with a standard set of critical review criteria: (a) the purpose of the study, (b) the characteristics of the population that was screened for SIB (i.e., the target population), (c) the sampling procedure, (d) the definition of SIB, (e) the assessment instrument and assessment process, and (f) the results. The results were broken down into two parts: (a) results that pertain to the SIB sample (e.g., relative prevalence of a certain SIB topography within all SIB cases, demographic composition of the index group) and (b) the results that pertain to the target population (e.g., prevalence of SIB cases in the total target group and various subpopulations; see Table 3.1). On several occasions the authors did not provide these statistics, so we had to calculate the values on the basis of the provided information.

Purpose of Data Collection

The studies reviewed in this chapter were conducted for different reasons, and the purpose influenced the methodology and, consequently, often the results. About three fourths of the papers reviewed were based on prospective, research-driven data collection processes that were designed and conducted to (a) estimate the prevalence or incidence rates of SIB or

(text continues on p. 69)

TABLE 3.1
Epidemiological Studies of SIB Among Individuals With Mental Retardation

Authors, year of publication	Purpose	Total population characteristics	Sampling procedure	SIB definition	Instruments & assessment	Results		
						SIB subsample	Total population[a]	
Ando & Yoshimura (1978)	Prevalence of SIB	Children at a school for mental retardation and autism in Japan N = 128 *Age (years):* x̄ = 10.6; range 6-14 *Gender:* 42% ♀, 58% ♂	Total population study	"... compulsively and consciously destructive behavior against himself such as head banging or hand biting"	A maladaptive behavior scale not further specified Evaluation of children by teachers and aides	SIB cases: *n* = 7 *Mental retardation level:* IQ x̄ = 31 ± 11	Global SIB prevalence: 5.5%	
Ballinger (1971)	Prevalence and nature of SIB	Patients in a hospital for individuals with mental retardation in Scotland N = 631 *Gender:* 44% ♀, 56% ♂ Mental retardation Level (IQ): 8% 68+, 23% 52-67, 23% 36-51, 23% 20-35, 23% <19	Total population study	"Any painful or destructive act, committed by the patient against his own body" Occurrence of SIB within the previous month	Examination of individuals by author	SIB cases: *n* = 93 *Gender:* 55% ♀, 45% ♂ *Mental retardation level (IQ):* 2% 68+ 9% 52-67 16% 36-51 28% 20-35 45% 0-19 *Topography:* 38% picking 22% striking 20% scratching 18% banging 15% biting	Global SIB prevalence: 14.8% *Prevalence mental retardation level (IQ):* 4% 68+ 6% 52-67 10% 36-51 18% 20-35 29% 0-19	

(continued)

TABLE 3.1
(Continued)

Authors, year of publication	Purpose	Total population characteristics	Sampling procedure	SIB definition	Instruments & assessment	Results SIB subsample	Results Total population[a]
Bodfish, Crawford, Powell, Parker, Golden, & Lewis (1995)	Description of compulsive and stereotypic behavior and SIB	Residents with severe to profound mental retardation living in a public residential facility $N = 210$ *Age (years):* $\bar{x} = 34.3$; range 18-26 *Gender:* 36% ♀, 64% ♂ *Medication:* 48% on psychotropic medication	Total population study with a two-step screening process: 1. Subjects from total public residential facility for individuals with mental retardation ($N = 448$) with severe/profound mental retardation, who were ambulatory and medically stable 2. Screened for target behaviors by caseload psychologists	"Repetitive movements that can cause tissue damage (e.g., hitting, slapping, biting self)"	Rated by teachers on: Stereotypy Checklist Self-Injury Checklist Compulsive Behavior Checklist	SIB cases: $n = 98$ *Multiple SIBs:* $\bar{x} = 2.9$ SIB per person 28% one SIB 22% two SIBs 16% three SIBs 34% three or more SIBs *Topography:* 27% biting 22% hitting body parts 21% hitting objects 16 % hitting with objects <10% pulling, rubbing or scratching, poking	Global SIB prevalence: 46.6%

| Borthwick-Duffy (1994a) | Prevalence of destructive behaviors

Administrative data survey | People served by California Department of Developmental Services in 1987

$N = 91,164$ | Total population study | *Frequency and Severity:* "Behavior causing severe self-injury and requiring physician's immediate attention at least once per month and/or behavior causing minor self-injury and requiring first aid at least once per week" | Client Development Evaluation Report (CDER)

Single SIB item | SIB cases: $n = 2,017$ | Global SIB prevalence: 2.2%

Dual diagnoses:
2% mental retardation only
6% dual diagnosis
9% severe dual diagnosis

Age (years):
1% 0-3
1% 4-10
2% 11-20
3% 21+

Gender:
2.1% ♀, 2.3% ♂

Mental retardation level:
<1% mild
2% moderate
3% severe
7% profound

Residential setting:
<1% independent living
<1% parental home
2% community care (1-6)
4% community care (7+)
2% intermediate care
3% skilled nursing
12% institution |

(continued)

TABLE 3.1
(Continued)

Authors, year of publication	Purpose	Total population characteristics	Sampling procedure	SIB definition	Instruments & assessment	Results	
						SIB subsample	Total population[a]
							Maladaptive behavior: <1% SIB and aggression 2% SIB and destruction <1% SIB, aggression, and destruction
Borthwick-Duffy (1994b)	Prevalence of destructive behaviors	People served by California Department of Developmental Services in 1987 *N* = 91,164	Total population study	*Frequency:* "SIB at least once a week"	Client Development Evaluation Report (CDER) Single SIB item	SIB cases: *n* = 8,444	Global SIB prevalence: 9.3%
5. Borthwick, Meyers, & Eyman (1981)	Prevalence of SIB	People receiving services for the developmentally disabled during 1979 in three states (Arizona, California, Colorado) *N* = 6,202	Total population study—three-state collection of information from all clients receiving developmental disabilities services in their state	"Does physical violence to self"	Behavior Development Survey (BDS) Single SIB item AAMD Adaptive Behavior Scale (ABS) shortened version	SIB cases: *n* = 1,228	Global SIB prevalence: 19.8% *Dual diagnoses:* 9% mental retardation only 16% dual diagnosis 22% severe dual diagnosis *Age (years):* 6% 0-3 10% 4-10 10% 11-20 9% 21+

Danford & Huber (1982)	Prevalence of pica	Individuals with mental retardation residing in an institution for 2 years N = 991 Age (years): range 11-88 Gender: 44% ♀, 56% ♂	Total population study—staff interviews and direct observation	Pica definition: "Frequent consumption of nonfood items (nonfood pica) and the excessive, compulsive eating of food and food-related substances (food pica)"	Not indicated	Pica cases: n = 256 Mental retardation level: <1 % borderline 2 % mild 4 % moderate 17 % severe 78 % profound	Gender: 9% ♀, 10% ♂ Mental retardation level: 4% mild 7% moderate 15% severe 25% profound Residential setting: 38% institution 18% convalescent 8% boarding home 13% family home 8% own home Maladaptive behavior: <1% SIB and aggression 2% SIB and destruction <1% SIB, aggression, and destruction
Emberson & Walker (1990)	Prevalence of SIB	Hospital residents for people with mental retardation N = 525 Age (years): x̄ = 43	Total population study Contact letters sent to hospital wards asking if anyone exhibited SIB in past 4 months; then interviewed care staff	"Repeated behavior that is self-inflicted, nonaccidental injury producing bruising, bleeding or other temporary or permanent tissue damage"	Not indicated (author checklist)	SIB cases: n = 163 Age (years): x̄ = 37 Gender: 50% ♀, 50% ♂ Medication: 53% anti-psychotic 32% other medications 26% anticonvulsants 13% sedatives 4% anxiolytics	Global pica prevalence: 25.8%

(continued)

TABLE 3.1
(Continued)

Authors, year of publication	Purpose	Total population characteristics	Sampling procedure	SIB definition	Instruments & assessment	Results	
						SIB subsample	Total population[a]
			Obtained demographics, description of SIB, when it was first noticed and last displayed, and whether physical restraint was involved			*Mental retardation level:* 18% mild/moderate, 64% severe, 17% profound *Multiple SIBs:* 38% one SIB, 38% two SIBs, 24% three or more SIBs *Topography:* 37% biting, 29% face slapping, 16% scratching, 16% skin picking, 13% head butting, 12% scratching face, <10% head banging, hair pulling, throwing self *Frequency:* 19% <once a week, 31% >once a week, 33% >once a day, 17% ≥once per hour	17% nonfood pica, 5% food pica, 4% combined *Mental retardation level:* 11% borderline, 10% mild, 11% moderate, 16% severe, 33% profound Global SIB prevalence: 31%
Eyman & Call (1977)	Prevalence of behavior problems	Individuals with mental retardation receiving services	Total population study	"Does physical violence to self"	Adaptive Behavior Scale (ABS)	SIB cases: n = 103	Global SIB prevalence: 15%

from two regional centers in California and Colorado community and institution centered services for mental retardation and from the Nevada Division of Mental Hygiene and Mental Retardation

N = 6,870

Age (years):
25% 0-12 years
76% 13 or older

Gender:
44% ♀, 56% ♂

Mental retardation level:
61% mild/moderate
21% severe
18% profound

Residential setting:
27% institution
30% community facility
43% family

Ratings by direct-care personnel for the institutions and social workers for the community placements

Single SIB item

Age (years):
15% ages 0-12
15% ages 13+

Mental retardation level:
8% mild or moderate
20% severe
36% profound

Residential setting:
34% institution
10% community facility
8% family settings

(continued)

TABLE 3.1
(Continued)

Authors, year of publication	Purpose	Total population characteristics	Sampling procedure	SIB definition	Instruments & assessment	Results: SIB subsample	Results: Total population[a]
Fovel, Lash, Barron, & Roberts (1989)	Prevalence of SIB	Residents of a state-supported school for mental retardation in Massachusetts in 1985 and 1988 $N = 669$ *Age (years):* $\bar{x} = 43$; range 17-85 *Gender:* 46% ♀, 54% ♂ Mental retardation level: 9% mild 21% moderate 40% severe 29% profound	Total population study of persons who self-restrain	"The occurrence of behavior(s) that produces redness, irritation, swelling, or bruising of one's own body *and* requires medical attention (e.g., cleaning or bandaging by a nurse and examination or treatment by a physician) at least once within the last year"	Not indicated (author checklist)	SIB cases: $n = 187$	Global SIB prevalence: 28.0%
Griffin, Ricketts, Williams, Locke, Altmeyer, & Stark (1987)	Prevalence, nature, and treatment of SIB	Children and adolescents with developmental disability in a metropolitan school district $N = 2,663$	Total population study Survey distributed within each school district to schools with target population	"Repetitive or isolated acts toward oneself that had resulted in physical harm during the preceding 12 months" *or*	Self-Injurious Behavior Identification Survey (SIB-I)	SIB cases: $n = 69$ *Topography:* 46% biting 42% head hitting 30% head banging 25% scratching 20% arm hitting 15% eye gouging 15% hair pulling	Global SIB prevalence: 2.6%

Study	Purpose	Sample	Procedure	Definition	Instrument	Results
		Age (years): x̄ = 10.2; range 2-20 *Gender:* 41% ♀, 59% ♂ Mental retardation level: 17.4% mild/moderate 82.6% severe/profound *Other treatments:* 53.6% restraints 0.7% psychotropic medication	Survey completed by teachers with students identified as self-injurious	"Repetitive acts toward oneself during the preceding 12 months that were typically considered to represent a SIB response" *or* "Restrained or having received psychoactive medication during the preceding 12 months for causing or attempting to cause injury to oneself"		13% orifice digging 12% mouthing 10% ruminating <10% pica, throat gouging *Frequency:* 72% at least daily 18% every 30 minutes 11% hourly 43% daily 19% weekly 8% monthly 1% once in last year
Griffin, Williams, Stark, Altmeyer, & Mason (1986)	Prevalence, nature, and treatment of SIB	Clients in residential facilities or state schools for mental retardation in Texas N = 10,000 *Age (years):* x̄ = 32.2 *Gender:* 44% ♀, 56% ♂	Total population study. Sent survey to facility coordinators. Survey completed by unit psychologists; reviewed by other members of clients interdisciplinary team	BDC1: n = 376 "Repetitive acts that resulted in frequent tissue damage" BDC2: n = 41 "Isolated acts (resulting in tissue damage) that the clients directed toward themselves" BDC3: n = 439 "Repetitive acts	Self-Injurious Behavior Identification Survey (SIB-I)	SIB cases: n = 184 *Age (years):* x̄ = 29.5; range 3-84 *Gender:* 44% ♀, 56% ♂ *Mental retardation level (by IQ):* <1% mild 9% moderate 19% severe 66% profound Global SIB prevalence: 13.6%

(continued)

TABLE 3.1
(Continued)

Authors, year of publication	Purpose	Total population characteristics	Sampling procedure	SIB definition	Instruments & assessment	Results	
						SIB subsample	Total population[a]
		Maladaptive behaviors: 55% aggression 47% personal aberrant behavior 30% destruction 30% avoidance behavior 51% motor idiosyncracies 17% sleep disturbances	Placed clients into 1 of 4 behavioral definition categories (BDC)	that did not result in visible tissue damage" BDC4: *n* = 455 "Clients who were mechanically restrained and/or receiving psychoactive medication specifically to prevent the occurrence of SIB" SIB occurred in last 12 months		*Maladaptive behaviors:* 55% any aberrant behavior *Multiple SIBs:* 58% one+ SIB 28% two SIBs 16% three SIBs 15% four or more SIBs *Frequency:* 5% every 30 minutes 6% hourly 55% daily 26% weekly 33% monthly or less *Topography:* 39% biting 37% head hitting 29% head banging 26% scratching 15% mouthing 14% arm hitting 13% pica 10% orifice digging < 10% hair pulling, eye gouging, ruminating, throat gouging	

Hill & Bruininks (1984)	Prevalence of maladaptive behavior	Residents in 236 public institutions and private community facilities throughout the United States $N = 2,271$	Random sampling of public institutions and private community facilities from entire 1977 list maintained by the National Association of Superintendents of Public Residential Facilities	None provided	Personal Record Sheet	SIB cases: $n = 323$	Global SIB prevalence: 14.2% *Residential setting:* 11% community residential 22% public residential
Hillery & Mulcahy (1997)	Prevalence of SIB	People in community care in Ireland $N = 429$ *Age (years):* $\bar{x} = 25.7$; range 2-84 *Gender:* 46% ♀, 54% ♂ *Mental retardation level:* 73% moderate 22% severe 5% profound *Residential setting:* 64% at home 36% residential center	Total population study Traced all individuals with IQ less than 50, within the geographical borders of a single community care area, for one month	"Behavior that is self-injurious and nonaccidental, producing bruising, bleeding, or other temporary or permanent tissue damage, or behavior that would produce bruising, bleeding, or tissue damage were it not for the use of protective devices or restraints"	Completion of special record sheet by staff once a day indicating whether SIB occurred within a 24-hour time period, its type, and its severity	SIB cases: $n = 62$ *Age (years):* $\bar{x} = 23.6$; range 3-60 *Gender:* 42% ♀, 58% ♂ *Mental retardation level:* 42% moderate 53% severe 5% profound *Topography:* (from most to least) Biting Slapping Head banging Eye poking	Global SIB prevalence: 14.4% *Residential setting:* 53% of those that lived at home

(continued)

TABLE 3.1
(Continued)

Authors, year of publication	Purpose	Total population characteristics	Sampling procedure	SIB definition	Instruments & assessment	Results	
						SIB subsample	Total population[a]
Jacobson (1982)	Prevalence of destructive behaviors	Individuals with mental retardation in New York N = 30,578 11.6% (N = 3,555) of which also have psychiatric disabilities and will be excluded in this summary *Age (years):* 71%: 21-44 29%: 5-20 *Gender:* 45% ♀, 55% ♂ *Mental retardation level:* *Ages 0-21 years:* 27% mild 30% moderate 21% severe 22% profound *Ages 22-45 years:* 27% mild 26% moderate 23% severe 24% profound	Total population study Protocols completed by clinical staff with experience in developmental disabilities services	"SIB that poses a serious impediment to independent functioning"	Developmental Disabilities Information Survey (DDIS) Single SIB item	SIB cases: n = 2,507	Global SIB prevalence: 8.2% *Age (years):* 8% 0-21 9% 22+ *Mental retardation level:* *Ages 0-21:* 2% mild 3% moderate 9% severe 14% profound *Ages 22-45:* 3% mild 3% moderate 6% severe 18% profound *Residential setting:* *Ages 0-21:* 0% independent 4% parents 2% family care 9% community 16% dev center *Ages 22-45:* 1% independent 2% parents 2% family care 5% community 15% dev center

Study		Population		Definition	Instrument	Findings	Prevalence
Johnson, Day, & Hassanein (1988)	Prevalence of SIB	Trainable mentally retarded (TMR) N = 857 *Other disabilities in survey:* Deafness, blindness, Severe multihandicaps, Personal and social adjustments, Autism and other health impairments	Total population study Surveys mailed to all school districts of Kansas	"Chronic persistent, self-directed behaviors, frequently noted among (but not limited to) children with autism and developmental delays children, that would be expected to cause pain in the average person or that cause immediate or eventual tissue damage. Examples include, but are not limited to: hitting scratching, or biting self; . . . The self-injury may be either mild or severe in nature"	Survey instrument developed for study	SIB cases: $n = 120$ *Topography:* 58% striking 52% pinching, scratching, poking, pulling 45% biting 17% pica <1% vomiting	Global SIB prevalence: 14%
Kebbon & Windahl (1985)	Prevalence of SIB	Persons receiving services for mental retardation in 22 of 25 counties in Sweden	Total population study Superintendents, social workers, psychologists,	Must have displayed SIB within the past 5 months "Behavior including an overt motor component, one part of the body being moved against	Not indicated (author questionnaire)	SIB cases: $n = 1,198$ *Gender:* 44% ♀, 56% ♂	Global SIB prevalence: 4.2% *Mental retardation level:* <1% mild

(continued)

TABLE 3.1
(Continued)

Authors, year of publication	Purpose	Total population characteristics	Sampling procedure	SIB definition	Instruments & assessment	Results — SIB subsample	Results — Total population[a]
		$N = 28,215$ *Gender:* 44% ♀, 56% ♂ *Mental retardation level:* 24.7% mild 34.6% moderate 28.6% severe 13.2% profound *Residential setting:* 26% institutions 74% integrated setting	and physicians responsible for gathering information Assumed informants knew the daily living conditions of the individual	another or against objects in the individual's surroundings" Excluded other behaviors such as pica, vomiting, and rumination		*Mental retardation level:* 1% mild 12% moderate 48% severe 41% profound *Residential setting:* 15% own home 7% group home 7% boarding school 64% residential home 8% special hospital	1% moderate 7% severe 13% profound *Residential setting:* 1% own home 3% group home 6% boarding school 11% residential home 15% special hospital *Frequency:* 75% daily or weekly
MacKay, McDonald, & Morressey (1974)[a]	Prevalence of SIB	Inpatient population of a British hospital $N = 600$ *Mental retardation level:* 33% moderate 48% severe 19% profound	Observations for 1 year	". . . painful or destructive act committed against own body" such as head banging, face slapping, skin picking, hair pulling, and regurgitation	Questionnaire	SIB cases: $n = 114$	Global SIB prevalence: 19%

Study	Purpose	Sample	Design/Measure	Definition	Instrument	SIB cases	Results
Maisto, Baumeister, & Maisto (1978)	Prevalence of SIB	Individuals in a state residential training center N = 1,300 Age (years): x̄ = 33.5; range 10-70 Gender: 44% ♀, 56% ♂ Mental retardation level: 5.2% mild 8.7% moderate 28.5% severe 47.6% profound	Total population study Personnel identified individuals who exhibited any type of SIB Questionnaire that was completed by the unit psychologist for each of these residents	"Repetitive acts by individuals directed towards themselves that result in physical harm or tissue damage"	Not indicated (author checklist and questionnaire)	SIB cases: n = 182 Age (years): x̄ = 28.3; range 10-62 Gender: 55% ♀, 45% ♂ Mental retardation level: 4% moderate 96% severe/profound	Global SIB prevalence: 14.0% Mental retardation level: 0% mild 3% moderate 21% severe/profound
Maurice & Trudel (1982)	Prevalence of SIB	Individuals residing in three institutions (two psychiatric, one mental retardation) in Quebec N = 2,858 Age (years): x̄ = 45.8 Gender: 47% ♀, 53% ♂ Diagnosis: 43.7% mental retardation 48.5% psychotic	Total population study Every ward in institutions completed initial short questionnaire that identified individuals with SIB Persons in charge of ward identified residents engaging in SIB; interview met with direct care personnel and completed main questionnaire	"Movement emitted voluntarily or involuntarily in a repetitive or stereotyped manner that contributed to a corporeal damage to the person who emitted the movement" SIB within last 2 years	Not indicated (author questionnaire)	SIB cases: n = 403 Mental retardation level: 10% mild 37% moderate 53% severe/profound Multiple SIBs: 41% one SIB 29% two SIBs 30% three or more SIBs	Global SIB prevalence: 14.1% 14% institutionalized population 23% population with mental retardation

(continued)

TABLE 3.1
(Continued)

Authors, year of publication	Purpose	Total population characteristics	Sampling procedure	SIB definition	Instruments & assessment	Results	
						SIB subsample	Total population[a]
Miller, Canen, Roebel, & MacLean (2000)	Prevalence of behavior problems including SIB	Archival data from individuals with mental retardation in Wyoming and South Dakota receiving Medicaid Waiver services *N* = 4,006 *Age (years):* x̄ = 35.2; range 3–96 *Gender:* 43.3% ♀, 56.7% ♂ *Mental retardation level:* 50% mild 20% moderate 12% severe 18% profound *Residential setting* 33.4% group home 23.8% family 22% independent 9.9% semi-independent 9.6% institution	Total population study	"Hurtful to self"	Inventory for Client and Agency Planning Single item	SIB cases: *n* =1502	Global SIB prevalence: 37.5% *Mental retardation level:* 27% mild 37% moderate 49% severe 60% profound

Source	Purpose	Sample/Design	Definition	Measures	Results
Mulick, Dura, Rasnake, & Callahan (1986)	Prevalence of SIB	Residents in an Intermediate Care Facility for Mental Retardation (ICFMR) for nonambulatory patients with severe and profound mental retardation N = 102 *Age (years):* x̄ 35; range 21–68 *Gender:* 47% ♀, 53% ♂ Total population study	"Behavior that causes physical damage to the person's own body" (Tate & Baroff, 1966)	Behavior Problems Inventory (BPI) Vineland Adaptive Behavior Scales	SIB cases: n = 55 *Multiple SIBs:* 51% one SIB 31% two SIBs 18% three or more SIB *Topography:* 13% head hitting 12% biting 11% pica 11% teeth grinding < 10% stuffing fingers in body orifices, scratching, rumination, hitting, hair pulling, etc. Global SIB prevalence: 54%
Murphy, Hall, Oliver, & Kissi-Debra (1999)	Identification of early emergence of SIB	Children with severe mental retardation (learning disability) and/or autism in the United Kingdom N = 614 Selected students with *potential* for exhibiting SIB; did not include students that were exhibiting SIB for more than 3 months *Age (years):* <11 Prevalence and incidence study—students selected from schools listed in Education Authorities' Yearbook (1991) Schools for children with severe intellectual disabilities and/or autism only Interviewed teachers who identified children; families contacted for consent	"Behavior that causes physical damage to the person's own body" (Tate & Baroff, 1966) Potential topographies were hitting head on objects, hitting objects to head, hitting body/head or kicking body, biting, scratching, pinching, eye poking, hair pulling, inserting objects into orifices	Vineland Adaptive Behavior Scales Childhood Autism Rating Scale (CARS) Aberrant Behavior Checklist (ABC) Teacher Concern Scale Naturalistic observations at 3-month intervals for 18 months	SIB cases: n = 154 Global SIB prevalence: 25.1% *Global SIB incidence:* 3% within 3 months 22% exhibit SIB >3 months 3% with potential SIB

(continued)

TABLE 3.1
(Continued)

Authors, year of publication	Purpose	Total population characteristics	Sampling procedure	SIB definition	Instruments & assessment	Results	
						SIB subsample	**Total population[a]**
		Matched control group	Participating children matched (with help from teachers) with another child in their class without SIB, who had similar age and adaptive level				
Oliver, Murphy, & Corbett (1987)	Prevalence of SIB	Residents with IQs < 70 from one health region in the United Kingdom N = 616	Total population study in a single health region in the United Kingdom (population size not reported)	"Repeated, self-inflicted, nonaccidental injury, producing bruising, bleeding, or other temporary or permanent tissue damage; also, any such behavior that would produce bruising, bleeding, or tissue damage were it not for protective devices, restraints, specific medical, or psychological interventions in use"	Screening questionnaire Interview with an individual who knew subject well	SIB cases: n = 596 *Age (years):* x̄ = 24.8; range 2-88 *Gender:* 42% ♀, 58% ♂ *Mental retardation level (IQ):* 12% mild 49% moderate/ severe 40% profound *Residential setting:* 51% Mental retardation hospitals 28% hostels 21% home 12% within hospital	Global SIB prevalence: N/A

60   ROJAHN AND ESBENSEN

Study	Purpose	Sample	Procedure	Definition/Instrument	Results
			Referred to the project individuals engaging in SIB in the past 4 months by professionals in the field Also visited mentally handicapped hospitals and interviewed staff		*Medication:* 36% antipsychotics 4% sedatives/ hypnotics 10% anxiolytics 20% central nervous system drugs *Multiple SIBs:* 54% more than one SIB *Topography:* 39% skin picking 38% biting 36% head slapping 28% head banging 10% body banging 10% other SIB
Reid, Ballinger, Heather & Melvin (1984)	Prevalence of maladaptive behaviors in comparison to a 1975 sample	Adults with severe and profound mental retardation in a hospital in the United Kingdom N = 86 *Age (years):* x̄ = 41.3; range 24-78 *Gender:* 57% ♀, 43% ♂ *Mental retardation level:* 52% severe 48% profound	Reexamined original cohort of 100 residents 6 years later in 1981 Subjects rated by nurses and psychiatrists	"Self-injury" Modified Manifest Abnormalities Scale of the Clinical Interview Schedule	SIB cases: *n* = 16 (nurse ratings) SIB cases: *n* = 6 (psychiatrist ratings) Global SIB prevalence: 19% nurse ratings 7% psychiatrist ratings

(continued)

TABLE 3.1
(Continued)

Authors, year of publication	Purpose	Total population characteristics	Sampling procedure	SIB definition	Instruments & assessment	Results	
						SIB subsample	Total population[a]
Rojahn (1984)	Prevalence of SIB	Adults in a residential institution for people with severe and profound mental retardation (Germany)	Sample of people with mental retardation who were low functioning	"Behavior that causes physical damage to the person's own body" (Tate & Baroff, 1966)	Behavior Problems Inventory (BPI)	SIB cases: n = 60	Global SIB prevalence: 65.9%
						Gender:	
			Checklists on selected residents completed by direct-care staff			54% ♀, 46% ♂	
		N = 91				*Multiple SIBs:*	
						25% one SIB	
						20% two SIBs	
		Age (years):				55% three or more SIBs	
		x̄: ♀ = 35; range 19-49					
		x̄: ♂ = 34; range 21-49				*Topography:*	
						70% hitting	
						40% biting	
						25% scratching	
						17% pinching	
						15% mouthing and sucking	
						13% pica	
						12 % aerophagia	
						<10%: gouging self, pulling out own hair, stuffing orifices, ruminative vomiting, coprophagia, polydipsia	

| Rojahn (1986) | Prevalence of SIB | Individuals with mental retardation in Germany

N = 13,313

From 134 participating facilities | Nationwide mail survey of individuals registered in schools/training centers, workshops, and group homes of a large national service provider

Materials to local service facilities distributed by local societies

Questionnaires for people who exhibited listed SIB within last 2 weeks filled in by staff

Second mailing to 98 local societies for reliability assessment

Control sample:
Gender:
41% ♀, 57% ♂

Mental retardation level:
20% mild
38% moderate
36% severe
7% profound | "Behavior that causes, or at least has the potential to cause, manifest damage to the person's own body" (Tate & Baroff, 1966)

Behavior Problems Inventory (BPI)

Vineland Social Maturity Scale | SIB cases: n = 431

Gender:
48% ♀, 51% ♂

Mental retardation level:
13% mild
28% moderate
43% severe
16% profound

Residential setting:
61% natural parents
2% foster home
34% group home
3% other

Multiple SIBs:
24% only one SIB

Topography:
45% biting
45% head-body
42% scratching
31% body-body
30% head-object
19% pinching
17% body-object
16% stuffing fingers in cavities
15% pulling hair
15% pica
14% teeth grinding
11% extreme drinking
< 10% rumination, stuffing objects in cavities, air swallowing | Global SIB prevalence: 1.7%

Setting:
8% schools/training centers
3% sheltered workshops
8% group homes |

TABLE 3.1
(Continued)

Authors, year of publication	Purpose	Total population characteristics	Sampling procedure	SIB definition	Instruments & assessment	Results	
						SIB subsample	Total population[a]
Rojahn, Borthwick-Duffy, & Jacobson (1993)	Prevalence of destructive behavior and psychiatric diagnoses	People served by the Department of Developmental Services in 1990 $N = 89,419$ People served by New York State Office of Mental Retardation and Developmental Disabilities in 1990 $N = 45,683$	Total population studies involving the entire database of individuals who received developmental disabilities services at the time	California: "SIB at least once a week" New York: "SIB that poses a serious impediment to independent functioning"	California: Client Development Evaluation Report (CDER) Single SIB item New York: Developmental Disabilities Information Survey (DDIS) Single SIB item	California SIB cases: $n = 7,866$ New York SIB cases: $n = 3,613$	Global SIB prevalence: California: 8.8% New York: 7.9% *Dual diagnosis:* Low levels of correlations between SIB and Diagnostic and Statistical Manual of Mental Disorders diagnoses
Rojahn, Matson, Lott, Esbensen, & Smalls (1999)	Prevalence of destructive behavior	People served by the developmental disabilities lead agencies in California and New York in 1990 $N = 135,102$	Total population studies involving the entire database of individuals who received developmental disabilities services at the time	California: "SIB at least once a week" New York: "SIB that poses a serious impediment to independent functioning"	California: Client Development Evaluation Report (CDER) Single SIB item New York: Developmental Disabilities Information Survey (DDIS) Single SIB item	SIB cases: $n = 11,479$	Global SIB prevalence: 8.5% *Mental retardation level:* 4% mild 7% moderate 16% severe 25% profound

Study	Purpose	Population	Sampling	Definition	Instrument	SIB cases	Results
Rojahn, Matson, Lott, Esbensen, & Smalls (under review)	Psychometric study of the Behavior Problems Inventory	Developmental center in Louisiana $N > 650$ *Age (years):* x̄ = 49.9; range 14-91 *Gender:* 46% ♀, 54% ♂ *Mental retardation level:* 2% mild 5% moderate 20% severe 72% profound	Random sample	"Behavior that causes, or at least has the potential to cause, manifest damage to the person's own body" (Tate & Baroff, 1966)	Behavior Problems Inventory (BPI)	SIB cases: $n = 317$	Global SIB prevalence: 43.3%
Ross (1972)	Prevalence of SIB	State hospital residents with mental retardation $N = 11,139$	Total population study of a hospital population through the California census	"Self-destructive behavior"	Census form Single SIB item	SIB cases: $n = 2,562$	Global SIB prevalence: 23% *Mental retardation level:* 13% mild 18% moderate 25% severe 26% profound
Schroeder, Schroeder, Smith, & Dalldorf (1978)	Prevalence and incidence of SIB	Residents of a developmental center for mental retardation over a 3-year period (1973, 1975, 1976) $N = 1,150$	Total population study Cases of SIB referred by social workers Interviewed social workers	"Repetitive acts by individuals directed towards themselves that result in physical harm or tissue damage" (Tate & Baroff, 1966)	Not indicated (author questionnaire and checklist)	SIB cases: n = 208	Global SIB prevalence: 18.1% *Age (years):* x̄ = 22.3 *Gender:* *Mild SIB, (severe SIB):* 49% (47%) ♀ 51% (53%) ♂ *Mental retardation level:* 2% mild 9% moderate 14% severe/profound

(continued)

TABLE 3.1
(Continued)

Authors, year of publication	Purpose	Total population characteristics	Sampling procedure	SIB definition	Instruments & assessment	Results	
						SIB subsample	Total population[a]
		Age (years): x̄ = 25.6; range 5–85 *Gender:* 55% ♀, 45% ♂ Mental retardation level: 4% mild 11% moderate 85% severe/prof	Searched medical and programming files for each referral Questionnaire in a group interview with ward staff			*Mental retardation level:* Mild SIB, *(severe SIB):* 1% (0%) mild 8% (6%) moderate 91% (94%) severe/profound	*Maladaptive behaviors:* Mild SIB, *(severe SIB)* 35% (37%) stereotyped behavior 30% (25%) other misbehavior
Singh (1977)	Prevalence of SIB	Patients in a hospital and training school for mental retardation in New Zealand N = 368	Studied all patients for 6 months	"Self-inflicted behavior that leads to lacerations, bruising, or abrasions of the patient's own body"	Not indicated (author checklist)	SIB cases n = 85 *Gender:* 40% ♀, 60% ♂ *Mental retardation level:* 8% mild 36% moderate 48% severe 8% profound *Multiple SIBs:* 74% one SIB 26% multiple SIBs *Topography:* 43% other 26% head banging 23% biting	Global SIB prevalence: 23.1%

| Smeets (1971) | Prevalence of SIB | Residents of a private residential school for mental retardation children and adults

N = 400 | Total population study | Self-mutilation: as "any behavior displayed by the individual that can cause direct physical damage to himself, which may or may not be repetitious, rhythmical, or stereotyped in nature, and which are not necessarily aversive to the individual himself but certainly would be aversive to 'normal' individuals" | Not indicated | SIB cases n = 35

Age (years):
x̄: ♀ = 19.9
x̄: ♂ = 16.3

Gender:
40% ♀, 60% ♂

Maladaptive behaviors:
86% temper tantrums
80% stereotyped behavior
74% hyperactive behavior
57% aggressive towards peers
43% destructive behavior
40% aggressive toward staff

Topography:
66% biting
57% head banging
46% pinching
26% scratching
23% face slapping
<10% orifice gouging, severe skin rubbing, throwing one's self to the floor | 19% skin picking
18% face slapping
8% hair pulling

Global SIB prevalence: 8.75% |

(continued)

TABLE 3.1
(Continued)

Authors, year of publication	Purpose	Total population characteristics	Sampling procedure	SIB definition	Instruments & assessment	Results	
						SIB subsample	Total population[a]
Soule & O'Brien (1974)[b]	Prevalence of SIB	Residents of state mental retardation facility N = 966	Unspecified	"Self-injurious behavior such as biting and head banging"	Not indicated	SIB cases: n = 74	Global SIB prevalence: 7.7%
Whitney (1966)[b]	Not indicated	Residents of mental retardation facility N = 950	Unspecified	"Mutilated bodies to the extent to require restraint"	Not indicated	SIB cases: n = 84	Global SIB prevalence: 8.8%

[a] Prevalence refers to the number of cases that are present within a population at a designated point in time. The prevalance rate is the number of cases within the target population in which the cases were indentified (Kiley & Labin, 1983).
[b] These studies were unavailable to the authors. The presented data were extrapolated from Johnson and Day (1992, Table 2.3).

(b) identify characteristics of individuals with SIB and the factors associated with the problem behavior. We make this distinction primarily to show the contrast with the analyses of large, administrative data sets (Borthwick, Meyers, & Eyman, 1981; Borthwick-Duffy, 1994; Eyman & Call, 1977; Jacobson, 1982; Rojahn, Borthwick-Duffy, & Jacobson, 1993). Although administrative data sets also yield interesting information, they are quite different from research studies and have their own problems. They are developed and maintained by state agencies for developmental disabilities with the primary purpose of fiscal accountability of the agency. None of the reports on administrative data sets listed in Table 3.1 include additional data collection or quality control procedures by the authors. The purpose of two studies differed from the rest. The one by Murphy, Hall, Oliver, and Kissi-Debra (1999) presented data on the emergence of and early stages of SIB, whereas the primary purpose of the study by Rojahn, Matson, Lott, Esbensen, and Smalls (in press) was to explore psychometric properties of a survey instrument for challenging behaviors in mental retardation.

Sampling and Target Populations

In this chapter, the term *target population* refers to the group of individuals that were surveyed for SIB cases. Table 3.1, column 3 shows the target populations identified by our review. Target populations are either the result of sampling strategies (*sampled target populations*), or they represent existing—albeit often arbitrary—populations (*total target population*). The majority of studies reviewed were based on total target populations. In 20 of the reports the target populations were residents of segregated facilities known as *developmental centers, public institutions, congregate care facilities*, or *specialized hospitals*. Administrative databases are typically also total populations. They were drawn from several states (Rojahn et al., 1993), single states (Borthwick-Duffy, 1994; Jacobson, 1982), or regions in several states (Borthwick et al., 1981; Eyman & Call, 1977). Two European studies were based on nationwide total population samples. Researchers in a Swedish study (Kebbon & Windahl, 1985) screened for SIB everybody in 22 of 25 counties who received public services for developmental disabilities (including individuals in integrated and nonintegrated residencies). In the second study, a mail survey conducted in former West Germany, the researchers screened only individuals who received community integrated services through a nationwide provider organization (Rojahn, 1986).

The majority of studies surveyed in this chapter relied on some form of "total population" (see Table 3.1, column 4). By definition, these studies did not use sampling strategies and screened everyone within that population. Only a few studies used a well-designed sampling strategy. Hill and Bruininks (1984) used a two-stage probability sample to identify their target population, the first stage of which involved the sampling of certain community programs and public residential facilities around the United States, whereas the second stage consisted of SIB case identification.

Definition of SIB and Assessment Instruments

A wide variety of SIB definitions was used in all studies to identify SIB cases (see Table 3.1, column 5). Some researchers relied on simple, often circular, definitions developed only for a particular study (e.g., Ando & Yoshimura, 1978; Ballinger, 1971); others identified cases through scores on one or two global SIB items that were part of comprehensive evaluation survey instruments such as the Client Development Evaluation Report (CDER; Borthwick-Duffy, 1994; Borthwick et al., 1981; Eyman & Call, 1977; Rojahn et al., 1993) or the Developmental Disabilities Information Survey (DDIS; Jacobson, 1982; Rojahn et al., 1993). Others used more detailed definitions and identified specific SIB topographies as prerequisites to being classified as a person with SIB (see Table 3.2). A frequently used definition or derivative thereof was the one by Tate and Baroff (1966), which refers to SIB as behavior that causes physical damage to the person's

TABLE 3.2
Comprehensive List of Identified SIB Topographies

Behaviors	Target area	Tool of injury
Aerophagia, air swallowing		
Banging	Unspecified, body, head	
Biting		
Butting	Head	
Coprophagia[a]		
Digging	Orifice	
Drinking (extreme amounts), polydipsia		
Gouging	Unspecified, eye, cavities, orifices, throat	Fingers
Grinding	Teeth	
Hitting	Unspecified, arm, body parts, body, head	Body, objects
Mouthing, mouthing & sucking		
Pica		
Picking	Skin	
Pinching		
Poking	Unspecified, eye	
Pulling	hair	
Pulling		
Rubbing	Unspecified, skin	
Ruminating, ruminative vomiting		
Scratching	Unspecified, face	
Slapping	Unspecified, face, head	
Stuffing	Body orifices, cavities, orifices	Objects, fingers
Throwing	Unspecified, self to the floor	

[a] Was listed separately in a study but could be considered as a special form of pica (Danford & Huber, 1982).

own body, with the emphasis on the consequences of the behavior. The wide variety of definitions is probably the main source of the large discrepancies in SIB prevalence rates across studies.

Column 6 in Table 3.1 shows the variety of assessment instruments that were used to assess SIB and associated characteristics. Assessment procedures ran the gamut from informal interviews by the authors, to single items within comprehensive behavior rating scales such as the CDER and the DDIS, to entire instruments dedicated to the assessment of behavior problems such as the Behavior Problems Inventory (BPI; Rojahn et al., in press). The BPI is a multi-item instrument with known psychometric properties featuring a two-step decision process: To meet the criteria for a score on a specific SIB item, the behavior has to fit a generic, functional SIB definition (Tate & Baroff, 1966), and it must match one of the specific topographical SIB items with operational definitions. The BPI and some of its derivatives have already been used in several epidemiological studies (Bodfish, Symons, Parker, & Lewis, 2000; Murphy et al., 1999; Rojahn, 1984, 1986; Rojahn et al., 1999, in press).

DESCRIPTIVE EPIDEMIOLOGY

Global Prevalence Rate

Global SIB prevalence rates are presented in the last column of Table 3.1. *Prevalence* refers to the number of cases that are present within a population at a designated point in time. The prevalence rate is the relative number of cases within the target population in which the cases were identified (Kiley & Lubin, 1983). The rate of prevalence in this chapter is expressed as a percentage rate ($[n_{SIB}/N] \times 100$), where n_{SIB} is the number of SIB cases, and N is the total number of individuals in the target population. Most of the studies we reviewed reported some sort of global SIB prevalence estimate. Considering the variety of populations, sampling strategies, settings, and assessment procedures, it is not surprising that global SIB prevalence rate estimates varied greatly, ranging from 1.7% (Rojahn, 1986) in a community-based sample of people with mental retardation to 93% (Anderson & Ernst, 1994) among a cohort of individuals with Lesch–Nyhan syndrome. However, as will be shown, global SIB prevalence depends on several factors, which explains in part the large range of global SIB estimates.

Global Incidence Rate

Incidence refers to the number of new cases that emerge within a specific time (Kiley & Lubin, 1983). Although several studies covered extended times in longitudinal research designs, researchers of only one investigation took advantage of that and explored incidence rates. Murphy et al. (1999) explored the predictive validity of a risk marker for newly developing SIB in young children by following two cohorts of children—one that was described as being at risk for SIB and one that was not. For 18 months, each child was evaluated every 3 months with multiple rating scales and direct observations. Researchers estimated that among 614 children 10 years old or younger with severe intellectual disability, 3% of new SIB cases emerged within 3 months.

Relative Prevalence Rates of Specific Topographies

Relative SIB prevalence refers to the number of cases with a certain SIB topography within the total SIB sample at the time of the survey. These data are shown in the next-to-last column in Table 3.1. The types of SIB topographies we encountered are listed in Table 3.2. The relative prevalence rate is defined as ($[n_{top}/n_{SIB}] \times 100$), where n_{top} is the number of cases with a specific SIB topography, and n_{SIB} is the total number of SIB cases identified. Unless the target population is representative of a meaningful population group, relative prevalence in itself is not a meaningful statistic because it strongly reflects the composition of the target population with regard to SIB.

Fourteen of the 38 reports presented data on the relative prevalence of specific SIB topographies. The types and number of topographies varied from study to study, and so did the relative prevalence estimates. All studies that collected data on specific SIB topographies included some form of hitting. Unfortunately, it is particularly difficult to compare prevalence rates for hitting behaviors in people with different types of SIB and in different studies because of alternative terms that may or may not be synonyms (e.g., butting, hitting, striking, slapping). To complicate matters, some researchers distinguished hitting even further by specifying the body part that is likely to be injured (e.g., arm, body, face, head) and the object that was used in the act (hands, objects). A similar problem exists with the semantic similarities between digging, gouging, poking, and stuffing. It is thus difficult to draw any firm conclusions about the relative prevalence of different SIB topographies.

Biting was reported as the most prevalent form of SIB in six different studies, yet only 10 of the 14 studies that presented data on the relative prevalence of specific SIB topographies even surveyed biting. The relative prevalence rate of biting ranged from 12% to 93%. Other frequently represented and relatively high rate behaviors were scratching (reported in eight studies, with a relative prevalence rate ranging from 4% to 42%), hair pulling, rumination, and different types of gouging.

Global Prevalence Rate as a Function of Mental Retardation Level

Table 3.3 presents two perspectives of prevalence rates of SIB as a function of mental retardation level: (a) prevalence rate within the target population and (b) relative prevalence of mental retardation levels among the SIB cases. Eleven studies reported the global prevalence rate of SIB as a function of the level of mental retardation. Despite the great variation

TABLE 3.3
Prevalence Rate of SIB as Function of Level of Mental Retardation

	Prevalence			
	Mild	Moderate	Severe	Profound
Ballinger (1971)	6	10	18	29
Borthwick-Duffy (1994)	1	2	3	7
Borthwick et al. (1981)	4	7	15	25
Eyman & Call (1977)	— (8)[b] —		20	36
Jacobson (1982), ages 0–21	2	3	9	14
Jacobson (1982), ages 22–45	3	3	6	18
Kebbon & Windahl (1985)	1	1	7	13
Maisto et al. (1978)	0	3	— (21)[b] —	
Miller et al. (2000)	27	37	49	60
Rojahn et al. (1999)	4	7	16	25
Rojahn et al. (under review)	2	5	19	66
Ross (1972)	13	18	25	26
Schroeder et al. (1978)	2	9	— (14)[b] —	
M[a]	5	9	16	27
Range	0–27	1–37	3–49	7–66

	Relative prevalence			
	Mild	Moderate	Severe	Profound
Ballinger (1971)	9	16	28	45
Danford & Huber (1982)	2	4	17	78
Emberson & Walker (1990)	— (18)[b] —		64	17
Griffin et al. (1986)	1	9	19	66
Hillary & Mulcahy (1997)	0	42	53	5
Kebbon & Windahl (1985)	1	12	48	41
Maisto et al. (1978)	0	4	— (96)[b] —	
Maurice & Trudel (1982)	10	37	53	
Oliver et al. (1987)	12	— (49)[b] —		40
Rojahn (1986)	13	28	43	16
Schroeder et al. (1878), mild SIB	1	8	— (91)[b] —	
Schroeder et al. (1878), severe SIB	0	6	— (94)[b] —	
Singh (1977)	8	36	48	8
M[a]	5	18	41	35
Range	0–13	4–42	17–64	5–78

[a] Means and ranges were calculated only for studies that had values reported for each of the four levels of mental retardation.
[b] Authors reported on combined levels of mental retardation.

across studies, the trend of increasing prevalence rates with decreasing level of mental retardation was uniform.

Global Prevalence Rate as a Function of Gender

The three studies that probably best estimated the extent to which the gender of the individual may be a predictor of the occurrence of SIB are the ones by Borthwick (1994), Borthwick et al. (1981), and Rojahn et al. (1999). The first two were based on two different administrative data sets from California. Rojahn et al. analyzed a combined California and New York data set. The prevalence rates vary greatly across studies, and it seems that the global SIB prevalence does not differ greatly between genders (see Table 3.4). The lower panel of Table 3.4 shows the relative prevalence of gender within the SIB samples. There does seem to be a trend toward a higher representation of males in SIB samples, yet that can easily be a function of uneven group sizes in the sampled population. Comparisons of gender ratios within certain SIB topographies are not explored here.

TABLE 3.4
Prevalence Rates of SIB as Function of Gender

| | Prevalence (percent) | |
	Female	Male
Borthwick-Duffy (1994)	2	2
Borthwick et al. (1981)	9	10
Rojahn et al. (1999)	5	8
M	5	7
Range	2–9	2–10
	Relative prevalence (percent)	
	Female	Male
Emberson & Walker (1990)	50	50
Griffin et al. (1986)	44	56
Hillary & Mulcahy (1997)	42	58
Kebbon & Windahl (1985)	44	56
Maisto et al. (1978)	55	45
Oliver et al. (1987)	42	58
Rojahn (1984)	54	46
Rojahn (1986)	51	48
Schroeder et al. (1978), mild SIB	49	47
Schroeder et al. (1978), severe SIB	47	53
Singh (1977)	40	60
Smeets	40	60
M	47	53
Range	40–55	45–60

Global Prevalence Rate as a Function of Residential Setting

Researchers from several studies addressed the prevalence of SIB according to the residential circumstances, or the relative degree of restrictiveness, of the residential environment. Table 3.5 is an attempt to document this trend on the basis of four studies conducted in the United States, three of which were administrative database analyses (except for Hill & Bruininks, 1984). The difficulty in tabulating these kinds of data across studies is heterogeneity of definitions of residential programs. Although some terminological similarities exist within the United States, comparing results from different countries is much more difficult. Hence, studies from outside the United States were not included in Table 3.5. One interesting and unexpected finding is the trend of SIB prevalence from 1981 (Borthwick et al.) to 1994 (Borthwick). Without drawing any firm conclusions, prevalence of SIB in segregated institutions seems to have steadily decreased from 38% in 1981 to 12% in 1994. With the current trend of closing down institutions and integrating people into community residences, it was generally assumed that institutionalized populations would become smaller but that the proportion of people with severe behavior problems would increase—because they were the ones who were either not released into community-integrated programs or had to be readmitted to the institutions. These data are not consistent with such an assumption.

TABLE 3.5

Prevalence Rates of SIB as a Function of Residential Settings[a]

	Setting (percent)				
	Independent living	Parents/ family	Community care	Intermediate care/nursing home/ convalescent hospital	Institution
Borthwick-Duffy (1994)	<1	<1	6	5	12
Borthwick et al. (1981)	8	13	8	18	38
Hill and Bruininks (1984)	——————— (11)[b] ———————				22
Jacobson (1982), ages 0–21	0	7	9	(no data)	16
Jacobson (1982), ages 22–45	1	3	5	(no data)	15
M[c]	3	6	7	12	13
Range	<1–8	<1–3	5–9	5–18	12–38

[a] Only studies conducted in the United States were included.
[b] The authors of this study distinguished only between institutional and non-institutional residence.
[c] Means and ranges were calculated only across those studies that had separate values reported for each of the four levels of mental retardation.

CONCLUSION

Perhaps the main conclusion of this review is that the definitive epidemiological study on SIB has yet to be conducted. Only few of the reviewed studies met methodological standards required for drawing firm and generalizable conclusions. However, on the basis of cumulative evidence, we can make some general inferences.

The relationship between SIB prevalence and the level of cognitive functioning is probably the most solid, consistently replicated epidemiological finding to date. However, because of the variability in absolute estimate levels across different data sets, we still do not know seemingly basic facts, such as the SIB prevalence rates for different levels of mental retardation or whether the relationship between levels of mental retardation and SIB prevalence rates follows a linear or curvilinear function. The restrictiveness of the residential situation is also positively related to the prevalence of SIB. Whether restrictive residential circumstances contribute to the occurrence of SIB or this is just an assortative selection phenomenon cannot be explained from the existing data. We can assume at this point that gender is probably not a very strong predictor of SIB in the general population of people with mental retardation, although it is obviously a very strong predictor in X-linked chromosomal conditions such as Lesch–Nyhan disease (Anderson & Ernst, 1994).

Internal validity in epidemiological studies, the sine qua non without which empirical data are not interpretable (Campbell & Stanley, 1963), largely depends on the quality of the case classifications, the assessment of the target behavior, or both. Many SIB definitions, behavior assessment tools, and case classification procedures were used in all studies, and in some of these studies the authors devised methods for their particular study only—without psychometric quality control. Some reports did not even specify the assessment instrumentation. This heterogeneity may explain in part the large variation of reported results. Obtaining reliable and valid epidemiological data requires high-quality case classification and assessment instruments. At this point, it seems as if the BPI (Rojahn et al., in press), a multidimensional behavior rating instrument with known psychometric properties, may represent such an instrument. It can be recommended as a viable choice for future epidemiological studies of SIB.

External validity refers to how representative the results of a particular study are for people who are not part of the study population (Campbell & Stanley, 1963). In epidemiological findings, generalizability relies on strong internal validity and the identification of the target population. The target population must be representative of the groups of individuals for whom researchers want to make predictions on the basis of the epidemiological findings. As far as target populations in the reviewed literature are concerned, the three most common population selection approaches were (a) total populations from developmental centers, schools, or hospitals; (b) total populations from statewide administrative data sets; and, in some cases, (c) sampled populations. The advantage of total population studies is the potential for good internal validity. Their problem, particularly for regional populations, is the external validity of the results or the extent to which one can generalize the obtained results to any other population. From the standpoint of generalizability, well-designed random or probability sampling techniques from clearly identified samples are preferable to total population studies. The typical advantage of statewide administrative data sets is the large number of clients. Power exists in numbers insofar as they may cancel out some of the measurement errors. One of the weaknesses of large client numbers is typically the lack of quality control at the level of data collection. The small number of SIB items that are typically used in such instruments raises questions about the reliability of the assessment and about the sensitivity and specificity of case classifications. Very few researchers actually employed random or probability sampling techniques in their studies to identify individuals who were screened for SIB cases, and not a single researcher made the attempt to sample from the national population of people with mental retardation. Even those who did use random sampling strategies did so on preselected populations (e.g., individuals receiving state services for people with developmental disabilities), which diminishes their generalizability to the individuals with mental retardation in general (many of whom do not receive public services). Another typical weakness of this literature is that very few researchers provided even basic demographic descriptions of the target population, such as group size, gender ratio, ratios of mental retardation levels, and age groups.

To achieve real progress in epidemiological research on SIB in mental retardation, researchers must avoid the methodological problems just mentioned. Researchers know that SIB is a highly heterogeneous phenomenon that is the outcome of the interplay of many contributing factors (Schroeder, Reese, Hellings, Loupe, & Tessel, 1999). To enhance existing knowledge about SIB and its causes, treatment, and prevention through an epidemiological research approach, high-quality analytical research studies are required, preferably combining cross-sectional and longitudinal strategies. Researchers in such studies should go beyond estimating descriptive prevalence and incidence rates of SIB in arbitrary populations and explore the multitude of behavioral, biological, and environmental risk and protective variables and their complex patterns of interaction from a developmental perspective. Research of that caliber would be relatively expensive to conduct and is hardly conceivable without special funding. We can assume that most researchers of the studies reviewed were well aware of the limitations of their results. The problem is not that scientists in this field lack talent but that it is so difficult for them to obtain the level of financial support needed for a high-quality epidemiological study.

II

ENVIRONMENTAL
MECHANISMS AND
INTERVENTION STRATEGIES

The beginning of the modern era of investigation into the assessment and intervention of self-injurious behavior (SIB) can be traced to two seminal papers: one by Lesch and Nyhan (1964) describing Lesch-Nyhan syndrome, a genetic disorder with a high incidence of vicious self-biting, and one by Lovaas, Freitag, Gold, and Kassorla (1965), in which they showed that SIB could be increased or decreased directly by manipulating its antecedents and consequences. These two lines of research proceeded relatively independently until the early 1980s, when Cataldo and Harris (1982) described various biological and behavioral interactions that contribute to SIB. In chapter 4, Iser G. DeLeon, Vanessa Rodriguez-Catter, and Michael F. Cataldo trace the progress of these biobehavioral interventions and suggest standards of care and research for the future.

In chapters 5 and 7, Brian A. Iwata and colleagues trace the basic mechanisms of learning by which SIB can be acquired and maintained by use of experimental assessment methods called *functional analysis*. This burgeoning technology also shows promise for biobehavioral studies, such as screening for environmentally induced biological effects, evaluation of drug-behavior interactions, assessment of physical anomalies, and the change from biologically to environmentally mediated SIB.

The authors of three other chapters address SIB's possible biobehavioral relationships to self-restraint (Rachel L. Freeman, Robert H. Horner, and Joe Reichle; chapter 6), to stereotyped behavior (Craig H. Kennedy; chapter 8) in humans, and to isolate-rearing in monkeys (Melinda A. Novak, Carolyn M. Crockett, and Gene P. Sackett; chapter 10). The chapter by Gershon Berkson and Megan Tupa (chapter 9) includes groundbreaking work on the incidence of stereotyped behavior and SIB among infants and toddlers in the early preschool programs in Chicago. This research is the first of its kind for a population in this age group.

4

TREATMENT: CURRENT STANDARDS OF CARE AND THEIR RESEARCH IMPLICATIONS

ISER G. DELEON, VANESSA RODRIGUEZ-CATTER,
AND MICHAEL F. CATALDO

As recently as a few decades ago, people with significant levels of mental retardation were destined to live out their lives in institutions, far removed from the rest of society. Little was offered to promote development of skills or afford the residents the means to improve the quality of their lives. Custodial care was the norm. In contrast, if the same individuals were born today, they would be identified early in life by medical professionals, extensively evaluated by psychologists and educators, afforded early intervention (e.g., stimulation, education), and allowed into and even financially supported by the broader community. Today, these individuals live with their families, attend school, and receive skills and job training. When they become adults, they live and work as independently as their level of retardation allows. This dramatic change in so short a time has occurred as a result of scientific advances, legal precedents, legislative action, and changes in social policies and attitudes.

The current state of services and societal priorities is not without its challenges. Perhaps most challenging are people with significant levels of mental retardation and severe behavior disorders such as aggression and self-injurious behavior (SIB). A 1991 estimate suggested that 200,000 individuals with developmental disabilities in the United States exhibited significant degrees of destructive behavior, and the annual cost to society of care and services exceeded $3 billion (National Institutes of Health [NIH], 1991). The most extreme cases involve people with serious SIB—perhaps 20,000 to 25,000 individuals (NIH, 1991). These individuals exhibit behaviors that include repeated, self-inflicted, nonaccidental injuries producing bleeding and permanent tissue damage, eye gouging leading to blindness, and swallowing of dangerous substances or physical objects. All forms of destructive behavior are difficult to treat and when untreated have serious social and personal consequences for individuals with developmental disabilities. Such behaviors are major barriers to inclusion in the broad range of societal opportunities that most individuals without severe behavior problems now enjoy.

Because of the effort, expense, and risk involved in treating these destructive behaviors, as well as the comparable effort required to maintain treatment gains, scientists and practitioners alike continually seek more effective and efficient approaches. In the health care industry, the *standard of care* is an important concept; it is the prevailing acceptable and reimbursable treatment approaches. All new treatments considered must be compared to current standards in terms of safety, efficacy, and eventually costs before a new treatment "raises the bar," or creates a new standard. The standard of care for the treatment of SIB has continually evolved over the past three decades, largely as a function of research from the field of behavior analysis. In tandem with the advances in evaluation, educational services, legal and legislative activities, and societal changes, the standard of care for treating severe behavior disorders has also changed. This chapter includes a discussion on the evolution of the current standard and how it establishes agendas for research on behavioral and biological variables related to severe behavior disorders.

BEHAVIORAL MANAGEMENT AND TREATMENT STRATEGIES

During the past several decades, behavioral researchers have invested a great deal of effort in developing and evaluating procedures to decrease SIB. During this time, the goal of treatment has not changed significantly. The general strategy has always been to decrease SIB while increasing levels of adaptive responses. What has changed is the complexity and cost related to the way this approach is carried out. Initial attempts to suppress SIB were often based on punishment, or basic reinforcement procedures that aimed to increase primarily nonspecific alternative behaviors and remove putative sources of social reinforcement for SIB (e.g., Azrin, Gottlieb, Hughart, Wesolowski, & Rahn, 1975; Corte, Wolf, & Locke, 1971; Lovaas & Simmons, 1969; Romancyzk & Goren, 1975). Reinforcers were selected rather arbitrarily and were typically based on what intuitively seemed reinforcing for many individuals or had been successful in treatments with other individuals demonstrating similar problems.

Since then, an important series of standards has been progressively added to treatment approaches, and the accumulation now comprises our current standards. The progression of treatment approaches includes

- obtaining baseline data,
- using behavioral interventions,

- basing behavioral interventions—and changes in those interventions—on changes in objective, quantified data,
- using a variety of treatment designs to demonstrate that the treatment thought to be effective is indeed necessary and sufficient,
- training positive and replacement behaviors,
- requiring that treatments produce a rapid change in the destructive or dangerous behavior,
- changing behavior to clinically significant levels,
- protecting clients and patients from harm during the behavior change process, and
- generalizing treatment gains across situations; etc.

The current standard is defined further by advances in assessment methodology (e.g., Carr, 1977; Iwata, Dorsey, Slifer, Bauman, & Richman, 1982; Repp, Felce, & Barton, 1988). Whereas developers of previous interventions sought to demonstrate that SIB could be modified regardless of its causes, changes in assessment technology cleared the path for interventions based on empirically derived hypotheses regarding the contingency arrangements that maintain problem behaviors (Carr, 1994; Mace, 1994). New assessments using a controlled simulation of actual situations revealed that SIB can be maintained, for example, by negative reinforcement contingencies in the form of escape from instructional contexts, positive reinforcement contingencies in the form of caregiver attention or access to tangible reinforcers, and sensory reinforcement independent of reactions from caregivers (i.e., automatic reinforcement). Armed with these testable hypotheses, researchers began to explore treatments that form the basis of the current behavior management philosophy.

Under the current standard of care, reinforcers are no longer selected arbitrarily and delivered for nonspecific alternative behaviors. Rather, selection of reinforcers is typically based on their known functional properties in maintaining SIB or after extensive evaluation of their actual, as opposed to presumed, effectiveness in changing behavior (e.g., Fisher et al., 1992; Pace, Ivancic, Edwards, Iwata, & Page, 1985). Alternative behaviors have become highly specific, chosen or established to help individuals procure functional reinforcers under the circumstances in which SIB tends to occur. Thus, individuals whose behavior is found to be maintained by escape from instructional demands receive specific training in alternative responses that permit them to request breaks from work (e.g., Lalli, Casey, & Kates, 1995) or request assistance in completing tasks (e.g., Carr & Durand, 1985). When SIB is found to be maintained by socially mediated positive reinforcement, individuals are trained to request caregiver attention (e.g., Durand, 1993) or tangible reinforcers (e.g., Durand, 1999; Kern, Carberry, & Haidara, 1997) appropriately. For individuals in whom SIB is not found to be sensitive to socially mediated reinforcers, current treatments are often based on promoting appropriate engagement of stimuli carefully chosen for their ability to displace or match the purported sensory function of SIB (e.g., Favell, McGimsey, & Schell, 1982; Piazza, Adelinis, Hanley, Goh, & Delia, 2000).

The promotion of alternative behavior is sometimes insufficient in reducing SIB that continues to be reinforced (e.g., Fisher et al., 1993; Shirley, Iwata, Kahng, Mazaleski, & Lerman, 1997). Thus, another critical contribution of functional assessment technology has been to identify appropriate and effective forms of extinction. Although using extinction to treat SIB was paramount from the start, functional assessment has enabled the development of extinction procedures tailored to the variables hypothesized to maintain the behavior (Iwata, Pace, Cowdery, & Miltenberger, 1994). Scientists and therapists now routinely individualize extinction procedures for behavior maintained by escape (Iwata, Pace, Kalsher, Cowdery, & Cataldo, 1990), attention (e.g., Mazaleski, Iwata, Vollmer, Zarcone, & Smith, 1993), and even sensory reinforcement through the use of methods that attenuate stimulation (e.g., Luiselli, 1991).

These advances have brought about significant changes in the approach to SIB treatment. Yet, restrictive and intrusive procedures such as restraint, seclusion, and punishment still seem to remain necessary to prevent extreme harm in some people (Brown, Genel, & Riggs, 2000). However, even the use of restrictive and intrusive procedures has evolved over the years in ways that minimize the undesirable effects on quality of life and maximize treatment effects. Thus, although restraint continues to be a part of the management of SIB for some individuals, behavioral researchers have begun to examine carefully the conditions under which restraint can be decreased systematically in response to improvements in behavior (e.g., Fisher, Piazza, Bowman, Hanley, & Adelinis, 1997; Oliver, Hall, Hales, Murphy, & Watts, 1998). The use of punishment also continues to be necessary in some cases (NIH, 1991). However, the number of published reports on the treatment of SIB that involve reinforcement have begun to outnumber significantly those that involve punishment, possibly as a function of increasing ethical reluctance to use punishment procedures for individuals with disabilities but alternatively as a result of the refinement of functional assessment technology (Pelios, Morren, Tesch, & Axelrod, 1999). Moreover, punishment procedures can now be selected based on systematic assessments that predict their effectiveness in addressing the problem behavior of each given individual (e.g., Fisher, Piazza, Bowman, Hagopian, & Langdon, 1994).

Contemporary behavioral interventions have proven effective in various settings with various response forms and for children with a great variety of diagnoses, some of whose associated self-injury is often thought to be biological rather than behavioral (e.g., Lesch–Nyhan syndrome; see Olson & Houlihan, 2000, for a review). Despite these advances, several aspects of the behavioral management of SIB need further exploration. Researchers do not yet have a good understanding of measures to prevent individuals with severe disabilities from developing SIB. In addition, although the sorts of interventions described are often successful in reducing SIB to a great extent, rarely do they lead to the total elimination of SIB. We randomly sampled 42 recent (from 1995 to 2000) behavioral treatment studies (consisting of 76 cases), including many of those previously cited (a full list of references is available from the authors). We found that SIB was eliminated entirely in only 12 cases (15.8%). In the remaining cases that used response rate as a dependent measure, the range of treatment effects deemed successful yielded extrapolated hourly rates of SIB between 0.12 to 480 responses per hour. In 17 of the 46 individuals for whom rate measures were available, mean response rates during the treatment condition were greater than 10 per hour. The lack of treatment maintenance and generalization data has been noted repeatedly by reviewers (e.g., Johnson & Baumeister, 1978; Lundervold & Bourland, 1988; Sturmey, 1997). In relation, treatment evaluations were frequently confined to small samples of behavior, often consisting of a limited number of brief sessions. Treatment evaluations in 85.7% of the 70 cases whose interventions were conducted in 15-minute (or less) sessions (in contrast to over several days or weeks), and the average number of sessions used to evaluate the final treatment was 25. Unfortunately, it is sometimes observed that the effects found in brief treatment sessions do not always predict effects over more extended periods (e.g., DeLeon, Anders, Rodriguez-Catter, & Niedert, 2000). Finally, although behavioral interventions represent the standard of care, little can be used for comparison. The list is not meant to be exhaustive.

BIOBEHAVIORAL INTEGRATION IN THE EVOLVING STANDARD OF CARE

Much of this volume is devoted to discussions of the most recent findings and thinking on the biological basis for self-injury. However, unlike 20 years ago and despite the limitations noted, researchers know a good deal more today about how to quantify and analyze SIB in relation to environmental variables. Furthermore, clinical standards of care are vastly different in terms of complexity, sophistication, and effectiveness. It is into this evolving standard that new, promising approaches stemming from basic research on brain-behavior relationships will be evaluated. What then are the implications for future clinical research arising from basic neuroscience research when applied against current standards?

When addressing this question, one important theme is the utility of retaining behavior analytic thought in emerging treatment models. Not only can users of alternative approaches benefit from the lessons learned through the evolution of the behavioral treatment of SIB, but users of new approaches will have to consider what is valid and effective about behavioral treatment as conceptual models, diagnostic procedures, and treatment evaluations are developed. As such, the sections that follow include highlights of a few areas in which joint biobehavioral endeavors might help to raise the standards. The foundation for these improvements has already been laid.

Methodologically Sound Drug Evaluations

Despite the success of behaviorally based approaches to treatment, because of the demographics and comorbidity associated with SIB, biological factors are most certainly significant to our understanding of this problem. Several biological mechanisms in the etiology and maintenance of SIB have been proposed over the years (Baumeister, Frye, & Schroeder, 1984; Cataldo & Harris, 1982). The hypothesized relationships among SIB and abnormalities in three essential components of central nervous system function (i.e., dopamine production, serotonergic transmission, and abnormalities of the endogenous opioid system), which were identified about two decades ago, continue to be the focus of current inquiries. Support for these hypotheses stem from animal studies, drug studies, and medical conditions such as Lesch-Nyhan syndrome, all of which implicate neurochemical dysregulation (Clarke, 1998; Pies & Popli, 1995; Winchel & Stanley, 1991). These findings have influenced past and current trends in the pharmacological treatment of SIB in individuals with mental retardation.

As is the case with the behavioral literature on the treatment of SIB, the shortcomings of the pharmacological treatment literature are readily apparent. Perhaps most notable among these is a lack of methodological rigor in evaluating the effects of pharmacological agents on SIB. Reviews of the effects of psychotropic drugs on SIB are fraught with concerns that evaluations have been methodologically flawed (e.g., Baumeister & Sevin, 1990; Matson et al., 2000). Many analyses are conducted under poorly controlled conditions and reported as loose clinical case studies. In contrast, clinical behavioral researchers rely on convincing demonstrations of experimental control and sound observation and measurement. In clinical behavior analysis, rigorous experimental design and compelling evaluations of treatment effects are synonymous. One clear benefit of the marriage of behavioral and biological research would be the careful analysis of drug effects using single-subject designs, and researchers are beginning to note the utility of using behavioral measurement methods and experimental designs in the evaluation of drug effects (Kalachnik, Hanzel, Harder, Bauernfeind, & Engstrom, 1995; Piazza et al., 1994).

Hypothesis-Driven Prescriptive Models

Much as functional assessment has led to highly specific and individualized behavioral treatments for SIB, users of alternative approaches will need to provide rational bases for prescribing one intervention instead of another. Neurological and pharmacological research has provided many hypotheses but has rarely led to treatment outcomes that are comparable or superior to behavioral approaches, especially in terms of specificity and magnitude of effect. Schaal and Hackenberg (1994) noted that although virtually every class of psychotropic treatment has been used with individuals with developmental disabilities, drugs are administered with little regard to the pharmacological basis for their effectiveness. Thus, they concluded that "researchers and clinicians are still largely unable to specify with certainty what a drug should be given for, to whom it should be given, and why it should be expected to help" (p. 124).

SIB is not a homogeneous phenomenon. Behavioral researchers have learned that although SIB can take similar forms in various individuals, it also can have highly variant functional properties, necessitating individualized, assessment-based treatments. The same observation clearly holds true for pharmacological treatment (Aman, 1993; Cataldo & Harris, 1982). Pies and Popli (1995) noted that there is no single, well-established drug of choice for individuals displaying SIB. Whereas many pharmacological agents have been effective in reducing SIB in some individuals, one can just as easily identify other individuals for whom each class of drug has failed. In our view, as well of the view of other researchers (e.g., Sturmey, 1995), the key to improving the standard of care involves establishing and evaluating the selective, diagnosis-based use of psychotropic medication using reliable indicators that separate responders from nonresponders.

Various approaches can now be described in which behavioral methods and practices can facilitate the formulation of hypothesis-driven prescriptive models. For example, some evidence has led researchers to suggest that behavior maintained by different forms of behavioral functions would be differentially responsive to specific pharmacological agents. Schaal and Hackenberg (1994) pointed out that although the environmental causes of behavior disorders are rarely considered when drugs are prescribed, relevant relationships have been discovered in the basic drug literature. Neuroleptics, for example, seem to exert selective weakening effects on signaled avoidance behavior (Fielding & Lal, 1978), which in some cases is analogous to behavior that occurs during demands to complete various tasks for individuals with developmental disabilities. It is therefore possible that the selection of pharmacological interventions can be guided not only by biologically driven hypotheses but also by consideration of the environmental variables that influence SIB. Others have discovered potentially important relations between drug effects and the topography of SIB (e.g., Herman et al., 1989; Thompson, Hackenberg, Cerruti, Baker, & Axtell, 1994), suggesting that to some extent the selection of pharmacological interventions can be guided by the form of the behavior.

Several other promising steps in this direction can now be noted. Sandman, Hetrick, Taylor, and Chicz-DeMet (1997) have begun to determine behavioral and biological correlates of individuals whose SIB responds favorably to treatment with opiate antagonists. Perhaps just as promising is the emerging practice of combining drug evaluations with the sorts of functional assessments conducted by behavioral researchers. For example, researchers have begun to discuss and evaluate biobehavioral treatment decision models based jointly on the formal properties of SIB, its similarities to symptoms of other psychiatric diagnoses, and the possible role of environmental determinants of the behavior (e.g., Mace & Mauk, 1995; Sturmey, 1995). In the model suggested by Mace and Mauk, pharmacological treatment becomes the focus when environmental determinants of SIB have been ruled out (i.e., for cases of automatic reinforcement). Automatic reinforcement may have emerged as a "default" category, indicating that no clear relationship between social variables and SIB can be identified. It is perhaps in this functional category that the merger of biological and behavioral approaches to assessment and treatment can be most fruitfully exploited.

Extending the Conceptual Model for Biobehavioral Explanation of SIB

Behaviorally based interventions for SIB are firmly rooted in decades of basic research regarding behavior-environment relationships. A direct line between principle and practice prevents a clinical discipline from becoming a mere "bag of tricks" and promotes extensions and improvements along the same rational bases (Baer, Wolf, & Risley, 1968). Biological models of treatment are perhaps even more securely grounded in this approach, having been derived from much basic neurological and neurochemical research and subsequent extrapolations to human conditions based on formal similarities. However, it seems that behavior-environment interactions are often overlooked in biological models of SIB, especially in individuals in whom SIB is highly correlated with biological abnormalities that are already partially understood. A comprehensive model of a phenomenon that clearly has multiple causes can benefit from both biological and operant input.

In the most simplistic form, five conceptual approaches can be used to understand SIB. Four have been discussed, and the fifth is included in the following list as a new possibility.

$$E \rightarrow SIB$$

$$B \rightarrow SIB$$

$$BE \rightarrow SIB$$

$$B \rightarrow E \rightarrow SIB$$

$$E \rightarrow B \rightarrow SIB$$

where E represents environmental variables, and B represents biological variables.

In the first instance, E → SIB, environmental variables are presumed to cause SIB. For example, chance differential reinforcement of very early instances of SIB may produce over time a repertoire of SIB that is highly resistant to extinction. This hypothetical explanation is plausible, especially when one considers that severe levels of retardation and significant language deficits could produce almost insurmountable barriers to a child developing in a world of more capable peers with superior language skills, and with potentially inappropriate parental and other adult expectations. Daily activities would require significant effort and be aversive and frustrating—all variables that in experimental settings have been associated with aggression toward others or self.

The second conceptual explanation, B → SIB, implies that biological variables directly produce SIB. That is, SIB is biologically driven. Biological variables produce seizures, high activity levels, and innumerable other specific behaviors. Genetic, neuroanatomical, and neurochemical processes directly produce SIB, independent of any environmental factors.

In the third characterization, BE → SIB, biological and environmental variables are directly related to SIB. Variables can be exclusively biological or environmental. Therefore, in the previous two examples, differential reinforcement or biologically driven SIB are possible. Differential diagnosis and treatment strategies are thus called for. Much of the current thinking in the field of behavior analysis has moved from E → SIB to B *or* E → SIB. Automatic reinforcement is an attempt to attribute SIB to biological factors when no maintaining socially mediated variables can be implied. Of course, B *and* E → SIB is also a possibility, and at least two variants of this equation exist.

One can argue that a biological factor, such as hypersensitivity to endogenous opiates, provides the potential for the development of SIB. When an individual with this hypersensitivity engages in developmentally normal head banging, which is commonly seen in infants, it produces an internally reinforcing event sufficient to rapidly condition SIB—it is an example of B → E → SIB. The key here is less the order of biological and environmental variables than the predisposing abnormality. In this instance, the biological variable is the key to the disorder. Environmental variables contribute only insofar as they represent normally occurring circumstances that would not produce SIB unless they were combined with the opioid sensitivity.

In contrast is an alternative set of relationships, E → B → SIB, which is common in other explanations for many disorders but not discussed in terms of SIB to our knowledge. In this condition, a special set of environmental situations, aberrant and predisposing, must occur to trigger a biological variable to produce the problem. The relationship between stomach ulcers and stressful environmental situations has been scientifically validated for several decades. Only recently has the reason been made clear. The mechanism is a bacterium found commonly in the gut, and it can only cause symptoms when stress reduces immune competence below a critical level, allowing the bacteria to propagate to significant levels.

Simplistic treatment approaches are preferable, but simplistic explanations are rare. Not all people with conditions such as severe mental retardation, autism, and Down's syndrome demonstrate SIB. The conceptual models need to account for the incidence of SIB both within and across diagnostic categories.

ADVANCING BIOBEHAVIORAL RESEARCH ON SELF-INJURY

Aside from the array of ideas and findings detailed in this volume, by now people may have expected more research and biobehavioral-based evaluation and treatment approaches given that the investigative blueprint for this line of inquiry was advanced almost two decades ago (Cataldo & Harris, 1982). This slow knowledge growth may be caused by the rather clear division between two camps of scientists: clinical behavioral and basic biomedical. The behavioral scientists pursue a research agenda designed to address treatment safety and efficacy. This clinical research agenda is dictated by the practical (albeit dramatic) problems encountered in community and residential settings by parents, teachers, and others and for which professional responsibility is often assigned to behavioral psychologists. With the exception of occasional clinical pharmacology studies, the second camp of scientists carry out basic research at various levels (e.g., genetic, cellular, neuroimaging) using models involving animals and clinical syndromes designed primarily to identify underlying mechanisms responsible for the etiology of self-injury as well as rates of occurrence.

The precision of the first camp is high with regard to variables of clinical importance, such as measurement of behavior (e.g., self-injury; other problem behaviors; positive, desirable, replacement behaviors) and procedures that produce rapid changes in behavior. The precision of the second camp obviously focuses on biological dependent and independent variables; behavior is of interest primarily because it validates the relevance of the research. The first camp has focused on an E → SIB model, whereas the second camp has focused on a B → SIB model. Much could be gained if outstanding members of both camps lent their talents and the precision of their science to understanding biobehavioral relationships relevant to self-injury.

Insofar as the role of NIH is relevant, from time to time NIH has specified interdisciplinary research collaboration as a funding priority. For example, this approach was employed a decade ago by the Heart, Lung, and Blood Institute to advance the research agenda in behavioral cardiology—eventually producing new standards of care for preventing and treating cardiovascular disease that added lifestyle (e.g., diet, exercise, stress reduction) to medical and surgical approaches. For the present purposes of advancing research on severe behavior disorders such as self-injury, priorities could be established for applications that have a research team of both basic biological and clinical behavioral scientists.

CONCLUSION

Unlocking the box that holds the secrets to the causes of self-injury and aggression is as exciting as it is challenging. To do so by understanding the biological mechanisms that underlie the development and maintenance of these behaviors is not only logically intuitive but also more possible than ever before with the recent scientific breakthroughs in genetics and brain imaging. As behavioral scientists use their methods to understand the function of behavior in relation to environmental variables (i.e., consequences), biomedical scientists are adding comparable knowledge about the function of chromosomes and the function of the brain in relation to behavior. The clinical endpoints for such basic research are now set by four decades of advances in the field of behavior analysis—advances that now set a standard for the rapid and safe reduction of problem behaviors and the establishment of necessary behavioral skills. Future comparable advances will, therefore, most likely come not only from understanding the biological basis for self-injury and aggression but also from the integration of such knowledge with that from behavior analysis.

5

ENVIRONMENTAL DETERMINANTS OF SELF-INJURIOUS BEHAVIOR

BRIAN A. IWATA, EILEEN M. ROSCOE,
JENNIFER R. ZARCONE, AND DAVID M. RICHMAN

Attempts to identify the causes of and effective treatments for self-injurious behavior (SIB) have generated a great deal of research over the past three decades (see Schroeder et al., 2001, for an overview). Much of this work has involved extensions of methodology derived from experimental research on learning—research known as *applied behavior analysis*—which has provided a systematic basis for studying the environmental context in which SIB occurs and for evaluating treatment effects. This chapter is a review of the behavioral research on the environmental determinants of SIB and its implications for intervention.

SIB AS LEARNED BEHAVIOR

There is strong evidence that many behavior disorders, including SIB, are learned. As such, these behaviors are acquired through an individual's history of interaction with the environment and are influenced by the same types of contingencies—positive and negative reinforcement—that account for the maintenance of nonpathological forms of behavior.

Positive Reinforcement

Social Reinforcement

Lovaas and colleagues provided the earliest demonstrations that SIB can be influenced by social consequences. In one study (Lovaas, Freitag,

Preparation of this chapter was supported in part by a grant from the Florida Department of Children and Families.

Gold, & Kassorla, 1965), it was observed that a child's SIB increased when adults made sympathetic statements following its occurrence. In a later study (Lovaas & Simmons, 1969), a child's SIB was observed to occur at high rates when adult attention was delivered contingent on SIB, but SIB occurred at very low rates when attention was either unavailable or delivered continuously. SIB often produces immediate reactions on the part of caregivers, which may include expressions of concern, redirection to preferred activities, and even reprimands. These inevitable social consequences may interrupt SIB temporarily; however, their continued occurrence may strengthen and maintain SIB through inadvertent positive reinforcement.

Automatic Reinforcement

Berkson and Mason (1963, 1965) observed a relationship between repetitive, "stereotyped" movements and environmental events that did not involve the manipulation of social contingencies. They noted that individuals with mental retardation engaged in higher rates of stereotypy when access to leisure materials was restricted. SIB has also been observed to occur, sometimes exclusively (e.g., Cowdery, Iwata, & Pace, 1990), in the absence of any social consequences. The source of reinforcement for such behavior may be perceptual stimulation (Lovaas, Newsom, & Hickman, 1987) or, in the case of SIB, highly specific biological events such as the release of endogenous opioids (Sandman & Hetrick, 1995). Collectively, these nonsocial contingencies have been described as *automatic reinforcement* (Vaughan & Michael, 1982) as a means of distinguishing them from social forms of reinforcement.

Negative Reinforcement

Social Reinforcement

It has been observed that both SIB (Carr, Newsom, & Binkoff, 1976) and aggression (Carr, Newsom, & Binkoff, 1980) may occur more often when demands to perform educational tasks are present than when they are absent, and that SIB can increase in frequency when its occurrence terminates ongoing instructional activities (Iwata, Pace, Kalsher, Cowdery, & Cataldo, 1990). These data indicate that SIB may be strengthened by negative reinforcement, which involves escape from (or avoidance of) aversive situations that may include a variety of academic and work requirements or even social interaction in general.

Automatic Reinforcement

The occurrence of SIB has been linked to a variety of painful medical conditions (Bosch, Van Dyke, Smith, & Poulton, 1997). For example,

DeLissovoy (1963) observed a higher incidence of head banging among children with otitis media. More recently, O'Reilly (1997) demonstrated that the SIB of one child occurred only during episodes of otitis media. These findings suggest that, in some cases, SIB may directly alleviate ongoing pain or discomfort and persist over time as a result of automatic negative reinforcement.

FUNCTIONAL ANALYSIS MODEL OF ASSESSMENT

When applied to behavior, the term *functional analysis* refers to empirical demonstrations of cause–effect (functional) relationships between environment and behavior (Skinner, 1953). Thus, functional analysis approaches to assessment involve attempts to identify which of several sources of reinforcement (see previous section) maintain behavior. Although many techniques have been developed for this purpose (see Iwata, Kahng, Wallace, & Lindberg, 2000, for an extensive review), most procedures can be classified under one of three general categories: (a) experimental (functional) analyses, (b) descriptive analyses, and (c) indirect assessments.

Experimental Analysis

The experimental analysis approach to assessment involves repeated observations of behavior under one or more test conditions in which variables suspected of influencing behavior are directly manipulated. Response rates under these conditions are compared to those observed under a control condition in which the variables of interest are absent. In the most common type of experimental analysis, the test conditions represent reinforcement contingencies that are likely to maintain behavior (see previous section) combined with their relevant antecedent events. For example, Iwata, Dorsey, Slifer, Bauman, and Richman (1982, 1994) described a general assessment protocol in which an individual is usually exposed to three basic test conditions. In the "attention" condition, the therapist ignores the client's behavior (antecedent event) except when the client exhibits a target behavior (e.g., SIB), at which time the therapist briefly delivers attention (consequent event). This arrangement provides a test for behavioral sensitivity to social-positive reinforcement. In the demand or escape condition, the therapist presents learning trials or other task demands to the client (antecedent event) except when the client exhibits a target behavior, at which time the therapist briefly terminates the trial (consequent event). This condition provides a test for behavioral sensitivity to social-negative reinforcement. In the "alone" condition, the client is observed under conditions of social deprivation, in which access to leisure materials is restricted. The basis for this condition is somewhat indirect: Because persistence of behavior during the alone condition is unlikely to be maintained by social reinforcement (positive or negative), automatic-positive reinforcement (sensory stimulation) is implicated through a process of elimination. (There is no direct test for the influence of automatic-negative reinforcement because it would require exposure to painful stimulation.) A control condition (play or leisure) is also included in which variables manipulated during the test conditions are absent. Attention is available on a frequent and noncontingent basis, demands are absent, and access to leisure materials is continuous.

In the described arrangement, higher rates of behavior in a particular test condition indicate behavioral maintenance by the variables manipulated in that condition. Figure 5.1 shows the results of three functional analyses expressed as responses per minute of SIB across conditions. Rates of SIB in the top panel are highest under the attention condition, indicating maintenance by social-positive reinforcement. SIB in the middle panel is highest under the demand condition, indicating maintenance by social-negative reinforcement. SIB in the bottom panel occurs at very high rates across all conditions, which could indicate the influence of several processes: (a) maintenance by automatic reinforcement, which is available in all conditions; (b) control by multiple sources of reinforcement; or (c) lack of discrimination among the different conditions. Additional sessions conducted only under the alone condition show persistence of SIB and indicate maintenance by automatic reinforcement. (The precise source of sensory stimulation that maintains SIB remains unknown but could be identified through more detailed analyses.) Numerous variations and extensions of the previous model have been reported in the literature (e.g., Hagopian, Fisher, & Legacy, 1994; Mace & Lalli, 1991; Northup et al., 1991; Vollmer et al., 1995). In the most extensive experimental analysis of SIB to date, Iwata et al. (1994) summarized the results of 152 assessments and reported the following prevalence rates for different functions:

- social-positive reinforcement, 26.3%
- social-negative reinforcement, 38.1%
- automatic reinforcement, 25.7%
- multiple controlling variables or uncontrolled outcomes, 9.9%.

Descriptive Analysis

As is the case with the experimental analysis, the descriptive analysis involves repeated observations of behavior across varying environmental conditions. However, researchers do not attempt to manipulate specific variables; instead, naturally occurring sequences of events (antecedent events, behaviors, and subsequent events) are recorded in an attempt to identify recurring patterns. Data are collected in a variety of ways, although interval and time sampling procedures (Bijou, Peterson, & Ault, 1968) are most common, and results can be analyzed by simple frequencies of

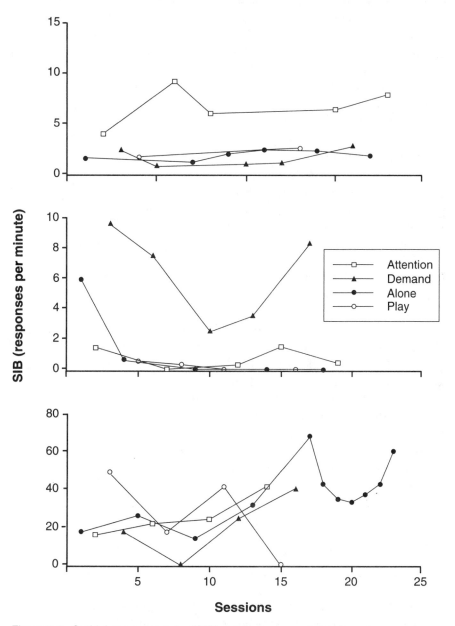

Figure 5.1. Self-injurious behavior (SIB) responses per minute in various assessment conditions (attention, demand, alone, and play) of an experimental analysis. Data in each panel illustrate maintenance of SIB by source of reinforcement.

occurrence (Mace & Belfiore, 1990), conditional probabilities (Repp & Karsh, 1994), or more complex techniques such as lag-sequential analysis (Emerson et al., 1996).

The underlying assumption of a descriptive analysis is that observed correlational relationships are suggestive of functional relationships, which may not always be true. Few comparisons between the outcomes of descriptive and experimental analyses have been reported in the literature; the most thorough of these (Lerman & Iwata, 1993; Mace & Lalli, 1991) suggest that the descriptive analysis adequately distinguishes between behavior maintained by social versus automatic reinforcement because of the high likelihood of caretaker presence or absence associated with these functions. However, distinctions between social–positive and social–negative reinforcement are not as clear.

Indirect Assessment

Indirect methods of assessment do not involve direct observation of behavior. Instead, information about behavioral function is gathered through structured questionnaires, rating scales, or checklists. For example, one frequently used questionnaire, the Motivation Assessment Scale (MAS), consists of 16 statements describing conditions under which behavior may occur. The respondent (parent or teacher) scores each item on a Likert-type numerical scale, indicating the extent to which the behavior does or does not occur under the conditions described.

The principal advantage of indirect assessments is their simplicity. However, as is the case with many verbal report measures, the reliability of these instruments has been found to be low (Sturmey, 1994). For example, although the original report on the MAS (Durand & Crimmins, 1988) presented interrater reliability correlations ranging from .89 to .98, subsequent attempts to replicate these findings have been unsuccessful. Zarcone, Rodgers, Iwata, Rourke, and Dorsey (1991) analyzed pairs of MAS data sets via multiple comparisons, which yielded correlations ranging from -.80 to .99 (M = .41) and item-by-item percentage agreement scores ranging from 0% to 63% (M = 20%). Thus, indirect assessments should be considered a preliminary, informal means of generating hypotheses and should be followed by descriptive or experimental analyses.

IMPLICATIONS FOR BEHAVIORAL INTERVENTION

By focusing greater attention on the functional characteristics of behavior (i.e., what maintains behavior) rather than on its structural characteristics (i.e., what the behavior looks like), clinicians have been able to identify the environmental determinants of SIB and, as a result, to systematically alter environmental circumstances with a higher degree of precision. Most often, environmental change is induced through a variety of reinforcement-based techniques, which generally produce behavioral suppression in one of three ways: (a) modification of antecedent conditions, (b) elimination of reinforcement for problem behavior, or (c) strengthening of competing behavior.

Modification of Antecedent Conditions: Establishing Operations

Michael's (1982, 1993, 2000) extensive discussion of antecedent influences on learned behavior emphasized the effects of establishing operations. An *establishing operation* is an antecedent event that (a) alters the extent to which a given consequence serves as effective reinforcement for behavior and, as a result, (b) alters the frequency of behavior that historically produced the consequence. The establishing operation for behavior maintained by positive reinforcement is often some form of deprivation, whereas the establishing operation for behavior maintained by negative reinforcement is aversive stimulation. Thus, water deprivation increases the reinforcing effects of drinking water (positive reinforcement) and occasions water-seeking behavior; exposure to intense noise increases the reinforcing effects of escape from noise (negative reinforcement) and occasions escape behavior.

Through identification of the contingency that maintains SIB, results of a functional analysis yield information that can be used to attenuate the influence of establishing operations via noncontingent reinforcement. For example, the noncontingent delivery of attention to individuals whose SIB is maintained by attention (positive reinforcement) has been shown to produce rapid and almost complete behavioral suppression (Hagopian et al., 1994; Vollmer, Iwata, Zarcone, Smith, & Mazaleski, 1993). By contrast, noncontingent reinforcement used with people displaying SIB maintained by escape from task demands (negative reinforcement) would involve either access to escape on a response-independent basis (Vollmer, Marcus, & Ringdahl, 1995) or the alteration of tasks to reduce their aversive characteristics (Smith, Iwata, Goh, & Shore, 1995). Finally, the noncontingent delivery of sensory stimulation has been shown to decrease SIB maintained by sensory (automatic) reinforcement (Piazza, Adelinis, Hanley, Goh, & Delia, 2000; Shore, Iwata, DeLeon, & Kahng, 1997).

Discontinuation of Reinforcement: Extinction

The most direct method for reducing the frequency of learned behavior involves eliminating its reinforcing contingency, *extinction*. Results of a functional analysis are particularly relevant to the design of extinction procedures because they identify the source of reinforcement to be discontinued. SIB maintained by attention is extinguished by withholding attention or terminating it when SIB occurs (Lovaas & Simmons, 1969); however, the same procedure would exacerbate SIB maintained by escape. Escape extinction involves the continuation, rather than the termination, of ongoing events (Steege, Wacker, Berg, Cigrand, & Cooper, 1989; Zarcone, Iwata, Smith, Mazaleski, & Lerman, 1994). Extinction of behavior maintained by automatic reinforcement is more difficult because it requires interrupting reinforcement that is a direct product of responding. To achieve this effect, experimenters have usually relied on the use of response blocking (Smith, Russo, & Le, 1999) or physical devices worn by the individual that attenuate sensory stimulation produced by SIB (Roscoe, Iwata, & Goh, 1998).

Strengthening of Competing Behavior: Differential Reinforcement

Treatment procedures based on the alteration of establishing operations and on extinction may be highly effective in reducing SIB, but they do not explicitly strengthen appropriate alternative responses. Behavioral replacement is accomplished through *differential reinforcement*, and the results of a functional analysis may be used to identify reinforcers to strengthen competing behavior (i.e., those reinforcers that currently maintain behavior). For example, after observing that problem behavior was apparently maintained by either attention or escape from task demands, Carr and Durand (1985) taught individuals alternative responses that produced these same consequences. By contrast, the ideal replacement for SIB maintained by automatic reinforcement would consist of an alternative self-stimulatory behavior, with object manipulation being the most common example. Favell, McGimsey, and Schell (1982) demonstrated that mere access to alternative sources of stimulation occasioned play behavior that competed with SIB, whereas Lindberg, Iwata, and Kahng (1999) found that toy play increased only when SIB was also interrupted.

IMPLICATIONS FOR BIOBEHAVIORAL INTERVENTION

Although functional analysis methodology is most directly pertinent to the development of learning-based interventions for behavior maintained by contingencies of reinforcement, its ability to isolate environmental determinants of SIB suggests a broader application. More specifically, functional analysis may be helpful as a screening tool when attempting to ascertain whether SIB has a biological component or as a means of establishing standard baselines in the evaluation of drug effects.

Screening for Environmental Sensitivity

In a recent discussion of biobehavioral influences on SIB, Mace and Mauk (1995) suggested that functional analysis methodology can supplement medical diagnosis by ruling out environmental sensitivity as a maintaining variable. If results of a functional analysis indicate that SIB is maintained by social reinforcement, behavioral interventions should first be implemented. On the other hand, undifferentiated or cyclical responding during a functional analysis might reflect the influence not only of sensory stimulation but also of a medical condition with associated pain or discomfort that occasions SIB. For example, Bosch et al. (1997) conducted a retrospective data review for seven individuals who engaged in SIB and were suspected of having previously undiagnosed medical conditions. The researchers summarized their general findings by providing data on three representative individuals. After results of functional analyses indicated that SIB was not maintained by social contingencies, more detailed medical evaluations revealed the presence of oral-motor dysfunction, hernia, constipation, and related problems. Medical treatment of these conditions was associated with decreases in participants' SIB.

In a related study, O'Reilly (1997) conducted a functional analysis of an individual's SIB in the presence and absence of otitis media. Results showed that no SIB occurred when otitis media was absent; however, when otitis media was present, SIB occurred at high rates only in a noisy environment (i.e., when a radio was playing). Thus, it seemed that noise from the radio was an aversive event (establishing operation), the effects of which were exacerbated by another painful condition.

Evaluation of Drug Effects

Standardization of Baselines

The effects of pharmacological treatments for SIB are often evaluated globally (i.e., through general rating scales) or against a background of uncontrolled variability (when directly observed). These sources of data may be either (a) influenced by a number of unidentified environmental factors or (b) insensitive to relatively small changes in behavior that suggest a partial therapeutic effect. Thus, the collection of data under controlled conditions both before and during drug administration may provide a uniform baseline against which the drug effects can be measured. Moreover, the use of several baselines may be helpful in evaluating drug effects under different environmental conditions.

Identification of Interaction Effects

Inconsistent findings reported with drug treatments for SIB can result from several factors (Schaal & Hackenberg, 1994). One possibility rarely explored by researchers is that some drugs may be selective for particular functions of SIB. The opiate antagonists (naltrexone and naloxone), which have been found to be the most effective pharmacological treatment for SIB (Sandman, Barron, & Colman, 1990; Sandman et al., 1983, 1993, 2000), provide perhaps the best example of a potential interaction effect between drugs and the environment. Opiate antagonists block the uptake of endogenous opioids, which may be a source of positive reinforcement for some types of SIB. Thus, one might predict that the opiate antagonists would be more effective in people with SIB that is apparently maintained by automatic reinforcement. Researchers in two recent studies examined this possibility. Gibson, Hetrick, Taylor, Sandman, and Touchette (1995) found no correlation between changes in the SIB of 20 individuals who were administered naltrexone and scores on the sensory scale of the MAS. Garcia and Smith (1999) conducted functional analyses of two participants' SIB during placebo and naltrexone conditions. Results indicated that naltrexone resulted in decreased rates of SIB in all conditions for one participant but only during demand sessions for the second participant. Although results of these studies did not provide evidence of a function-selective effect for naltrexone, the methodological innovation in both studies is noteworthy and suggests further refinements in the integration of environmental and biological assessment.

CONCLUSION

Research on the environmental determinants of SIB has shown that the behavior is often sensitive to operant contingencies in the form of positive and negative reinforcement. Numerous methodologies have been developed for identifying the influence of these contingencies individually. Collectively known as *functional assessment* or *functional analysis approaches*, these methods differ considerably from one another with respect to the degree of control that is exerted over the assessment context and the types of data collected. Whereas experimental or functional analyses involve observation of behavior under predetermined test and control conditions, descriptive analyses involve uncontrolled observation under naturally occurring conditions, and indirect assessments are based on information provided by an informant. The common goal of researchers using these methods is to identify (a) significant environmental events (antecedents) that occasion problem behavior and (b) sources of reinforcement (consequences) that maintain problem behavior.

The application of functional analysis methodology has led to a reconceptualization of the fundamental ways in which reinforcement-based interventions reduce the frequency of problem behavior: (a) through the elimination of establishing operations or noncontingent reinforcement, (b) through the discontinuation of reinforcement (extinction), or (c) through the strengthening of competing responses (differential reinforcement). Each approach influences behavior differently, but all can be combined to yield maximum treatment strength.

Because of its precision in isolating environment–behavior interactions, functional analysis methodology may also contribute to the further development of biobehavioral interventions. Functional analysis baselines may be used to rule out environmental sensitivity, to provide a standardized context in the evaluation of drug effects and identify possible drug-environment interaction effects.

6

FUNCTIONAL ASSESSMENT AND SELF-RESTRAINT

RACHEL L. FREEMAN, ROBERT H. HORNER, AND JOE REICHLE

Individuals who perform self-injurious behavior (SIB) sometimes engage in behaviors described as *self-restraint* (Fovel, Lash, Barron, & Roberts, 1989; Schroeder & Luiselli, 1992). Examples of self-restraint include sitting on hands; holding objects; and wrapping limbs in clothing, around furniture, or other people's clothing (Lerman, Iwata, Smith, & Vollmer, 1994; Powell, Bodfish, Parker, Crawford, & Lewis, 1996). Some individuals seek mechanical restraints such as arm or leg guards, pinch guards, and helmets (Schroeder & Luiselli, 1992). Others ask for or independently put on contingent electric shock devices (Linscheid, Pejeau, Cohen, & Footo-Lenz, 1994; Mudford, Boundy, & Murray, 1995). Self-restraint is most often correlated with the presence of SIB (Fisher & Iwata, 1996; Fovel et al., 1989; Isley, Karsonis, McCurley, Weisz, & Roberts, 1991; Luiselli, 1993; Schroeder & Luiselli, 1992; Smith, Iwata, Vollmer, & Pace, 1992). In fact, authors of a recent review of published research found no reported incidences of individuals engaging in self-restraint without engaging in SIB (Fisher & Iwata, 1996). Isley et al. (1991) conducted a survey of 858 institutionalized individuals and found the incidence of self-restraint to be 4%. In a smaller sample of 99 adults with severe or profound mental retardation, 46% of the individuals engaged in self-restraint (Powell et al., 1996).

Although self-restraint seems to reduce the occurrence of SIB, it is problematic in many ways (Smith et al., 1992). Self-restraint can cause restriction of blood circulation, interfere with daily activities, and hinder habilitation sessions (Isley et al., 1991). In more extreme cases, self-restraint can cause muscular atrophy and arrested motor development (Smith, Lerman, & Iwata, 1996). As a result of these possible outcomes, self-restraint can seriously impede a person's quality of life.

Current efforts to understand the relation between SIB and self-restraint have focused primarily on operant explanations—predominantly the use of functional analyses to explore the variables maintaining both behaviors (Derby, Fisher, & Piazza, 1996; Fisher, Grace, & Murphy, 1996; Smith et al., 1992; Smith et al., 1996; Vollmer & Vorndran, 1998). In some cases, SIB and self-restraint may be closely tied to internal events, and the addition of physiological assessment measures could provide valuable insight contributing to the functional assessment process. The purpose of this chapter is to (a) discuss the importance of developing models that acknowledge the complex relation between the environmental and biological factors influencing SIB, (b) describe how problem behaviors such as SIB and self-restraint could be investigated by incorporating physiological assessment strategies into functional assessment procedures, and (c) explore how this information could lead to environmental as well as physiological interventions.

ASSESSMENT OF ENVIRONMENTAL
AND BIOLOGICAL FACTORS

A strong body of research includes documentation that SIB is maintained by different social functions (Iwata et al., 1994; Mace, Lalli, & Shea, 1992). An individual may engage in self-injury to communicate a need to escape from demands or nonpreferred tasks (Carr, Newsom, & Binkoff, 1980), obtain tangibles within their environment (Durand & Crimmins, 1988), and/or gain the attention of others (Iwata et al., 1994). Numerous functional analyses, however, do not yield conclusive findings (Vollmer, Marcus, & LeBlanc, 1994). Consequently, interventionists are placed in a position where they are expected to identify effective interventions based on inconclusive results.

In a summary of 152 functional analyses of SIB, Iwata et al. (1994) reported that 30% involved automatic reinforcement (sensory stimulation, pain attenuation, and undifferentiated high responding). That is, 30% did not show sensitivity to socially mediated reinforcement (Vollmer et al., 1994). Derby and colleagues (1992) found that 34% of their clients engaged in problem behavior that appeared to be maintained by automatic-sensory consequences. These data suggest that in 30% of the instances, a functional analysis was unable to identify a socially mediated function that maintained problem behavior.

Research on problem behaviors maintained by automatic-sensory reinforcement supports the influence of both environmental and neurobiological factors (Carr, 1977; Demchak & Halle, 1985; Guess & Carr, 1991; Lewis, Baumeister, & Mailman, 1987). For instance, automatic positive reinforcement may be caused by an internal physiological process such as the production of endogenous opiates (Sandman, Barron, & Colman, 1990) or due to environments that are under- or overstimulating (Brusca, Nieminen,

Carter, & Repp, 1989: Guess & Carr, 1991; Hutt & Hutt, 1970). Problem behaviors may originate from an organic disorder but later be maintained by environmental events (Demchak & Halle, 1985; Guess & Carr, 1991). Conversely, some people may engage in SIB that was originally maintained by social contingencies but over time and with extensive exposure to SIB experienced changes in their body's release of dopamine or endogenous opiates (Schroeder, Reese, Hellings, Loupe, & Tessel, 1999).

To fully understand and treat SIB, professionals need a model that incorporates physiological factors into the functional assessment process (Mace & Mauk, 1999). For instance, Thompson and Symons (1999) recommend that careful selection of psychotropic medications be made by considering how specific pharmacological treatments may influence an individual's response to environmental stimuli that maintain both adaptive and problematic behavior. Thompson and Symons (1999) reported how drugs such as benzodiazepines used to treat anxiety may decrease SIB maintained by negative reinforcement. In addition, the administration of benzodiazepine may result in an increase in socially maintained SIB because the value of punishers that previously suppressed SIB may decrease. Laboratory animal research literature supports this hypothesis (Cook & Catania, 1964; Heise & Boff, 1962; Randall, Schallek, Heise, Keithh, & Bagdon, 1960).

Assessment strategies that systematically analyze the impact psychotropic medications have on altering the effects of controlling environmental variables can contribute to a better understanding of treatment efficacy. A study by Northup, Fusilier, Swanson, Roane, and Borrero (1997) assessed the drug–behavior interaction effects of methylphenidate (MPH), a stimulant prescribed for attention deficit hyperactivity disorder (ADHD). In this study the subjects received MPH or a placebo alternatively across days within a multielement design. Three environmental conditions were alternated within the school day to assess the effects of teacher attention in the form of reprimands, escape from difficult tasks, and peer attention. Results indicated that disruptive behavior increased during the peer attention condition on days when a placebo was given. The authors suggested that medications such as MPH may act as an establishing operation that alters the reinforcing value of environmental stimuli.

Mace and Mauk (1999) have been developing and piloting a biobehavioral model for the classification of self-injury. In the model proposed, the authors have included a biomedical classification system in addition to the already identified operant functions maintaining problem behavior. This biomedical model creates classes of SIB based on observable symptomatology that may correlate with presumed disordered neurotransmitter systems. Five clinical subtypes are described, including (a) extreme self-inflicted injury, (b) repetitive and stereotyped SIB, (c) high-rate SIB with agitation when interrupted, (d) co-occurrence of SIB with agitation, and (e) multiple clinical features. The authors are currently conducting research to analyze clinical features and neurochemical markers to further refine their assessment model using a cluster analysis. One area of research that may benefit from assessment strategies that include physiological measurement is the relation between two highly correlated behaviors: SIB and self-restraint.

RELATION BETWEEN SIB AND SELF-RESTRAINT

Although researchers have shown growing interest in the possible functions of self-restraint and its relation to SIB, they still know very little about this behavior (Isley et al., 1991; Schroeder & Luiselli, 1992). Many suggestions for possible functions of self-restraint rely primarily on operant principles (Luiselli, 1993). Several theories have been proposed to explain the function maintaining self-restraint (Fisher & Iwata, 1996; Isley et al., 1991; Luiselli, 1993; Schroeder & Luiselli, 1992; Smith et al., 1992).

One theory states that self-restraint and SIB are affected by similar reinforcement and punishment contingencies (Fisher & Iwata, 1996). In other words, SIB and self-restraint are part of the same response class (Luiselli, 1993; Smith et al., 1992). If a person engages in SIB to escape from performing tasks, he or she could use self-restraint to serve the same function. Smith and his colleagues proposed a theory that self-restraint and SIB may be part of different response classes. For example, the function of SIB for an individual may be to escape from difficult or nonpreferred tasks, whereas self-restraint may be maintained by attention. In addition, the authors suggest that the current function of self-restraint may be different from its establishing function. For instance, although self-restraint may have functioned as a means of avoiding SIB, sensory function, such as comfort, or socially maintained attention may currently be maintaining the behavior.

One of the most popular theories (Luiselli, 1993) is that self-restraint is negatively reinforced by the avoidance of pain induced from self-injury (Fisher et al., 1996; Isley et al., 1991; Luiselli, 1993; Schroeder & Luiselli, 1992; Smith et al., 1992). The high correlation between SIB and self-restraint lends credence to this theory (Luiselli, 1993). One explanation for the reason individuals engage in self-restraint instead of choosing to stop engaging in self-injury is based on an approach-avoidance paradigm in which the variables that affect the probability of a response are in competition (Fisher & Iwata, 1996; Miller, 1959). That is, a response may be associated with both positive and negative consequences. The consequences maintaining SIB are not constant and depend on various factors, such as schedule and quality of reinforcement, deprivation and satiation conditions, and the degree of perceived aversiveness of the negative consequence (Fisher & Iwata, 1996).

The negative-reinforcement hypothesis has been difficult to confirm because the expected reinforcer is escape from or avoidance of SIB, which is an automatic consequence of self-restraint (Fisher & Iwata, 1996). However, some studies are consistent with this theory (Fisher et al., 1996; Silverman, Watanbe, Marshall, & Baer, 1984; Smith et al., 1992). For instance, Fisher et al. (1996) demonstrated that blocking an individual's attempts to self-injure resulted in a decrease in self-restraint. The negative reinforcement theory incorporates the physiological variable pain within an operant paradigm for explaining the relationship between self-injury and self-restraint. Future researchers studying the relation between self-injury and self-restraint may need to consider physiological factors more directly. The next section of this chapter describes the way SIB and self-restraint may be associated with both respondent and operant learning. Operant variables integrated with the elements of physiology (reflex behaviors and arousal levels) are presented.

RESPONDENT LEARNING

Physiological changes in an individual during the period in which he/she engages in problem behavior may increase the likelihood that some form of respondent learning has occurred in addition to any operant factors involved (Schwartz, 1989). In discussing the relation between operant and respondent conditioning, Margin and Pear (1988) assert that any behavioral sequence is likely to include both types of learning. An operant model may be able to explain why a boy bitten by a dog no longer plays with any dogs, but doesn't explain why the boy becomes frightened, has an increased heart rate, and sweats profusely when he sees a dog nearby.

Numerous researchers have proposed that SIB may be elicited by emotional events (Frankel & Simmons, 1976; Newsom, Carr, & Lovaas, 1977; Romanczyk, 1977; Romanczyk & Goren, 1975). Initial development of SIB may occur through simple classical conditioning in which a specific emotional stressor then becomes generalized to other situations (Romanczyk, Lockshin, & O'Conner, 1992). Romanczyk (1987) combines operant and respondent variables to describe the function of SIB. According to his theory, SIB is aversive to the person. When they experience pain from SIB, they become aroused and seek escape to reduce arousal. The unconditioned stimulus—pain—is followed by the unconditioned response, which in this case is an increase in arousal. Individuals engaging in SIB do not want to hurt themselves, so they are often physiologically aroused when confronted with situations that elicit SIB. Self-injury becomes reinforced by staff restraint, which calms the individuals and returns them to physiological equilibrium. Creators of this theory suggest that at times SIB may be preceded by an aversive emotional state, which may provide insight into the origins of self-restraint.

PROPOSED MODEL OF SELF-RESTRAINT

To prevent severe self-injury, individuals with developmental disabilities are often placed in some kind of physical restraint. Isley et al. (1991) suggest that mechanical or physical restraint may be an essential part of an individual's history if self-restraint is to occur. Researchers have found that self-restraint appears to reduce SIB (Luiselli, 1993; Smith et al., 1992), whereas other investigators have found that self-restraint can function as a reinforcer (Favell, McGimsey, & Jones, 1978; Favell, McGimsey, Jones, & Cannon, 1981; Smith, Lerman, & Iwata, 1996; Vollmer & Vorndran, 1998).

According to Romanczyk's (1987) model, self-restraint also is the result of respondent learning. An individual engages in self-restraint to avoid SIB and the corresponding increase in physiological arousal. Figure 6.1 describes the possible development of self-restraint based on the assumption that self-restraint occurs as a result of both operant and respondent learning (Martin & Pear, 1988; Romanczyk et al., 1992; Schwartz, 1989). After the occurrence of SIB in the operant model, staff members immobilize the individual, self-injury terminates, and the person calms down. This relaxed condition may be incompatible with the conditions that evoked SIB (Schroeder, Peterson, Solomon, & Artley, 1977). After this pattern has occurred repeatedly, the person begins to request restraints from staff members. Eventually, because staff members are not always available, the person attempts to self-restrain to obtain the same calming response. Releasing restraints may serve as a discriminative stimulus for an individual who frequently engages in SIB. Over time, increases in arousal may become paired with the release of restraints, whereas a decrease in arousal becomes paired with self-restraint. In some cases the degree to which overt arousal is observed may decrease because of active avoidance of SIB (Romanczyk & Mathews, 1998).

The success of treatment using stimulus fading and transfer techniques (Schroeder & Luiselli, 1992) might be explained by higher order learning in respondent conditioning. This type of treatment often involves changing the self-restraint topography by utilizing symbolic clothing items such as a hat, a pair of glasses (Fox & Dufrense, 1984), wristbands, or pants with pockets (Pace, Iwata, Edwards, & McCosh, 1986). The symbolic clothing items are paired with the absence of pain, leading to a conditioned response—a decrease in arousal. Over time, observable arousal related to SIB may decrease given the success of self-restraint as a means of arousal reduction (Romanczyk & Mathews, 1998). Further research in this area may focus on the relation of SIB and self-restraint to both neurochemical and environmental factors (Fisher & Iwata, 1996).

If SIB occurs for different reasons, one might expect self-restraint to occur in some but not all of the discussed patterns. For instance, if the function of SIB were predominantly operant, the occurrence of self-restraint would not be expected, assuming that both operant and respondent models are correct. If SIB appears to have a sensory–automatic function, the likelihood of self-restraint may be higher. A certain type of neurochemical dysfunction also may indicate whether self-restraint would be more likely to

Operant learning model

Respondent learning model

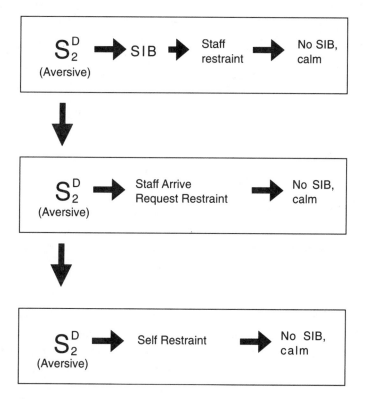

Figure 6.1. Operant and respondent models of self-injurious behavior (SIB) and self-restraint.

occur. For instance, self-restraint may be more likely in people in whom dopaminergic and serotonergic dysfunction is suspected. Individuals who engage in SIB to release endogenous opiates would be less likely to engage in self-restraint because self-restraint is incompatible with SIB. Experimental designs similar to those of Northup et al. (1997) may provide additional insight regarding these theories.

The use of psychotropic medications in the treatment of SIB also might explain how the function maintaining self-restraint changes over time. For instance, consider the previous example regarding the effects of benzodiazepine, which may eliminate the aversive effects of specific environmental events. In this scenario, the administration of a benzodiazepine results in an increase in socially maintained SIB because the value of punishers that previously suppressed SIB may decrease. Likewise the administration of certain psychotropic medications also could have an impact on the functions maintaining self-restraint by acting as an establishing operation. Changes in the value of the aversive consequences of SIB could contribute to the development of socially maintained factors for both SIB and self-restraint. Researchers systematically investigating the interaction between pharmacological treatment and environmental variables may provide insight into the relation between SIB and self-restraint. In addition, adding physiological measurement strategies into the functional assessment process may provide important clinical information for intervention purposes (Freeman, Horner, & Reichle, 1999; Romanczyk & Mathews, 1998; Romanczyk et al., 1992).

PHYSIOLOGICAL MEASUREMENT

Physiological measurement approaches incorporated into the functional assessment process may lead to a deeper understanding of SIB and self-restraint. Psychophysiological measurement strategies identify the occurrence of internal events that may be correlated with behavior (Surwillo, 1990). Patterns in physiological events may provide insight that is not directly observed. If physiological arousal immediately precedes the occurrence of self-injury, then this information can be used to design proactive intervention strategies (Romanczyk & Mathews, 1998). Romanczyk et al. (1992) described three case studies in which heart rate and skin conductance were used as indicators of arousal. The data were used to "enhance and confirm" observational and performance information. In other cases, increases in arousal preceding the occurrence of problem behavior were detected using galvanic skin conductance (GSC) for two children with disabilities (Romanczyk & Mathews, 1998) and increases in muscle tension for two adults engaging in severe self-injury utilizing data from an electromyogram (EMG; Schroeder et al., 1977).

The two hypotheses presented in Figure 6.2 may explain the link between arousal and problem behavior. In the first hypothesis, problem behavior serves as a discriminative stimulus for increases in arousal. In this scenario, increases in arousal would be expected to follow the occurrence of problem behavior. The second hypothesis suggests that some individuals may have increases in arousal that precede problem behavior. Individuals who consistently react to situations and events with increased physiological arousal preceding problem behavior may be more anxious, and this anxiety may be an establishing operation for problem behavior (Bijou & Baer, 1961; Kantor, 1959; Wahler & Graves, 1983). Evidence that increases in arousal can both precede and follow the occurrence of problem behavior have been verified, although these findings need to be replicated (Freeman et al., 1999; Romanczyk & Mathews, 1998; Schroeder et al., 1977). The next section of this chapter describes important issues related to heart rate, a physiological measure that can be used to explore these two arousal hypotheses.

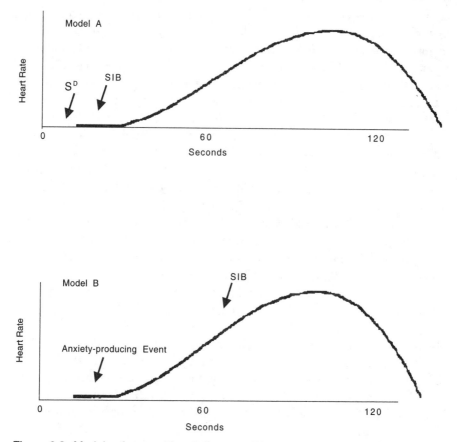

Figure 6.2. Models of arousal in relation to self-injurious behavior (SIB).

Cardiovascular Measurement Issues

Cardiac activity has been utilized by psychophysiologists to study such diverse subjects as information processing, biofeedback, and emotional states (Romanczyk et al., 1992). The relation between stress and increased cardiovascular function is now widely accepted in medical practice (Hassett & Danforth, 1982). Measurement of heart rate is one of the most commonly used indices of arousal (Romanczyk et al., 1992), partly because it can be measured easily and accurately (Cacioppo & Petty, 1982a; Turner, 1994). Several important issues should be considered when using cardiovascular measurements.

The normal heart beat starts with the discharge of an electrical impulse from the sinoatrial node, the heart's natural pacemaker, thereby producing the rhythmic contraction of the entire heart. Heart rate is simply the measurement of frequency of contractions per unit of time (Romanczyk et al., 1992). Increases in heart rate are related to the activation of the sympathetic branch of the autonomic nervous system (ANS), whereas decreases in heart rate are related to the parasympathetic branch of the ANS. The cardiovascular system is responsible for major life support—controlling metabolic functions that include distributing oxygen to tissues, removing metabolic waste, controlling temperature, and balancing fluids and electrolytes (Obrist, 1982). Caution interpreting heart rate changes is warranted since researchers must try to separate heart rate responses associated with problem behavior from natural physiological and physical factors that systematically affect this measure (Tursky & Jamner, 1982).

Although somatic activity (i.e., physical movement) is closely linked to heart rate (Obrist, 1982; Obrist, Webb, Sutterer, & Howard, 1970), researchers investigating active avoidance demonstrated that participants placed in a situation where they could actively avoid a threatening stimulus found that active coping resulted in increases in heart rate exceeding any possible metabolic demand (Obrist, 1976). In one experiment, those who could avoid shocks showed greater increases in systolic blood pressure, cardiac rate, and performance when compared with those passively exposed to shocks (Light & Obrist, 1980). In another experiment, participants showed greater increases in heart rate when led to believe they could avoid shock by modifying an undesignated bodily activity (Obrist, 1976).

Fowles (1982) has described heart rate measurement as a "noisy index of anxiety" (p. 113). Increases in heart rate can be attributed to many variables, including mental effort, affective states, feeding, and physical exertion (Shapiro & Reeves, 1982). Consequently, additional assessments are needed to understand the relation of heart rate increase to the occurrence of problem behavior. Cacioppo and Petty (1982a, 1982b) argued that physiological responses must be interpreted within the context of the individual's reportable state. Individuals with severe intellectual disabilities may not be able to verbalize positive or negative affective states; however, observers may be able to capture this phenomenological information effectively. The link between anxiety or other emotional states and heart rate may, in some cases, be directly related to the occurrence of problem behaviors.

Strong evidence exists regarding individual differences in heart rate patterns and other physiological responses (Freeman et al., 1999; Romanczyk & Mathews, 1998; Romanczyk et al., 1992; Turner, 1994). Individuals in the same situation show significant variations in their cardiovascular reactivity (Turner, 1994). Heart rate increase may serve as a cue for emotionality (Shapiro & Reeves, 1982). By understanding individual patterns of heart rate reactivity to environmental stressors, researchers can create specific interventions to reduce reactivity, which may successfully decrease the frequency and severity of problem behaviors and contribute to the individual's general state of health.

In one study, researchers collected data on covariation and rate of SIB, physiological measurement of heart rate, and the occurrence of events and activities in real time (Freeman et al., 1999). Sequential analysis procedures (Bakeman & Gottman, 1986; Gottman, 1981; Gottman & Roy, 1990; Whitehurst, Fischel, DeBaryshe, Caulfield, & Falco, 1986) were used to examine the relation between heart rate and the occurrence of problem behaviors (Freeman et al., 1999). The data collected in this study suggested that for one individual, heart rate patterns differed according to the type of problem behavior, even though these behaviors were thought to be part of the same response class.

Use of Data

At this time, the clinical use of physiological data in relation to behavior is still tentative (Romanczyk & Mathews, 1998; Turpin & Clements, 1993). Discrepant findings in arousal research have been reported (James & Barry, 1980) because of numerous factors, including inconsistencies in terminology and classification, differing strategies for reducing movement, and difficulties in using physiological measurement in the real environment (Romanczyk & Mathews, 1998). However, continued efforts in developing methodological approaches and recent advances in psychophysiological measurement devices are making it possible to explore the link between physiology and problem behavior (Romanczyk et al.,1992). Utilizing knowledge of psychotropic medication effects and incorporating physiological measures into functional assessment may provide important information regarding the relation between SIB and self-restraint. For instance, measurement strategies may identify key arousal patterns that support the negative reinforcement hypothesis in self-restraint and provide additional insight. Intervention strategies based on psychophysiological measurement can be used to evaluate both environmental and physiological variables.

Implementing Interventions Based on Physiological Data

A number of pharmaceutical and environmental strategies addressing physiological arousal are described in the literature (Cautela & Baron, 1973; Cautela & Groden, 1978; Chandler, Gualtieri, & Fahs, 1988; King, 1991; Mace & Mauk, 1999; Steen & Zuriff, 1977; Thompson & Symons, 1999). Pharmacotherapy with medication for the co-occurrence of SIB and agitation has included lithium carbonate, propranolol, and benzodiazepines (Chandler, Gualtieri, & Fahs, 1988; Greendyke, Kanter, Scuster, Verstreate, & Wooten, 1986; Lader, 1988; Thompson & Symons, 1999). The treatment of agitation related to obsessive-compulsive disorder has included serotonin-reuptake inhibitors including fluoxetine and clomipramine (King, 1991; Markowitz, 1992).

Evaluating the efficacy of psychotropic medications by utilizing physiological measurement strategies may contribute to more effective treatment plans. For instance, a study could be implemented exploring whether the use of propranolol with subjects who clearly have heart rate increases preceding problem behavior reduces the magnitude of heart rate change during stress (T. A. Thompson, Director of the Institute for Child Development at the University of Kansas Medical Center, personal communication, June 7, 2000). Validation of this treatment approach could include involving a comparison group of individuals who engage in SIB but do not show a large heart rate increase preceding the behavior. Other interventions may use physiological measurement to design effective relaxation interventions or environmental modifications.

If physiological arousal is a cue for emotionality, reduced heart rate may be less compatible with a negative affective response (Shapiro & Reeves, 1982). Individual heart rate patterns may be an important focal point of functional assessment allowing for the design of interventions aimed at decreasing heart rate through relaxation approaches and environmental manipulation. The use of relaxation as an intervention for problem behavior has been recognized for some time (Cautela & Baron, 1973; Cautela & Groden, 1978; Groden & Baron, 1991; Schroeder et al., 1977; Steen & Zuriff, 1977). However, physiological measurement procedures are rarely used to assess arousal directly (Romanczyk & Mathews, 1998). Physiological measurement strategies may be able to assess specific situations or times of day associated with high arousal levels so that relaxation programs can be implemented. In one situation, Romanczyk and Mathews (1998) used GSC to assess arousal levels of one child engaging in self-injury. Arousal levels increased in response to close physical contact with others. A multicomponent intervention approach, including systematic desensitization to physical proximity, task demands, social interaction, and noisy environments, was implemented based on this information.

Researchers from one study did report the use of physiological measurement to facilitate a relaxation intervention that included the use of biofeedback (Schroeder et al., 1977). The authors demonstrated that the use of EMG feedback and contingent restraint resulted in decreasing amplitude and increasing duration of low amplitude muscle activity for two individuals engaging in self-injury. Future intervention strategies could include the use of an athlete's heart rate monitor as a biofeedback device. An individual with mild disabilities may be able to respond to an alarm indicating that his heart rate has risen above normal levels, by initiating a self-management relaxation strategy. Knowing the time an episode of increased arousal usually lasts also might provide clues on how to interrupt the usual pattern of arousal and bring about faster heart rate decreases.

Researchers have identified patterns of rhythmic cycles and SIB (Carlson, 1988; Francezon, Visier, & Mennesson, 1981; Lewis, MacLean, Johnson, & Baumeister, 1981; Romanczyk et al., 1992; Romanczyk, Gordon, Crimmins, Wenzel, & Kistner, 1980). Understanding these rhythmic cycles of arousal could lead to more effective medical treatment and behavior support strategies. For instance, if physiological arousal is higher at a certain time of day and an individual is more likely to engage in problem behaviors when heart rate increases, an interventionist can schedule more relaxing or pleasurable activities during periods of high arousal.

CONCLUSION

Functional assessment has had significant advances in behavioral technology during the past decade (Carr, 1994; Horner, 1994). The major focus of functional assessment research has been determining the way environmental variables affect behavior, while less time has been spent studying the relation between biological and environmental factors. A gap persists between the medical and behavioral models explaining SIB, although some professionals have made significant contributions in this area (Guess & Carr, 1991; Mace & Mauk, 1999; Schroeder et al., 1999; Thompson & Symons, 1999). Future research on the relation between physiological factors and SIB is needed to build conceptual bridges between biological and environmental factors (Guess & Carr, 1991).

SIB involving self-restraint prevents clear identification of controlling variables (Isley et al., 1991). The negative reinforcement hypothesis has been difficult to confirm because the expected reinforcer is escape from or avoidance of SIB, which is an automatic consequence of self-restraint (Fisher & Iwata, 1996). A model of self-restraint that builds on the negative reinforcement hypothesis by melding both operant and respondent learning paradigms has been proposed. In some cases, the occurrence of SIB may be perceived as aversive, stimulating an avoidance response that results in self-restraint. If operant and respondent conditioning occur in most behavioral sequences (Martin & Pear, 1988; Schwartz, 1989), then measurable physiological changes will be apparent. Following this logic, self-injury may be triggered by arousal, which then becomes maintained by environmental stressors (Romanczyk et al., 1992). Further research is needed to identify and develop more sophisticated approaches for studying the link between arousal and self-injury within the natural environment.

If the most difficult cases of SIB are those cases in which behavior is both neurochemically and environmentally related (Oliver & Head, 1990; Oliver et al., 1993; Thompson, Egli, Symons, & Delaney, 1994), then cooperation among professionals is imperative. The development of interdisciplinary research teams consisting of professionals who specialize in medical, biological, and social sciences fields is needed to better understand the complexity of problem behavior (Guess & Carr, 1991). "The ultimate value of functional analysis will be realized when all potential determinants of SIB (operant and other) can be evaluated separately and interactively" (Linscheid, Pejeau, Cohen, & Footo-Lenz, 1994, p. 89).

7

THE IMPACT OF FUNCTIONAL ASSESSMENT ON THE TREATMENT OF SELF-INJURIOUS BEHAVIOR

SUNGWOO KAHNG, BRIAN A. IWATA, AND ADAM B. LEWIN

Results of more than 30 years of research on the assessment and treatment of self-injurious behavior (SIB) indicate that, in the majority of cases, SIB is maintained through environmental contingencies in the form of positive and negative reinforcement (Carr, 1977; Iwata, Pace, et al., 1994; Lovaas, Freitag, Gold, & Kassorla, 1965). During the past 15 years, researchers have become increasingly interested in the development of methods to identify the contingencies that account for SIB on an individual basis. As a group, these methods have come to be known as *functional assessment* procedures and have enhanced the ability to develop effective behavioral interventions in several ways (Iwata, Vollmer, & Zarcone, 1990; Mace, Lalli, & Lalli, 1991). First, the antecedent conditions under which behavior occurs (i.e., establishing operations and discriminative stimuli) can be identified and altered to reduce the likelihood of SIB. Second, identification of the maintaining contingencies allows one to minimize or eliminate the source of reinforcement (i.e., through extinction). Third, the same reinforcer that maintains SIB may be used to establish an alternative response. Finally, knowledge of behavioral function may permit one to eliminate reinforcers and treatment components that may be irrelevant to the overall reduction of SIB.

The success of functional assessment procedures has led to their widespread endorsement by researchers and clinicians. For example, the National Institutes of Health (NIH) convened a consensus panel in 1989 on the treatment of destructive behaviors associated with developmental disabilities. One of the panel's recommendations was that treatment of

This research was supported in part by a grant from the Florida Department of Children and Families. We thank Marc Branch, Shari Ellis, Tim Hackenberg, and Cecil Mercer for comments on previous versions of this chapter.

severe behavior disorders should be based on the results of functional analyses (NIH, 1989). Subsequently, the 1997 reauthorization of the Individuals with Disabilities Education Act contained a provision requiring the use of some form of functional behavioral assessment before initiating a change of placement for students who have behavior disorders. Mandates such as these have had a clear impact on practice. Desrochers, Hile, and Williams-Moseley (1997) surveyed members of the Psychology Division of the American Association on Mental Retardation. Using a scale labeled *always*, *often*, *seldom*, or *never*, respondents ($N = 125$) indicated that treatment decisions were always (47%) or often (46%) based on a functional assessment.

This increased emphasis on the use of functional assessment has also led to a change in the way researchers evaluate treatments for SIB (Mace, 1994). Before the development of this technology, treatments were often implemented arbitrarily without regard to the contingencies that maintained problem behavior. When these interventions failed to produce positive outcomes, researchers often turned to default technologies, such as punishment, without analyzing the conditions necessary for successful behavior change (Iwata, 1988). Functional assessment has been directly responsible for the development of many new treatment procedures based on the empirical examination of environmental changes that weaken existing response-reinforcer relationships while strengthening new ones (Mace, 1994). Finally, functional assessment has allowed researchers to systematically identify factors that may result in treatment failure. For example, numerous studies have suggested that the ineffectiveness of some interventions may partly be caused by a mismatch between behavioral function and treatment (Durand & Kishi, 1987; Repp, Felce, & Barton, 1988) or a change in the function of the problem behavior over time (Lerman, Iwata, Smith, Zarcone, & Vollmer, 1994) rather than the need for a more intrusive intervention (i.e., punishment).

Several reviews of the literature contain summaries of the research on behavioral approaches to SIB treatment. All contain important information that remains timely in many respects; however, each has certain limitations. For example, some reviews were conducted many years ago, before the refinements in assessment just described were established (Johnson & Baumeister, 1978). Other reviews did not include any information on the use of functional assessment (Gorman-Smith & Matson, 1985), examined research from a relatively brief period of time (Sternberg Taylor, & Babkie, 1994), or included a small number of journals in the sample (Pelios, Morren, Tesch, & Axelrod, 1999). Therefore, the purpose of the present review was to examine research conducted during the past three decades on behavioral approaches to SIB, with special emphasis on the use of functional assessment and its relationship to treatment selection and outcome.

Literature Search

A database of research articles on the assessment and treatment of SIB and other related behavior disorders was compiled through searches of *Current Contents*. Additional articles were identified through examination of the PsycINFO and ERIC databases using the keywords *self-injurious behavior* and *SIB*. Inclusion of articles was based on the following criteria:

1. The article had to include data on a behavioral treatment for either SIB alone or with other problem behaviors (e.g., aggression, property destruction) in individuals diagnosed with developmental disabilities (e.g., mental retardation, autism).
2. If the article included multiple participants, only those individuals who engaged in SIB (alone or in conjunction with other destructive behaviors) were included in the analysis.
3. To ensure that information (e.g., type of treatment, behavior graphs) about each participant was readily available, only articles incorporating single-subject experimental designs (Kazdin, 1982) were included.

The following types of studies were excluded from the data analysis:

1. studies that presented only assessment of SIB but did not include a treatment condition
2. studies using group designs (i.e., "large-*N*" studies) that did not report individual data
3. studies utilizing pharmacological treatments

Functional Assessment

Type

Data were collected on whether the study included a pretreatment functional assessment. Functional assessments are generally classified under three categories: (a) indirect assessment, (b) descriptive analysis, and (c) functional (experimental) analysis. Indirect methods of assessment consisted of structured interviews and rating scales (e.g., Durand & Crimmins, 1988) that did not involve direct observation. Descriptive analyses involved direct observation of behavior in an attempt to identify environmental antecedent and consequent events that were correlated with the occurrence of SIB (Bijou, Peterson, & Ault, 1968). Finally, functional analyses involved the arrangement of specific assessment conditions to test for maintaining contingencies for SIB (Iwata, Dorsey, Slifer, Bauman, & Richman, 1982, 1994).

Behavioral Function

Behavioral research has characterized sources of reinforcement for SIB in various ways, including reference to specific stimuli (e.g., contingent attention) or to larger classes of contingencies (e.g., social-positive reinforcement). We used the latter method in this chapter to allow comparisons with data presented in a large-scale study on the functional analysis of SIB in which results from 152 participants were summarized (Iwata, Pace, et al., 1994). Therefore, each article (individual data set) included in this chapter that contained a functional assessment was scored based on the authors' interpretation of the assessment outcome, and the resulting functions were placed into the following categories: (a) social-positive reinforcement (access to attention, food, or other tangible items), (b) social-negative reinforcement (escape from task demands, social interaction, or other environmental stimulation), (c) automatic reinforcement (sensory stimulation), (d) multiple control (two or more of the previous functions), and (e) unknown.

Treatment

Type

Treatment type was divided into seven main categories: (a) antecedent manipulation, (b) extinction, (c) reinforcement, (d) punishment, (e) restraint, (f) response blocking, and (g) other. Response blocking was not included in any of the other treatment categories because it is often unclear whether blocking suppresses behavior through punishment (Lerman & Iwata, 1996) or extinction (Smith, Russo, & Le, 1999). In cases of the simultaneous application of multiple interventions, each component of the treatment package was counted separately.

Effectiveness

Treatment outcomes were estimated by comparing data at the end of a baseline phase with those at the end of a treatment phase. We initially determined the value of each of the last five data points from the baseline and treatment phases. If the phase consisted of fewer than five data points, values of the data points were determined for the maximum yet equal number of data points available for the baseline and treatment phases. For example, if a baseline phase only consisted of three data points, those three baseline points were compared to the last three data points of the treatment phase. If a study contained multiple replications of baseline, treatment conditions, or both (e.g., reversal designs), data were taken from the last phase of each condition.

An approximate value for each data point was calculated with the aid of an academic divider, which is a device similar to a compass but with needlepoint tips on both ends (rather than a tip on one end and a pencil on the other). The divider was used to determine the distance between each data point and the x-axis of the graph. The distance between the tips of the divider was then measured against the y-axis of the same graph to obtain an approximate value. Using these data, a mean was calculated for the baseline and treatment data points.

To determine treatment effectiveness, the mean value of the treatment data was subtracted from the mean value of the baseline data. This number was then divided by the mean baseline value and multiplied by 100% to obtain a reduction or increase percentage. Thus, a reduction of 100% reflected total elimination of the response based on comparison of the specified treatment data points, whereas a reduction of 0% reflected no change from baseline. A negative percentage reflected an increase in response during treatment relative to baseline. Percentage effectiveness was not calculated for those data sets in which the data were presented as averages or based on rating scales. In addition, if the data set failed to include a baseline, intervention effectiveness was not calculated.

Interobserver Agreement

Agreement on scoring all of the previous categories was assessed by having a second rater independently review 13.6% of the articles. Comparisons were then made of the two raters' entries for each separate category (e.g., treatment). An *agreement* was defined as both raters making the same entry for the same category (e.g., exact agreement on the type of treatment), and an agreement percentage was calculated for each category by dividing the number of agreements by the number of agreements plus disagreements and multiplying by 100%. A different calculation was used for the treatment efficacy category: The smaller number (percentage change) was divided by the larger number and multiplied by 100%. Mean agreement scores were as follows: functional assessment type, 96.8%; behavioral function, 97.3%; treatment type, 96.4%; and treatment efficacy, 97.6%.

FINDINGS

Literature Search

We identified 396 articles from 63 journals covering the years 1964 to 2000.[1] These articles included 706 data sets (i.e., participants) that met the criteria for inclusion in this chapter (see Table 7.1). The *Journal of Applied Behavior Analysis* had the largest number of articles and data sets, which accounted for nearly a third of all articles and data sets.

Functional Assessment

The majority of the data sets (62.2%) did not provide information on the use of functional assessment, which was taken as an indication that no assessment was done. These data correspond to findings of other reviews on

---

[1] A complete list of articles is available from the first author.

TABLE 7.1
Distribution of Journals Publishing Articles on the Treatment of SIB

Journal	Number of articles	Number of data sets
Journal of Applied Behavior Analysis	121	263
Journal of Behavior Therapy and Experimental Psychiatry	34	41
Research in Developmental Disabilities[a]	24	50
Behavioral Interventions[b]	22	36
American Journal on Mental Retardation[c]	16	35
Journal of Intellectual Disability Research[d]	16	20
Behavior Modification	14	23
Behavior Therapy	14	18
Journal of Developmental and Physical Disabilities[e]	11	17
Mental Retardation	10	12
Behaviour Research and Therapy	9	23
Journal of Autism and Developmental Disorders[f]	8	11
Psychological Reports	7	7
Journal of the Association for Persons with Severe Handicaps[g]	6	10
Behavioural and Cognitive Psychotherapy[h]	5	11
Journal of Visual Impairment and Blindness	5	10
Other (fewer than 5 articles)	74	119
Total (N = 63 journals)	396	706

[a] Applied Research in Mental Retardation merged with Analysis and Intervention in Developmental Disabilities to become Research in Developmental Disabilities.
[b] formerly Behavioral Residential Treatment
[c] formerly American Journal of Mental Deficiency
[d] formerly Journal of Mental Deficiency Research
[e] formerly Journal of the Multihandicapped Person
[f] formerly Journal of Autism and Childhood Schizophrenia
[g] formerly the Journal of the Association for Education of Persons with Severe and Profound Handicaps
[h] formerly Behavioural Psychotherapy

the treatment of problem behavior in general (e.g., Lennox, Miltenberger, Speigler, & Erfainian, 1988; Lundervold & Bourland, 1988). The top panel of Figure 7.1 shows the number of data sets that did and did not include a functional assessment during the various years. The number of data sets published without functional assessments steadily increased from the mid-1970s through the mid-1980s. Thereafter, the number of data sets without functional assessments decreased, as more studies incorporating functional assessments were published. Most pronounced is the dramatic increase in the number of data sets with functional assessments, starting near the end of the 1980s. This appears to be a direct function of a significant increase in the number of data sets that incorporated experimental (functional) analyses (see Figure 7.1, bottom panel). Indirect assessments, descriptive analyses,

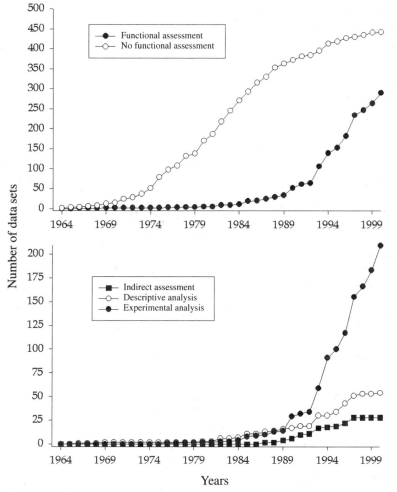

Figure 7.1. Cumulative number of data sets incorporating a functional assessment (top panel) and the type of functional assessment chosen (bottom panel).

and experimental (functional) analyses were conducted for 3.9%, 7.5%, and 28.9% of the data sets, respectively.[2] Whereas these data indicate that two thirds of those studies including functional assessment used functional (experimental) analyses, Lennox et al. (1988) and Lundervold and Bourland (1988) reported much lower percentages in the use of functional analyses (6% and 13%, respectively). This discrepancy seems to be a result of the dramatic increase in the use of functional analyses after the publication of the Lennox et al. and Lundervold and Bourland reviews.

The increasing trend in the use of functional assessments since the 1980s noted in our data corresponds to that found by Pelios et al. (1999) and is probably attributable to two factors. First, the development of a general methodology for conducting functional analyses (Iwata et al., 1982/1994) and the design of interventions based on the outcomes of such analyses (Carr & Durand, 1985) first appeared around that time period. Second, a general emphasis since the 1980s has favored the use of reinforcement-based rather than punishment-based interventions, and the systematic design of reinforcement procedures is more heavily dependent on information about behavioral function (Axelrod, 1987).

Reported Functions of SIB

Based on results of functional assessments (including indirect assessment, descriptive analysis, and functional analysis) conducted in studies included in this chapter, the most prevalent behavioral function of SIB was social negative reinforcement (31.3%, see Table 7.2). It is interesting to note that our summary of assessment results across a large number of independently conducted, small-N studies corresponds closely to that presented by Iwata, Pace, et al. (1994), who summarized data on behavioral function for a large group of individuals with SIB ($N = 152$) from a single setting, all of whom were assessed via functional analysis. (Those data are also shown in Table 7.2 for purposes of comparison.) Both the rankings of behavioral function in terms of prevalence (e.g., escape function most common) and the percentages reported for each behavioral function were remarkably sim-

---

[2] Some data sets may include more than one type of assessment.

TABLE 7.2
Functions of SIB Identified Through Assessment

Function	Number of data sets	Percent	Iwata, Pace et al. (1994)
Social negative reinforcement	83	31.3%	38.1%
Social positive reinforcement	70	26.4%	26.3%
Automatic reinforcement	73	27.5%	25.7%
Multiple function	18	6.8%	5.3%
Unknown	21	7.9%	4.6%

ilar. Thus, results of two large-N summaries of functional assessment data indicate that the majority of SIB is maintained by social consequences. (The combined proportion for SIB maintained by social reinforcement was 57.7% in our sample and 64.4% in the Iwata, Pace, et al. sample.)

Treatment Selection

When preceded by a functional assessment, the use of both reinforcement and punishment show an upward trend starting in the mid-1980s (see Figure 7.2, top panel), although the trend is much steeper for reinforcement-based interventions than for punishment (these results are similar to those

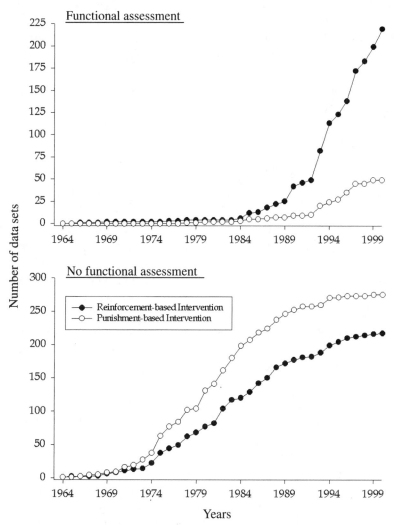

Figure 7.2. Cumulative number of data sets using reinforcement-based versus punishment-based interventions when preceded by a functional assessment (top panel) and not preceded by a functional assessment (bottom panel).

reported by Pelios et al., 1999). Although punishment was more likely to be used without a functional assessment than was reinforcement (see Figure 7.2, bottom panel), there was no marked difference in trends between the number of data sets that incorporated either intervention in the absence of a functional assessment. Both data sets show a relatively steady increase through the mid- to late 1980s, after which both begin to show a decreasing trend. By contrast, Pelios et al. noted a relatively stable trend across years in the number of studies (using reinforcement or punishment) that were not preceded by a functional assessment. This discrepancy is most likely a result of differences in sampling and calculation. Pelios et al. confined their literature search to five journals that "publish a large body of research on the treatment of self-injurious and aggressive behavior" (p. 7), which accounted for approximately 40% of the articles included in this chapter. In addition, Pelios et al. based their results on the number of articles published rather than the total number of data sets contained in those articles. Thus, in addition to the fact that our chapter contains many more articles, small trends reflected by numbers of articles may have been magnified by taking into account every published data set.

Treatment Efficacy

The extent to which interventions based on functional assessments are more effective than those selected either arbitrarily or through some other means has not been well established (for an exception, see Iwata, Pace, et al., 1994). Although the clinical utility of functional assessments has been established in a number of studies containing small numbers of participants, the generality of this finding is unknown because, on a large scale, any method used for selecting an intervention could produce positive outcomes overall. Therefore, we examined intervention effectiveness based on whether or not it was derived from the outcome of a functional assessment. These data must be interpreted with caution because of selection bias, in that researchers may be reluctant to submit articles containing "failure" data, and journal editors may be reluctant to accept such articles for publication (Johnson & Baumeister, 1978).

Table 7.3 shows the mean percentage reduction in SIB for different classes of intervention when these interventions were implemented with or without a functional assessment. Not shown in the table are the overall percentage reductions achieved from the use of reinforcement-based interventions (including extinction) versus punishment, which were 76.5% and 83.3%, respectively. These figures are consistent with results from numerous reviews indicating that punishment is more effective than reinforcement or extinction as a treatment for SIB. However, different results are obtained when the use of functional assessments is taken into account. When reinforcement alone, reinforcement combined with extinction, or extinction

TABLE 7.3

Effectiveness[a] of Treatment either alone[b] or in Conjunction with Another Intervention[c] Based on the Use of Functional Assessment

	Antecedent		Extinction		Reinforcement		Punishment		Response block		Mechanical restraint	
	No	Yes	No	Yes	No	Yes	No	Yes	No	Yes	No	Yes
Functional Assessment												
Antecedent	76.9% (n=20)	98.1% (n=19)										
Extinction			47.0% (n=2)	85.6% (n=24)	47.5% (n=5)	82.3% (n=31)						
Reinforcement					61.6% (n=92)	83.5% (n=103)	82.4% (n=75)	89.5% (n=17)	57.3% (n=3)	81.8% (n=5)		
Punishment							84.9% (n=121)	67.8% (n=29)				
Response block												
Mechanical restraint											87.5% (n=14)	94.2% (n=19)

[a] Mean percentage reduction in SIB
[b] Identical column and row labels
[c] Different column and row labels

alone was implemented without a functional analysis, percentage reductions in SIB were generally low (61.6%, 47.5%, and 47%, respectively). However, when these same interventions were implemented with a functional assessment, percentage reductions in SIB exceeded 80%, which was comparable to the 83.3% reduction associated with punishment (all combinations aggregated). Thus, as has been suggested by several authors (e.g., Axelrod, 1987; Iwata, Pace, et al., 1994), the primary benefit of functional assessments has been to increase the precision and resulting effectiveness of reinforcement-based interventions.

CONCLUSION

Results of the present analysis indicate that research on behavioral approaches to the treatment of SIB shows a marked increase in the use of functional assessments, particularly functional analyses, and that this trend has occurred primarily during the past decade. Results of such assessments, when aggregated, indicate that most SIB appears to be maintained by social contingencies. When functional assessments are used as the basis for intervention, treatment procedures are more likely to consist of reinforcement than punishment. Finally, the effectiveness of reinforcement-based interventions is enhanced when they are implemented in conjunction with functional assessments.

Aside from the trends noted, the most obvious implication of the present data is that the development and evaluation of treatments may be heavily influenced by the use of functional assessments. This should be taken into account in future reviews of the literature as a potential determinant of both treatment selection (see Figure 7.2) and treatment outcome (see Table 7.3).

An unexpected finding was the fact that the overwhelming majority of functional assessments (two thirds of all those reported) consisted of functional (experimental) analyses. This result was surprising in light of suggestions that simpler and more efficient forms of assessment (e.g., indirect assessments, descriptive analyses) may be adequate for identifying the functions of problem behavior (Durand & Crimmins, 1988; Touchette, MacDonald, & Langer, 1985). The reasons for such heavy reliance on the use of functional analysis are speculative but may include the following. First, because this chapter focused on published research, it might be expected that a larger proportion of treatment data would be based on more rigorous methods of assessment. In other words, researchers, but not clinicians, may be more likely to use functional analyses than other forms of assessment, and this possibility is supported by results from practitioner surveys (e.g., Desrochers et al., 1997). Second, given the superior precision of the functional analysis, it is possible that assessments of this type enhance treatment outcome which, in turn, has a selective effect on publication (see previous comments). Finally, the many components of a functional analysis (i.e., the qualitative and quantitative characteristics of a number of antecedent and consequent variables) are well suited to a variety of methodological variations and extensions.

Research on the use of functional analysis also seems to be growing much more quickly than is research on indirect or descriptive assessments. Thus, one interesting area for future research would entail more systematic efforts at refining these latter methods. For example, although several questionnaires and rating scales (i.e., indirect methods) have been developed, little is known about the conditions under which respondents can reliably or accurately describe the functional characteristics of problem behavior or about the types of questions that are more likely to yield useful information. Similarly, although many methods are available for conducting direct observations of behavior (descriptive analyses), much less is known about ways to structure such observations to increase the likelihood of identifying functional influences.

Finally, results of the present analysis are limited to SIB. Because of its dramatic nature, SIB may be more likely to involve inadvertent social reinforcement, the use of more sophisticated forms of assessment, treatment with punishment, and so on. Because research on the treatment of other significant problem behaviors (e.g., aggression, stereotypy) in people with developmental disabilities may reveal different emphases or trends, researchers need to perform large-scale studies of these disorders and meta-analyses of research across time.

8

EVOLUTION OF STEREOTYPY INTO SELF-INJURY

CRAIG H. KENNEDY

Although knowledge about the environmental and biological variables that can *maintain* self-injurious behavior (SIB) is increasing, less is known about the conditions that *create* it. Researchers have identified a range of reinforcers, stimulus controls, and establishing operations that cause self-injury to reoccur and have developed new assessment and treatment approaches based on these maintaining variables (see DeLeon, Rodriguez-Catter, & Cataldo, chapter 4; and Iwata, Roscoe, Zarcone, & Richman; chapter 5; both this volume). However, researchers have fewer answers to an apparently simple question: How do behaviors such as self-biting, eye gouging, and head hitting originate?

The answer to this question is undoubtedly complex and multifaceted. Developing a complete answer to questions about the genesis of SIB will involve integrating knowledge of behavioral phenotypes, neural mechanisms, and environmental events that coincide to create this group of behaviors. However, to answer this larger question, researchers will need to pose a series of simpler questions. They need to identify the environmental events that give rise to SIB.

Given the apparent maladaptive (and even life-threatening) nature of SIB, most people conclude that the behavior is "psychotic" and driven by forces that are not part of everyday events that impinge on their own behavior. Researchers have demonstrated that the maintenance of self-injury can be attributed to specific, but quite ordinary, events in a person's environment. The environmental conditions that maintain SIB are typical events, present in our everyday lives, that become linked with self-destructive behavior.

It has long been known that behavioral processes that are part of behavior-environment interactions can give rise to "psychotic" behaviors that when behaviorally analyzed are demonstrated to be lawful (Sidman,

1960). Behaviors such as SIB that seem irrational are proving to be quite normal in the sense that they occur for identifiable and predictable reasons. Given that researchers suggest ordinary environmental events can maintain SIB, it seems reasonable to propose that similarly ordinary events can create it. However, very little research has been done on the origins of SIB.

This chapter's focus is on the ideas that a frequently occurring pattern of behavior—referred to as *stereotypy* —can be the genesis for SIB under certain environmental conditions. The basis of this idea rests on the following logic. First, it has been shown that the majority of children with developmental disabilities engage in stereotypy (Berkson, 1983). Second, researchers have noted that (a) most people with developmental disabilities who engage in SIB also engage in stereotypy, and (b) in many cases, it seems that the stereotypy developed before the self-injury (Guess & Carr, 1991). Finally, researchers have shown that stereotypy may serve a range of complex environmental functions that are similar to SIB (Kennedy, Meyer, Knowles, & Shukla, 2000).

To begin answering questions about the origin of self-injury, this chapter is an exploration of possible behavior-environment mechanisms that contribute to the development of SIB. The rationale for focusing on behavior-environment mechanisms is that substantial basic research has been done on the environmental causes of arbitrary responding (Lattal & Perone, 1998). This research has yielded a great deal of information about how environmental feedback mechanisms can differentially shape patterns of complex responding. In addition, the majority of experimental analyses of SIB suggest an important role for environmental events in its maintenance. However, little empirical or theoretical work has been done on the linkage of basic behavioral processes to the genesis of self-injury. Therefore, it may be useful to synthesize information regarding (a) well-established basic behavioral processes and (b) environmental conditions that allow stereotypy to evolve into SIB.

NATURE OF STEREOTYPED RESPONSES

That stereotypy may serve as a bridge to SIB is a relatively new idea first tendered by Guess and Carr (1991). These authors theorized that because of the ubiquitous occurrence of stereotypy in some children with developmental disabilities, self-injury may emerge as a topographically distinct response to similar environmental conditions. Such conjectures seem plausible and heuristic. However, before elaborating on behavior-environment mechanisms that may facilitate stereotypy evolving into SIB, it may be propaedeutic to elaborate on what is known about stereotypy and the conditions under which it occurs.

Stereotypy is characterized by repetitive behaviors that occur as a highly consistent topography (Berkson & Tupa, chapter 9). Examples of stereotypy include body rocking, hand waving, finger flicking, and tongue clicking. Stereotyped behaviors occur across intellectual functioning levels, but researchers have found that an increased prevalence of these behaviors is an inverse function of intellectual ability (Berkson, Rafaeli-Mor, & Tarnovsky, 1999). These behaviors tend to emerge early in development and are more likely to persist into adulthood if a significant developmental disability is present (Berkson, McQuiston, Jacobson, Eyman, & Borthwick, 1985). In addition, researchers have repeated analyses demonstrating that stereotyped behaviors are more likely to occur if (a) low levels of environmental stimulation are present, or (b) excessive levels of stimulation are present (Repp, Karsh, Deitz, & Singh, 1992). These general characteristics of stereotypy suggest that the behavior tends to occur at high rates, tends to persist over the course of development, and is sensitive to environmental events.

Stereotypy theorists tend to focus on the perceptual stimulation received by the person participating in the behavior. For instance, Lovaas, Newsom, and Hickman (1987) posited a perceptual reinforcement hypothesis suggesting the causes of stereotypy are twofold. First, stereotyped behaviors occur in response to diminished environmental stimulation. As the top panel of Figure 8.1 shows, these behaviors can occur when the appropriate establishing operations set the occasion for stereotypy to produce positive reinforcement in the form of perceptual stimulation. For example, children may wave their hands in front of their eyes to produce visual stimulation when little other stimulation is present. Second, stereotypy can enter into a negative feedback function with its environment. As shown in the bottom panel of Figure 8.1, stereotypy may reduce environmental stimulation when excessive stimulation is present. An example of this negative reinforcement function is a child covering the ears to reduce noise levels as an ambulance drives by. The perceptual reinforcement hypothesis suggests that stereotypy is an operant behavior (i.e., is sensitive to environment stimulation and feedback) that is positively reinforced, negatively reinforced, or both by perceptual stimulation (Lovaas et al., 1987).

However, recent research suggests that the causes of stereotypy may be more complex than this theory posits. Along with perceptual reinforcement for stereotypy, researchers have demonstrated that these behaviors are sensitive to reinforcement from social events (Kennedy et al., 2000). This research suggests that stereotypy not only occurs because of perceptual reinforcement but also because of reinforcers that are mediated by others in a person's environment (see also Durand & Carr, 1987; Mace & Belfiore, 1991). For example, a child's stereotypy might be positively reinforced by being provided access to a computer game when he flicks his fingers in front

Positive feedback mechanism

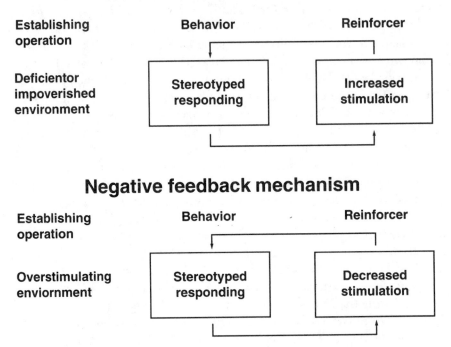

Establishing operation

Behavior

Reinforcer

Deficient or impoverished environment

| Stereotyped responding | Increased stimulation |

Negative feedback mechanism

Establishing operation

Behavior

Reinforcer

Overstimulating enviornment

| Stereotyped responding | Decreased stimulation |

Figure 8.1. Environmental feedback mechanisms and the establishing operations that maintain stereotypy.

of his eyes. Conversely, the child's finger flicking might be negatively reinforced by withdrawal of adult attention when the stereotypy occurs. These findings suggest that stereotypy is a form of operant behavior that can be multiply determined by perceptual and social stimuli.

EVOLUTION OF STEREOTYPY INTO SELF-INJURY

The emerging picture of the functional causes of stereotypy suggests that this behavior is part of typical developmental processes, but the behavior may become susceptible to control by additional variables that cause its transformation into self-injury. Several fundamental properties of stereotypy make this scenario possible. First, stereotyped behaviors tend to occur at relatively high rates and are present largely during waking activities. Given the often ubiquitous nature of stereotypy, the probability of it occurring with adventitious contingencies of reinforcement is high (e.g., Clark, 1962; Sidman, 1958). If a behavior occurs 3 to 5 times per minute during 40% of a person's day, the likelihood of other events either occurring after a stereotyped response or being removed as the behavior occurs is high. Therefore, stereotyped responses routinely occur simultaneously with events that could function as positive or negative reinforcers, and this correlation may establish adventitious contingencies of reinforcement for the behavior.

Second, stereotyped behaviors tend to be invariant. That is, they tend to persist over time, with a consistent topography. This characteristic of stereotypy allows for repeated occurrence of the behavior with adventitious contingencies of reinforcement. This aspect of stereotypy creates increased adventitious reinforcement and can place the behavior on intermittent schedules of reinforcement. Both of these dimensions of reinforcement schedules are known to establish and maintain responses (Catania & Keller, 1981).

Finally, stereotyped responses are highly susceptible to control by socially mediated reinforcers (Kennedy et al., 2000). Although researchers and practitioners have historically viewed (if not defined) stereotyped responses as behavior maintained by events apart from the social environment, these behaviors seem to be very sensitive to social reinforcement. The social reinforcement can directly relate to social interaction (e.g., social attention) or changes in stimulation that require another person (e.g., access to music). This stereotypy characteristic means that it may be maintained by multiple forms and functions of reinforcing stimuli.

The remainder of this section includes an exploration of possible mechanisms associated with the emergence of stereotypy into self-injury. This process is discussed within the context of four stages that reflect what may empirically prove to be critical phases in the transformation of stereotypy into SIB. The goal is to provide a proscriptive treatment of this phenomenon that may suggest potential mechanisms for researchers to study. Given the theoretical nature of this endeavor, the following discussion is likely to be incomplete once empirical evidence is forthcoming. However, in the spirit of empirical advance, the following behavioral processes may be involved in the genesis of self-injury from stereotypy.

Emergence of Perceptual Reinforcement

As noted by Guess and Carr (1991), stereotypy's origin appears to be rooted in its perceptual consequences. This observation is consistent with the theoretical work of Lovaas et al. (1987) and the empirical work of Berkson and colleagues. As discussed previously in this chapter, the perceptual consequences maintaining early forms of stereotyped responding seem to be the two generic feedback mechanisms that maintain operant behavior—positive and negative reinforcement. How these events come to maintain the response depends on changes in stimulation in relation to behavior, the ability of the stimulus to function as a reinforcer, and the existence of establishing operations that evoke or inhibit stimuli as reinforcers (see Figure 8.1).

Evidence supporting the perceptual reinforcement hypothesis includes (a) a relation between high and low levels of stimulation and the occurrence of stereotypy (Berkson & Mason, 1963), (b) sensory deprivation effects that increase the occurrence of stereotypy (Lichstein & Sackett, 1971), (c) extinction-like processes that occur when the hypothesized perceptual cause of stereotypy is eliminated (Rincover, Cook, Peoples, & Packard, 1979), and (d) the occurrence of response substitution when one type of stereotypy is suppressed (Rollings, Baumeister, & Baumeister, 1977). Although direct evidence for perceptual reinforcers in stereotypy is notably lacking (Kennedy, 1994), primarily as a result of difficulties in measuring these events, indirect evidence supports the role of perceptual reinforcement in the maintenance of stereotypy (Kennedy et al., 2000).

Response and Perceptual Reinforcement Differentiation

A second process likely involved in the evolution of stereotypy into other forms of responding is the differentiation of behavior. If an individual learns to engage in a response to produce a perceptual reinforcement (e.g., visual or vestibular stimulation), that response comes under the control of specific positive reinforcers, negative reinforcers, or both. For example, body rocking may produce vestibular stimulation functioning, which would serve as positive reinforcement when low levels of environmental stimulation were present. Placing the hands over the ears and humming may be negatively reinforced by a reduction in subjective noise levels. Once these reinforcement processes are established, it is likely that response differentiation will be induced via differential reinforcement.

To draw an analogy from evolutionary biology, in many respects differential reinforcement affects behavior in the same way selective reproduction affects the differentiation of animal species (Skinner, 1971). Various response types may occur, but only certain behaviors may be reinforced. The responses that prompt reinforcement are selected (i.e., reinforced) and more likely to occur in the future than responses that do not prompt reinforcement (i.e., they are extinguished). For example, a person who is highly sensitive to auditory frequencies higher than 1 kHz would find typical ambient noise at these frequencies noxious. At some point, ear covering in the presence of noise may reduce its subjective level, thus negatively reinforcing the ear covering. Hence, ear covering is selected instead of other responses (e.g., body rocking, closing the eyes) and is more likely to occur in the future. However, as is often the case with differential reinforcement (Catania, 1991), these selective processes continue to alter and modify the response, the conditions under which the response, and the types of stimulation the response produces. These processes may make stereotypy more sensitive to environmental input through a history of differential reinforcement.

Response-reinforcer differentiation may occur through several possible behavior-environment mechanisms. First, stereotypy is likely to be sensitive to the types of stimulation it produces; therefore, specific response topographies are selected. For example, a person whose body rocking produces vestibular stimulation that is positively reinforcing learns that certain types of body postures, rates of rocking, and degrees of movement more effectively and efficiently produce the reinforcing stimulation. This process leads to more refined forms of stereotypy and perhaps greater topographic rigidity as the behavior is performed and selectively reinforced over time (Newell and Bodfish, this book).

Coincident with response topography selection via differential reinforcement is the establishment of stimulus control over responding. As pointed out in initial discussions of operant behavior (e.g., Skinner, 1938), differential reinforcement is necessary to establish stimulus control, and the process itself tends to differentiate responding under some stimulus conditions and not others. This process relates to stereotypy. For example, consider a person whose hand waving is reinforced by the visual stimulation it produces. Initially, specific hand waving motions are selected because they produce the requisite visual stimulation. However, along with response differentiation, certain stimulus conditions are selected. For example, consider a person engaging in hand waving in lighted and darkened rooms. If visual stimulation is the reinforcer maintaining the response, then the response will be extinguished in darkened rooms. Lighted rooms will become necessary for the visual stimulation reinforcement. Likewise, certain people or activities may also have a differential effect on the availability of reinforcement.

Response-reinforcer differentiation is also affected by adventitious reinforcement of stereotypy by perceptual events other than those initially maintaining the behavior. Because of the ubiquitous nature of stereotypy, the behavior is likely to produce another form of stimulation that might function as a positive or negative reinforcer. For example, if a person engaging in hand waving accidentally knocks something off a table with the hand, the sound of the object falling on the ground could function as a positively reinforcing event, and the hand waving would be adventitiously reinforced. This process could establish new operant functions for stereotypy in addition to its functional origins.

Emergence of Social Control

As stereotypy comes under differential control through selective reinforcement processes, it may become more sensitive to other environmental contingencies. Stereotypy not only may directly produce stimulation that could function as reinforcement but also might be affected by the behavior of other people. Clinical assumptions regarding the causes of stereotypy have historically focused on perceptual reinforcement—or self-stimulation. However, there is increasing evidence that the functions of stereotypy are also social.

Durand and Carr (1987) showed that some cases of stereotypy are affected by the attention of adults. Similarly, Mace and Belfiore (1990) demonstrated in a case history that stereotypy could be negatively reinforced by withdrawal of attention. These studies suggest that social stimuli could serve as reinforcers for stereotypy. Kennedy et al. (2000) recently demonstrated that most cases of stereotypy in children with autism between the ages of 6 and 18 years served multiple operant functions. For these individuals, stereotypy was often used to gain adult attention (positive reinforcement), to avoid carrying out demanding instructions (negative reinforcement), to provide perceptual stimulation (of unknown operant function), or all of these.

This cumulative evidence strongly suggests that stereotypy is a more complex set of behaviors than previously considered. In addition, it suggests that stereotypy is sensitive to social reinforcement in much the same way that other forms of behavior are. This observation means that stereotypy not only occurs for perceptual reinforcement, but for social or communicative reasons. So far, researchers have demonstrated that social attention and access to preferred activities or items (e.g., music, a computer) can function as positive reinforcers for these behaviors, whereas demands, social attention, and loud noises can function as negative reinforcers (see also Carr, Schriebman, & Lovaas, 1975; Kennedy, Tang, Koppekin, & Caruso, 2000).

Possible mechanisms accounting for this increase in operant functions for stereotypy include (a) differential reinforcement of stereotypy as a form of communication and (b) adventitious reinforcement of stereotypy in social interaction contexts. Apparently, stereotypy is affected by social stimuli, as well as access or withdrawal of tangible stimuli through the social mediation of others. The accumulating data on the social and communicative functions of stereotypy (Prizant &Wetherby, 1989) suggest that these behaviors are very sensitive to the actions of others and can readily come under the control of socially mediated reinforcers.

Transition From Stereotypy Into Self-Injury

If stereotypy can evolve into behavior that obtains or avoids reinforcers through the behavior of others, this social control provides a range of opportunities for stereotypy to turn into self-injury. Although researchers have tended to categorize stereotypy separately from self-injury, the observation that stereotypy can come under social control suggests a greater continuity between these behaviors than previously thought and suggests possible behavior–environment mechanisms that cause this shift in response topography. In essence, once stereotypy comes under the control of social behavior, it becomes a communicative operant response just like talking, signing, or pointing and, like those behaviors, is amenable to control by well-known behavioral processes.

One set of mechanisms that might induce a shift from stereotypy into self-injury is based on *matching theory* (Herrnstein, 1970). The matching law specifies the conditions under which behavior is allocated to various response options. For example, if Response A is positively reinforced by attention for every 20th occurrence and Response B is positively reinforced by attention for every 5th occurrence, with other variables being constant and equal, a person will tend to emit Response B.

Typically, researchers discuss four dimensions of behavior-environment relations related to the matching law that predict the occurrence of specific responses: (a) magnitude of reinforcement, (b) frequency of reinforcement, (c) delay of reinforcement, and (d) response effort (see Catania, 1966). *Magnitude of reinforcement* refers to the amount of reinforcement that a response prompts. For example, if Response A allows a person to avoid noxious stimuli for 30 seconds and Response B allows the person to avoid these stimuli for 5 seconds, Response A is more likely to occur. *Frequency of reinforcement*, as was described in the previous paragraph, refers to the schedule of reinforcement that a response follows. *Delay in reinforcement* refers to the time that elapses between the response and the onset (positive reinforcement) or offset (negative reinforcement) of stimulation. For example, if Response A produces attention within 2 seconds and Response B produces attention within 15 seconds, Response A is more likely to occur. Finally, *response effort* refers to the physical effort required to emit a response. For example, if Response A requires 50 N of force to emit and Response B requires 500 N of force, then Response A is more likely to occur.

The relations between these behavior-environment dimensions can be summarized as follows:

Response probability = (Magnitude x Frequency) / (Delay x Effort)

That is, the greater the magnitude or frequency of reinforcement and the less the delay of reinforcement or response effort, the more likely a response (e.g., SIB) is to occur, relative to other responses (e.g., stereotypy). Although this is a simplified version of the matching law, it illustrates the basic relationship between behavior and its environment. In terms of stereotypy and SIB, if stereotypy is less efficient than self-injury in terms of, for example, magnitude or frequency of reinforcement, then SIB is more likely to occur. This theory suggests that if self-injury is more likely to induce the desired results than stereotypy, it is the preferred response option for obtaining positive and negative reinforcers. For example, if hand waving rarely produces attention from others but head slapping frequently and quickly produces attention, then under the appropriate establishing operations a person uses head slapping to obtain attention. Given that people are more likely to react to SIB than to stereotypy, it is likely that the matching law explains how self-injury could be preferred to stereotypy for obtaining reinforcers that already control stereotypy.

Matching theory also provides the structure for suggesting how chains of behavior might be established. This process can be demonstrated by juxtaposing one variable against the others. For example, if hand waving requires little effort and prompts reinforcement, and head slapping requires a lot of effort but produces the same reinforcement as hand waving, hand waving is more likely to occur. However, if hand waving is placed on an extinction or intermittent reinforcement schedule, head slapping might become more likely (Sprague & Horner, 1994). To the casual observer, this behavioral process might appear as follows: A girl waves her hand when she is alone, and she becomes increasingly agitated. She slaps her head, and her teacher comes over and hugs her. In other words, when satiated by the stimulation produced by hand waving and deprived of social attention, the girl may eventually learn to simply slap her head a few times to get somebody's attention.

However, the matching law includes nothing about how self-injury might emerge from stereotypy—only why it might be more likely to occur than stereotypy when seeking reinforcement. Although multiple mechanisms undoubtedly cause a shift from stereotypy into SIB, one behavioral process is a likely candidate: shaping. *Shaping* acts on behavior by differentially reinforcing successive approximations to some other response and is an important mechanism in creating new behaviors (Catania, 1992).

Shaping can act on stereotypy by gradually changing the response into one that is self-injurious. For example, if a boy taps his chin and learns that this causes his father to rush over and interact with him, the chin tapping might come under the control of positive reinforcement in the form of attention from his father. However, if over time his father stops paying attention to the chin tapping, the tapping would be on an extinction schedule. As a result the child may tap his chin more vigorously or change the topography of the response (both behaviors that are well-documented effects of extinction), causing his father to pay attention to the new variation in chin tapping. This behavioral process can lead to rapid changes in response topography and create SIB from other more benign response topographies such as stereotypy. An important part of this behavioral process, however, is that the reinforcement is only provided or removed for select behaviors—something to which responses under social control are very amenable (as opposed to responses that produce their own responses, such as perceptual reinforcement).

Together, shaping and matching theory provide plausible behavioral mechanisms for the genesis and maintenance of SIB from stereotypy, respectively. Undoubtedly other behavior-environment mechanisms play a role in this evolutionary process, but these two behavioral processes may provide a parsimonious explanation for the emergence of SIB.

CONCLUSION

Current evidence suggests that the phylogeny and ontogeny of SIB are determined by interactions of genes, neurobiology, and environment. This chapter has focused on the etiology of SIB in relation to environmental influences on behavior—in particular, how self-injury may have its genesis in the behavior-environment relations entered into by stereotypy. Emerging evidence suggests that stereotypy occurs not only for perceptual reinforcement but also for reinforcement mediated by the behavior of others. It is unclear how early this reinforcer differentiation occurs, but initial data suggest that stereotypy may readily come under multiple operant control.

It has been suggested in this chapter that stereotypy evolves into SIB through a set of well-known behavioral processes. These behavior–environment mechanisms may offer future researchers a parsimonious, predictable, and testable set of hypotheses to use when studying the transfer of behavioral functions from stereotypy to self-injury. Researchers know that once SIB is present, it is highly sensitive to environmental reinforcement contingencies, but less is known about the genesis of these behaviors. Perhaps the mechanisms outlined in this chapter will be of assistance to future researchers in understanding the functional origin of self-injury, which may lead not only to a more robust scientific understanding of this phenomenon but also to improved and humane approaches to its remediation.

9

INCIDENCE OF SELF-INJURIOUS BEHAVIOR: BIRTH TO 3 YEARS

GERSHON BERKSON AND MEGAN TUPA

To learn about abnormal stereotyped and self-injurious behavior (SIB) in the period before age 3 years, we have been studying babies with severe disabilities. The work builds on papers by Kravitz et al. (1960), MacLean et al. (1991), and Wehmeyer (1991), who showed that such abnormal behaviors exist in the period before age 3 and can interfere with adaptation. Beyond that we have referred to the research of Lourie (1949), Sallustro and Atwell (1978), and Thelen (1981), whose well-known studies established that normal transitory stereotyped behaviors are characteristic of most typical infants. In this chapter, we include data only on SIB.

Our studies depend on the fact that, although there has been substantial research about behavioral and pharmacological approaches to treatment of these abnormalities when they are well-established, the occurrence of these behaviors early in development has hardly been recognized (see Berkson & Tupa, 2000, for a review). It is hoped that increased attention to these problems will lead to greater alertness to their developmental aspects. Consequently, infants and toddlers might be able to begin appropriate therapies while their abnormalities are emerging rather than when they are well-established.

Before proceeding, it is important to clarify two points. The first is that, although abnormal stereotyped and self-injurious behaviors can begin during infancy, they can also emerge later. The work of Murphy et al. (1999) makes this point clear. Consequently, a developmental perspective might also be applicable for children older than age 3.

The second preliminary point is that we include in our studies noninjurious behaviors that have the same general form as SIB. Thus, children

This research was supported by a grant from the National Institute of Child Health and Human Development (HD R01-27184). Thanks to Lauren Sherman for her help in data collection and analysis.

145

who bang their head but do not injure themselves are engaging in a behavior that might develop into a habit that does cause an injury. Therefore, we take these potential, or *protoinjurious*, behaviors seriously, although we do distinguish them from the more traditionally defined SIB.

We worked in several early intervention programs in the Chicago area. After a training session on stereotyped behaviors, we asked staff members to refer to us those children who seemed to be appropriate for the research. In particular, we asked them to consider children who are severely delayed, visually impaired, seemed autistic, already were showing stereotyped behavior (such as body rocking) or SIB (such as head banging). Staff members who observed such a child used our parental permission document. After the parent had consented, one of us observed the child to verify the existence of a behavior of interest. Although we worked with some children who were younger, we ordinarily began observations of our sample when the children were about a year and a half old and continued until they were age 3 years, unless they left the program earlier.

Because we visited each program at least once a week, we were able to collect several 5-minute video samples of each child's behavior. We also wrote log notes about our observations and talked with the parents and staff members about changes in the behaviors of interest. Both during and before our meeting with the family, we checked the child's records for clinical note references to stereotyped and self-injurious behaviors.

Thus, we have multiple data sources from a significant period of the child's development. We organize the data by using the checklist presented in Exhibit 9.1. Note that the categories include stereotyped behaviors, SIB, whether an injury is evident, the context in which the behavior occurred, and various subcategories of motor development and interaction.

When analyzing the data, we ensured that the people who were filling out the checklist from the various data sources were doing so reliably. Thus, we trained observers on each of the data sources. In most cases, interobserver reliabilities exceeded 85% immediately. However, with some of the video records, observers required additional training until two of them agreed on the video at least 85% of the time. Once interobserver agreement was adequate, we arranged all of each child's monthly data on a master data sheet. Using the checklist, we noted which behaviors occurred during each month.

The results presented in this chapter provide a general picture of the data we have currently for proto-SIB and SIB. Of the 457 children, some of whom lived with their biological families and some of whom were adopted, the staff chose 64 children as candidates for the research. Of these 64, only 48 were deemed appropriate for the research, and we could not use 9 others because of poor attendance and a 4-month project suspension when all research at our university was stopped.

EXHIBIT 9.1
Video Checklist for Stereotypy or Self-Injurious Behavior (SIB)
During Child Development

Stereotypy

Body rocking style
- Back and forth
- Side to side
- Bounce

Form
- Prone/supine
- Four-point posture
- Seated
- Standing

Head roll
Hand or finger gazing or staring
Hand flapping
Thumb or finger sucking
Pacifier sucking
Other repetitive behaviors
- Pokes object with digits
- Scratches surface
- Twirls or spins object
- Moves hand or object in front of eyes

Self-Injury

Head banging or hitting
- Hits head against object
- Hits head using object
- Hits head using digit
- Hits head with fist

Self-scratching
Skin picking
Self-slapping or hitting
- Fist or palm

Hair pulling (own hair)
Eye poking
Eye pressing

Motor Development

Supine/prone form
- Lifts head
- Rolls over
- Props on arms

Crawling
- Slithers on floor
- Assumes four-point posture
- Crawls in four-point posture

Sitting
- Sits with support
- Sits without support (<15 seconds)

W sitting
- Sits without support (<15 seconds)
- Raises to sitting without assistance

Standing
- Pulls to stand holding on
- Pulls to stand alone
- Stands with support (holding on)
- Stands without support (<15 seconds)
- Stands without support (>15 seconds)

Walking
- Walks with hands held
- Walks with support
- Walks with wide gait
- Walks alone (<10 steps)
- Walks alone (>10 steps)
- Walks up or down stairs
- Walks on toes
- Runs

Evidence of Injury (if SIB)

Bruise
Scab or lesion
Bump
Hair loss
None

Context for Stereotypy or SIB Occurrence

Music
Tantrum
Sickness
High chair or restraining chair
Meal
Crib

Prehension

Holds object in one hand
Holds object in both hands
Holds one object in each hand
Bangs objects together
Claps hands together
Bangs hands on object or substrate
Bangs object on object or substrate
Shakes toy
Turns book pages singly
Puts puzzle pieces together or in place
Puts object on stick without assistance

The remaining 39 children constitute our total sample to date. Of these individuals, 22 engaged in one or more behaviors that were protoinjurious, transient, or self-injurious. *Protoinjurious* behaviors were never accompanied by any tissue damage. *Transient* behaviors were accompanied by an injury on 1 to 4 occasions. *Self-injurious* behaviors were associated with an injury on 5 or more occasions. Occurrence of any of these classes of behaviors constituted an overall incidence rate of 4.8% of the original 457 children.

The details of the overall incidence are shown in Table 9.1, which provides a picture of the individual participant. Note that specific children sometimes had more than one type of SIB-like behavior. Note also that the ages of onset sometimes were younger than the age at which we began intensive observations of the children. We recorded a younger age of onset from information in the clinical records or from the parents' retrospective accounts of the onset of the behavior.

Table 9.2 includes a summary of some of the information in Table 9.1. Eleven children, or 2.4% of the total number of children in the schools, showed protoinjurious behaviors. Twelve children showed 12 behaviors that were transient, which is an incidence of 2.6%. Six children showed relatively chronic SIB, which was an incidence of 1.3%. The incidence of transient behavior, SIB, or both (i.e., behaviors in which an injury resulted) was 15 children, or 3.3%.

The second section of the table displays the distribution of the number of SIBs shown by different children. The modal number was a single behavior, but children could have as many as five behaviors. The categories of the behaviors are familiar because they are the categories used in studies of typical children as well as of older children and adults who have mental retardation. The most remarkable thing about the list in this table is that almost all of the behaviors are directed toward the head. The exceptions are two children who engaged in arm biting.

CONCLUSION

First, a caveat. Our sample consists of no children in foster care. Inclusion of children in foster care is important for future studies because differences in social history might produce different rates of stereotyped and self-injurious behaviors. We did attempt to compare staff ratings of a large group of children in foster care and children living with their biological families. However, the reliabilities of staff ratings were so low that the data were not reportable. Thus, although such a comparison is desirable, future investigators should attend more adequately to reliability and validity issues than we were able to.

The incidence of behaviors with actual injuries was either 1.3% or 3.3%, depending on which measure was used. This incidence is similar to the prevalence rates of 1.7% and 2.6% reported in older, noninstitutionalized

TABLE 9.1
Topographies of SIB for Each Child

Child	Age in project (in months)	Behavior	Age of onset (in months)	Type
101	9–29	Head banging	11	Protoinjurious
104	21–35	Head banging	25	Transient
105	18–35	Head banging	18	Transient
106	24–51	Head banging	27	Protoinjurious
		Eye pressing	27	Protoinjurious
107	23–36	Head hitting	26	Protoinjurious
		Head banging	35	Protoinjurious
109	21–36	Head banging	9	Self-injurious
		Head hitting/poking	21	Self-injurious
		Hair pulling	26	Transient
110	22–35	Head banging	22	Protoinjurious
		Self-biting	29	Transient
111	17–34	Eye poking	15	Self-injurious
115	23–35	Eye pressing	6	Self-injurious
117	35–38	Hair pulling	13	Self-injurious
		Head banging	14	Transient
		Face slapping	14	Protoinjurious
		Self-scratching	14	Self-injurious
		Head hitting/poking	30	Protoinjurious
120	24–36	Arm biting	25	Transient
123	38–40	Head banging	11	Transient
125	3–24	Head hitting	12	Protoinjurious
129	19–31	Hair pulling	19	Transient
130	19–36	Arm biting	18	Transient
133	19–24	Face hitting/slapping	18	Protoinjurious
136	16–36	Eye poking	4	Self-injurious
		Head banging	17	Transient
		Self-slapping	23	Protoinjurious
		Self-scratching	23	Transient
		Head hitting	24	Transient
137	30–36	Head banging	12	Transient
139	16–30	Head hitting/poking	22	Protoinjurious
		Head banging	22	Protoinjurious
140	32–36	Eye poking	20	Self-injurious
149	20–30	Face slapping	21	Protoinjurious
		Head banging	21	Transient
		Head hitting	28	Protoinjurious

TABLE 9.2
Frequency and Form of SIB-Related Behaviors

Behavior Associated With Injury

Type	Definition	No. of children	% Incidence
Protoinjurious	No self-injury	10	2.2
Transient	1–4 occurrences	12	2.6
Self-injurious	>4 occurrences	6	1.3
Transient and/or self-injurious		15	3.3

Behavior Frequency

No. of behaviors	No. of children
1	13
2	4
3	2
4	0
5	2

Behavior Form

Behavior[a]	No. of children
Head banging	14
Head hitting	7
Eye pressing	2
Eye poking	3
Hair pulling	3
Self-biting	3
Self-scratching	2
Self-slap	4

[a]All but self-biting are directed at the head.

populations of children and adults with developmental disabilities (Griffin et al., 1987; Rojahn, 1986). Note first that our incidence figure and the prevalence figures of others refer to children with developmental disabilities, not the general population. Previous studies of typical children have found the prevalence of head banging to be about 5%, or about the same as our incidence of protoinjurious, transient, and self-injurious behaviors combined.

Many of the children who engage in these behaviors to express anger or frustration may give up this mode of expression as they develop language skills. On the other hand, some of the behaviors seem to be self-stimulatory, so perhaps these behaviors are the ones that persist.

We are continuing to collect data from some of the children that we have already located, and we plan to add a few more participants to the sample. The longitudinal character of our research ultimately allows us to learn more about the crucial role of the determinants of the behaviors' abnormal character, as well as learn something about their fate. In addition, we will be analyzing the records for body rocking and other stereotyped behaviors in relation to motor development.

10

SELF-INJURIOUS BEHAVIOR IN CAPTIVE MACAQUE MONKEYS

MELINDA A. NOVAK, CAROLYN M. CROCKETT, AND GENE P. SACKETT

Abnormal behavior in captive primates was intensively studied between 1955 and 1985. A thorough review of many of these studies was conducted by Capitanio (1986). Research by Harlow and his students and colleagues (Harlow and Harlow, 1969; Sackett, 1972a) on rhesus monkeys underlined the importance of environmental stimulation during primate infancy for the development of species typical behaviors. Rhesus monkey infants were studied using four basic rearing environments: (a) *mother–peer*, in which infants were reared with mothers and had daily social interaction with agemates (i.e, monkeys of the same age); (b) *peer only*, in which infants were reared in agemate social groups without mothers; (c) *partial isolation*, in which infants were reared in single cages with visual, auditory, and olfactory social contact but no physical contact; and (d) *total isolation*, in which infants were reared asocially in enclosed cages precluding visual, tactile, and sometimes auditory social contact, with or without cloth surrogate mothers.

Relative to the first two conditions, both isolation conditions produced numerous behavioral anomalies, the severity of which depended on the duration of isolation from birth.

During rearing periods lasting more than 3 months after birth, isolated rhesus monkeys developed a repertoire of self-directed clasping, oral behavior, and rhythmic stereotyped motor patterns that were rarely seen in socially raised animals. After the rearing period, monkeys raised in total isolation were rehoused in single cages allowing visual access to other rhesus monkeys. The animals were tested daily for social interaction in groups of four or more in a playroom containing toys and climbing and swinging structures.

Research conducted at the New England Regional Primate Research Center was supported by National Institute of Health (NIH) Grants RR00168 and RR11122 from the National Center for Research Resources. Research conducted at the Washington Regional Primate Research Center was supported by NIH grant RR00166 from the NCRR.

151

Groups usually contained both socially and asocially reared monkeys, but in some studies groups were composed of animals reared in the same condition. Regardless of grouping type, asocially raised animals showed a repertoire of atypical behaviors that came to be called the *isolation syndrome*. Monkeys with this syndrome spent long periods exhibiting self-directed and stereotyped motor behaviors, showed little interest in exploring their environment or in playing with other monkeys, and had a high probability of reacting fearfully and withdrawing when approached socially.

The studies just discussed were conducted on rhesus monkeys, but the effects of isolation rearing were also studied in pigtail and longtail monkeys and compared with rhesus monkeys. All three species were reared and tested postnatally under the same conditions (Sackett, Ruppenthal, Fahrenbruch, Holm & Greenough, 1981). During the rearing period, rhesus infants developed a strong repertoire of isolation syndrome behaviors, which occupied about 50% of the time they were observed. Longtail macaques were more moderate in their display of these behaviors, whereas pigtail infants spent less than 5% of their time displaying isolation syndrome behavior. On postrearing social behavior tests with socially reared controls, the same ranking of isolate activity was observed. Surprisingly, longtail macaques did not differ significantly from socially reared controls in positive social behaviors such as play and grooming, yet they had high levels of isolation syndrome behaviors when not socially engaged. This work suggests that macaque species differ in their vulnerability to developing abnormal behavior during asocial rearing, and that the behavioral repertoire following asocial rearing also differs by genotype.

Researchers in follow-up studies assessed the long-term impact of isolation rearing on juvenile and adult rhesus monkeys (reviewed by Capitanio, 1986). Most of these studies revealed a continued absence of positive social behavior by monkeys that had been previously reared in total isolation (total isolates). Monkeys reared in partial isolation (partial isolates) often showed a modest improvement in social behavior with social experience. However, both total and partial isolates continued to show fear, withdrawal, and little exploration in novel settings (Sackett, 1972b). In contrast, Suomi, Harlow, & Novak (1974) showed that the isolation syndrome could be reversed if asocially reared rhesus monkeys were paired with much younger monkeys. It appeared that persistent attempts by the young "therapist" monkeys led isolates to eventually accept physical contact. This acceptance was followed by a progression of increasingly complex social interactions, eventually forming a social behavior repertoire that was somewhat similar to that of socially raised monkeys (Novak & Harlow, 1975; Novak, 1979). The key to this form of therapy lies in socializing monkeys on the basis of developmental stage and social experience rather than on chronological age. Thus, the isolate-reared monkeys were subsequently exposed to therapist monkeys who were chronologically younger but socially more comparable to the isolates. No studies in which total isolates received their initial social contacts with competent agemates have produced this normalizing effect on juvenile or adult behavior.

The most conspicuous aspect of the adult isolate monkey repertoire is self-directed behavior, primarily finger or toe sucking, and elaborate stereotyped locomotor patterns. Researchers in follow-up studies also revealed that isolate females usually make poor mothers (Ruppenthal, Arling, Harlow, Sackett, and Suomi, 1976) and that isolate males apparently show reproductive deficits because they cannot perform the "double foot-clasp mount," a posture crucial for intromission and conception (Harlow & Harlow, 1965).

The most extreme effect of isolation rearing was the development of a behavioral pathology that primarily affected adult males with total isolates being more affected than partial isolates (Mitchell, 1968, 1979). This behavior consisted primarily of monkeys biting their own limbs or torsos. Although self-directed biting sometimes occurred in situations in which socially reared animals acted aggressively toward other monkeys or humans, it often appeared to be spontaneous and unrelated to any obvious external stimuli. Such behavior caused great concern for researchers and veterinarians. Many instances of self-biting did not cause actual injury and should probably be called potentially self-injurious behavior (SIB). However, some animals actually wounded themselves severely enough to require medical treatment. A few did so repeatedly.

The following list summarizes some of the major findings concerning risk for abnormal behavior and risk for self-injury as a result of asocial rearing of macaque monkeys:

- Adult rhesus monkey males had a greater incidence of abnormal behavior, including self-injury, than did adult females.
- During and after the rearing period, macaque species differed in the extent of abnormal behavior and the specific dimensions of behavior that were affected.
- The more time spent asocially during infancy, the greater the expression of abnormal behavior.
- Serious self-injury requiring medical treatment occurred only in adult macaques, with the exception of trauma induced by extreme self-sucking and mouthing behavior in younger monkeys.
- Abnormal behavior could be largely overcome when asocially raised monkeys were later socialized with much younger monkeys.
- Socially reared monkeys who continued to be housed socially after the rearing period rarely developed SIB.

Although it was rare for adult asocially raised monkeys to engage in repeated episodes of self-inflicted wounding, such behavior was repugnant to all people involved in studying or caring for monkeys. Primate studies addressing the physiological and behavioral causes and maintenance of abnormal personal behavior produced by total social isolation rearing had completely ceased by the mid-1980s. Potential development of SIB was a major reason for this decline and it is certainly understandable in light of issues concerning humane treatment and psychological well-being of animals (e.g., National Research Council, 1998; Novak & Petto, 1991; Novak & Suomi, 1988). However, these issues have precluded all attempts to study isolation reared primates as a proven valid and relevant primate model of human SIB—a major problem in individuals with mental retardation and other developmental disabilities.

Recently, researchers have identified another potential primate model—a small percentage of monkeys housed in individual cages in captivity—for studying the factors causing and maintaining SIB and other abnormal behaviors. Because of experimental requirements, these monkeys may live asocially for long periods after infancy. As described in the next section, even when reared socially during infancy, a small percentage of these animals develop a repertoire of abnormal behavior somewhat similar to that of asocially raised monkeys. The repertoire includes both potential and actual SIB.

CORRELATES OF ABNORMAL BEHAVIOR IN CAPTIVE MONKEY COLONIES

Most of the data described in the following section is derived from studies of macaque monkeys at the New England Regional Primate Research Center (NERPRC) and Washington Regional Primate Research Center (WaRPRC). Like most primate facilities, both centers have developed programs for enhancing the psychological well-being of their captive primates. This program includes provision of both nonsocial and social enrichment. However, some monkeys in biomedical studies involving the long-term effects of teratogens, viruses, and other disease-causing agents cannot be housed socially or receive direct social contact because of experimental protocols. Although these monkeys are a minority of the total population, the numbers are substantial. Stereotyped and self-directed behaviors are observed in some of these monkeys when they are housed individually for long periods. In the interest of identifying animals with these abnormalities and providing enriched nonsocial stimulation that may have therapeutic benefits, researchers have begun to examine demographic, environmental, and physiological correlates. Following are the summarized results from some of the current studies.

Subjects

Demographic studies based on retrospective data at the NERPRC involved 188 adult rhesus monkeys that had been reared socially as infants but then lived in single cages with limited or no social contact (Jorgensen, Kinsey & Novak, 1998). Experimental studies at the NERPRC involved 14 adult males with a history of confirmed SIB and 9 controls with no SIB, matched for housing history, age, and sex. Studies at the WaRPRC involved 92 monkeys exhibiting abnormal behaviors identified by the veterinary staff or researchers involved in the center's Psychological Well-Being Program (Bellanca, Heffernan, Grabber, & Crockett, 1999). These animals were referred for any combination of excessive self-directed or stereotyped loco-motor behaviors and potential or actual self-injury. A subgroup of 29 referred pigtailed macaque males (from ages 4–11 years) and 58 age-matched controls, all singly housed, were observed to describe typical daily behavior patterns.

Demographic Data

NERPRC

Table 10.1 shows the dramatic SIB differences in male and female rhesus monkeys at the NERPRC. Although 22.4% of males housed individually had histories of self-inflicted wounding requiring medical treatment, only 1.4% of females (a single animal) had this history. Self-injury by the affected animals had an incidence of less than 1 per 2 years. However, among the 27 monkeys with a history of SIB, direct observations revealed that 21 were habitual self-biters and had at least one daily bout of noninjurious self-biting activity.

Three other correlates, each significant at $p < .05$, appear to be etiological factors. Among these, age at initiation of individual cage housing was most important. Animals with SIB histories were separated from their rearing social group and placed into individual cage housing at a younger age

TABLE 10.1
Sex Differences in Self-Injurious Behavior
Among Individually Housed Adult Rhesus Monkeys.

Veterinary record of self-inflicted wounding	Males	Females
Yes	26	1
No	90	71
Total	116	72

(14.2 months) than were animals with no SIB (25.4 months). Animals with SIB histories were also moved into new cages in the same room more often (3.54 moves per year) than were animals with no SIB history (1.79 moves per year), suggesting that even subtle housing changes may be a risk factor for SIB in longterm caged rhesus adults. Animals with SIB histories had more clinical treatment procedures for a variety of conditions (26.2 lifetime average), excluding wound treatments, than did those with no SIB history (15.3). This latter finding suggests that animals with SIB may be at greater risk for compromised immune functioning, may have had greater nonexperimental exposure to disease, or may have been on research protocols requiring more clinical treatment.

WaRPRC

Figure 10.1 presents prevalence data for two species of adult macaques referred to the center's Psychological Well-Being staff because of abnormal behaviors. Observed numbers are compared with expected numbers based on the percentage of animals of each sex-species grouping in the population at risk on January 1, 1999, approximately the median date of the referrals. No significant differences between observed and expected numbers of referred adult female or adult male longtailed monkeys (*Macaca fascicularis*)

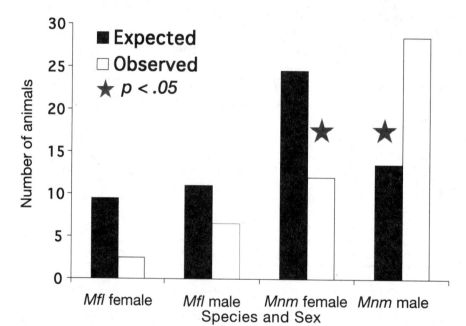

Figure 10.1 Number of observed and expected *Macaca fascicularis* (*Mfl*, long-tailed macaques) and *Macaca nemestrina* (*Mnm*, pigtailed macaques) female and male adults referred to the Washington Regional Primate Center Psychological Well-Being program because of excessive abnormal behavior. Expected numbers are based on the percentage of each type of animal in the colony.

were observed. However, among pigtailed macaques (*Macaca nemestrina*), females had significantly fewer referrals than expected whereas males had more than double the expected number of referrals. The WaRPRC pigtailed macaques show the same sex difference found in NERPRC rhesus macaques. The longtail–pigtail difference may reveal a species by sex interaction in abnormal behavior prevalence among adults, because the recent environmental conditions were the same for each species.

Observational Data

NERPRC

The 23 male rhesus SIB and matched control monkeys were observed for 300 5-minute sessions each. Figure 10.2 presents behaviors showing significant ($p < .05$) differences in rates of occurrence. Males with a history of self-biting did exhibit self-biting during these observations while controls showed little, if any, of this behavior. The SIB monkeys also had a higher rate of vocalization, threatening the observer or other monkeys, and drinking water. The latter category is especially interesting, because rhesus monkeys that had been reared in total social isolation for 12 months after birth

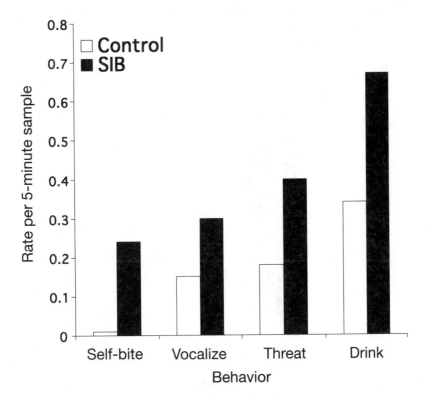

Figure 10.2. Rate of statistically different behaviors by adult rhesus monkeys with SIB and their matched controls during observations in the home cage.

also exhibited excessive water intake (polydipsia) when 8–10 years old (Miller, Caul, and Mirsky, 1971).

WaRPRC

The 29 referred and 58 matched control male pigtail monkeys were observed in their home cages on 4 days (four 10-minute observations for at least 2 weeks). Referred monkeys were significantly more active and had twice the probability of abnormal behavior than the nonreferred monkeys (Bellanca & Crockett, 2000). A greater proportion of abnormal behaviors for referred monkeys took the form of locomotor stereotypies and potentially self-injurious behaviors (see Figure 10.3). As in the NERPRC control animal data, the potential SIB category was almost never seen in nonreferred monkeys.

For further examination of factors underlying the incidence of abnormal behavior, the behavioral data from all 29 referred and 58 controls were combined (Bellanca & Crockett, 2000). Figure 10.4 shows the proportion of scan samples containing any abnormal behavior plotted against the proportion of days that the animal was housed in an individual cage during its first four postnatal years. A Pearson correlation of .50 (p<.001) shows that individual cage housing time was an important risk factor for developing abnormal personal behaviors. This finding is similar to an NERPRC finding on rhesus monkeys which showed that postinfancy individual-cage housing duration was related to SIB.

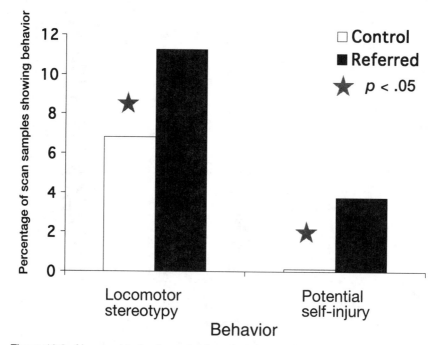

Figure 10.3. Abnormal behaviors of referred and control adult male pigtail monkeys during home cage scan sampling.

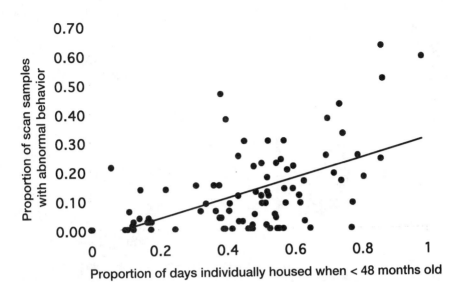

Figure 10.4. Scattergram illustrating the positive correlation between percentage of scan samples of adult male pigtailed macaques containing abnormal behavior and proportion of days individually housed between birth and 4 years.

Experimental Data

The NERPRC SIB and control monkeys were studied for heart rate differences in response to the stress of being fitted with a cloth jacket containing telemetry equipment (Chase, Marius, Jorgensen, Rasmussen, Suomi, & Novak, 1999). The SIB monkeys had significantly lower heart rates on the morning after the start of this stressor. This surprising result suggested that the SIB animals were either less aroused by the situation, or recovered from arousal faster than did controls. Stress responsivity was further assessed by measuring cortisol after capturing, restraining, and sedating these monkeys for blood sample collection (Tiefenbacher, Novak, Jorgensen, & Meyer, 2000). Figure 10.5 shows that cortisol levels were lower in the SIB monkeys after this procedure compared to controls. Samples taken after nonstressful conditions showed no differences between groups. Combined, these two sets of results suggest that animals exhibiting SIB have a blunted stress response, which is indicated by less arousal when exposed to external stressors than controls. If this is the case, then SIB may function to increase stimulation from a typically low level of arousal or conversely may serve to keep animals from becoming too aroused.

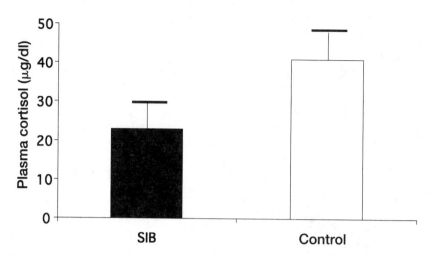

Figure 10.5. Plasma cortisol levels of SIB and matched control adult rhesus monkeys after restraint, sedation, and venipuncture.

CONCLUSION

SIB and stereotyped locomotor activity in macaque monkeys has been correlated with both brain serotonin and dopamine abnormalities. Kraemer, Schmidt, and Ebert (1997) reviewed this literature and suggested ways that nonhuman primate neurochemistry might be related to brain abnormalities in humans exhibiting SIB. Martin, Spicer, Lewis, Gluck, and Cork (1991) showed that compared with socially raised controls, aged rhesus monkeys that had been reared asocially had abnormal anatomical brain features that were related to dopamine deficits in the striatal cortex. This work raises the question of whether abnormalities seen near the end of life were present during the rearing period or developed during juvenile or adult life phases. This research, in addition to other studies of normal and abnormal aggression in primates (e.g., Kalin, 1999), suggest that primate models can yield important clues concerning the neurochemistry and neuroanatomy of SIB in humans.

The New England and Washington colonies are typical of most institutions housing large numbers of primates under captive, individual cage conditions. Six other national primate centers exist in the United States, in addition to numerous large colonies run by private companies and nonprofit institutions. Each of these centers houses monkeys with clinical problems caused by abnormal behavior, including SIB. The veterinarians, behavioral scientists, and researchers in these facilities generally welcome scientists interested in studying animals with abnormal behavior both to develop nonhuman primate models of human conditions and to better the lives of captive primates. Research includes clinical studies aimed at therapy for abnormal behavior as well as studies of mechanisms underlying these behaviors. An excellent source of information for identifying potential research resources for these studies can be found at the Primate Information Network Website, *http://www.primate.wisc.edu/pin/*. Go to the topic of *Resources*, then *Research*, then *Primates in Research*.

The primate literature suggests that the etiology and maintenance of self-injury in juvenile and adult macaques consist of gene-environment interaction processes. Like monkeys, human males with various conditions, including mental retardation with unknown etiology, are at higher risk for SIB than are females (e.g., Buitelaar, 1993). In addition, like monkeys, only a small percentage of humans exposed to impoverished stimulation because of sensory disabilities or environmental deprivation actually develop SIB. Many of the primate colonies housing at-risk monkeys have family history data on self-injury that is useful for pedigree analyses. Researchers could use these data to facilitate genetic research to identify genes involved in development of SIB among those at environmental risk. In summary, the study of macaque monkeys in captive colonies can provide models for studying genetic and environmental factors involved in the etiology and maintenance of SIB, as well as physiological correlates of SIB and drug and behavior therapy for these behaviors.

III

NEUROBIOLOGICAL FACTORS

The advent of animal models of stereotyped behavior and self-injurious behavior (SIB) was an important development of the late 1970s and early 1980s in exploring the neurobiology of SIB. An important review paper by Lewis and Baumeister (1982) implicated dopamine supersensitivity in the nigrostriatal pathway of the basal ganglia. In chapter 11, Cortney A. Turner and Mark H. Lewis provide an integrated update of the many dopaminergic and serotonergic hypotheses related to SIB. In chapter 12, Brian H. King's rat model of pemoline-induced SIB permits exploration in an unlesioned animal. In 1983, Sandman et al. discussed suppression of SIB with naloxone, a blocker of β-endorphin, and implicated the opioid peptide system. Curt A. Sandman and Paul Touchette update and extend this work in chapter 13.

Three other chapters cover behavioral and biological interactions that are important components of SIB. In chapter 14, Wayne W. Fisher, Cathleen C. Piazza, and Henry S. Roane explore the disruptive effects of disturbances in sleep and circadian rhythms on SIB. In chapter 15, Frank S. Symons provides an update of pain mechanisms and SIB. Karl M. Newell and James W. Bodfish present an intriguing analysis of the force dynamics of head banging in chapter 16. The study of kinetics and kinematics allows assessment of the relation of SIB to other dynamic movement disorders. Assessing movement control, variability, coordination, ballism, and feedback-based regulation of the limbs and the body may provide a noninvasive way to study common underlying neuropathology of SIB and other movement disorders.

11

DOPAMINERGIC MECHANISMS IN SELF-INJURIOUS BEHAVIOR AND RELATED DISORDERS

CORTNEY A. TURNER AND MARK H. LEWIS

Although relatively little is known about the neurobiological basis of self-injurious behavior (SIB), evidence from both clinical and animal studies implicates alterations in basal ganglia dopamine and associated neurotransmitter systems (see chapter 2). The objective of this chapter is to examine the nature of the evidence supporting dopaminergic mechanisms associated with the occurrence of SIB. We first examine evidence from clinical studies. These findings, which are frequently indirect or correlative, come from psychopharmacological studies as well as neuropathological, neuroimaging, and neurochemical investigations, largely of individuals with Lesch–Nyhan syndrome. Next, we review evidence from animal models that implicates dopamine in self-injury. These data come from studies of intact and lesioned animals as well as early socially deprived nonhuman primates. For their expression, complex behaviors such as self-injury require alterations of circuitry that involve multiple brain regions and multiple neurotransmitter systems. Thus, we also review evidence supporting the more complex chemoarchitecture in which alterations in dopamine function are thought to play a role in the mediation of the genesis and expression of SIB. Finally, we attempt to identify research initiatives that will help establish a clear role for dopamine in the pathogenesis and maintenance of SIB.

DOPAMINE DEFICIENCY MODEL OF SIB: CLINICAL EVIDENCE

Lesch–Nyhan Syndrome

The strongest and earliest link between SIB in humans and alterations in dopamine function comes from the work of Lloyd et al. (1981), who examined postmortem brain tissue from three individuals with Lesch–Nyhan syndrome (see chapter 17). Self-injury in people with Lesch–Nyhan syndrome is characterized by self-biting of the fingers and lips, a behavior that typically starts around age 3 years. Lloyd et al. (1981) were the first to show markedly lower dopamine concentrations in caudate-putamen (striatum) in patients with Lesch–Nyhan syndrome. Consistent with this postmortem study was the observation of decreased cerebrospinal fluid (CSF) concentrations of the dopamine metabolite homovanillic acid (HVA) made by Castells et al. (1979). The seminal observation by Lloyd et al. had gone unconfirmed for many years until two positron emission tomographic (PET) studies substantiated dopaminergic deficits in people with Lesch–Nyhan syndrome. Ernst et al. (1996) demonstrated a 31% to 57% reduction in presynaptic accumulation of fluorodopa F^{18}, a radiolabeled analogue of the dopamine precursor levodopa. These results reflect substantial loss of dopamine synthesis capacity in caudate, putamen, and frontal cortex, as well as in regions containing dopamine cell bodies (e.g., substantia nigra, ventral tegmental area). Consistent with these findings is the work of Wong et al. (1996), who also used PET scanning and demonstrated a 50% to 75% loss of dopamine transporter sites in caudate and putamen, reflecting a substantial loss of dopamine neurons and presynaptic nerve terminals in striatum. Finally, a second postmortem study (Saito et al., 1999) confirmed a loss of dopamine in the caudate accompanied by an up-regulation of both D_1 and D_2 dopamine receptors in the same brain region. A recent magnetic resonance imaging (MRI) study has demonstrated decreased basal ganglia volumes (34%) in people with Lesch–Nyhan syndrome versus control patients. Although indirect, such an observation is consistent with previous work and suggests loss of striatal innervation (Harris et al., 1998).

We are unaware of other neuropathological or neuroimaging studies that have measured indices of dopamine function in individuals who display SIB. Therefore, researchers are still not certain whether dopamine deficiency is a generalized neurobiological mechanism mediating SIB or is specific to the neuropathology of Lesch–Nyhan syndrome. The severity and specific topographies of self-injury associated with Lesch–Nyhan disorder (lip and digit biting) may indicate a different neurobiological mediation than that associated with other forms of SIB.

Blink Rate

However, evidence does suggest an association between dopamine deficiency and stereotyped behavior in adults with mental retardation, some of whom also exhibited SIB. The first of these studies used blink rate and other behavioral measures to index dopamine function. Numerous animal and human studies support the conclusion that spontaneous blink rate is mediated by central, probably striatal, dopamine (Karson, 1983; Karson et al., 1981). For example, it has been known for more than 30 years that people with Parkinson's disease exhibit significantly reduced blink rates that normalize after L-dopa therapy. Blink rate also appears to be among the most sensitive behavioral indices of dopamine receptor activation, particularly in dopamine-depleted animals (Elsworth et al., 1991; Lewis et al., 1990). Individuals who exhibit stereotypies have been shown to exhibit significantly lower blink rates compared to matched control individuals (Bodfish et al., 1995; MacLean et al., 1985). Moreover, significant inverse correlations were found for blink rate and severity of repetitive behavior disorder, as well as for blink rate and ratings of motor slowness (Bodfish et al., 1995).

Stereotypy

The association between stereotypy and dopamine function has also been examined using a biochemical measure. Lewis et al. (1996) compared plasma concentrations of HVA, a major metabolite of dopamine, between individuals with mental retardation and stereotypy and matched individuals without stereotypy. Alterations in plasma concentrations of HVA reflect alterations in the synthesis, release, and metabolism of dopamine in the central nervous system (CNS; Bacopoulos et al., 1978, 1979, 1980; Kendler et al., 1981, 1982). Significantly lower plasma HVA concentrations were found in individuals exhibiting motor stereotypies compared with matched controls.

Rett Syndrome

Additional support for a dopamine deficiency model of repetitive behavior disorders comes from studies of Rett syndrome, a genetic disorder observed only in females and associated with severe mental retardation. Hand stereotypies are an early and defining feature of this syndrome and co-occur with Parkinsonian-like symptoms. This syndrome is of particular interest because neuropathological (Brucke et al., 1987), neurochemical (Perry et al., 1988; Riederer et al., 1985; Zoghbi et al., 1985), neuroimaging (Chiron et al., 1993; Harris et al., 1986), and pharmacological (Zappella & Genazzani, 1986) studies of Rett syndrome have all found evidence for dopamine involvement in the pathophysiological features of this disorder. Specifically, evidence exists for hypodopaminergic function, although alterations in other monoamines have also been described. In addition, the use of a dopamine agonist, bromocriptine, in children with Rett syndrome had positive results (Moodley, 1993; Zappella & Genazzani, 1986). Interestingly, in an open trial involving six young children with autism, bromocriptine (7.5 mg daily for 6 to 36 months) was also reported to be well tolerated and result in marked improvement of stereotypies as well as withdrawal, communication, attention, and bizarre reactions (Simon-Soret & Borenstein, 1987).

We have completed a double-blind placebo controlled trial of the bromocriptine in the treatment of stereotypy in an adult with Rett syndrome (unpublished observations). In our trial, bromocriptine (in both the 5-mg and 7.5-mg doses) was associated with a significant reduction in frequency of hand stereotypy and a significant increase in blink rate.

Dyskinesia and Akathisia

The dopamine deficiency hypothesis of repetitive behavior disorders is also based on the association of stereotyped behavior with dyskinesia and akathisia. The occurrence of stereotypy has been shown to be associated with both increased dyskinesia scores and an increased prevalence of tardive dyskinesia (Bodfish et al., 1996, 1997). Increased dyskinesia scores were also found for patients displaying stereotypy who had no recent history of neuroleptic treatment. Similarly, in individuals with stereotypies who were receiving neuroleptics, the occurrence of tardive dyskinesia and stereotypic movements were significantly associated with an increased occurrence of akathisia. Thus, the presence of stereotypy is a risk factor for the development of neuroleptic-related movement disorders and suggests a common pathophysiology associated with dopamine deficiency in basal ganglia function.

In summary, several studies have presented converging lines of evidence for a dopamine deficiency hypothesis of SIB and associated repetitive behavior disorders in humans. Evidence from people with Lesch–Nyhan syndrome, Rett syndrome, mental retardation and stereotypies, as well as individuals with stereotypy who are receiving neuroleptic treatment all implicate basal ganglia dysfunction in the development of SIB. Nevertheless, clinical evidence is quite limited for dopamine deficiency as an important mechanism in the pathogenesis or expression of SIB. This is particularly true given the reliance on the association between dopamine deficiency and stereotypy rather than SIB.

SIB, DOPAMINE, AND RELATED DISORDERS

Given the paucity of direct information about the neurobiological basis of SIB, it is helpful to consider the disorders associated with SIB. Both stereotypy and compulsion are associated with SIB. SIB is frequently coexpressed with stereotypy in individuals with mental retardation (Rojahn, 1986) and is frequently co-expressed with compulsions in individuals with Tourette's syndrome (Trimble, 1989) (see chapter 2). In addition, several SIBs, such as trichotillomania and onychophagia, have been considered by some to be part of what are now termed *obsessive–compulsive spectrum disorders* (Wise & Rapoport, 1989). Recently, King (1993) hypothesized that some forms of SIB in individuals with mental retardation may be manifestations of obsessive–compulsive disorder (OCD; see chapter 2). These similarities among SIB, stereotypy, and compulsion may extend from the phenomenological to the pathophysiological because evidence shows that both stereotypy (Lewis, Baumeister, & Mailman, 1987) and the various obsessive–compulsive spectrum disorders (Rapoport, 1988) are mediated, at least in part, by basal ganglia dysfunction. Obsessive–compulsive spectrum disorders that are self-injurious (e.g., trichotillomania) are known to involve pathological basal ganglia features and dopamine mediation (e.g., exacerbation of trichotillomania by methylphenidate). Thus, the comorbidity and co-occurrence of stereotypy, SIB, and compulsions suggest a common or overlapping pathophysiology involving alterations in the excitability of specific circuits traversing the basal ganglia.

SIB is also frequently observed in people with Tourette's syndrome, a disorder also linked to alterations in basal ganglia dopamine. Specifically, motoric and verbal tics in people with Tourette's syndrome are known to be comorbid with OCD and SIB. Initial reports indicated that HVA, a major dopamine metabolite, is reduced in the CSF of individuals with Tourette's syndrome (Butler et al., 1979; Cohen et al., 1978). In addition, a decrease in the size of the left putamen has been found to be associated with tics (Peterson et al., 1993; Singer et al., 1993). Clinically, the treatment of choice for tic disorders is dopamine antagonists, particularly haloperidol. Dopamine antagonists have also been used to treat the SIB associated with this disorder (Sandyk, 1987). This work initially supported the view that dopamine receptors in affected individuals were hypersensitive or supersensitive (Koslow & Cross, 1982). In both postmortem tissue and neuroimaging studies, increases in the number of dopamine uptake sites in the striatum have been documented in individuals with Tourette's syndrome (Muller-Vahl et al., 2000; Singer et al., 1991; Wong et al., 1994). More directly, SIB in people with Tourette's syndrome was found to be significantly associated with an increase in dopamine transporter binding (Muller-Vahl et al., 2000). Other studies have yielded conflicting data, however, finding no differences in uptake site density compared with controls (Heinz et al., 1998; Schindler et al., 1999). The observation of an increased density of dopamine transporter sites associated with the expression of SIB in Tourette's syndrome is intriguing. Such an observation may be interpreted as reflecting an increased density of dopamine nerve terminals (hyperinnervation) in striatum. This could indicate hyperdopaminergic function rather than dopamine deficiency. Conversely, increased numbers of transporter sites without a concomitant increase in dopamine nerve terminals may result in decreased synaptic concentrations of dopamine. These observations underscore the potential importance of differing neurobiological mechanisms subserving SIB as a function of different disorders or etiologies.

PSYCHOPHARMACOLOGY OF SIB:
EVIDENCE FOR DOPAMINE MEDIATION?

Historically, dopamine antagonists have been the mainstay of psychotropic drug treatment for individuals with mental retardation. Lewis et al. (1996), Aman (1997), and Baumeister et al. (1998) have reviewed the major behavioral effects of typical neuroleptics (e.g., thioridazine, haloperidol) in people with developmental disabilities. Among the published controlled studies, the most consistently reported finding involves a reduction in stereotyped behavior (Aman et al., 1984, 1999; Campbell et al., 1978, 1982; Singh & Aman, 1981). Although neuroleptic treatment has also been shown to produce reductions in SIB, this effect has been less consistent. Despite the clear overreliance on this single class of medication in this population, only a small number of well-controlled studies of neuroleptic treatment effects in individuals with developmental disabilities exist. Inconsistent outcomes and small effects leave the issue of selective SIB effects of neuroleptics unresolved, and there is a lack of controlled studies in the field.

Conversely, treatment with dopamine agonists may prove efficacious in reversing repetitive behaviors associated with dopamine depletion. Although a single acute administration of a dopamine agonist may increase repetitive behavior, carefully titrated chronic administration should reverse the dopamine receptor supersensitivity associated with dopamine deficiency. Thus, dopamine agonist administration should down-regulate dopamine receptors, and stereotyped and self-injurious behaviors should decrease. The previously mentioned results obtained with bromocriptine support this view.

The newer class of neuroleptics, termed *atypical antipsychotics*—drugs that block D_2 dopamine receptors and also block 5-HT_2 receptors—seem to have some efficacy in treating self-injury. Only a few atypical neuroleptic studies have been completed, limiting the ability to assess the efficacy of these compounds to ameliorate SIB (Aman & Madrid, 1999). Of the existing studies, however, (18 open trial studies, most case reports, and two placebo-controlled studies), there are reports of selective improvements in self-injury (Hammock et al., 1995; Lott et al., 1996), as well as other repetitive behaviors, including compulsions (McDougle et al., 1997; Potenza et al., 1999) and stereotypies (McDougle et al., 1998; Purdon et al., 1994).

A common practice in the psychopharmacological management of individuals with mental retardation is to change their drugs from typical antipsychotics (e.g., haloperidol, thioridazine) to atypical antipsychotics (e.g., risperidone, olanzapine). We are currently assessing the effects of this shift on repetitive behaviors. We have examined the efficacy of the atypical neuroleptic olanzapine in 10 participants with abnormal repetitive behaviors. Six of the participants exhibited SIB, the rate of which was decreased by at least one third in 3 of the 6 participants. The group also experienced a significant decrease in dyskinesia and stereotypy scores on olanzapine. In a separate group (n = 8) whose drug was switched to risperidone, we observed similar effects for SIB.

ANIMAL MODELS OF SIB: PHARMACOLOGICAL EVIDENCE FOR DOPAMINE MEDIATION

Several lines of evidence in the preclinical literature implicate altered dopamine function in the mediation of self-injury. Administration of dopamine uptake inhibitors such as pemoline and GBR-12909 have been shown to induce SIB in rats. Mueller et al. (1980, 1982, 1986) were the first to describe the effects of chronic low doses of pemoline. These rats exhibited stereotyped grooming and self-biting commonly directed at the forelimbs, with the severity and latency of self-biting being dose related. This behavioral phenotype was accompanied by hyperactivity, stereotyped behaviors, and abnormal social and sensorimotor behaviors. Lower, chronic doses have a longer latency of onset and are associated with less severe self-biting behavior. In terms of interactions with other neurotransmitter systems, naltrexone, an opiate antagonist, decreased the self-biting behavior but only at low doses (King et al., 1993), whereas paroxetine, a selective serotonin uptake inhibitor, increased the severity of self-biting behavior (Turner et al., 1999). King has also shown that pretreatment with MK-801, a glutamate antagonist, prevented the development of SIB. Cortical ablation increased the severity and onset of self-biting behavior in this model (King et al., 1995, 1998). The effects of GBR-12909 have been less well studied but indicate that repeated doses induce SIB in rats (Sivam, 1995). This regimen has also been shown to reduce the steady-state levels of dopamine by 30% in the striatum. These results also support a dopamine deficiency as mediating SIB in rodent models.

Although neither pemoline nor GBR-12909 have been observed to induce SIB in mice, a recent report has documented the ability of methamphetamine to induce self-biting behavior in adult BALB/c mice (Shishido et al., 2000). The SIB produced was completely blocked by pretreatment with a N-methyl-D-aspartate (NMDA) antagonist as well as a D_1 antagonist. The serotonin precursor, 5-hydroxy-L-tryptophan, also somewhat reduced the observed SIB. Neither an opiate antagonist nor a D_2 antagonist had any effect on the SIB produced. Interestingly, this single report of pharmacological induction of SIB in mice was accomplished using a mouse strain considered to be highly aggressive. Clinical evidence suggests a significant association between SIB and aggression (Lewis et al., 1995).

SIB can also be induced in animals using either a direct acting dopamine agonist or a dopamine precursor. This behavioral supersensitivity is particularly apparent in rats treated neonatally with 6-hydroxydopamine

(6-OHDA), a neurotoxicant that results in chemical lesioning of dopamine pathways. These animals exhibit intense stereotyped and self-injurious behaviors when treated with apomorphine or L-dopa (Breese et al., 1984; Creese & Inversen, 1973; Ungerstedt, 1971) at a dose of L-dopa that failed to induce such behavior in adult lesioned animals. Moreover, interactions with adenosine, purine, and glutamate have been observed in this model. Furthermore, adult rats having bilateral lesions of the substantia nigra induced by 6-OHDA exhibited stereotyped and self-injurious behaviors at doses that did not produce such behavior in control animals (Mileson et al., 1991). Goldstein et al. (1986) have also shown that SIB can be induced by a dopamine agonist in monkeys that had sustained lesions of the ventral tegmental area (an area rich in dopamine cell bodies) early in development.

One animal model noteworthy for the absence of self-injury is the hypoxanthine phosphyribosyltransferase (HPRT) knockout mouse (i.e., a mouse in which the HPRT gene has been turned off) generated to model the phenotype observed in Lesch–Nyhan syndrome. Although several neurochemical markers of dopamine were reduced in the striatum of these mice, no SIB was observed (Jinnah et al., 1990, 1994). These findings do not rule out the role of dopamine in SIB, as the dopamine content does not decline until later in development in this model.

Our studies of a nonhuman primate model of stereotyped movement disorder also support dopamine deficiency as pathogenic for stereotypies and SIB. An invariant consequence of early social deprivation in rhesus monkeys is stereotyped behavior (Suomi & Harlow, 1971), with self-injury being less frequently observed. Using older adult monkeys who experienced early social deprivation, we tested the association of SIB and stereotypy with increased dopamine receptor sensitivity (Lewis et al., 1990). Significant increases in dopamine-mediated behaviors (e.g., eye blinking, whole body stereotypies) in response to apomorphine challenge were observed in socially deprived monkeys. This observed dopamine receptor supersensitivity was thought to be the result of loss of presynaptic innervation by dopamine nerve terminals. This hypothesis was tested directly by examining brain tissue from socially deprived and control monkeys using immunocytochemical techniques to visualize specific types of neurons (Martin et al., 1991). Tyrosine hydroxylase immunoreactivity (a marker for dopaminergic neurons) was significantly and selectively reduced in the striatum and substantia nigra of socially deprived animals.

SIB can also be observed in individually housed monkeys. There is little information about the pathobiology or treatment of these spontaneous behaviors, which occur in about 10% of individually caged animals (Novak et al., 1998). One report indicated the serotonergic precursor L-tryptophan may be useful in treating this behavior (Weld et al., 1998).

INTERACTION OF DOPAMINE AND OTHER
NEUROTRANSMITTER SYSTEMS

As mentioned previously, the expression of self-injury requires recruitment of circuitry involving multiple brain regions and neurotransmitter systems. It is not surprising, therefore, that SIB can be induced by numerous pharmacological agents acting on nondopaminergic target proteins. For example, SIB has been induced in rats by activation of a striatal efferent pathway mediated by γ-aminobutyric acid (GABA; Baumeister & Frye, 1986; Scheel-Kruger et al., 1978, 1980). This strionigral pathway directly modulates the activity of the ascending dopaminergic nigrostriatal pathway.

In high doses, methylxanthines such as caffeine or theophylline have been shown to induce SIB in rodents (Mueller, 1982). These effects appear to be caused by blockade of adenosine receptors that are found in high concentrations in striatum and interact with D_2 dopamine receptors (Ferre et al., 1991).

Serotonin uptake inhibitors have been shown to be efficacious in the treatment of SIB. For example, McDougle et al. (1992) showed increased sociability, as well as decreased aggression, severeity of OCD, and SIB in young adults with autistic disorder after treatment with clomipramine. We have also tested the efficacy of clomipramine in the treatment of SIB in individuals with severe and profound mental retardation (Lewis et al., 1996). Eight individuals with severe SIB who had failed to improve with other interventions (e.g., contingent shock) completed a double-blind, placebo-controlled crossover trial. Six of the eight people exhibited a clinically significant improvement (50% or greater reduction from placebo) in the frequency of SIB. Clomipramine treatment also reduced by 50% or greater ratings of SIB intensity in three of the eight people.

McDougle et al. (1996) observed an exacerbation of stereotyped motor behavior (e.g., whirling, rocking, self-hitting) following reduction of 5-HT by depletion of its precursor tryptophan. Because reduction of whole blood 5-HT by fenfluramine has failed to ameliorate behavioral problems in individuals with autism, the attenuation of stereotypies appears to be caused by the loss of central rather than peripheral serotonin. If exacerbation of stereotypies following tryptophan depletion was a reliable and selective outcome, it would be the first direct link between repetitive behavior and 5-HT transmission in humans.

More evidence supporting a serotonergic role in the mediation of SIB is provided by studies using ligands that increase serotonergic neurotransmission. For example, administration of the serotonin precursor 5-HTP, as well as drugs that inhibit the uptake or facilitate the release of 5-HT or act as direct 5-HT agonists, have been reported to induce stereotyped head weaving and forepaw treading in rats (Curzon, 1990). Several lines of evidence suggest that these behaviors are dependent on 5-HT_{1A} receptors and the interactions of these receptors with dopamine. For example, 5-HT agonist-induced head weaving and forepaw treading in rodents are blocked by lesions of the nigrostriatal and mesolimbic dopamine pathways or administration of the dopamine blocker haloperidol (Curzon, 1990). Turnover rates of dopamine and serotonin appear to be highly correlated in numerous brain regions in animals. Indeed, as Hsiao et al. (1987) have pointed out, the substantial correlation between CSF concentrations of 5-hydroxyindoleacetic acid (5-HIAA) and HVA is one of the most consistent and robust findings in the clinical literature. Psychopharmacological experiments have shown that serotonin inhibits stereotyped behavior in animals that is induced by dopamine agonists (Korsgaard et al., 1985; Weiner et al., 1975). Serotonin uptake inhibitors also potentiate neuroleptic-induced catalepsy (Carter & Pycock, 1981). The anatomical locus of such interactions may be axo-axonal synaptic connections of 5-HT and dopamine pathways in several brain regions including the striatum. Moreover, 5-HT uptake sites are found in high concentrations in the substantia nigra and ventral tegmental area, the nuclei of origin of the major dopamine pathways in brain. Stimulation of 5-HT neurons in the median raphe reduces the firing rates of cell bodies in substantia nigra. Finally, lesions of central dopamine systems in infant rats, such as those used to model Lesch–Nyhan disorder, induces a pronounced "sprouting" of serotonergic nerve terminals.

A possible mediating role for opioid peptides in autistic and self-injurious behaviors has been postulated by numerous investigators (e.g., Thompson et al., 1994). Indirect tests of this model have involved assessing the efficacy of the opiate antagonists naloxone or naltrexone. Of the therapeutic targets for these drugs, SIB has received the most attention. Although previous reports suggested the efficacy of naloxone and naltrexone, more recent studies (e.g., Gillberg, 1995) have failed to support these claims. The available data do suggest, however, that naltrexone is efficacious for some individuals with SIB, perhaps 50% according to a recent review (Baumeister et al., 1993), although the precise factors that may be related to a positive response to naltrexone have not yet been established.

Opiate administration can induce intense stereotypies and self-mutilative behavior in rodents (Iwamoto & Way, 1977), whereas opiate antagonists can inhibit certain forms of stereotypy in movement-restricted farm animals (Dantzer, 1986). Numerous investigators have described the opiate–dopamine interactions in the brain, including the observation of dense concentrations of opioid receptors in dopaminergic terminal fields (e.g., striatum; see Angulo & McEwen, 1994). There are also important enkephalin projections to substantia nigra and ventral tegmental areas. Thus, opiate–dopamine interactions may be important in the mediation of some forms of SIB.

Stereotyped behavior in both humans and laboratory animals has been induced by anticholinergic drugs (Kulik & Wilbur, 1982). Undoubtedly, these observations involve modulation of a polysynaptic circuit that involves dopamine projections from substantia nigra (pars compacta) to striatal cholinergic interneurons expressing D_2 receptors. These interneurons, in turn, synapse on GABAergic medium spiny neurons, which project either back to substantia nigra or to globus pallidus, regulating the output of the neural pathways of the basal ganglia.

Also of interest are the interactions of the serotonin system with stress hormones and the mediation of stereotypies and self-injury. This is mentioned because the functional integrity of the 5-HT system is reciprocally regulated by levels of stress hormones (De Kloet et al., 1996). Furthermore, chronic stress has been shown to induce supersensitivity of dopamine receptor systems (Prasad et al., 1995). Verhoeven et al. (1999) recently found interactions between serotonin and the stress hormones in a group of individuals with mental retardation who displayed stereotypy and self-injury. The results support lower cortisol values in the SIB group and higher 5-HIAA values in the stereotypy group versus matched control individuals with mental retardation.

CIRCUITRY INVOLVED IN SIB

The animal and clinical pharmacology findings are consistent with other findings documenting significant interactions in striatum among dopamine, opioid peptides, adenosine, glutamate, and serotonin. The mechanisms used by these systems to interact depend on the localization of the neurotransmitters. Specifically, dopamine receptors are colocalized with adenosine and opioid peptides. Furthermore, dopamine projections from the substantia nigra pars compacta interact with both serotonin projections from the dorsal raphe and glutamate projections from the cortex. To understand the role of the basal ganglia in SIB, an understanding of the cortico–striato–thalamo–cortical motor circuits is imperative, because this circuitry integrates the actions of multiple neurotransmitter systems (Graybiel, 1990). Activation of these motor loops is thought to facilitate the maintenance of motor programs initiated by the motor cortex. This is accomplished via disinhibition of thalamo–cortical relay neurons that stimulate neurons of the supplementary motor cortex to provide positive feedback to active regions of the primary motor cortex.

Neuroimaging studies performed in individuals with Lesch–Nyhan syndrome clearly implicate the ventral tegmental complex (substantia nigra and ventral tegmentum), as well as the caudate and putamen (Ernst et al., 1996). Because input from the nigrostriatal dopamine pathway helps to modulate the activity of GABAergic medium spiny neurons in the striatum, abnormal activity along this pathway alters the output of these medium spiny neurons, having an impact on the positive feedback loop described. Because activation of this feedback loop helps to maintain the activity of motor programs, elevated output through this circuit is expected to result in behavioral perseveration and possibly SIB. Thus, it is likely that the striatum is an important neuroanatomical locus in the mediation of self-injury.

In addition to the impact of nigrostriatal dopamine input to the striatum, activity of striatal medium spiny neurons is influenced by excitatory glutamatergic input from the cerebral cortex. The possibility that the cerebral cortex may also mediate SIB has been furthered by two recent studies. In humans, Ernst et al. (1996) found evidence for reduced dopaminergic activity in the frontal cortex of individuals with Lesch–Nyhan syndrome. By comparison, depletion of dopamine levels in the medial prefrontal cortex is expected to result in disinhibition of cortical–striatal projections and has been shown to result in exacerbation of stereotypic behavior in mice (Karler et al., 1998). Also in rodents, King et al. (1998) demonstrated that cortical ablation exacerbated the severity of self-injury in a model of SIB.

Of the individual cortico–striato–thalamo–cortical loops that traverse the basal ganglia, the motor and limbic circuits (for a review, see Rauch & Savage, 1997) have been proposed to play predominant roles in SIB. The motor system comprises activity predominantly in the putamen and matrix component of the dorsal striatum and projects to the substantia nigra pars reticulata and the globus pallidus, which then sends projections to the ventral anterior and ventral lateral thalamus, which are known to project to motor cortices. The limbic loop, by contrast, comprises activity in the caudate and striosomal part of the ventral striatum and projects to the substantia nigra par compacta and dorsal medial thalamus, which sends projections to the associative and limbic areas of cortex.

Neuronal circuitry has been proposed for disorders in which SIB is a component of the behavioral phenotype including OCD, Tourette's syndrome, and Lesch–Nyhan syndrome. Based on imaging and neurosurgical studies, the hypothesized circuitry mediating OCD involves projections linking orbitofrontal cortex, caudate nucleus, globus pallidus, and thalamus (Wright & Hewlett, 1994). Structural neuroimaging studies in people with OCD have found alterations in metabolic activity in the head of the caudate nucleus and the orbitofrontal cortex (Modell et al., 1989). Neuroimaging of people with Tourette's syndrome has revealed volumetric abnormalities in the putamen that may underlie the disorder, whereas involvement of the caudate may indicate the severity of the disorder (for review, see Rauch & Savage, 1997). Furthermore, functional imaging of cortical areas implicates the sensorimotor cortex in Tourette's syndrome (for review, see Rauch & Savage, 1997). Clinical studies of Lesch–Nyhan syndrome also implicate the involvement of the limbic and motor circuits.

Recent studies have found significant reductions of dopamine levels in the caudate, putamen, and nucleus accumbens of people with Lesch–Nyhan syndrome (for a review, see Visser et al., 2000).

The striatum is the one component of the implicated motor loops through which both the limbic and motor circuits pass; therefore, it may be the locus found to be responsible for the self-injury observed clinically. This region has a distinctive cytoarchitectural organization involving strio-somes, or "patches" that represent dense or weak innervation relative to the matrix. These compartments differ, for example, in the dopamine receptor subtypes expressed and metabolic activity (Graybiel, 1990). Canales et al. (2000) induced stereotypy in rats with a dopamine agonist and examined changes in the expression of the immediate early genes *fos* and *jun* B. These authors found an increase in the ratio of striosomal to matrix compartments of the striatum in gene activation that correlated with the observed motor stereotypies. These results suggest that the specific organizational components of striatum may be involved in the expression of stereotypy and, by extension, SIB.

RESEARCH INITIATIVES

Limited progress has been made in our understanding of the role played by dopamine in the pathogenesis and expression of SIB. This can be generalized to the overall understanding of the neurobiological basis of SIB. Psychotropic drug studies provide important, albeit limited, information about pathobiology. Nevertheless, it is possible to elucidate the mechanisms of abnormal repetitive behavior in the context of treatment studies. As stated by Rutter (1997),

> Treatment studies provide an invaluable means of testing causal mech-anisms if there is within group analysis to determine whether the out-come gains are a function of changes in the postulated mediating mechanism. This constitutes one of the key challenges for the future and provides the essential link between causal research and studies of treatment efficacy.

Such treatment studies are sorely needed.

Pharmacological challenge paradigms may be a useful adjunct in estab-lishing pathophysiology. The pharmacological challenge strategy permits a more direct approach to testing specific biological hypotheses and poten-tially to predicting pharmacotherapeutic efficacy. The objective of the phar-macological challenge is to administer a drug selective for a specific neurotransmitter system to uncover a dysregulation in that system. The functional responsivity of the neurotransmitter system can be assessed by measuring changes in plasma concentrations of a hormone, release of which is regulated, at least in part, by the neurotransmitter targeted by the challenge agent. Although it is unlikely that alterations in a neurochemical system will be observed under basal conditions, a pharmacological challenge test may uncover functional abnormalities in an activated system. For example, although individuals with major depression do not differ in basal plasma prolactin levels from healthy control individuals, they have been shown to have a blunted prolactin response to fenfluramine (Coccaro et al., 1989).

In neurology, challenge procedures have been used to examine dopaminergic function in patients with Parkinson's disease. Various challenge drugs have been used, including the dopamine agonists, apomorphine, bromocriptine, and L-dopa (e.g., Barker et al., 1989; Hughes et al., 1990). In addition, this dopaminergic challenge has been found to predict reliably subsequent positive response to drug therapy in Parkinson's patients. Although pharmacological challenge paradigms are now a standard tool in biological psychiatry research, to date there has been little research using these paradigms in individuals with mental retardation. Furthermore, although many previous researchers have examined the potential effectiveness of various pharmacotherapies in the treatment of the behavioral and psychiatric disorders of individuals with mental retardation, none have established a protocol for the a priori determination of probable drug treatment response.

Establishing the pathophysiology of SIB in people with Lesch–Nyhan syndrome has been aided dramatically by neuroimaging studies. These studies need to be extended to people who show SIB but do not have Lesch–Nyhan syndrome. Although the SIB in the two groups differs in etiology, one might expect overlap in its pathophysiology that could be confirmed by this technology. The generalization of dopamine depletion as a cause of SIB could be tested in people who do not have Lesch–Nyhan syndrome using the techniques described by Wong et al. (1996) and Ernst et al. (1996). Neuroimaging studies of SIB also need to be developmental so that they control for alterations in neuronal structure and function that may be caused by the behavior's repetitious nature or its potential for CNS damage. Furthermore, neuroimaging techniques will be useful in establishing the pathophysiology of disorders in which SIB is a component of the disorder, although not a defining feature, such as Tourette's syndrome. In this regard, overlapping pathophysiological features of disorders that include SIB may help identify candidate neurobiological mechanisms.

SIB is likely not to be a homogenous behavioral category but rather discrete behaviors that are likely to be associated with differing etiologies and pathophysiological conditions. Identification of discrete neurobiological mechanisms associated with different forms of SIB (e.g., skin picking in Prader–Willi syndrome, digit biting in Lesch–Nyhan syndrome) is an important research direction to pursue. Work directed at establishing behavioral phenotypes of specific genetic etiologies will be helpful in this regard (Dykens et al., 1997).

Examination of animal models of SIB using modern molecular biological techniques and approaches should provide important candidate mechanisms for self-injury. The mechanisms in turn can lead to the development or application of novel treatment approaches. Similarly, molecular genetic studies of behavioral phenotypes that include self-injury may lead to identification of candidate genes implicated in SIB.

Using treatment studies to identify mechanisms, expanded use of neuroimaging techniques, application of molecular techniques to animal models of SIB and use of molecular genetic methods will allow us to test more rigorously neurobiological hypotheses. Specifically, such techniques will allow testing of the hypothesis that dopamine plays an important role in the mediation of SIB. Effective somatic therapies for SIB require such an empirical base.

CONCLUSION

Repetitive behavior disorders are not only highly prevalent but often dominate the repertoire of individuals with severe developmental disorders, significantly interfering with daily functioning. Self-injury is particularly distressing and presents a formidable challenge in terms of clinical management. The current data implicate dysregulation in dopamine and numerous other neurotransmitters that constitute integrated circuits within the basal ganglia as the pathophysiological basis for SIB. Neuropathological and neuroimaging studies of people with Lesch–Nyhan syndrome strongly implicate basal ganglia dopamine deficiency as an important causative factor of SIB. These observations are consistent with evidence from individuals with stereotypy. A dopamine deficiency hypothesis of SIB is supported by studies of intact and dopamine-denervated animals treated with dopamine agonists. Other disorders with SIB as a part of their behavioral phenotype also seem to involve significant basal ganglia pathological features. Specific neuronal circuitry involving discrete cortico–stirato–thalamo–cortical loops are likely to be involved in the pathogenesis of SIB. Because SIB and related repetitive behavior disorders are associated with multiple etiologies, pathophysiological features, and behavioral correlates, it is unlikely that any single neurobiological mechanism or treatment will explain or be effective for all manifestations of these disorders.

12

PEMOLINE AND OTHER DOPAMINERGIC MODELS OF SELF-BITING BEHAVIOR

BRYAN H. KING

Animal models of self-injurious behavior (SIB) in the rodent seem to have emerged in the context of broader attempts to understand the role of dopamine in the production of stereotyped behaviors (Randrup & Munkvad, 1968). With the discovery of the selective monoamine neurotoxin 6-hydroxydopamine (6-OHDA) and its intracerebral injection, it became possible to isolate the behavioral effects of stimulation and ablation of the nigrostriatal dopamine system (Ungerstedt, 1968; 1971; see also chapter 19).

In one of the early studies using this technique, Ungerstedt (1968) injected 6-OHDA bilaterally into the substantia nigra of young adult male rats. Three days later, after receipt of a single dose of the dopamine agonist apomorphine (5 mg/kg), he described a sequence of behaviors commencing with

> increased motility and sniffing that changed into licking and biting. (The rats) soon developed a furious compulsive gnawing which was far more violent than after the same dose of apomorphine administered to a normal animal. The operated (6-OHDA treated) animals even "chewed up" their front paws, bit off their fingers or ate themselves into their abdomen. (p. 108)

At about the same time, a group in Milan (Genovese et al., 1969) reported a similar phenomenon occurring in both mice and rats after the administration of very high doses of 5-phenyl-2-imino-4-oxo-oxazolidine, or pemoline. These investigators characterized the behavior as *self-aggressiveness* and noted that it was like nothing that had "been described for any other drug in such an evident form and high incidence" (p. 513).

Noting the reliability of this drug-induced phenomenon, Mueller and Hsiao (1980) selected pemoline instead of other agents such as caffeine and clonidine, which had also been linked to self-biting behavior in rodents (Boyd et al., 1965; Jones & Barraclough, 1978; Peters, 1967; Razzak et al., 1975). These investigators were the first to describe the behavioral response to high-dose pemoline (140 and 220 mg/kg) in detail. They noted that in addition to persistent self-biting, primarily of the medial foreleg, the rats exhibited hyperactivity, stereotypy, abnormal social and sensorimotor behavior, and unresponsiveness or avoidance of moderate levels of sensory stimuli. Pemoline-challenged rats were noted to exhibit increased locomotor activity within 2 hours of drug receipt. Thereafter, animals engaged in increasing degrees of stereotypy culminating in the emergence of self-biting in as few as 3 hours or as many as 2.4 days. Once self-biting had commenced, the animals generally persisted in this behavior despite being challenged by prodding with a cotton swab, the introduction of highly palatable food, the introduction of another (nondrugged) cagemate, banging on the cage with a metal coffee can, or even being soaked in water (Mueller & Hsiao, 1980). The investigators proposed that pemoline-induced self-biting behavior represented a fragmented grooming response because the biting itself was behaviorally indistinguishable from some elements of the normal grooming sequence and because the areas groomed initially in a typical sequence were the areas of most likely injury.

Noting similarities between this constellation of behaviors and patients with Cornelia de Lange syndrome—specifically hyperactivity, stereotypy, abnormal social behavior, avoidance of physical contact, and self-mutilation—in a manner suggestive of grooming, Mueller and colleagues suggested that pemoline may provide a useful animal model for the de Lange (Mueller & Hsiao, 1980) or Lesch–Nyhan syndrome (Mueller & Nyhan, 1982). As such, pemoline was the first rodent model specifically used in an effort to investigate the pathogenesis of self-injury in people with mental retardation.

PHARMACOLOGY OF PEMOLINE-INDUCED SELF-BITING

In collaboration with Nyhan, Mueller reported experiments designed to determine whether pemoline-induced self-biting, believed to be primarily dopaminergically mediated, could be modified pharmacologically by manipulation of other transmitter systems as well (1982). These authors observed that the dopamine antagonist haloperidol was very effective in normalizing pemoline-induced behaviors. Interestingly, another dopamine antagonist, pimozide, also prevented self-biting, but in contrast to haloperidol it had little effect on pemoline-induced stereotypy or hyperactivity. Pretreatment with the serotonin neurotoxin, p-chloroamphetamine (PCA), or the serotonin synthesis inhibitor p-chlorophenylalanine (PCPA), had no effect on pemoline-induced self-biting behavior. The benzodiazepine diazepam was also without consistent effect on self-biting. The authors concluded that in spite of the very high doses of pemoline used in this model and the attendant possibility of pharmacological effects on nondopaminergic receptor populations, self-biting appeared to be mediated primarily by dopaminergic mechanisms. Furthermore, given the relative selectivity exerted by pimozide on self-biting and not on other stereotyped behaviors, they posited that self-biting may require mechanisms other than those involved in the production of stereotypy alone. That is, contrary to the notion that self-biting is just a form of extreme stereotypy—an idea implicit in scoring self-biting as severe stereotypy (e.g., Eichler et al., 1980; Mason et al., 1978)—self-biting may indeed represent a distinct phenomenon.

Stereotypy and Self-Biting Behavior

In a subsequent study, Mueller, Saboda, Palmour, and Nyhan (1982) used two different paradigms, chronic caffeine and chronic amphetamine, to better characterize the relationship between stereotypy and self-biting behavior. Animals receiving daily caffeine injections displayed self-biting within 3 days. Coadministration of haloperidol decreased the likelihood of self-biting and delayed its onset. In animals treated with continuous-release amphetamine pellets, self-biting occurred frequently and within the first 48 hours of exposure. On the other hand, "such obvious examples of stereotypy as head weaving, continuous sniffing or repetitive licking of the cage were virtually never observed" (p. 616). The authors postulated that continuous administration of lower doses of pemoline would also likely produce self-biting in the absence of intense stereotypy, a prediction that was subsequently confirmed in their laboratory with weanling rats (Mueller et al., 1986).

Elaboration of the Pemoline Model

Since Mueller's early work, numerous investigators have confirmed that pemoline, when administered in sufficient doses over sufficient time, reliably produces SIB in the rat (Turner et al., 1999). Pemoline-induced biting behavior in the mouse has not been replicated since the initial report of Genovese et al. (1969). In addition to obvious species and even possible strain differences, mice were much less sensitive to pemoline than rats (requiring 1,000 mg/kg doses), and subsequent data with other challenge paradigms (e.g., clonidine) has revealed that sex, individual versus group housing, wire versus plastic cages, and the presence of alternative objects to bite all influence the likelihood of self-biting behavior in the mouse (Razzak et al., 1975).

Interestingly, pemoline has been associated with motoric hyperactivity and athetoid and choreiform movements in humans, including prominent orofacial movements and tongue protrusion (Bonthala & West, 1983; McNeil, 1979; Nausieda et al., 1981; Sallee et al., 1989; Singh et al., 1983).

Pemoline's Mechanism of Action

Although important data regarding its precise mechanism of action are lacking (Abbott Laboratories, 1975), the preponderance of evidence suggests that pemoline acts at least in part through dopaminergic mechanisms (Dren & Janicki, 1977; Everett, 1975; Molina & Orsingher, 1981). Cromwell et al. (1996) caused unilateral 6-OHDA lesions of the medial forebrain bundle and subsequently challenged rats to a single high dose of pemoline (250 mg/kg). This paradigm is useful in distinguishing direct from indirect dopamine agonists, because animals rotate away from the side of greater dopaminergic activation. In this preparation, a direct dopamine agonist such as apomorphine would prompt rotational behavior toward the intact (i.e., unlesioned) side because of stimulation of supersensitive dopamine receptors on the side of the lesion. In contrast, Cromwell et al. (1996) observed that the lesioned animals rotated away from the unlesioned side, suggesting that the pemoline effect is indirect, requiring the release or blocking the reuptake of dopamine. The same investigators later used in vivo microdialysis to measure intrastriatal pemoline levels after a single subcutaneous injection (250 mg/kg; King et al., 1998). Interestingly, perhaps because of its relative insolubility, peak levels of pemoline in the dialysate are reached at approximately 4 hours and remain at that level for the next 24 hours. The investigators concluded that the large dose of pemoline probably serves as a reservoir for continuous infusion, not unlike the amphetamine pellet used by Mueller et al. (1982).

GBR-12909 and Pemoline

GBR-12909 is a potent and selective dopamine reuptake inhibitor (Andersen, 1989). If such blockade is essential to the mechanism of action of chronic pemoline or amphetamine exposure, one would predict that chronic GBR-12909 administration to the rat would also lead to self-biting behavior. Indeed, Sivam (1995) has observed that 100% of rats treated with daily doses of GBR-12909 (20 mg/kg) exhibited self-injury after 4 days of this regimen. Analysis of striatal dopamine content revealed significant reductions in both dopamine and DOPAC (3,4-dihydroxyphenyl acetic acid) in the GBR-12909-treated animals. In the case of dopamine, values were reduced to 67% (±4.3%) of control values. GBR-induced self-biting could be prevented by both D_1 (SCH23390) and D_2 (spiperone) selective antagonists in this paradigm (Sivam, 1995). Animals given lesions as neonates with 6-OHDA (see following section) did not exhibit self-biting when later challenged with the GBR compound.

Striatal dopamine depletion after pemoline administration has also been observed in animals that self-bite. Zaczek et al. (1989) observed self-biting in rats after repeated injection of lower doses (70 mg/kg every 12 hours for 3 days). These investigators noted that in animals with self-biting after pemoline administration (in contrast to animals treated with lower doses that did not self-bite), neostriatal dopamine levels were significantly reduced (to 60% of control values), as were midbrain and hypothalamic norepinephrine levels, whereas 5-HIAA levels were elevated. Interestingly, the reductions in striatal dopamine levels are remarkably similar to those reported for GBR-12909. Is dopamine depletion a prerequisite for subsequent self-biting behavior? Review of other models certainly suggests that supersensitivity to dopamine is a common theme.

NEONATAL 6-OHDA

The neonatal 6-OHDA model, often referred to as the *6-OHDA model of self-injury*, has been the most thoroughly studied and is covered in chapter 19. Briefly, rats treated with intracisternal 6-OHDA as neonates and challenged as adults with dopamine agonists (e.g., L-dopa, apomorphine) manifest SIB, whereas animals given intracisternal 6-OHDA as adults, or control animals, do not self-injure when similarly challenged (Breese et al., 1984). The likelihood of self-biting increases with repeated exposure to the dopamine challenge, a reverse-tolerance phenomenon that has been termed *priming* (Breese et al., 1985, 1994). The finding that the timing of the 6-OHDA lesion is critical is particularly intriguing because in humans, self-injury in the context of developmental disorders typically starts in childhood. On the other hand, pemoline, GBR-12909, and chronic amphetamine all produce the same behaviors within hours to days in adult animals.

It may in fact be that the timing of the 6-OHDA lesion has less of an impact on developmental consequences than on the severity of the lesion produced. Erinoff, Kelly, Basure, and Snodgrass (1984), for example, suggested that ICV (intracerebroventricular) administration of 6-OHDA in neonates resulted in a more complete depletion of dopamine than for adult animals, and Marshall and Ungerstedt (1977) noted the critical relationship between degree of 6-OHDA-induced dopamine loss and the degree of dopamine supersensitivity that ensues. Moreover, adult animals pretreated with 6-OHDA may exhibit self-biting after a dopamine challenge.

Dopamine Depletion Methods

Neostriatal Dopamine Depletion by Direct Injection of 6-OHDA and Subsequent Challenge With Dopamine Agonists

When the nigrostriatal dopaminergic system in adult animals receives lesions by direct infusion of 6-OHDA into the nigra (Price & Fibiger, 1974; Ungerstedt, 1971) or striata (Hartgraves & Randall, 1986), an apomorphine challenge produces self-biting. On the other hand, it does seem that the timing of lesions within the neonatal period can influence the propensity for biting behavior with later challenge. Neal-Beliveau and Joyce (1999), for example, recently observed that intrastriatal 6-OHDA-induced lesions received 7 days after birth—but not 1 day after—could produce self-biting if given a dopamine challenge in adulthood. Lesions induced at the latter time had a more significant effect on D_1-mediated behaviors. These investigators interpreted their findings in light of possible and different critical periods for the expression of D_1 and D_2 receptor subtypes, with attendant differential windows of vulnerability. Interestingly, following intracisternal administration of 6-OHDA to neonates, D_1 receptor number (B_{max}) increases in the substantia nigra in animals that exhibit L-dopa-induced self-biting (Yokoyama & Okamura, 1997).

In these supersensitivity paradigms, considerable time must elapse before biting behavior is elicited with a dopamine challenge. Is there reason to believe that pemoline or GBR-12909 could produce states of supersensitivity within hours after administration?

Rapid Dopamine Depletion by Exposure to Reserpine and AMPT and Subsequent Challenge With Dopamine Agonists

Moody and Spear (1992) found that treatment with reserpine and alpha-methyl-p-tyrosine (AMPT) could result in intense self-mutilation with subsequent (5 hours later) administration of combined D_1 (SKF38393) and D_2 (quinpirole) agonists. When the same dopamine agonists were administered separately, however, self-biting was much less likely. This response was evident in animals challenged as weanlings (21 days after birth) but not 10 days after birth. The degree of acute dopamine depletion was correlated with the likelihood of self-biting behavior, which the investigators believe is related to the magnitude of possible receptor up-regulation following the dopamine depletion paradigm (Moody & Spear, 1992).

Additional data on the respective roles of D_1 and D_2 receptor subtype stimulation, as well as anatomical influences, have accumulated from the intracerebral injection of specific drugs. These data add support to Mueller and Nyhan's contention (1982) that the self-biting response is qualitatively distinct but not necessarily the most severe form of stereotypy.

SPECIFICITY AND NEUROANATOMICAL CHARACTERISTICS OF SELF-BITING IN THE RAT

Delfs and Kelley (1990), having localized oral stereotypy in the rat to the ventrolateral striatum (VLS; Kelley et al., 1988), were interested in the relative contribution of selective D_1 and D_2 stimulation in this region. Microinjection of the D_1 agonist SKF 38393 did not produce any changes in behavior during their formal 30-minute test period. However, the investigators noticed that some 3 hours later, intense self-biting ensued. This response could also be elicited with infusion of dopamine or amphetamine into the VLS, and the biting response could be blocked by the nonselective dopamine antagonist haloperidol, as well as by the relatively D_1-selective antagonist SCH23390 and the D_2-selective antagonist raclopride.

More recently, Canales et al. (2000) began to map the neural pathways that mediate amphetamine-induced stimulation of the VLS. These investigators have shown that oral stereotypy produced by amphetamine microinjection is attenuated by lidocaine-induced inactivation of the substantia nigra pars reticulata (SNr). Interestingly, stimulation of the SNr by direct injection of the GABA agonist muscimol also produces self-biting behavior in the rat (Baumeister & Frye, 1984). Baumeister and Frye (1986) also demonstrated that the self-biting response in this paradigm required an intact midbrain reticular formation because bilateral electrolytic lesions of the latter area ventrolateral to the periaqueductal gray matter, including the pedunculopontine nucleus, selectively blocked self-biting but not other stereotypies. Interestingly, Mathur et al. (1997), have observed stereotypy including self-biting and grooming, in rats treated with bilateral microinjections of scopolamine into the pedunculopontine tegmental nucleus. Self-biting in this paradigm was attenuated with parenteral haloperidol administration, leading the investigators to posit that scopolamine acts by blocking muscarinic receptors on mesopontine cholinergic neurons, causing their disinhibition and subsequent activation of dopamine neurons.

In addition to subcortical structures exerting an influence on self-biting behavior, the frontal cortex may be important as well. Cromwell et al. (1999) recently observed that bilateral frontal cortical lesions decreased self-biting latency and increased the incidence of pemoline-induced self-biting behavior. These findings are in keeping with others who have shown that cortical lesions enhance amphetamine-induced behavior (Braun et al., 1993; Iversen, 1971) and are of particular interest given that individuals with cortical pathological features (severe mental retardation) are more likely to exhibit SIB (King, 1993).

Considerable work remains with regard to the mapping of the neuroanatomical features of self-biting behavior. Regardless, it is already clear that numerous different neurotransmitter systems can exert an influence on the expression of this behavior.

ELABORATION OF THE PHARMACOLOGY OF PEMOLINE-MEDIATED SELF-BITING

In keeping with Mueller and Nyhan (1982), King, Turman, Cromwell, Davanzo, and Poland (1994) reported that the dopaminergic antagonists haloperidol, spiperone, and SCH 23390 significantly attenuate or completely prevent pemoline-induced biting behavior. Perhaps because of its pharmacokinetic profile, SCH 23390 is more effective if it is administered closer to the time of onset of SIB, whereas spiperone retains its efficacy if given before pemoline administration or later in the course of the pemoline challenge (King et al., 1995).

Considerable interest in opioidergic influences on self-injury has emerged as a result of clinical experience with the antagonists naloxone and naltrexone (see chapter 13). King et al. (1993) and Turner et al. (1999) studied naltrexone as a potential antagonist of pemoline-induced self-biting behavior.

The former group identified a low (0.01 mg/kg), probably μ-selective, dose of naltrexone that modestly but significantly attenuates SIB (King et al., 1993). Larger doses, including 0.1 and 1 mg/kg, did not significantly alter pemoline-induced self-biting, a finding replicated by Turner et al. (1999) for 0.1 mg/kg of naltrexone in a paradigm involving repeated administration of smaller doses of pemoline.

Turner et al. (1999) also explored a single dose of the serotonin reuptake inhibitor paroxetine (1 mg/kg) in their paradigm and found that it actually increased self-biting severity in the pemoline-treated animals. A permissive if not facilitative role for serotoninergic function in pemoline and GBR-12909-induced self-biting has been suggested on the basis of measured levels of serotonin and its primary metabolite in self-biters (Sivam, 1996; Zacek et al., 1989).

Interesting data regarding the importance of glutamatergic influences on self-biting derives from electrophysiological studies in pemoline-treated animals as well as treatment with the NMDA antagonist MK 801. Cromwell, King, and Levine (1997) observed that pemoline treatment alters the direction of the modulatory action of dopamine on synaptic responses recorded in neostriatal neurons only in rats that display self-biting. In control animals, dopamine causes an attenuation in synaptic response size. After pemoline, the same dopamine treatment potentiates the amplitude of the response, however, and this enhancement can be blocked by the NMDA receptor antagonist 2-amino-5-phosponopentanoic acid (Cromwell et al., 1997).

King, Au, and Poland (1995) had previously observed a protective effect in studying the NMDA antagonist dizocilpine (MK-801) on pemoline-induced biting. Pretreatment with MK-801 could completely block subsequent expression of self-biting behavior. Interestingly, delaying the administration of MK-801 from 1 hour before pemoline administration until 8 hours into the pemoline response (but still typically hours before the onset of self-biting) resulted in the complete loss of the ability of MK-801 to suppress the behavior. The authors concluded that different mechanisms may be involved in the induction and expression or maintenance of the biting behavior.

Sivam (1996) has advanced a similar argument for the dissociation of causal and maintenance factors that is supported by the chronology of tachykinin, particularly Substance P, biosynthesis after GBR-12909 challenge.

CONCLUSION

Study of the pemoline and other dopaminergic models has been useful in elucidating mechanisms underlying the neuropathology of self-biting behavior in the rodent. Clearly in humans, no unitary neurotransmitter or anatomical diathesis can account for self-injury in its varied forms. By the same token, even with a relative paucity of data available on factors that influence pemoline and other models of self-biting, the mechanism is clearly complex. Nevertheless, there is a fascinating convergence of data highlighting specific brain regions and even neurotransmitter receptor subtypes in the expression of self-biting in the rat. Further elaboration of these models and the development of new animal models, specifically to incorporate new knowledge about human conditions in which self-injury is common, may yield important insights into the pathogenesis and possible treatment of a devastating clinical problem.

13

OPIOIDS AND THE MAINTENANCE OF SELF-INJURIOUS BEHAVIOR

CURT A. SANDMAN AND PAUL TOUCHETTE

Our studies on self-injurious behavior (SIB) span 20 years. During this period, we have been impressed with a collection of features unique to this mysterious behavior. For instance, SIB has compulsive features that frequently become ritualized. Self-injury often is the culmination of a behavioral repertoire that appears driven by an anonymous motive. Some individuals who repeatedly and intentionally injure themselves appear to be immune to the normal experience of pain. Indeed, the apparent elevated pain threshold is the most remarkable aspect of SIB. By definition, SIB involves harm to the self, but some people seek objects and methods of harm that result in major tissue damage and can cause death. Generally, SIB has remained resistant to treatment. In some patients in certain contexts, behavioral interventions have been effective (Iwata, Dorsey, Slifer, Bauman, & Richman, 1982; Lovaas & Simmons, 1969; Matson & Taras, 1989; Matson & Keyes, 1990; Rincover & Devaney, 1982; Rincover & Koegel, 1975; Romanczyk & Goren, 1975). In some patients, pharmacological approaches have been effective. We discuss one such approach in this chapter. However, individuals exhibiting SIB also respond in unpredictable ways to medications, and paradoxical reactions have been reported to classes of neurotropic agents (Barron & Sandman, 1983).

Two opiate hypotheses of SIB have been reviewed extensively (Cataldo & Harris, 1982; Deutsch, 1986; Farber, 1987; Sandman, 1990/1991, 1988; Sandman & Hetrick, 1995; Sandman, Spence, & Smith, 1999; Sandman et al., 1998). One hypothesis is that SIB reflects general sensory depression and an insensitivity to pain, perhaps related to chronic elevation of endogenous opiates (Barron & Sandman, 1983, 1985; Cataldo & Harris, 1982; Davidson, Kleene, Carroll, & Rockowitz, 1983; Deutsch, 1986; Farber, 1987; Sandman, 1988; Sandman, Datta, Barron, Hoehler, Williams, & Swanson, 1983). This possibility is supported by findings that opiate blockers reverse congenital insensitivity to pain (Dehen, Willer, Boureau, & Cambier, 1977) and hypothalamic dysfunction coexisting with elevated pain threshold (Dunger, Leonard, Wolff, & Preece, 1980). These observations are consistent with an extensive body of literature demonstrating the hyperalgesic influence of naloxone on animals (Grevert & Goldstein, 1977; Walker & Sandman, 1979). Unfortunately, pain threshold remains difficult to assess among people with developmental delays, despite several attempts (Davidson et al., 1983; Richardson & Zaleski, 1983).

Alternatively, it is plausible that the function of SIB is to release β-endorphin and thereby achieve an opiate "high" (Sandman, 1990/1991; Sandman & Hetrick, 1995). In this perspective, SIB may be viewed as an addiction because it supplies the "fix" for tolerant, down-regulated opiate receptors. This possibility is supported by findings that repeated β-endorphin administration results in tolerance (Lal, 1975; Madden, Akil, Patrick, & Barchas, 1977), physical dependence (Wei & Loh, 1976), and euphoric-like effects (Belluzzi & Stein, 1977).

Since the beginning, our studies have focused on identification of plausible biological mechanisms that could account for these features of SIB. Recently, we completed a program of research that had three primary components: naturalistic observations of behavior, determination of biological markers, and pharmacological intervention. Each component makes a contribution to the understanding of SIB. In this chapter, we discuss results in these three areas of research that have led us to conclude that (a) behavioral patterns suggest internal (biological) motives are responsible for SIB in most individuals, (b) the endogenous opioid system is dysregulated among individuals exhibiting SIB, and (c) pharmacological interventions that target the endogenous opioid system reduce and sometimes eliminate SIB in a significant fraction of individuals.

NATURALISTIC OBSERVATIONS SUPPORT BIOLOGICAL MOTIVATIONS FOR SIB

Advances in computer hardware and software have provided new opportunities for the direct observation and measurement of behavior (Thompson, Felces, & Symons, 2000). Direct observations of behavior are critical for biobehavioral studies because clinical scales, questionnaires, and staff impressions do not have the temporal resolution, precision, or accuracy necessary for determining reliable associations with physiological state (Sandman, Hetrick, Taylor, & Chicz-DeMet, 1997; Sandman, Touchette, Ly, Marion, & Bruinsma, 2000; Thompson, Felce, & Symons, 2000; Wiethoff et al. 2000).

We have developed a computer-assisted method that has allowed us to collect extensive (40 hours of) direct observations of maladaptive behavior and environmental conditions in a large group of participants (see details in Sandman et al., 2000). Moreover and most importantly, we have adapted analytical methods to determine the relationships (transitional probabilities) among behaviors. Our primary aim was to develop a metric that characterized complex target behaviors for which a distribution of individual differences could be generated. Previous findings from our project indicated that SIB described a contagious distribution (McCleary, Ly, & Bruinsma, 1997). To capture this phenomenon, we examined the probability that a target SIB event would follow another SIB event (Sandman et al., 2000). This result is highly relevant for studies of the biological basis of behavior because the most parsimonious explanation of a contagious distribution of maladaptive behavior is that internal (i.e., biological) mechanisms provoke and maintain the behavior.

Naturalistic observations were collected for 53 people who exhibited SIB and were resistant to treatment. Among the participants various traditional behavioral and pharmacological treatments had been attempted but proven unsuccessful. Behavior of each person was observed in natural settings without disruption or intrusion for continuous 2-hour periods, 2 times a day (morning and afternoon), 4 days a week for 2 consecutive weeks—a total of 40 hours per patient. Real-time data (frequencies or durations) were entered on palm-top computers (Sandman et al., 2000) by key presses that recorded the occurrence of an event (target behavior) and the time at which each behavior occurred. These data were downloaded to a host computer for analysis. Interobserver agreement estimates of .80 to .90 were generated between two observers with independent recording systems observing the same participant for extended periods.

The relationships among classes of behavior were determined with lag sequential analyses to generate transitional (conditional) probabilities. By analyzing relationships between a target behavior (SIB) and other recorded behaviors, a preferred behavioral pathway was constructed. The pathway was defined as the probability that an observed behavior would occur after an antecedent behavior. For our purposes, the relationship of interest was between SIB events—in other words, did one SIB episode predict a subsequent SIB episode? Both state (or event) and time (single and double transitions) lag analyses were done with several time windows for each participant; however, for this discussion, only event and 30-second time lags are considered. We discovered that the Q statistic (Yoder & Fuerer, 2000) generated unusual outcomes when testing the transitional probabilities of the same event (e.g., SIB following SIB). There is no a priori reason for choosing one of several solutions for determining the probability of behavioral transitions. We chose to use the conditional probability solution because it is the most inclusive and most conservative:

$$\frac{\text{SIB transitions}}{\text{Number of SIB transitions} + \text{Number of SIB transitions between all other behaviors, including no behaviors.}}$$

The distribution of transitional probabilities is illustrated in Figure 13.1 for event (top panel) and for both single (middle panel) and double (bottom panel) transitions at a 30-second lag. On the abscissa is the probability (in 10% increments) that SIB will follow SIB. On the ordinate is the number of participants at each probability range. For example, in the event

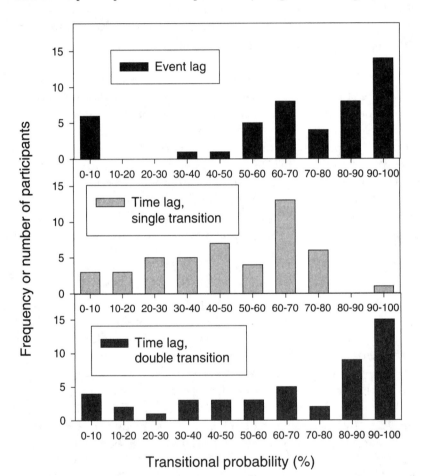

Figure 13.1. Comparison of results from three types of sequential lag analyses. Each panel illustrates the distribution of the transitional probability of SIB following SIB for our participants. The top panel is the event lag; the second panel is a single transition for a 30-second time lag; and the bottom panel is a double transition, 30-second time lag. For each type of analysis, a significant number of participants exhibit SIB as the primary antecedent for subsequent SIB. The lower probability for the single transition solution suggests that the findings are not the result of short bursts of SIB.

lag, 14 participants had a transitional probability between 90% and 100%, and 6 participants were between 0% and 10%. Comparison of the event and time lags indicates that this metric is not redundant and produces a distribution of individual differences for each solution. The finding of interest, however, is that SIB is contagious, because the probability that SIB follows SIB is highly significant ($p < .01$) for each lag (Sandman et al., 2000).

Moreover, transitions between SIB episodes are significantly higher than SIB following any of several other behavioral or environmental events recorded. This is illustrated for the event lag in Figure 13.2. On the abscissa are listed several behaviors and environmental events recorded for all participants, and on the ordinate is the average transitional probability of SIB following any of the listed behaviors or events. SIB is clearly the best predictor of subsequent SIB. These data establish in a large sample the contagious nature of SIB and as such provide reliable measures and methodology to test the biological hypothesis.

SIB AND THE ENDOGENOUS OPIOID SYSTEM

After it was established that the body had its own opiate system (Pert & Snyder, 1973), the endogenous opiates became prime suspects as being responsible for maintaining SIB. Their analgesic properties explained elevated pain thresholds, and their addictive qualities (i.e., euphorigenic effects) could account for behavior that appeared "driven" to commit self-harm. However, previous studies either of resting levels of various opioids in plasma or cerebrospinal fluid from patients exhibiting SIB generated inconclusive results. This was not surprising because there was little consistency

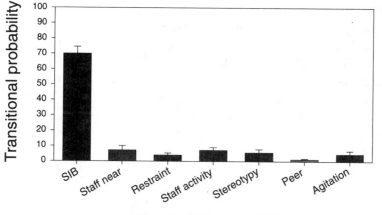

Figure 13.2. Average transitional probability of several events following SIB. SIB is the most probable event following SIB compared with other behaviors and events recorded.

among studies regarding the rigor of diagnosis, the peptides measured, or the conditions assessed (Coid, Allolio, & Rees, 1983; Ernst et al., 1993; Gillberg, Terenius, Hagberg, Witt-Engerstom, & Eriksson, 1990; Gillberg, Terenius, & Lonnerhom, 1985; Ross, Klykylo, & Hitzemann, 1987; Sandman, Barron, Chicz-DeMet, & DeMet, 1991; Weizman, Weitman, Tyano, Szekely, & Sarne, 1984).

In the search for a biological marker to distinguish SIB, contemporary studies have included the pro-opiomelanocortin (POMC) system. In humans, most POMC is produced in the pars distalis of the anterior pituitary. POMC also is produced by hypothalamic neurons and neurons in the amygdala and pituitary stalk. Three POMC fragments with opioid activity have been identified, including a highly specific β-endorphin component (β-endorphin$_{1-31}$), a smaller opioid sequence (β-endorphin$_{1-23}$), and another opioid fragment highly cross-reactive with the larger β-LP$_{1-91}$ peptide. In addition to the opioids, POMC gives rise to various neuropeptides including ACTH, melanocyte stimulating hormone (MSH), and lipotrophic hormone (LPH) and plays a prominent role in the hypothalamic-pituitary-adrenal (HPA) stress response system (Sandman, Spence, & Smith, 1999).

Dysregulation in the opioid region of POMC is manifested among subgroups of people with SIB (and some with autism) by (a) elevated resting levels of the C-terminal of β-endorphin$_{20-29}$ (Cazzullo, Musetti, Musetti, Bajo, Sacerdote, & Panerai, 1999; Leboyer, Bouvard, Recasens, et al., 1994; Leboyer, Philippe, Bouvard, et al.,1999;), (b) elevation of β-endorphin$_{1-31}$ after a target behavior (Sandman et al., 1997), and (c) uncoupling of the POMC fragments (β-endorphin) and adrenocorticotropic hormone (ACTH$_{1-39}$) after challenge and at rest (Bouvard et al.,1995; LeBoyer et al., 1994, 1999; Sandman et al., 1997; Sandman, Hetrick, Taylor, Marion, & Chicz-DeMet, 2000). Disruption of the corelease of β-endorphin and ACTH in the plasma is uncommon and not evident after various physical and psychological stresses (Forman, Cavalieri, Estilow, & Tatarian, 1990; Giuffre, Udelsman, Listwak, & Chrousos, 1988; Holson, Scallet, Ali, Sullivan, & Gough, 1988; Knigge, Matzen, Bach, Bang, & Warberg, 1989; Oltras, Mora, & Vives, 1987; Recher, Willis, Smit, & Copolov, 1988; Shutt, Smith, Wallace, Connell, & Fell, 1988). Mutti et al. (1989), however, reported a similar dissociation between β-endorphin and ACTH among heroin addicts in response to stress, providing inferential support for the connection between SIB and addiction (Barron & Sandman, 1983; Cataldo & Harris, 1982; Deutsch, 1986; Farber, 1987; Sandman, 1990/1991; Sandman et al., 1983).

Leboyer et al. (1994) reported a massive difference between resting levels of N-terminal β-endorphin($_{1-23}$) and C-terminal β-endorphin($_{20-29}$) POMC fragments in people with autism, some of whom exhibited SIB. They found that the β-endorphin$_{20-29}$ fragment level was elevated in plasma resting levels, but the β-endorphin$_{1-23}$ fragment level was depressed or no different than in control patients. Moreover, they reported that other fragments of POMC (e.g., ACTH) were not abnormal (further evidence of uncoupling of this system). This research team (Bouvard et al., 1995) subsequently reported that β-endorphin$_{20-29}$ levels were decreased in plasma after treatment with a centrally active opiate blocker in people categorized as positive responders. More recently this group (Leboyer et al., 1999) replicated their finding of elevated plasma C-terminal β-endorphin levels among autistic probands. Moreover, they reported that mothers, but not fathers, of the probands expressed significantly elevated C-terminal β-endorphin. These findings are the first to suggest a maternal influence for POMC fragment variations. The authors concluded that these differences may be evidence of abnormal processing of the POMC gene among individuals with mental retardation and developmental delay (MRDD).

Our most recent results strongly support the relationship between dysregulation of POMC and SIB. In Figure 13.3, the transitional probability of SIB is on the abscissa, and POMC dysregulation on the ordinate. A positive

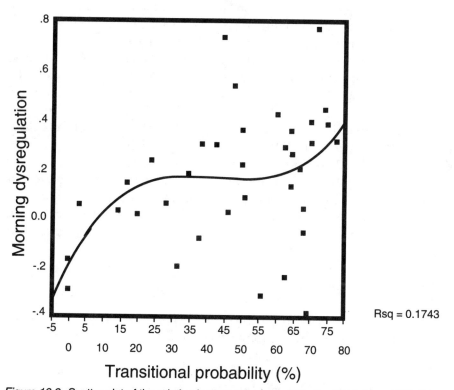

Figure 13.3. Scatter plot of the relation between the probability the SIB followed SIB (30-second, single transition) and an index of morning POMC dysregulation (DI). Results indicate that an elevated β-endorphin level is associated with SIB following SIB.

dysregulation index indicates higher β-endorphin levels relative to ACTH. This figure illustrates that high morning levels of β-endorphin predicted significantly the association between SIB events. We have argued that a contagious distribution of SIB is compatible with a biological explanation for this behavior. We found that for most but not all patients, SIB is the best predictor of subsequent SIB. The findings presented here, in preliminary form, provide evidence that those individuals with "contagious" SIB may represent a behavioral phenotype whose behavior is most likely provoked and maintained by the endogenous opioid system.

Researchers have made alternative proposals about the role of the opioid system in SIB. Verhoeven et al. (1999) have suggested that SIB is tightly linked to stereotypy, and these two behaviors may be part of stress regulation system. This intriguing hypothesis suggests that stereotypy is a "successful" means of stress reduction, but SIB is a maladaptive response to stress. This explanation is not incompatible with our findings or our hypothesis because POMC and the opiate system are intimately involved in the HPA stress axis. However, we have some difficulties with the assumptions of this alternative and how they were tested. Although many individuals who exhibit SIB also exhibit stereotypies, there are more individuals for whom this is not the case. More importantly, findings from our extended direct in situ observations indicate that the conditional probability between these behaviors is very low in our sample. That is, even individuals who exhibit both of these behaviors do not manifest them in a transitional sequence. Typically the "negative" studies (Verhoeven et al., 1999; Willemsen-Swinkels, Buitelaar, Nijhof, & van Engeland, 1995) have relied on questionnaires and staff interviews rather than direct and contemporary observations of the behavior. We (Sandman et al., 1993, 2000) and others (Thompson et al., 2000; Weithoff et al., 2000) have reported that data collected by staff reports are not consistent with real-time observations and are not sensitive (for reasons listed previously) either to pharmacological interventions or associations with endogenous state. Thus, the major problem with the stress hypothesis lies not in the plausibility of the argument but the methods used to support the argument.

SIB and Opiate Blockers

One source of support for the opiate hypotheses comes from the successful opiate blocker therapy for people who exhibited SIB but were treatment resistant. Because the opiate blockers naloxone and naltrexone have few effects in the absence of opiates (Reisine & Pasternak, 1996), effective treatment with these drugs must engage the endogenous opioid system. Initial reports indicated that injections of naloxone reduced SIB in a majority of adult patients (Sandman, 1990/1991). The consensus from more than 30 studies (including several large double-blinded protocols) is that between 30% and 50% of all patients treated with naltrexone reduce their SIB (reviewed in Sandman et al., 1998, 2000; Verhoeven & Tuinier, 1999). The percentage is higher for certain classes of people, including those with severe and frequent SIB, those who damage their heads, and among those who engage in self-biting (Sandman et al., 1993; Thompson, Hackenberg, Cerutti, Baker, & Axtell, 1994). It is important to acknowledge again that the significant effects of naltrexone especially are apparent in studies that directly observe SIB. Willemsen-Swinkels et al. (1995) examined global ratings of behavior by staff members and reported that a single, fixed dose of naltrexone in people with autism (11 with SIB) was ineffective in improving behavior. More recently, however, Willemsen-Swinkells et al. (1999), reversed their position and reported that about one third of their sample were consistently responsive to naltrexone. These results are consistent with our (Sandman et al., 1993) findings that naltrexone treatment had no observable effect on staff ratings of patient behavior, but the effects were highly significant when behavior was objectively and directly observed (Sandman et al., 2000).

A double-blind, placebo-controlled, cross-over, dose-finding study from our project (Sandman et al., 1993) reported that 18 of 21 individuals exhibiting SIB responded favorably to at least one dose (ranging from 0.5 mg/kg to 2 mg/kg) of naltrexone. A previous version of our behavioral observation system was used in this study. Videotaped observations were collected for 30 minutes per day (15 minutes in the morning and 15 minutes in the afternoon), 4 days a week for the 10-week period, resulting in 20 hours of direct observations for each patient and 2 hours for each dose of naltrexone. The videotapes were scored with a computerized observational program (Hetrick, Isenhart, Taylor, & Sandman, 1991). Acute treatment (1 week at each of three doses) with naltrexone reduced the frequency of SIB without major side effects. Specifically, the highest dose (2 mg/kg) was the most effective, confirming earlier results in this population (Sandman, Barron, Chicz-DeMet, & DeMet, 1990). Seven of the eight people responding best at the highest dose also responded favorably to the 1 mg/kg dose. Six of these eight people also responded at the 0.5 mg/kg dose. Eleven participants responded positively to both the 1- and 2-mg/kg doses. Finally, participants with the most frequently occurring SIB were the most positive responders to higher doses of naltrexone, consistent with previous findings (Herman et al. 1987; Sandman et al., 1990).

Another double-blind, placebo-controlled, fixed-dose study of eight adults with severe to profound mental retardation (Thompson et al., 1994) reported that treatment with naltrexone reduced head hitting, head banging, and self-biting. The eight individuals evaluated displayed 18 forms of SIB. Improvement was observed in 77% of the head hitting and head banging episodes and 100% of the self-biting forms. Episodes of high frequency

SIB also were more sensitive to treatment with naltrexone. The 100-mg (high) dose was more effective than the 50-mg (low) dose in reducing SIB. For several individuals, some forms of SIB decreased after naltrexone (e.g., head hitting and self-biting), but other forms (e.g., throat poking) did not change. Four of the participants in this trial received concomitant treatment with clonidine (an alpha-2-adrenergic agonist), but no effects on SIB or interactions with naltrexone were observed. These findings complement previous studies and reveal that although naltrexone is effective in reducing SIB, not all self-inflicted harm may be controlled by the opioid system.

These two relatively large studies of acute treatment with naltrexone came to similar conclusions. Opiate blockers appear to be an effective treatment for a significant number of individuals exhibiting SIB. Administration of naltrexone reduces high-frequency SIB episodes and some, but not all, self-destructive behavior. Both studies acknowledged that not all individuals expressing SIB were positive responders and that a small minority may increase SIB (see also Barrett, Feinstein, & Hole, 1989).

There are few controlled, long-term studies of naltrexone for treating SIB. Two types of clinical studies comprise the long-term evaluation of naltrexone, either (a) prolonged treatment with naltrexone or (b) extended observations after brief periods of treatment. With either procedure, about 70% of the people exhibited long-term benefits (in varying degrees) from exposure to naltrexone (Barrett, Feinstein, & Hole, 1989; Crews, Bonaventura, Rowe, & Bonsie, 1993; Panksepp & Lensing, 1991; Smith et al., 1995; Walter et al., 1990). In a retrospective study of 56 people, Casner et al. (1996) discovered that 57% of people treated with naltrexone for between 3 to 87 months were considered by clinical review to be responders; 25% of the people treated met objective criteria as responders.

In our project, we completed a placebo-controlled, double-blind, reversal design with a single (most effective) dose (Sandman et al., 2000). The single dose was chosen based on response to a previous acute challenge with naltrexone (Sandman et al., 1993). Fifteen minutes of observational samples each week (three 5-minute samples) were collected (videotaped) for each person for at least 28 to 32 weeks, generating between 420 and 480 minutes (7 to 8 hours) of direct observation for each person. This time was extended up to 70 weeks for people continuing the second 3-month naltrexone treatment, increasing the observation time up to 1,060 minutes (18 hours). The samples were collected on 3 days of each week for each person.

We found that a subgroup of people exhibited long-term or persisting effects of naltrexone after responding positively to an acute exposure to the drug a year previously. This group decreased their SIB after the acute treatment, and the decrease persisted for at least a year. A 70% or more reduction of SIB in five patients is consistent with placebo-controlled case reports (Barrett, Feinstein, & Hole, 1989; Crews et al., 1993; Walter et al., 1990) and the open study of several cases with multiple doses (Panksepp & Lensing, 1991; Smith, Gupta, & Smith, 1995). A reduction in SIB of this magnitude for the type of people enlisted in this study (i.e., treatment resistant) did not occur by chance as determined by the modified Monte Carlo forecast. However, without exception, these five patients increased their SIB when entered into the 3-month long-term treatment with naltrexone. In contrast, a second subgroup of patients increased their SIB over the 1-year period after acute treatment, but they decreased their SIB after both the first and second long-term treatment periods.

How and why naltrexone exerts persisting effects are not known. Normally, NTX and its metabolites are cleared within 48 to 96 hours (Gonzalez & Brogden, 1988); however, intermittent and chronic exposure to naltrexone produce different receptor dynamics. Chronic, or daily administration of naltrexone supersensitizes or up-regulates opiate receptors and increases the reinforcing effects of opioids. These effects retreat within days of cessation of treatment (Bardo & Neisewander, 1987; Brunello, Volterra, DiGiulio, Cuomo, & Racagni, 1984; Marley, Shimosato, Gewiss, Thorndike, Goldberg, & Schindler, 1995; Zukin et al., 1982). However, intermittent exposure to naltrexone (our acute study involved nine exposures during a 10-week period) results in long-lasting supersensitivity (at least 10 weeks after treatment subsides) and generates a more complex receptor binding pattern in the brain. In contrast to chronic treatment, which results only in up-regulation, intermittent naltrexone up-regulates opioid receptors in the hind brain and down-regulates midbrain receptors (Marley et al., 1995).

Moreover, there seems to be a dual modulation of cellular response to opioids (Crain & Shen, 1995; Shen & Crain, 1992). The same receptors may mediate both excitatory and inhibitory effects (Smart & Lambert, 1996). Chronic exposure to opioids results in tolerance to the inhibitory effects of high doses of opiates but in supersensitivity to the excitatory effects of extremely low doses of opiates and the effects of opiate antagonists (Crain & Shen, 1995; Shen & Crain, 1992). This suggests that patients with high levels of endogenous opiates should be the most responsive to treatment with naltrexone.

Endogenous Opioid Levels and Response to Opiate Blockers

In our initial study, we determined the relationship between endogenous opioids and response to naltrexone by collecting blood samples from 10 patients within 2 to 5 minutes of a self-injurious act and during a control period (Sandman et al., 1997). At least 1 month later the effects on SIB of naltrexone were examined in a double-blind, placebo-controlled cross-over study during a 10-week period. Patients with the highest change in plasma levels of β-endorphin after SIB had the most positive response to naltrexone ($p < 0.03$). These results are consistent with several other reports. First,

Ernst et al. (1993) reported that baseline levels of β-endorphin were positively related to changes in behavior (Clinical Global Impressions scale, CGI) after treatment with naltrexone in five young children with autism. Second, Bouvard et al. (1995) found that C-terminal β-endorphin decreased after naltrexone only in good responders. Third, Scifo et al. (1996) found that increases in SIB and response to naltrexone in some people were related to high levels of endogenous opiates (i.e., good responses to naltrexone were observed in patients with high levels of β-endorphin). Fourth, Cazzullo et al. (1999) reported that patients responding with decreased β-endorphin levels after treatment with naltrexone had better and more pervasive behavioral improvement than patients who did not have physiological changes after naltrexone.

We recently have made similar observations in our long-term studies of naltrexone and SIB (Sandman et al., 2000). POMC fragments were measured in 12 self-injurious patients before and after long-term (3-month) treatment with naltrexone. POMC fragments were sampled from blood collected at the end of the baseline and placebo-controlled treatment phases of the study. Two patterns emerged. One group (the responders) displayed persisting improvement in SIB and lower relative levels of β-endorphin$_{1-31}$ after initial exposure to naltrexone. Chronic administration of naltrexone to this group was associated with increased SIB and elevated relative levels of β-endorphin. Returning to receiving the placebo improved their behavior (reduced SIB), and their levels of β-endorphin returned to basal levels. The second group (the nonresponders) was characterized by absence of persisting improvement after acute treatment with naltrexone and by elevated basal β-endorphin levels. Chronic treatment with naltrexone improved their behavior but did not alter their β-endorphin levels. Analysis of the disregulation index (DI) indicated that the long-term positive response to acute doses of naltrexone was associated with less dysregulation of ACTH and β-endorphin.

Our newest and most encouraging findings are presented in Figure 13.4, illustrating the effects of naltrexone (QOD) on the transitional probability of SIB following SIB. These are the first data to our knowledge presenting the effects of treatment on transitional behavior. Behavioral observations were collected on the palm-top computer as described previously for consecutive 7-week periods for each patient in a double-blind, multiple-dose, cross-over design. On the ordinate is the change in transitional probability of SIB following SIB after treatment with naltrexone. A negative number represents improvement or a decrease in the probability that SIB will follow SIB as a function of treatment with naltrexone. The concentration of β-endorphin after an SIB event is represented on the abscissa A significant ($r = -.85$, $p < .01$) linear relationship was found between these variables, indicating that biological changes associated with SIB predicted

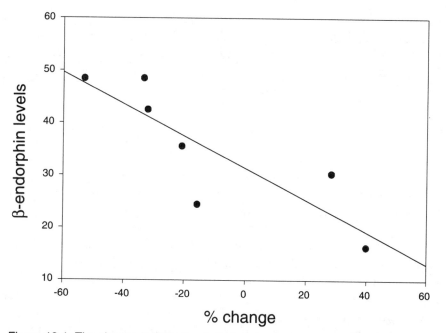

Figure 13.4. The change in SIB after 1 mg/kg of naltrexone compared to blind placebo is predicted by the levels of β-endorphin after a SIB episode. Higher levels of β-endorphin predict positive responses (decreased SIB) to naltrexone.

subsequent response to an opiate blocker. Higher levels of β-endorphin after a self-injurious act predicted positive response to a subsequent challenge with an opiate blocker.

SIB and the POMC Gene

Some individuals with SIB, perhaps the majority, exhibit altered POMC expression. It is reasonable to conclude that POMC is implicated in specific subtypes (phenotypes) of SIB. Identification of specific behavioral and neurochemical phenotypes is the goal of our future studies. We have collected preliminary results in a small pilot sample (5 adults with autism and SIB) suggesting that the fragment of the gene that codes for the opioid region of POMC is highly polymorphic (Sandman, Spence, & Smith, 1999). In one person, results of polymerase chain reaction (PCR) analysis of the sequence encoding opioid activity revealed that a deletion or mutation occurred. This is the first evidence we are aware of indicating that the opioid fragment of the POMC gene is defective in any patient. These findings complement the report (Krude, Biebermann, Luck, Horn, Brabant, & Gruters, 1998) of the first defect related to deletion in the MSH region of the POMC gene, defining a new monogenic disorder with early onset. These two findings suggested that the POMC region of chromosome 2 contains candidate genes for developmental and regulatory function, and it is reasonable to conclude that POMC is implicated in specific subtypes (phenotypes) among individuals exhibiting SIB. We view these encouraging findings as a small first step in characterizing a genetic anomaly associated with individuals who self-injure.

CONCLUSION

Our program of research has evolved from pharmacological studies of the opioid system to the search for genes that may be associated with a behavioral and neurochemical phenotype that may determine response to opiate blockers. Initially our studies addressed the effects of opiate blockers on the behavior of individuals who exhibited self-injury. In general, the results indicated that naltrexone is an effective treatment for some individuals (Sandman et al., 1998). However, the effects of naltrexone on SIB were not simple. We and others (Bouvard et al., 1995; Leboyer et al., 1994, 1999) have found that background POMC fragments, specifically opioid fragments, contribute to the symptoms of SIB and the response to treatment. The intact β-endorphin fragment is uncoupled from ACTH during self-injury, and the C-terminal β-endorphin fragment level is significantly depressed among some subgroups while at rest. Both of these findings are examples of POMC dysregulation, and both predicted efficacy of naltrexone treatment. Uncoupling of POMC fragments suggests an underlying basic, perhaps genetic, mechanism. The findings of a maternal influence on the C-terminal β-endorphin fragment among individuals with autism (Leboyer et al., 1999) supported this possibility. Our preliminary findings of a mutation in the opioid region of the POMC gene in an individual exhibiting SIB were encouragingly consistent with the prospect that a subgroup of patients will be identified who share this genetic defect.

14

SLEEP AND CYCLICAL VARIABLES RELATED TO SELF-INJURIOUS AND OTHER DESTRUCTIVE BEHAVIORS

WAYNE W. FISHER, CATHLEEN C. PIAZZA, AND HENRY S. ROANE

SLEEP DISTURBANCE AND SEVERE DESTRUCTIVE BEHAVIOR DISORDERS

Assessment of Sleep Disorders

Behavior Disorders and Sleep Disturbance.

In one of the first investigations conducted on sleep and destructive behavior, we showed that children with severe behavior disorders were much more likely to have markedly disturbed sleep than their typically developing peers and that the level of sleep disturbance was inversely correlated with intellectual functioning (Piazza, Fisher, & Kahng, 1996). In this study, a momentary time-sampling method was used to record the sleep–wake patterns of 50 children with mental retardation who displayed severe destructive behavior. That is, every half hour, an observer conducted a brief observation lasting a few seconds and recorded whether the individual was awake or asleep. These observations were conducted 24 hours a day, 7 days a week, while the individuals were in an inpatient unit specializing in the assessment and treatment of destructive behavior displayed by people with autism or mental retardation. During approximately one third of the

This investigation was supported in part by Grant MCJ249149-02 from the Maternal and Child Health Service and Grant 1 R01 HD37837-01 from the National Institute of Child Health and Human Development within the U.S. Department of Health and Human Services.

Epidemiological research has identified numerous environmental and biological correlates of severe SIB and other destructive behavior that may greatly influence the development, course, maintenance, and severity of these disorders. Two potentially important biological factors related to SIB are sleep and cyclical variables, which include certain mood disorders and other biological processes that are periodic and influence behavior (e.g., the menstrual cycle). In this chapter, we summarize a line of research on relationships between destructive behaviors such as SIB and sleep and cyclical variables.

observations, a second, independent observer also recorded the individual's sleep–wake patterns to ascertain the reliability of the data collection system. In this investigation and all subsequent investigations in which we have used this direct-observation method for measuring sleep–wake patterns, reliability coefficients have exceeded 90% agreement.

The results of this investigation showed that children with mental retardation who showed destructive behavior slept approximately 2 to 3 hours less per night than typically developing peers and were more likely to sleep at inappropriate times during the day. In fact, 88% of the children with mental retardation who showed destructive behavior met criteria for insomnia (i.e., they displayed difficulties in initiating or maintaining sleep during 3 or more nights per week).

Covariation Between Sleep and SIB

Although the prevalence of sleep disturbance is exceedingly high among all children with destructive behavior, we have noticed that children with severe SIB tend to show the most disturbed sleep–wake problems. Therefore, researchers wanted to determine whether sleep and SIB were relatively independent disorders that happened to co-occur frequently in this population or whether the two conditions were more intimately related. More specifically, researchers wanted to determine for individual participants whether day-to-day fluctuations in one problem (e.g., SIB) were correlated with similar or inverse changes in the other problem (e.g., sleep). In this investigation the momentary time-sampling procedure described was used to measure the sleep–wake patterns of 35 participants (Kuhn et al., 1996). Continuous, direct-observations methods were used to measure the daily rate of SIB. That is, each SIB response was recorded throughout the day, and the rate was calculated by dividing the daily frequency of SIB by the number of hours of observation each day. Next, individual lag correlations for each participant were calculated to determine whether daily fluctuations in SIB and sleep disturbance were related.

Lag correlations are sometimes used to generate hypotheses about potential causal relationships between two variables because they allow the investigator to determine the extent to which changes in one variable precede or follow changes in the other variable (based on the notion that causes tend to precede effects). Obviously, one needs to be cautious when interpreting such data, but lag correlations can be a good starting point for identifying potential causal relations.

Significant correlations ($p < .05$) between sleep and SIB were identified for 54% of the participants. That is, for 19 of the 35 participants, day-to-day fluctuations of one of the variables (e.g., sleep) were either positively or negatively correlated with day-to-day changes in the other variable (e.g., SIB). In some people the changes in sleep preceded the changes in SIB, whereas in other people the changes in SIB came first. In the following paragraphs, we summarize the various patterns that emerged from these analyses for different participants.

Among those with significant lag correlations, the most common finding was that higher levels of SIB occurred on or following days in which relative sleep deprivation occurred (42% of cases). That is, for these individuals, decreases in sleep were significantly associated with subsequent increases in SIB. These data are consistent with the recent case reports using functional analysis methods showing that destructive behavior reinforced by the termination of nonpreferred activities (i.e., escaped-maintained behavior) was more likely following nights in which the participants slept less (Horner, Day, & Day, 1997; O'Reilly, 1995). These case reports suggest that academic and other work tasks may become more aversive following sleep deprivation, thus increasing motivation to display escape-maintained problem behavior.

The next most common relation was that, for some individuals, increases in SIB occurred on or following days with increases in sleep (28% of cases). At first glance, this relation may seem somewhat counterintuitive. However, one possible explanation is that these individuals were more likely to display SIB following nights in which they slept more.

A third finding was that some individuals demonstrated increases in sleep following days with relatively higher levels of SIB (13% of cases). Perhaps these individuals needed increased rest following days in which higher levels of SIB occurred.

Future investigations should be directed toward testing each of these three hypotheses. For example, interventions that specifically target one problem (e.g., sleep) could be implemented for individuals who show the first relation (increased SIB following sleep deprivation) to determine whether the treatment not only increases sleep but also decreases SIB. We recently conducted a single-case experiment using this method, and manipulations of the individual's amount of sleep produced inverse effects on SIB. That is, during assessment, awakening the child early (which produced sleep deprivation) resulted in increased levels of SIB. Conversely, the faded-bedtime protocol—a treatment specifically designed to increase the amount of sleep (see description in following section)—not only regulated and increased the individual's sleep but also reduced destructive behavior almost completely.

Behavioral Treatment of Sleep Disorders

Piazza and Fisher (1991) evaluated the effects of a faded bedtime with response cost procedure for treating sleep problems displayed by four individuals with developmental disabilities and severe destructive behavior. The participants had multiple sleep problems, including difficulty initiating sleep, night and early wakings, and cosleeping (sleeping in a caregiver's bed). A momentary time-sampling procedure was used each half hour to record whether the participant was awake or asleep and in bed or out of bed. The treatment involved using the baseline data to determine a time when rapid sleep onset was likely (i.e., a time when the participant was typically asleep). The initial bedtime was established by calculating the average sleep onset time in baseline and adding 30 minutes. The fading component involved delaying or advancing the participant's bedtime based on the latency of sleep onset the previous night. If the participant fell asleep within 15 minutes of being placed in bed, the bedtime was 30 minutes earlier on the next night. If the participant failed to fall asleep within 15 minutes of being placed in bed, the bedtime was later on the next night. The response cost component involved taking participants out of bed and keeping them awake for 1 hour if they failed to fall asleep within 15 minutes. This procedure was repeated until the participants fell asleep within 15 minutes of being placed in bed. These procedures were used to fade the bedtime until the participants were falling asleep at an age-appropriate time.

Piazza and Fisher (1991) hypothesized that both classical and operant conditioning may contribute to the efficacy of the faded bedtime treatment. From the standpoint of classical conditioning, delaying the bedtime and thereby producing sleep deprivation increases the probability of rapid sleep onset. Presumably, the unconditioned stimulus is the physiological state associated with sleep deprivation and the unconditioned response is sleep. Because the participants are placed in bed when they are more likely to fall asleep, the behavior of lying in bed becomes the conditioned stimulus that increases the probability of sleep.

From an operant perspective, sleep deprivation (achieved through delaying the bedtime and removing the child from bed for long latency to sleep onset) may produce avoidance behaviors. During treatment, the participants are placed in bed at a time when they are likely to be tired. If they fail to fall asleep rapidly, they are removed from bed and kept awake. Being kept awake may become more aversive as sleep deprivation increases. Therefore, the individuals learn to avoid being removed from bed by falling asleep rapidly. During fading, a stimulus (the bedtime) is changed gradually such that the individuals do not detect the change and continue to respond to the earlier bedtime (the changed stimulus) as they did to the later bedtimes (the initial stimulus).

The faded bedtime with response cost procedure is a multicomponent treatment that consists of (a) bedtime scheduling (establishing a consistent sleep and wake time), (b) fading (gradually changing the bedtime), and (c) response cost (removing the child from bed when rapid sleep onset does not occur). To evaluate which of the components of the faded bedtime with response cost procedure were important in improving sleep, Piazza, Fisher, and Sherer (1997) conducted a comparison of (a) a bedtime scheduling procedure with (b) the faded bedtime with response cost treatment. The participants were 14 children with developmental disabilities. Participants were assigned randomly to either the faded bedtime with response cost or the bedtime scheduling procedure. The faded bedtime with response cost treatment was conducted as described previously (Piazza & Fisher, 1991). During bedtime scheduling, the participants were placed in bed at the same time every night and awakened at the same time every morning. The sleep and wake times were established based on norms in conjunction with parental input. The sleep of both groups improved following treatment. However, the sleep of the children in the faded bedtime with response cost group improved significantly more than those in the bedtime scheduling group. These results suggested that the bedtime scheduling component did not account for the effectiveness of the faded bedtime treatment and that the fading components were necessary to maximize treatment effectiveness.

The faded bedtime with response cost procedure capitalizes in part on establishing a regular sleep-wake cycle within the context of gradually moving the bedtime to an earlier time. An alternative method is to delay the bedtime until the individual is falling asleep at a socially acceptable time. Gradually delaying the bedtime is a procedure known as *chronotherapy*, a procedure that has been used with adults diagnosed with sleep cycle disorders (i.e., delayed sleep phase insomnia; Czeisler et al., 1981).

Piazza, Hagopian, Hughes, and Fisher (1998) used chronotherapy to treat the severe sleep problems of an 8-year-old girl with mental retardation. Irregular sleep onset times, frequent night and early wakings, and short total sleep times characterized her sleep. The chronotherapy procedure involved establishing a time at which rapid sleep onset was highly likely (in this case, 3:30 a.m.). The bedtime was advanced by 2 hours each night until the participant was placed in bed and falling asleep at 9 p.m. As a result of treatment, the participant's sleep improved as characterized by more consistent sleep onset and wake times and an increase in the total amount of sleep. These studies show that it is possible to regulate the sleep patterns of individuals with developmental disabilities and severe behavior disorders using behavioral principles and procedures.

CYCLICAL PATTERNS OF SIB AND OTHER DESTRUCTIVE BEHAVIORS

The research literature on SIB includes numerous references to patients who display episodic SIB that seems to dramatically worsen and improve over time, relatively independent of ongoing environmental circumstances (Iwata et al., 1994; Reid, 1972). For example, Reid described an individual with profound mental retardation who was normally subdued and withdrawn. The person showed four self-limiting phases characterized by excessive activity, sleep disturbance, irritability, and SIB, each of which lasted approximately 10–20 days. This situation is highly similar to numerous cases we have admitted to the neurobehavioral programs at the Kennedy Kreiger and Marcus Institutes in Baltimore, Maryland and Atlanta, Georgia, respectively. We admit a patient every year or so whose SIB (or aggression) seems to worsen and then get better relatively independent of the behavioral and drug interventions used. Most of the individuals display behavior that worsens, improves, and then begins to worsen again within 20–30 days, thus meeting one of the primary criteria for rapid-cycling bipolar disorder.

Cyclical destructive behavior represents an intriguing problem, but one that is exceedingly difficult to study with great fidelity. To determine whether an intrinsically controlled form of cyclical SIB is present, researchers must hold the relevant extrinsic variables constant. However, a sudden and dramatic worsening in SIB usually precipitates a treatment change (e.g., the psychiatrist alters a medication dosage, the behavior analyst manipulates a contingency, or both interventions are modified at once). Thus, our research on cyclical SIB has focused on the development of procedures for detecting and testing hypotheses about cyclical SIB in nonverbal individuals when so many extrinsic variable remain uncontrolled. We have also been interested in methods for identifying the biological processes that may be responsible for periodicity in this disorder.

Assessment of Cyclical Behavior Patterns

Individuals with cyclical SIB or other destructive behavior have various diagnoses. Among the 10 individuals we have admitted with cyclical SIB, the most common diagnoses were atypical bipolar disorder, intermittent explosive disorder, or temporal-lobe epilepsy. However, these diagnoses are also applied to people with various behavior disorders who do not show a predictable cyclical pattern. Thus, one of the first issues we attempted to address was better identification of the specific behaviors that should be monitored to detect the presence of cyclical behavior disorders in individuals with profound mental retardation.

We reviewed various cases in the literature describing cyclical behavior disorders among individuals with severe to profound mental retardation and identified 10 behaviors that were commonly reported in these individuals (Lewis, Silva, & Silva, 1995; Naylor, Reid, Dick, & Dick, 1976; Osborne, Baggs, Darvish, Blakelock, Peine, & Jenson, 1992; Reid, 1972; Taylor, Rush, Hetrick, & Sandman, 1993; Wieseler, Campbell, & Sonis, 1988). The behaviors identified were (a) agitation, (b) aggression, (c) food refusal, (d) food selectivity, (e) inappropriate laughter, (f) insomnia, (g) noncompliance, (h) vocal agitation, (i) restlessness, and (j) SIB. In our population of individuals with cyclical behavior disorders, these behaviors also were quite common, but not all of them increased and decreased in a predictable cyclical pattern. In fact, what we observed was that SIB, aggression, or both were the behaviors most likely to follow a cyclical pattern, so we now focus on the way we detected cyclical patterns in these specific responses.

Detecting Cyclical Patterns

One of the first issues we had regarding cyclical destructive behavior was determining which types of data collection systems were most sensitive to the detection of cyclical behavior patterns. We collect data on SIB using two primary methods. One data collection method is to set up highly controlled analogue situations and collect data on laptop computers, as is typically done when assessing and treating SIB using functional analysis methods. The major advantage of this method is that it is possible to accurately isolate the effects of specific antecedent or consequent stimuli. However, we have not found this method of data collection to be very sensitive to cyclical patterns of aberrant behavior in most cases, primarily because this method does not sample a sufficient amount of time each day.

The second data collection system we use is to collect frequency-within-interval data (usually blocked into half-hour intervals) all day long. In 9 of 10 cases, this method of data collection has been more sensitive to detecting cyclical behavior patterns. That is, the increase in the rate of SIB that characterizes the "up" portion of a cycle is generally not manifested continuously throughout each day. Rather, the individual may display several intense bursts of high-rate SIB during the "up" portion of a cycle and display fewer or lower rate bursts during the "down" portion of a cycle. Because this second data collection system measures each SIB response emitted throughout the day, the changes in the rate of SIB between the up and down portions of the cycle are more likely to be detected.

Another potentially important variable in detecting cyclical behavior disorders relates to the way the data are summarized and analyzed. There are various statistical techniques for detecting cyclical patterns in data, but we have generally found that simpler methods work as well or better. We begin by graphing each day's frequency of SIB or aggression as a single data point. In some cases, this is sufficient for detecting an exceptionally clear cyclical pattern, but more often, additional manipulations are required. For example, Figure 14.1 shows Jed's destructive behavior graphed as frequency per day. As can be seen, the data are highly variable, but it is not readily apparent from this graph whether a cyclical pattern is present. However, we then graphed these same data as weekly averages in Figure 14.2, and a much clearer cyclical pattern emerged. Another simple technique that we have used is to "smooth" the data series using a floating average in which each data point represents an average of that data point and a few adjacent data points (see Dee's data in Figure 14.9 for an example).

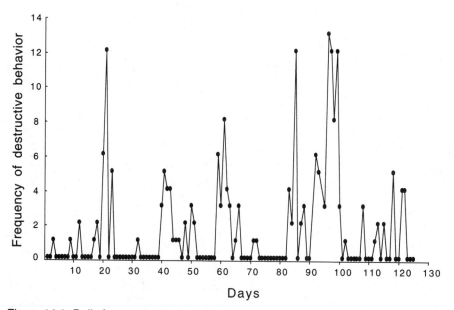

Figure 14.1. Daily frequency of Jed's destructive responses.

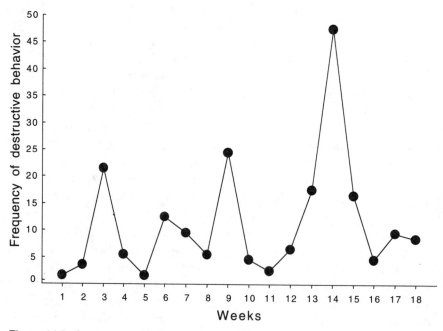

Figure 14.2. Average weekly frequency of Jed's destructive behavior.

FISHER, PIAZZA, AND ROANE

Testing Hypotheses About Cyclical Patterns

Another set of issues we have attempted to address relates to the predictability of cyclical SIB and aggression. Based on a hypothesized cycle, can one predict whether the next observable change in behavior will be an increase or a decrease? In addition, can one predict when an increase in behavior is going to occur?

With cyclical behavior, one generally predicts a pattern in which the rate of behavior increases and decreases repeatedly. That is, one would predict that a data point representing the mean of an up portion of the cycle should be followed by a lower data point (i.e., the mean of the down portion of a cycle), which in turn would be followed by another high data point, and so forth. In some ways, predicting the direction of the next change in behavior is similar to tossing a coin in that two outcomes are possible (an increase or decrease in behavior—heads or tails). Because two outcomes are possible, one can use the formula for a Bernoulli trial and determine how many successive data points have to follow the predicted pattern to show that it is highly improbable that the pattern occurred by chance. For example, if one is able to predict 5 consecutive data points (higher, lower, higher, lower, higher), the statistical test would reach the conventional cutoff point of $p < .05$, a sequence of 7 correct predictions would reach the significance level of $p < .01$, and a sequence of 10 would reach the significance level of $p < .001$.

Figure 14.3 shows Tony's average daily rate of aggression collapsed into our predicted 10-day cycles (10 days for a change in behavior, 20 days to

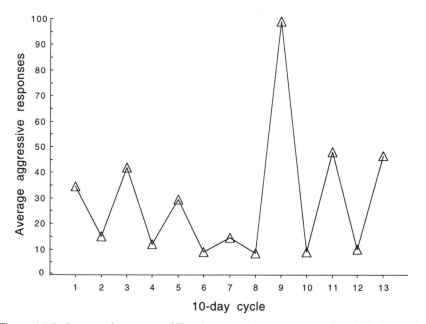

Figure 14.3. Average frequency of Tony's aggression across predicted 10-day cycles.

complete an up and down cycle). As can be seen, Tony's aggression followed the predicted pattern for 13 consecutive data points, and the probability of this occurring by chance was less than 1 in 1,000 ($p < .001$).

The second issue relates to whether one can accurately predict when destructive behavior is going to worsen. If researchers can consistently predict when an individual's behavior is going to change, then they can be fairly confident that the behavior is following a cyclical pattern. In the following case example, we chose a window of 5 days and calculated the chance probability that a marked increase in destructive behavior would consistently occur within the predicted window. We again applied the formula for a Bernoulli trial to determine how many times we would have to accurately predict the increase in SIB to reach statistical significance. Predicting three consecutive increases in SIB would produce a p value of less than .05, five consecutive predicted increases would produce a p value of less than .01, and seven correct predictions would produce a p value of less than .001.

Jan, age 16, had profound mental retardation and blindness. We first detected the cyclical pattern of her SIB based on some rather crude data collected by her mother at home during the months before her admission. Jan would be placed in restraints (with her wrists tied to her wheelchair) on days when her SIB was of a sufficient rate and intensity to produce tissue damage. Her mother kept track of whether Jan was restrained by placing a mark on the calendar on days when restraints were necessary. Figure 14.4 shows the times when Jan displayed SIB that produced tissue damage and necessi-

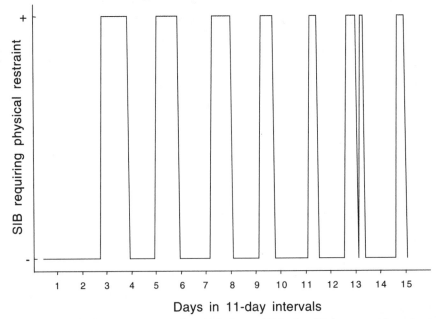

Figure 14.4. Eleven-day intervals in which Jan exhibited self-injury requiring physical restraint at home.

tated restraints. On days when restraints were necessary, the data point is up (i.e., at the + point on the y-axis); on days when restraints were unnecessary, the data point is down (i.e., at the − point on the y-axis). As can be seen, Jan would typically require restraints for multiple days in a row (M = 14.6), but then she would have multiple days in a row during which restraints were unnecessary (M = 8.1). That is, Jan's SIB worsened about every 22.7 days.

Next, we used Jan's data from home to determine whether we could predict increases in SIB that occurred on our inpatient unit. Figure 14.5 show Jan's average daily rate of SIB collapsed into our predicted 11-day cycles. That is, her behavior changed approximately every 11 days (or 22 days from one increase to the next). Moreover, using the data from Jan's home, which indicated when SIB was severe and she had to be restrained, we were able to accurately predict (within 5 days) the onset of each of the four cycles during her inpatient stay. The chance probability of getting all four predictions correct was less than .05.

Identifying Biological Correlates of Cyclical SIB

In the majority of people we have seen with cyclical SIB, we have not been able to identify a specific cause or biological correlate of the cyclical behavior disorder, so our presumption has been that these were atypical forms of rapid-cycling bipolar disorder. Therefore, we have begun to correlate changes in SIB or aggression with other variables, such as sleep (see previous

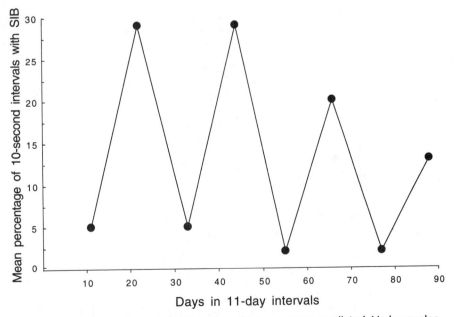

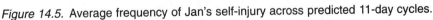

Figure 14.5. Average frequency of Jan's self-injury across predicted 11-day cycles.

section), mood, and the menstrual cycle. The following two case studies illustrate these methods.

June, age 12, had profound mental retardation and pervasive developmental disorder. Direct observation measures of her mood and destructive behavior were conducted throughout her school day in half-hour intervals. During each half-hour interval, observers scored whether June displayed negative affect (e.g., crying, screaming, groaning, frowning) or positive affect (e.g., cooing, smiling, laughing) and scored each occurrence of destructive behavior. Figure 14.6 shows the mean number of destructive behaviors per minute (closed circles) and the level of June's affect (open circles). Her level of affect was calculated by subtracting the percentage of intervals with negative affect from the percentage of intervals with positive affect for each day. As can be seen, changes in June's mood were inversely correlated with changes in her destructive behavior (Pearson Product-moment Correlation Coefficient $r = -.71$, $p < .05$).

Helen, age 16, had profound mental retardation and episodic, high-intensity SIB and aggression. She also destroyed property and frequently disrobed. Figure 14.7 shows the daily frequencies of these destructive

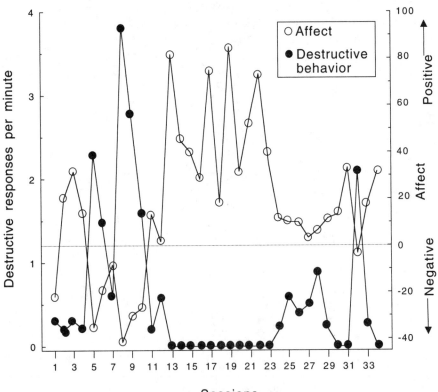

Figure 14.6. Destructive responses and daily ratings of affect during June's daily sessions.

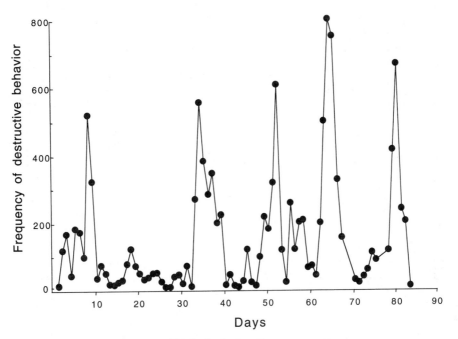

Figure 14.7. Daily frequency of Helen's destructive responses.

behaviors. As can be seen, the pattern is characterized by episodic, high-rate destructive behavior (as many as almost 700 responses per day during her up cycles). Figure 14.8 show the same data graphed in relation to Helen's menstrual cycle. The closed circles show the average daily rate of destructive behavior during 7-day periods at the time of ovulation. The open circles show the average daily rate of destructive behavior during 7-day periods at the time of menses. The closed triangles show the average daily rate of destructive behavior at times other than ovulation or menses. As can be seen, the vast majority of her destructive behaviors (almost 90%) occurred during the periods around ovulation and menses.

Treatment of Cyclical Behavior Disorders

Evaluating Treatments for Cyclical SIB and Aggression

Of the 10 individuals we have seen with cyclical SIB or aggression, all of them showed a rapid-cycling profile (i.e., at least four cycles in a year). All of the 10 individuals with cyclical SIB received multiple trials of psychotropic medications and behavioral interventions. We generally use a specific single-case experimental design to evaluate the additive and interactive effects of drug and behavioral treatments when cyclical patterns are present (Fisher, Piazza, & Page, 1990; Piazza et al., 1994). With this design, periods of behavioral treatments and behavioral baselines are alternated across days

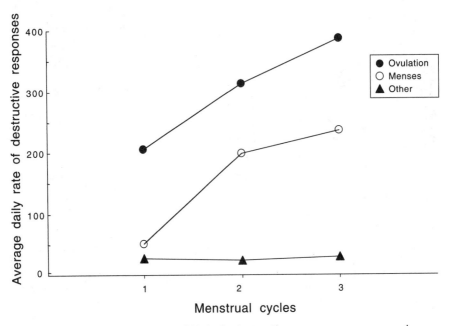

Figure 14.8. Average frequency of Helen's destructive responses across various stages of the menstrual cycle.

or shifts (i.e., day and evening shifts), whereas medication trials are introduced for multiple days or weeks (depending on the medication). The following case example illustrates the use of this design.

Dee, age 20, had profound mental retardation, pervasive developmental disorder, and cyclical SIB. Figure 14.9 shows a smoothed version (a floating average of each series of five consecutive data points) of the mean rates of her behavior during analogue sessions (i.e., the social attention condition of a functional analysis). During these sessions, Dee was given toys to play with while a therapist sat in the corner of the room reading a magazine. The therapist ignored Dee, except when she displayed SIB. The therapist delivered a verbal reprimand (e.g., "Don't do that, you'll hurt yourself") contingent on each occurrence of SIB.

Based on the cyclical pattern of SIB and the concomitant increases in agitation, a trial of lithium was initiated and a behavioral intervention was implemented. To evaluate the effects of lithium and the behavioral intervention concurrently, we used an alternating-treatments design. The results of this evaluation are shown in Figure 14.10. During the first phase, baseline contingencies were in effect during both the day and evening shifts. During this time, Dee's lithium levels varied slightly between 0.6 and 0.8 mmol/l. In the second phase, the behavioral intervention was introduced during the day shift (open circles), and baseline contingencies remained in effect during the evening shift. The behavioral intervention consisted of differential reinforcement of alternative behavior and contingent standing following

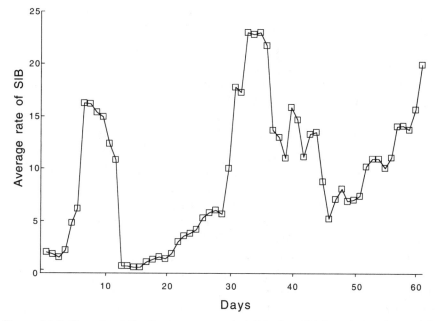

Figure 14.9. Smoothed (floating) average rate of Dee's self-injury during the social attention condition.

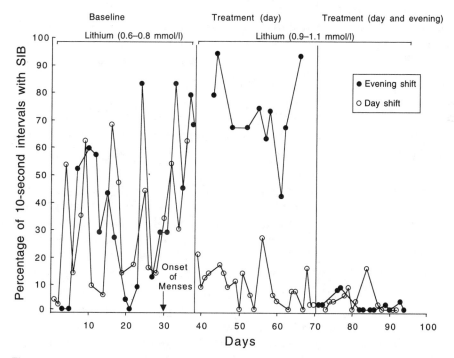

Figure 14.10. Percentage of Dee's intervals with self-injurious behavior during a lithium trial and behavioral baseline and treatment phases across day and evening shifts.

SIB. (Dee was physically guided to a standing position and required to remain standing for 15 seconds each time she displayed SIB.)

The behavioral intervention selected for Dee was developed based on the Premack (1971) principle, which states that high-probability responses can be used as reinforcing consequences to increase lower probability responses, and lower probability responses can be used as punishing consequences to decrease higher probability responses. During the up portion of Dee's cycle, SIB was a high-probability response, and standing was a low-probability response (she spent almost all of her time lying on the floor and resisted attempts to move her). Therefore, we guided her to a standing position (the lower probability response) each time she engaged in SIB (the higher probability response) to decrease SIB.

In addition, during the second phase, lithium levels reached the target dose of 1 and remained relatively stable (i.e., between 0.9 and 1.1 mmol/l) for the remainder of Dee's admission. As can be seen, during the second phase, Dee's SIB remained high during the evening shift with baseline contingencies in effect but decreased markedly during the day shift with the behavioral intervention in effect, suggesting that the behavioral intervention was effective at reducing SIB. The effectiveness of the behavioral intervention was further confirmed when treatment was introduced during the evening shift and SIB decreased almost completely, whereas lithium levels remained constant. The fact that SIB remained high during the evening shift, when lithium reached the target level and baseline contingencies were in effect, suggests that this medication was not helpful for controlling Dee's SIB. The design used in this case shows how behavioral and drug interventions can be systematically evaluated concurrently.

Overall Treatment Effectiveness With Cyclical SIB and Aggression

Rapid-cycling bipolar disorder among patients without developmental disabilities has been reported to be a treatment-resistant condition, with approximately 75% of patients failing to respond positively to lithium (Calabrese & Woyshville, 1995). We have had a similar experience with this population. The individuals who displayed SIB or aggression that had a cyclical pattern have tended to be the most treatment-resistant patients admitted to our program. We previously reported on a subgroup of these patients who showed statistically significant increases in destructive behavior when treated with lithium (Piazza et al., 1994). Moreover, all of the 10 patients we have seen with clear cyclical SIB or aggression had received multiple medications, and only one showed a clear and dramatic response to drug treatment. This adolescent girl had a dramatic response to risperidone. Her SIB decreased dramatically, and objective daily ratings of her mood stabilized.

As a group, these patients have also not responded well to behavioral interventions. Only 1 of the 10 individuals showed a clinically significant reduction in destructive behavior through treatment with reinforcement-based procedures (i.e., providing differential reinforcement for appropriate behavior and placing the destructive behavior on a social extinction schedule). In 8 of the 10 individuals, we were able to reduce destructive behavior by 70% or more using a combination of differential reinforcement and punishment. (The previous case of Dee provides such an example.) However, in most of these cases, the behavioral treatment decreased the frequency of the behavior, but the individuals continued to show cyclical patterns of intense and severe destructive behavior. Moreover, the treatments were often very difficult to implement, sometimes requiring two staff members when the behavior was at its most severe level.

CONCLUSION

Epidemiological research has identified both environmental and biological correlates of severe SIB or aggression that may greatly influence the development, course, maintenance, and severity of these disorders. Sleep and cyclical variables represent two potentially important biological factors related to destructive behavior, which include certain mood disorders and other biological processes that are periodic and influence behavior (e.g., the menstrual cycle). In this chapter, we have summarized a line of research on relations between destructive behavior and sleep and cyclical variables. One study showed that children with severe behavior disorders were much more likely to have markedly disturbed sleep than typically developing peers. Another study showed that day-to-day fluctuations in sleep and SIB are often inversely correlated, with decreased sleep (sleep deprivation) often followed by increased SIB. A series of studies showed that behavioral interventions designed to entrain sleep patterns in synchrony with the individual's biological clock could effectively treat sleep disorders in this population and, in rare cases, sleep treatment may significantly reduce SIB. With regard to cyclical variables in SIB, we have developed a set of procedures for detecting and testing hypotheses about cyclical SIB in nonverbal individuals and for identifying the biological processes that may be responsible for periodicity in this disorder. Further research is needed to identify treatments that will more effectively manage individuals with treatment-resistant cyclical behavior disorders.

15

SELF-INJURY AND PAIN: MODELS AND MECHANISMS

FRANK S. SYMONS

Self-injury is one of the most scientifically puzzling and clinically destructive behavior disorders among individuals with mental retardation and related developmental disabilities. In almost all cases of self-injurious behavior (SIB), the etiology of the behavior disorder is unknown, and the underlying pathophysiological features are only partly understood. Severe self-injury that occurs at high rates over long periods can result in irreversible mutilation, blindness, or brain injury. This suggests that the normal mechanisms for perceiving and responding to painful stimuli may be disordered (Barrera, Teodoro, Selmeci, & Madappuli, 1994; Corbett & Campbell, 1980). The abnormal sensory input associated with severe self-injury has not been studied systematically, nor has the relationship between the peripheral and central mechanisms of pain transmission and regulation and the tissue damage associated with chronic SIB. It is not known in most cases whether pain is a cause or consequence of self-injury. Furthermore, it is not clear whether resolving this issue would lead to changes in our approach to treating self-injury. Presumably, knowing whether self-injury was a consequence of pain or pain-related behavior would result in more specific treatments related to mechanisms of analgesia and pain regulation.

Sufficient evidence exists to show that aberrant pain experience occurs among people with developmental, psychiatric, and neurological disorders (Biersdorff, 1994; Lautenbacher & Krieg, 1994). It is therefore likely that pathological alteration in the basic mechanisms regulating pain experience may be common across disorders. Self-injury also occurs in many different

This work was supported, in part, by PHS Grant 35682 from the National Institute of Child Health and Human Development (NICHD). Part of this chapter was presented at the NICHD Workshop on Self-Injurious Behavior (December 1999) in Rockville, Maryland. The author is indebted to Jim Bodfish for his comments on a previous version of this manuscript and to David Lam for his skill and perseverance in conducting much of the library research necessary to write this chapter.

forms among people with developmental, psychiatric, and neurological disorders. Whether self-injury shares any common mechanisms related to altered pain transmission and regulation is unknown. The clinical parallels between self-injury in developmental disorders and self-mutilation in psychiatric disorders have not received serious attention, nor have bridging studies examined the possibility of shared mechanisms between the two clinical phenomena. Historically, SIB and self-mutilation have been regarded as distinct diagnostic entities with little or no shared characteristics. Similarly, the clinical relevance of self-injury associated with acquired and congenital neuropathies among various neurological disorders has been overlooked in many of the models of SIB in people with developmental disorders. From a pain perspective, individuals with neurological and psychiatric disorders tend to be verbal and can provide a unique perspective on the nature of any pain associated with self-injury. Similar information is not easily accessible in nonverbal individuals with severe and profound mental retardation. Indeed, it remains difficult to determine reliably and validly the nature of the pain response in relation to SIB among nonverbal individuals with severe disabilities because most current pain measurement relies, to some degree, on verbal report.

The purpose of this chapter is to review the evidence that pain mechanisms are involved, at least in part, in the pathogenesis and pathophysiological features of some forms of chronic self-injury in individuals with mental retardation and related developmental disorders. Neurological, psychiatric, and developmental disorders associated with self-injury are reviewed. For each of the disorders, the clinical phenomenology of self-injury and the mechanisms of pain regulation and transmission hypothesized to mediate self-injury are described. Based on this review, a general model of relief from aversive stimulation is discussed, and new directions in research are suggested. Throughout the chapter, the term *self-injury* is used, although it is recognized that different disciplines have and continue to use different terms such as *self-mutilation*, *deliberate self-harm*, *self-abuse*, and *auto-aggression*.

SELF-INJURIOUS BEHAVIOR, DISORDERS, AND PAIN MECHANISMS

Neurological Disorders

It has been known for some time that self-injury occurs in association with congenital sensory neuropathies and insensitivity to pain (Critchley, 1934; Kirman & Bicknell, 1968; Pinsky & Digeorge, 1966), and more recently it is recognized in acquired sensory neuropathies (Roach, Abramson, & Lawless, 1985; Swoboda, Engle, Scheindlin, Anthony, & Jones,

1998) and Tourette's syndrome (Robertson, Trimble, & Lees, 1989). Self-injury among people with neurological disorders tends to be directed toward the distal extremities (Swoboda et al., 1998), but reports also include head-directed and oral or facial SIB, as well as mutilation of the tongue and mouth (Rasmussen, 1996). Overall, the forms of self-injury seem best characterized by localized biting, scratching, and rubbing rather than nonspecific banging, hitting, or slapping (Zammarchi, Savelli, Donati, & Pasquini, 1994). Swoboda et al. reported a case of a typically developing 7-year-old boy self-mutilating the digits of his hand. Electromyogram evidence showed severe median nerve entrapment, and clinical evaluation suggested pain insensitivity in the hand region. In cases of SIB associated with acquired neuropathies, the onset is usually rapid with no prior history of self-injury or related repetitive movement disorder. Roach, Abramson, and Lawless (1985) documented the onset of SIB within days following acute trauma for two typically developing children with acquired peripheral neuropathies. Most clinical reports characterize the SIB associated with neurological dysfunction as intense and almost always associated with significant tissue damage (Mailis, 1996). Prevalence estimates of SIB associated with neurological disorders are unknown. Cases of self-injury co-occurring with documented neurological impairment in typically developing children and intellectually normal adults suggest that self-injury may be regulated by pathological pain mechanisms associated with neurological dysfunction of either central or peripheral origin.

Evidence for the relation between neurological dysfunction and chronic neuropathic pain associated with self-mutilation comes from experimental laboratory studies with animals and clinical reports from humans experiencing pain disorders. Rats typically engage in self-mutilation of a paw that has been denervated following transection of the sciatic and saphenous nerves (Coderre & Melzack, 1986). In nonhuman primates, experimental injury of the peripheral or central nervous system (CNS) leads to targeted SIB, producing various degrees of tissue damage from excoriations to mutilation and self-cannibalism of the denervated limb (autotomy; Mailis, 1996). Temporal-lobe and spinal cord lesions in macaques (bilateral dorsal rhizotomy) result in self-injury (Busbaur, 1974; Sweet, 1981), as do sectioning of the sciatic nerve and the lateral funiculus (Harris, 1995; Jones & Barraclough, 1978). In humans, self-injury has been reported in association with brachial plexus avulsions (Procacci & Maresca, 1990), alcohol injection into the gasserian ganglion (Schorstein, 1943), and following complete spinal cord injury (Dahlin, Van Buskirk, Novotny, Hollis, & George, 1985). Furthermore, there are clinical examples of intellectually normal individuals engaging in SIB related to neuropathic pain, targeting body sites characterized by thermoalgesia, allodynia, or hyperalgesia (Mailis, 1996).

Although various models accounting for self-injury associated with neurological dysfunction have been proposed, the specific mechanisms related to SIB and pain transmission and regulation are less clear and not universally accepted. In some cases with congenital or acquired sensory disturbances, self-injury is considered a pain response to relieve the dysesthesia (i.e., abnormal sensations) commonly accompanying the disorder. In some people, dysesthesia is associated with pain. In this model, intense rubbing, biting, scratching, or otherwise targeting the affected area reduces the discomfort associated with the underlying peripheral nerve dysfunction. This model is consistent with reports of SIB that is localized and patient reports of burning and itching of the extremities toward which they direct their self-injury. In other people, self-injury is considered a "side effect" of injury in a system that is characterized by diminished pain perception or complete anesthesia; therefore, the individual has no biological reason to avoid noxious stimuli.

It is unclear whether self-mutilation related to nerve damage or dysfunction is regulated by dysesthesia associated with pain or regulated by anesthesia associated with the absence of sensation. Coderre and Melzack (1986) showed that procedures that increase pain sensitivity also increase self-injury in rats, suggesting that self-injury in such cases was primarily a sensory phenomenon related to painful dysesthesia. The underlying mechanisms regulating this effect are not certain, but controlled studies suggest that the enhancement of self-mutilation in rats is not related to stress or a general increase in excitability. Rather, the self-mutilation is associated with an initial injury related to an increase in neural activity resulting in peripheral and central sensitization sustained for prolonged periods (Coderre & Melzack, 1986). In the human model, although the mechanism regulating self-injury related to chronic pain is unknown, Mailis (1996) concluded that the painful dysesthesia arising from peripheral or central somatosensory system lesions in the presence of idiosyncratic personality, neural, humoral, and environmental factors seem to release or facilitate the expression of SIB targeted to the painful body part. Because most of the evidence is based on collections of case reports, no studies have examined systematically the way unique intraindividual and contextual variables set the occasion for the expression of SIB. To date, the limited treatment data suggest that reducing pain leads to corresponding decreases of painful dysesthesia and termination of SIB in individuals with identified neurological disorders.

Psychiatric Disorders

Self-injury distinct from suicide attempts has been associated with numerous psychiatric illnesses, including schizophrenia (Feldman, 1988; Herpertz, 1995), eating and substance abuse disorders (Evans & Lacey, 1992; Favazza, DeRosear, & Conterio, 1989), and personality disorders (Kemperman, Russ, & Shearin, 1997). Self-injury among people with psychiatric disorders tends to occur under circumstances associated with stress (Walsh &

Rosen, 1988), pathologically altered mood or affect (Feldman, 1988), and dissociative experiences (Zlotnick, Mattia, & Zimmerman, 1999). The forms of self-injury most commonly reported or observed clinically include skin cutting, head banging, skin burning, and various topographies related to scratching, rubbing, and biting (Herpertz, 1995). In a study of psychiatric inpatients, more than half of a study sample reported more than one form of self-injury during a 2-year period (Herpertz, 1995). In cases of SIB associated with borderline personality disorder (BPD), the onset is usually reported during early adolescence, whereas onset appears later during young adulthood among individuals without BPD with no previous history of self-injury or related repetitive movement disorder. Clinical reports characterize SIB as intense and almost always associated with significant tissue damage and some degree of permanent scarring (Walsh & Rosen, 1988). Overall prevalence estimates of SIB associated with psychiatric disorders suggest that as many as 80% of patients with BPD report histories of self-injury, compared with prevalence estimates of approximately 4% in the general psychiatric population (Shearer, Peter, Quaytman, & Wadman, 1988). When Axis I disorders are examined directly, however, significant associations among people with self-injury and substance abuse, posttraumatic stress disorder, and intermittent explosive disorder have been reported, with the overall prevalence of reported SIB cases being comparable to that observed in people with BPD (Zlotnick et al., 1999).

Altered pain perception is prevalent in numerous psychiatric disorders, including schizophrenia, depression, anxiety, eating, and personality disorders (Lautenbacher & Krieg, 1994). Evidence for a possible relationship between psychiatric impairment and altered pain mechanisms associated with SIB comes primarily from studies of patients with BPD. Emerging evidence suggests that self-injury can have subtypes—painful and not painful—among patients with BPD. Kemperman et al., (1997) documented that many people with BPD and SIB report not feeling pain during self-injury. Ratings of affect and dissociative symptoms are higher in the people with BPD who report no pain when compared with those reporting pain. In addition, the same people have altered thermal responsivity to noxious stimuli, suggesting dysfunction in normal pain mechanisms.

Consistent with patient reports, experimental studies of acute pain using the cold pressor test (CPT) have also found that pain perception is altered in patients with BPD who do not experience pain during self-injury. Mood is also reported to improve following CPT in people with BPD who reported that they experienced no pain during self-injury. Alteration in responsivity to noxious stimuli and improvement of mood following CPT-induced analgesia may be related to activation of brain mechanisms thought to regulate both pain and affect (e.g., endogenous opioid peptide system, serotonergic systems; Russ et al., 1992). When the opioid peptide system is antagonized by administering naloxone hydrochloride, measures of reported pain during CPT increase in patients with BPD and SIB (Russ et al., 1994). In a study of circulating neuropeptides, Coid, Allolio, and Rees (1983) reported finding raised plasma metenkephalin levels in patients who habitually self-mutilated. The degree of elevation was related to the severity of the patient's illness but also to the time since the last act of self-injury. Russ et al. (1993) reported that individuals who reported no pain during SIB tended to have an earlier onset of self-injury with more repeated instances during long periods than those who reported feeling pain during SIB. It seems that, at least for people with BPDs, onset, time course, and severity of self-injury (and presumably tissue damage) may be important variables in determining whether pain mechanisms mediate SIB.

Not surprisingly, models accounting for SIB among people with psychiatric disorders are diverse. In some models, SIB is characterized as an arousal modulator or mood regulator, whereas others hypothesize SIB as failed impulse control. In the majority of models, specific mechanisms related to pain transmission and regulation are absent or not well developed. The Coid et al. (1983) report of elevated metenkephalin levels in the absence of elevated ACTH among people who repeatedly self-injured suggests that the finding is not simply a peripheral response to stress associated with psychiatric illness. Rather, it supports the notion of subtypes of self-injury regulated in part by feedback mechanisms occurring during repeated tissue damage associated with severe self-injury. This idea is consistent with a more general neurobiological model of self-injury based on alterations in neurochemistry related to repeated noxious stimulation and associated stress. Similarly, the finding that self-injury tends to occur primarily in people with Axis I disorders characterized by failed impulse control and impulsive aggression is suggestive of neurobiological regulation, specifically serotonergic dysfunction (Zlotnick et al., 1999). Zlotnick et al. made the observation that altered serotonin functioning has been associated with a range of impulse control disorders including self-mutilation (Simeon et al., 1992), substance abuse (Konopka et al., 1996), and posttraumatic stress disorder (van der Kolk, 1997). Altered serotonin function has also been reported in people who exhibit pain-elicited aggression (Jacobs & Cohen, 1976). The relation between impulsive aggression and pain-elicited aggression may warrant further study. In general, however, it remains difficult to determine with certainty the function of self-injury among people with psychiatric disorders because most study designs preclude statements about whether dissociative states or altered mood are a cause or consequence of repeated self-injury. Furthermore, it is likely that self-injury has multiple causes; therefore, a model is required that accommodates different pathways to SIB. On the other hand, reports suggest consistently that for approximately two thirds of study samples, SIB results in transient relief from aversive affective states.

Developmental Disorders

Self-injury is a relatively prevalent behavior disorder, occurring in as many as 30% of adults with severe intellectual and developmental disabilities in residential treatment facilities (National Institutes of Health [NIH], 1991). In these individuals, self-injury can occur in distinct patterns (Schroeder, Mulick, & Rojahn, 1980; Thompson, Symons, Delaney, & England, 1995). In some cases, times between successive acts of self-injury (intrabout times) vary, and consequently SIB seems intermittent and random. SIB also occurs in repeated bouts consisting of highly repetitive, invariant, rapidly occurring forms such as severe head blows or self-bites lasting for various durations of time.

Self-injury may not be directed indiscriminately on the body's surface (Rojahn, 1994). In study samples of children and adolescents with mental retardation, as much as 80% of self-injury is reported to occur on a very small percentage of the body surface, primarily on the hands, wrists, and head, whereas other equally accessible areas are not typically targeted as SIB sites (Symons & Thompson, 1997). Overall, self-injury varies widely in form and intensity and includes head banging, biting, scratching, pinching, gouging, rubbing, and other forms of self-destructive behavior (NIH, 1991).

An emerging evidence base supports the suggestion that some cases of severe, apparently intractable SIB among individuals with pervasive developmental disorders (e.g., autism) or developmental disabilities (e.g., mental retardation) may be related to the pain or discomfort associated with illness or untreated medical conditions. Intervention studies designed to prioritize the treatment of illness first have shown corresponding reductions in SIB. Ample evidence shows that SIB can be correlated with identified painful and uncomfortable conditions such as otitis media (O'Reilly, 1997), obstructed bowel (Roy & Simon, 1987), and menstrual cycles (Taylor, Rush, Hetrick, & Sandman, 1993). In some cases, the etiology of SIB is directly or indirectly related to an undiagnosed painful medical condition (Bocsh, Van Dyke, Smith, & Poulton, 1997; Gunsett, Mulick, Fenald, & Martin, 1989). Bosch et al. found that of 25 people showing self-injury in their study sample, 28% had previously undiagnosed medical conditions that would be expected to cause pain or discomfort. For six of the seven individuals, the daily rate of self-injury decreased following treatment of their medical conditions. Gunsett et al. suggested that SIB be used as a possible indicator for medical screening before behavioral programming for adults with severe and profound mental retardation. In their study, three people with SIB were referred and screened for medical problems. Each person was found to have a serious medical illness (urinary tract infection, ear infection, and impacted bowel) that when treated resulted in reported reductions in self-injury.

Self-injury is also associated with numerous identified syndromes related to developmental disorders that involve impaired or unknown pain sensitivity. In many syndromes associated with mental retardation, years of anecdotal reports discuss diminished sensitivity to painful stimuli, but very little empirical evidence exists. In people with autism and related pervasive developmental disorders, for example, it has long been recognized that many individuals have reduced sensation or responses to presumably painful stimuli (Ornitz, 1976). This observation is significant considering the estimated prevalence of self-injury is as high as 40%–50% in people with autism (Bartak & Rutter, 1976). People with Prader–Willi syndrome have a remarkable tendency for repetitious, persistent skin picking accompanied by little apparent pain response. Anecdotal reports suggest skin picking is often caused by an initial irritant, but the compulsive nature of Prader–Willi syndrome leads to chronic, extremely damaging SIB (Symons, et al., 1999). Brandt and Rosen (1998) showed that sensory nerve action potential amplitudes for people with Prader–Willi syndrome were on average only 40%–50% of the normal size of matched control individuals. Similar work has not been conducted with other groups of individuals with identified syndromes associated with mental retardation and self-injury (e.g., Lesch–Nyhan syndrome, fragile X syndrome, Cornelia de Lange syndrome, Smith–Magenis syndrome).

Pain can go unrecognized among individuals with severe and profound mental retardation and related developmental disabilities who are nonverbal. Although progress has been made in understanding the neuroanatomical, neurophysiological, and neurochemical mechanisms involved in pain transmission and regulation (Wall & Melzack, 1994), characterizing the subjective pain experience in individuals with severe disabilities presents both scientific and clinical challenges. The International Association for the Study of Pain defines pain as an unpleasant sensory and emotional experience associated with actual or potential tissue damage or described in terms of such damage (Porter, 1993). However, this definition includes both emotional and sensory components, which are difficult to assess in individuals with developmental disabilities who are nonverbal or have language and cognitive impairments. In other clinical populations who are nonverbal, measures have been used to identify pain based on coding of facial expression during minor invasive procedures (Ekman & Friesen, 1978; Grunau & Craig, 1987; 1990; Izard, Huebner, Risser, McGinnes, & Dougherty, 1980). In studies of individuals with developmental disorders, facial coding is beginning to be used in addition to assessments of biobehavioral responses during invasive procedures (LaChapelle et al., 1999; Oberlander et al., in press). From the perspective of studying a more general class of pain behavior, SIB may be considered a component part of a possible pain signal. Individuals may display unique behaviors associated with pain or discomfort that go unrecognized and for which self-injury may function, in part, as a signal or symptom.

Numerous models account for SIB among individuals with developmental disorders. In biologically oriented models, SIB has been hypothesized to be a compulsive behavior disorder (King, 1993), an arousal regulator (Baumeister & Forehand, 1973), or a consequence of altered neurotransmitter systems (Thompson & Schroeder, 1995). In behavioral models, SIB is considered a learned operant regulated by behavioral mechanisms. From a functional perspective, self-injury may be shaped by positive reinforcement such as parental or staff attention (Carr, 1977; Mace, Lalli, Lalli, & Shea, 1993), negative reinforcement such as termination of a demand following SIB (Carr, Newsom, & Binkoff, 1976; Fisher et al., 1993) or automatic reinforcement through the production of sensory stimulation (Lovaas et al., 1987). Iwata et al. (1994) reported an experimental epidemiological account of SIB from 152 single-subject analyses of the operant functions of SIB. Social contingencies accounted for the largest proportion of the sample (64%). Of the reported self-injury cases in the Iwata et al. sample, 25% were maintained by sensory reinforcement contingencies. However, the mechanisms regulating sensory reinforcement and the relation between automatic reinforcement and biological variables are poorly understood.

For individuals exhibiting high rates of tissue-damaging SIB, pain may function as a conditioned reinforcer, or it may indirectly influence operant mechanisms. From this perspective, pain may function as an establishing operation associated with basic biological circumstances that determine the momentary value of reinforcement available to the individual. The aversiveness of demands or the reinforcing effectiveness of attention may be altered by underlying painful conditions. In a model of SIB related to chronic pain, the biological circumstances may have an enduring rather than only a momentary impact on reinforcer effectiveness.

It is not clear, however, whether SIB in developmental disorders can be divided into the painful or not painful subtypes as it is in people with BPD. People who display SIB and experience associated pain may respond differently to treatment than people who display SIB and do not experience pain. Sandman (1988) suggested a model of SIB that assumes a congenital condition of permanently upregulated opioid receptors and high circulating levels of β-endorphin. Such a condition could result in the elevation of pain thresholds (hyperanalgesia) and is consistent with observations of an apparent lack of sensitivity to pain in many individuals exhibiting SIB. Moreover, opiate antagonists might attenuate SIB by making the consequences of the injurious behavior more painful. Alternatively, opioid antagonist treatment of SIB may disrupt a cycle related to a more general class of addictive behavior similar to substance abuse and regulated, in part, by opioid peptide binding. Emotional behavior is also partly regulated by similar neural substrates (Carr, 1984), and evidence shows negative affect correlated with SIB in people with developmental disabilities (Lindauer, DeLeon, & Fisher, 1999).

Treatment based on a model of environmental deprivation and enrichment resulted in reductions in both SIB and negative affect.

SELF-INJURY AS A MODEL OF RELIEF-MEDIATED BEHAVIOR

Severe SIB is associated with various neurological, psychiatric, and developmental disorders and disabilities. The relation between pain and self-injury within and among conditions is poorly understood. One common model for SIB in people with neurological, psychiatric, or developmental disorders is a *relief-from* model—that is, relief from pain of central or peripheral origin, relief from an affective or dissociative state, or relief from unidentified pain associated with an undiagnosed medical condition or illness. In a more general sense, it might be argued that many of the forms of SIB among individuals with developmental disorders are maintained by relief from aversive conditions associated with impoverished environments, impaired adaptive abilities, harsh punitive environments, or otherwise aversive external or internal conditions. Self-injury is attenuated when the aversive state or stimulus is taken away or prevented from occurring, either in the form of pain medication, psychotropic medication, or behavioral therapy or by acquiring a new skill that can prevent or reduce the occurrence of an aversive stimulus.

From a developmental psychopathology perspective, SIB may be viewed as part of a maladaptive process to counter the effect of a recurrent exogenous aversive stimulus or a persistent endogenous aversive state associated with a CNS compromised by prenatal or postnatal trauma. The timing (i.e., prenatal, perinatal, postnatal, early childhood, early adolescence) and duration of exposure to the trauma combined with the nature of the condition (i.e., developmental, neurological, or psychiatric disorder) may determine, in part, the risk status for later SIB. In some people, initial self-injury may possibly persist as a response in the absence of the initial aversive state or stimuli as a function of the duration of exposure to the initial aversive state or stimuli. The subsequent interplay between respondent and operant learning mechanisms in the context of stress and considerable plasticity in the sensory nervous system may also contribute to its early persistence.

Methodological and conceptual ideas from SIB research parallel research conducted from the learned helplessness and the stress-induced analgesia paradigms. In the stress-induced analgesia paradigm, an aversive context consisting of repeated exposure to an inescapable or unavoidable stressful event (i.e., unavoidable stress) results in opioid- and nonopioid-mediated analgesia. Chronic unavoidable stress can lead to the development of pathological change in mechanisms that regulate pain and affect, which consequently impairs adaptive behavior. In learned–helplessness models, individuals in inescapable situations are found to have escape-behavior deficits (i.e., impaired adaptive behavior) and altered nociception (i.e., pain perception), the expression of which is opioid modulated (Teixeira, Pereira, & Hermini, 1997). Moreover, in animal models, the analgesia associated with inescapable shock is reversible with naltrexone, suggesting opioid mediation (Hyson, Aschcraft, Drugan, Grau, & Maier, 1982). Similarly, people in chronic pain, a model of helplessness, have significant clinical problems related to affect regulation and dysfunctional pain responses, which is consistent with a general model related to opioid peptide effects on emotional regulation and altered responsiveness to inescapable aversive stimuli. Although not phenomenologically similar to individuals experiencing chronic pain or helplessness, chronic SIB in people with developmental disabilities and disorders may be regulated by similar neurobiological substrates and mechanisms that have gone awry after years of repeated self-injury in the context of relatively inescapable aversive stimuli (whether that be a recurrent but undiagnosed painful medical condition, an impoverished environment, etc.).

CONCLUSION

SIB and aberrant pain experiences are associated with various neurological, psychiatric, and developmental disorders. The nature of the relationship between self-injury and pain within and among disorders is unclear. In some people, pain may cause self-injury, whereas in others pain may be a consequence. Multiple models based on different assumptions have emerged to account for the emergence and maintenance of self-injury. Few models have incorporated mechanisms specific to pain transmission and regulation, despite the fact that self-injury involves tissue damage and related injury. Although little consensus exists as to whether common mechanisms regulate aberrant pain responses and self-injury, a majority of study outcomes are consistent with a *relief-from* model of self-injury related to pain and aversive states. From this perspective, numerous issues specific to pain and self-injury remain to be systematically examined.

The abnormal sensory input associated with self-injury and the mechanisms of pain transmission and regulation have been relatively unexplored. Given that most self-injury results in some tissue damage to specific areas of the body, it may be useful to conduct research focused on behavioral variables common to pain and self-injury (stimulus location, frequency, intensity, and duration), as well as bioactive peptides that play important roles in pain transmission and regulation. Further investigation of the opioid peptides or other neurochemical substrates regulating stress and pain mechanisms may be warranted to help identify treatment responders (Sandman, Hetrick, Taylor, & Chicz-DeMet, 1997).

Basic neurobiological research could be designed to study the long-term consequences of intractable self-injury on the synaptic organization and function of the neurotransmitters involved in pain transmission and regulation among different study populations. In this approach, regulatory mechanisms rather than diagnostic category would be studied. The obvious ethical issues and practical problems for studies of this sort in humans could be partially overcome by technology (e.g., positron emission tomography, magnetic resonance imaging) or animal models.

Clinical research examining the expression of pain associated with SIB and validating objective nonverbal pain measures is needed. Iwata et al. (1990) developed a scale to quantify tissue damage caused by SIB. Symons, Sutton, & Bodfish (2001) reported that the body sites targeted most frequently for self-injury among a sample of adults with severe mental retardation who were nonverbal were associated with altered skin temperature, whereas infrequent self-injury body sites were unaffected. During opioid antagonist treatment, self-injury directed toward the body site with altered skin temperature was most likely to be reduced. Further controlled studies of this type are needed to examine the value of assessing pain status in different ways for people with mental retardation or related developmental disabilities who are nonverbal and exhibit tissue-damaging SIB. More generally, further controlled studies examining the value of assessing pain and investigating the clinical utility of pain indices in predicting self-injury treatment response may be warranted. The overall goal is to develop a general model of SIB that can be reduced to general principles by recognizing commonalities of underlying processes and accommodating multiple developmental pathways.

16

TEMPORAL AND FORCE DYNAMICS OF SELF-INJURY

KARL M. NEWELL AND JAMES W. BODFISH

In this chapter, we focus on two aspects of self-injurious behavior (SIB) that have received little study to date: (a) the impact forces to the body that arise from self-injurious hits with the arm and hand, and (b) the temporal organization of sequential SIBs during various time scales, such as the distribution of discrete hits within a bout of SIB and the distribution of bouts during hours, days, and months.

TRADITIONAL MEASUREMENT AND ANALYSIS OF SIB: THE FUNCTIONAL PERSPECTIVE

The observable characteristics of SIB are (a) form (e.g., head hitting, skin picking), (b) rate (i.e., frequency of occurrence), (c) severity (i.e., extent of tissue damage), (d) location (e.g., head, torso), (e) intensity (i.e., impact force), and (f) temporal distribution (e.g., interbehavior interval). Of these, intensity and temporal distribution have received virtually no systematic investigation. Clearly, intensity and temporal distribution are crucial features of SIB in terms of the potential for injury and interference with learning or adaptive behavior. It seems that rate, severity, and location of SIB all interact with intensity and temporal distribution to produce the resulting clinical significance (Ducker & Seys, 1997; Iwata et al., 1990; Symons & Thompson, 1997).

Traditionally, SIB has been analyzed and conceptualized in terms of operant functions such as attention seeking, escape from demands (see chapter 5), and sensory reinforcement (Iwata, Dorsey, Slifer, Bauman, &

This work was supported in part by National Institute of Child Health and Human Development Grant HD-21212. The authors thank Robert Sprague, John Challis, Mark Lewis, and Frank Symons for their collaboration on many of the empirical studies reviewed in this chapter.

Richman, 1982; Iwata et al., 1994). A large body of applied behavioral research has demonstrated that for many individuals, self-injury can be effectively treated using procedures based on behavioral function. At the same time, however, many individuals who present what seems to be intractable SIB do not always fit any clear behavioral or social profile of self-injury. Furthermore, few of the treatments have proven efficacy in long-term treatment of self-injury. Perhaps most important is the often unrecognized fact that these traditional procedures for SIB were tested based almost exclusively on only one of the observable characteristics of SIB: rate. This represents a potentially serious limitation of the theoretical and clinical literature on SIB.

Furthermore, like all analyses based on a standard linear model, traditional analyses of SIB have typically ignored within-subject or within-condition variability in SIB rate by assuming that the variabilities are simply "noise" (random fluctuations) in the system. It is interesting to note that in the seminal study on the experimental functional analysis of SIB, the authors make a special point of reporting on the variability of SIB: "Considerable variability was observed within subjects across the different experimental conditions. The within-subject variability was evident regardless of a subject's overall level of responding" (Iwata et al., 1982). Indeed, in six of the nine SIB cases examined in this experimental functional analysis of SIB rate, the standard deviation was equal to or exceeded the mean level of SIB rate (i.e., the coefficient of variability was >1.0).

Since the time of the Iwata et al. (1982) study, extensive empirical effort has been directed toward the functional analysis of SIB rate, and such patterns of high within-subject SIB variability are routinely found but rarely addressed. The assumption that movement variability is a reflection of noise is being questioned in the motor behavior area (Newell & Molenaar, 1998; cf. Newell & Corcos, 1993), and studies have begun to systematically analyze the nature of behavioral variability as an important source of information about the organization and change of behavior in general (see reviews by Newell & Slifkin, 1998; Slifkin & Newell, 1999).

ORGANIZATIONAL CHARACTERISTICS OF SIB: A STRUCTURAL PERSPECTIVE

Self-injury by people with mental retardation seems to be manifest in unique temporal and spatial patterns. Intrabout times, or time between successive SIB instances, can vary considerably; a single instance of self-injury can be separated from a subsequent instance by several minutes or hours or even longer. SIB also occurs in repeated bouts of highly repetitive, rapidly occurring (e.g., more than one per second) head blows or self-bites, with bouts occurring in varying durations (e.g., from 30 seconds up to as long as

15 to 30 minutes without stopping for longer than a few seconds at a time). In some instances, a bout of self-injury is often evoked by environmental provocation (e.g., a parental or staff member request that the individual finds difficult to accomplish) but once initiated may continue for an extended period without further environmental perturbations (Luiselli, Matson, & Singh, 1992; Thompson, Symons, Delaney, & England, 1995). In some people the SIB bout may consist of several self-blows or bites and then cease, or the bout may escalate into rapid and intense repeated SIB continuing for prolonged intervals. The course of SIB often waxes and wanes, thus making SIB seem unpredictable and posing problems for determining the actual effects of treatment.

The characteristics of SIB suggest that its manifestation varies considerably both within and between individuals with the disorder. This variability has most often been overlooked as experimental studies lump together people with low- and high-rate, consistent and variable, and forceful and nonforceful SIB. Therefore, researchers have many unanswered questions about the potential meaning or functional significance of behavioral variability in SIB. Current models of behavior do not offer causal explanations of behavioral variability. In models that assume intrinsic control of behavior, variability in behavior is accepted a priori as also being of (unknown) intrinsic origin. In contrast, other models attribute behavioral variability to extrinsic causes, average out the variability using statistical transformations, and tolerate it as long as the prime experimental objective has been achieved. For a long time, prominent behavioral theorists have pointed out that neither position is fruitful in furthering researchers' understanding of basic behavioral processes (Skinner, 1953; Sidman, 1960) and have advocated experimental analyses of the structural characteristics of behavioral variability (e.g., Bernstein & Ebbesen, 1978).

SIB severity can be operationalized using structural characteristics as the resultant impact force of SIB actions. For example, a head-hitting bout involves a sequence of repetitive arm motions away from and then toward the head. Mechanical laws of motion can be used to derive the impact forces from sequential measures of the position and speed of the hand. Furthermore, sequential displacements of the hand during head hitting can be analyzed for degree of complexity of the hand's motions involved in SIB acts. The motions could be similar across cycles (low complexity) or markedly different across cycles (high complexity). Theoretically, force can vary independently of complexity of the motion that produces the force. Clinically though, to generate pathological extremes of impact force, the body may be constrained into only performing a small array of motions that are capable of producing excess impact force. If this is the case, then highly forceful SIB may be associated with less complex patterns of SIB motion; this is one hypothesis that we are currently investigating.

SIB frequency can be operationalized in terms of the temporal distribution of sequential occurrences of SIB. Within any given time scale, sequential instances of SIB possess a given temporal structure. For example, in a bout of SIB, sequential SIBs can cluster in well-defined periods (e.g., one per second) or can be distributed in a more random (less periodic) manner. The same is true for other time scales such as the distribution of SIB bouts within an hour, day, week, month, or year. Furthermore, the temporal distribution can be analyzed to isolate predominant frequencies or periodicities, and the SIBs of different people may differ in degree of periodicity. Thus, temporal distributions of sequential occurrences of SIB can be analyzed for the degree of inherent structure, patterning, or complexity. Theoretically, SIB frequency can vary independently of the complexity of the temporal distribution of SIB. Clinically, the temporal distribution may need to be constrained into simple, periodic patterns of successive occurrences to generate pathologically high frequencies of SIB. If this is the case, then high-frequency SIB may tend to be associated with less complex patterns of SIB temporal distribution. In the only studies of temporal dynamics to date, Lewis and colleagues have demonstrated that SIB is manifest most often in highly periodic patterns when examined during several time scales, including minutes (Bodfish, Symons, & Lewis, 1999), hours (Lewis, MacLean, Johnson, & Baumeister, 1981), and days (Lewis, Silva, & Silva-Gray, 1995).

In a majority of people, SIB seems to be chronic, with onset during childhood and a typical waxing and waning course through adolescence and adulthood. To date, there has been very little direct measurement of the chronicity of SIB and very little analysis of factors related to increased chronicity. In a structural perspective, chronicity may be related to the maintenance of certain structural characteristics over time such as increased impact force or increased periodicity. In a dynamic perspective, extremes of force or periodicity of SIB may be related to specific patterns of SIB organization that are inherently more resistant to change and therefore more likely to be persistent over time. Less complex patterns of SIB organization may be less adaptable in general and thus more prone to remain in the repertoire as a chronic disorder. Thus, the structural characteristics of SIB appear to provide a rich source of information that can complement traditional analyses of SIB based on form and function (Schroeder, Mulick, & Rojahn, 1980).

A DYNAMICAL DISEASE MODEL OF SIB

At the heart of the basic understanding of abnormal behavior lies an intriguing paradox: Although referred to as *disorders*, pathological conditions most often seem to involve strikingly "ordered," periodic, and predictable dynamics (Goldberger, 1997). Children with autism lose behavior variability and become locked in to highly repetitive, ordered actions; people with schizophrenia lose cognitive flexibility and instead manifest stereotypy of thought, speech, and posture; and people with depression or bipolar illness experience cyclic variations in extreme mood states (Gottschalk, Bauer, & Whybrow, 1995). Similar changes in dynamics occur in a range of disease states. People with Parkinson's disease lose variability of motor behavior and instead exhibit virtually indistinguishable tremors; leukemia is often indexed by abnormal cyclic oscillations of neutrophil counts (Gatti et al., 1973); various cardiac disorders are marked by a loss of structural complexity of the heart rate signal (Poon & Merrill, 1997); and sleep disorders (Ehlers et al., 1991) and epilepsy (Casdagli et al., 1997) are characterized by a loss of complexity in electroencephalogram (EEG) signals. In this context, SIB fits nicely into the concept of dynamical diseases (Glass & Mackey, 1988).

As a general principle, disease states are often marked by less complex dynamics than healthy ones (Bassingthwaighte, Liebovitch, & West, 1994; Glass & Mackey, 1988; Goldberger, 1997). In our preliminary work on SIB dynamics, we found that both the organizational dynamics of SIB motions and the temporal dynamics of SIB times series are typically highly structured, indicating that, like other diseases or disorders, SIB is often marked by less complex dynamics. When biological systems lose structural complexity, their information content is degraded, and they are less able to cope with the exigencies of a constantly and unpredictably changing environment. These kinds of findings have been taken as support for dynamical disease models in clinical science (Glass & Mackey, 1988; Goldberger, 1997) and point to the value of examining the structural characteristics of clinical conditions within the framework of nonlinear dynamics. This theoretical perspective has moved beyond conceptualization in some areas. The dynamical model has been used to develop improved predictive modeling algorithms to monitor the clinical course of the disorder (Goldberger et al., 1984; Poon & Merrill, 1997). In addition, dynamical analyses have been used to explore pathophysiological mechanisms (King, Barchus, & Huberman, 1984) and novel forms of treatment (Garfinkel et al., 1992).

Research Focus

A rigorous dynamical characterization of SIB is possible, as SIB involves discrete events whose occurrences in time or space can be precisely determined. Such an analysis would involve determinations of both the force and temporal characteristic of SIB.

A temporal dynamics analysis of SIB would involve coding the occurrence of SIB in real time to create a time series of interbehavior intervals. This would be accomplished over both short-term time scales (e.g., occurrence within a single bout, or episodes within an observation session) and long-term time scales (e.g., episodes across days, weeks, or months) to permit a complete characterization of the temporal evolutionary properties of SIB. Characterization of key temporal properties is achieved using standard linear statistical procedures (e.g., frequency distribution; autocorrelation; spectral analysis; ARIMA [autoregressive, integrated, moving-average]) and nonlinear statistical procedures (e.g., approximate entropy, dimensionality, first return maps; Hilborn 1994). Such an approach is now common in the physical sciences and is becoming increasingly used in the biomedical sciences (Glass & Mackey, 1988; Goldberger, 1997). Importantly, characteristics of a few behavioral disorders, such as tics in Tourette's syndrome (Peterson & Leckman, 1998) and mood in bipolar disorder (Gottschalk et al., 1995), have been examined using these types of dynamical analysis procedures.

A force dynamics analysis of SIB relies on classical mechanics and encompasses the measurement of the kinematic and kinetic properties of SIB (Winter, 1979; Zatsiorsky, 1997). *Kinematics* describes the motions of objects (such as the torso and limbs) in the dimensions of space and time and the various derivatives such as velocity and acceleration. Kinetics describes local causes of objects' motions by characterizing the force produced over time by a given object's mass. The kinetics and kinematics of movement have been used to study a wide range of everyday human actions and are increasingly being used to study stereotypies (Sprague & Newell, 1996). The measurement of movement dynamics can be examined over short- and long-term time scales to investigate questions about the persistent and transitory nature of the current state and change of impact forces of SIB over time.

During the past decade, our research program has focused on the analysis of the dynamics of aberrant repetitive movements and behaviors associated with mental retardation (Newell 1996a, 1996b; Newell, van Emmerik, & Sprague, 1993). This work has included the development of practical methods for the quantification of key dynamic aspects of repetitive actions such as frequency and amplitude relations, velocity and spatial displacement, temporal organization, and sequential dependency. Our empirical approach has been to (a) develop practical methods for objective measurement of structural characteristics using routine sources of behavioral data (e.g., videotape samples, direct observations recorded in real time), (b) identify the range of individual differences in the structural characteristics of the behavior or movement in question, (c) develop a comprehensive dynamical analysis of the behavior in question and identify common dynamic patterns associated with aberrant behavior or movement, and (d) explore the adaptability of the intrinsic dynamic in tests of responding over time in goal-oriented tasks or in response to treatment. We have applied these methods and analyses to the examination of natural stereotyped actions (Newell, Incledon, Bodfish, & Sprague, in press), drug-induced movements such as tardive dyskinesia (Newell, Gao, & Sprague, 1995; van Emmerik, Sprague,

& Newell, 1993), and akathisia (Bodfish, Newell, Sprague, Harper, & Lewis, 1997) and most recently have initiated this approach with SIBs (Newell, Sprague, Pain, Deutsch, & Meinhold, 1999).

A consistent finding of our work in people with various aberrant behaviors and movements, is that abnormal repetitive actions are associated with a pattern of periodic, low-dimensional dynamic organization. This pattern can be conceptualized as a constraint on the number of degrees of freedom that are available to organize action (Newell, 1996a, 1996b). The functional consequence is that conditions associated with repetitive and stereotyped repertoires are less adaptable to changing environmental demands because of the fewer active degrees of freedom that are regulated in the organization of action. Furthermore, the clinical implication is that valid treatments are those that can alter the underlying dynamic in such a way as to remove constraints on action and thereby enhance adaptability. An important methodological consequence is that studies relying on measures that do not provide insight into the dynamic mechanisms of behavioral organization are unlikely to identify these forms of valid treatments.

Because there has been little systematic study of SIB dynamics, our initial efforts have involved preliminary studies of observational methodology and measurement to examine the feasibility, reliability, and validity of various dynamic measures of the force and temporal distribution of SIB. The remainder of this chapter outlines our progress to date in evaluating the kinematic and kinetic (dynamic) properties of SIB hitting motions that impact the body.

Characterizing SIB Force and Temporal Dynamics

Clearly, the repeated blows to the body, and head in particular, can create injuries to the skin tissue and musculature, the skeletal system (bone), and the chemical-neural integrity of the brain. In general, many aspects of the central and peripheral nervous systems may be compromised by prolonged SIB. Most of the focus of SIB injuries has naturally been on the skin tissue and musculature. However, people with SIB also have the potential for developing health problems that are linked to concussion.

The acceleration the head experiences when being struck is reduced by the visco-elastic properties of the soft tissue and somewhat by the hair. Strikes to a less protected area, such as the chin, do not have their effects mediated to any functional degree. If the neck musculature is not suitably active during a SIB impact, then significant head motion is not induced. During such an impact, the skull starts to move and the brain, because of its inertia, does not move immediately. Therefore, because the skull moves at a different speed than the brain, it can cause distention of the veins between the brain and the superior sagittal sinus. Research has shown that oblique blows to the head induce greater rotation with the induced angular acceleration being proportional to the force applied and the distance from the impact point to the axis of the rotation. The axis of rotation depends on the type of blow but is the same regardless of the headgear used. The addition of headgear can reduce the force the head experiences, but oblique blows increase the moment (angular force) and therefore produce more angular acceleration. High angular accelerations of the head have been reported to be major causes of brain damage.

Ommaya et al. (1993) have reported that 50% of the potential for brain injury is directly proportional to the amount of rotation the impact causes, yet inversely proportional to the amount of translation. No guidelines exist for tolerable levels of head angular accelerations, but Ommaya et al. (1967) and Lowenhielm (1975) have reported levels at which concussion occurs. No research has been done on the nature and type of impact forces in the hitting motions of SIB.

We have developed a series of techniques for quantifying the force dynamics of SIB from routinely collected clinical videotapes (Newell, Challis, Boros, & Bodfish, 2000; Newell et al., 1999). From available videotapes, we selected trials for analysis largely on the basis of the length of the repetitive SIB trial sequence produced (i.e., the number of sequential hits that occurred). An additional criterion was to provide representative data for both single and double arm SIB motions.

The movements recorded on videotapes were manually digitized using a Peak 5 digitizing system, and standard inverse dynamic analysis techniques were applied (Winter, 1979; Zatoriorsky, 1997). Numerous body landmarks were used to define body segments and locations using standard anthropometric measures (Snyder, Schneider, Owings, Reynolds, Golomb, & Schork, 1977). The locations digitized were the middle finger tip, wrist (ulnar process), elbow (center of the joint), shoulder (external limit of the shoulder), sternum (middle of), midpoint between middle of the top of top lip and the bottom of the nose (septum), and eye (lateral corner of the left eye). Calibration was obtained from the known anatomical geometry and points of the face. These digitized points provided the basis for a kinematic analysis of the limb trajectories and a kinetic analysis of the forces of motion, particularly the impact forces of the hand on the head. The trajectories and impact forces were analyzed with respect to one and two hand motions.

The results from our original case study (Newell et al., 1999) and further additional tests (Newell et al., 2000) have revealed a high degree of cycle-to-cycle consistency in the qualitative dynamics of the limb motions, with one-hand motions being faster than two-hands motions (in-phase and antiphase). We have also recorded very low variability in the limb trajectory motions in some of the low-impact force subjects, as shown in the relative motion plots of Figures 16.1 and 16.2. Indeed, the relative variability of these trajectories as indexed by coefficient of variation measures is very low, apparently lower than much of the other movement variability work

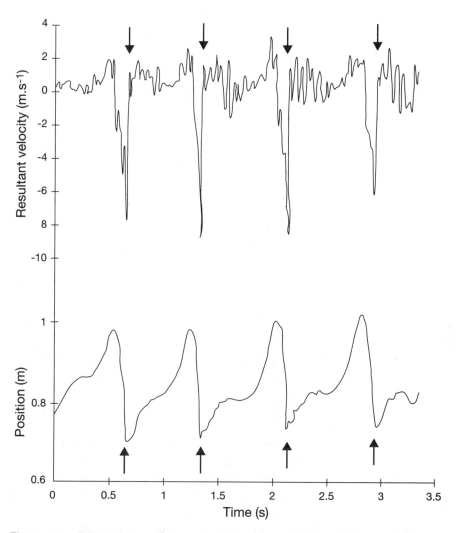

Figure 16.1. Bottom time series: A plot of the motion of the wrist in the X position (m) in the horizontal plane over time (seconds) for a sample segment of SIB; sample is of a girl (wearing a helmet) displaying one-hand SIB. The arrows show the point of initial hand–head contact for each blow in the SIB sequence. *Top time series:* The resultant velocity (m.s^{-1}) of the horizontal and vertical planes over time (seconds) for the same SIB segment as shown in the position–time time series. The arrows show the point of initial hand–head contact for each blow in the SIB sequence. (*Note:* From "Dynamics of Self-Injurious Behavior," by Newell et al., 1999, *American Journal on Mental Retardation,* 104, pp. 11–21. Adapted with permission.)

reported (Newell & Corcos, 1993). However, to date, we have analyzed too few people with SIB to state with confidence the generality of these findings for the force structure of SIB and its associated dynamics. The SIB trajectory data are also consistent with the complexity and degrees of freedom perspective outlined previously, but they do not provide a definitive test of the concept.

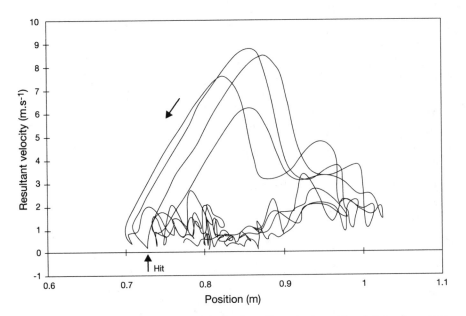

Figure 16.2. A plot of the resultant velocity (m.s⁻¹) against position (m) for the same trial segment as shown in Figure 16.1. The arrow shows the direction in time of the position-resultant velocity relationship. (*Note:* From "Dynamics of Self-Injurious Behavior," by Newell et al., 1999, *American Journal on Mental Retardation*, 104, pp. 11–21. Adapted with permission.)

Analysis of the rhythmical aspects of the repetitive limb motions and impact forces has also shown that numerous people have temporal relations between whether the SIB involves only single-limb (arm) hitting or two-limbs (right and left arms) hitting, in which the arms are making head contact either in phase or in an alternating sequence. The alternating pattern with two limbs tends to have a movement trajectory that has twice the frequency of the two-limb, in-phase impact motions. Similarly, single-limb SIB tends to have much higher (almost twice as high) impact force as the dual-limb SIB sequences. These temporal and force relationships to the sequential properties of SIB are intriguing and deserve a more thorough analysis than we have conducted to date. If these kinds of limb trajectory relations are shown to exist with some degree of generality, they will invite the suggestion that the impact forces are organized on the basis of either energy of output or energy of impact force.

The highest resultant impact forces, which were recorded in the case study of a young girl (Newell et al., 1999), were a single-limb SIB force of 95 N and a double-limb SIB force of 73.4 N. The ballistic-like motion and low between-blow variability of the arm trajectory before contact reveals a highly consistent self-injurious action within a given condition.

The impact forces of SIB as a percentage of body weight are near the low end of forces generated in boxing blows and karate hits based on available normative data for these actions. These preliminary direct estimates of the impact forces of SIB highlight the feasibility of our proposed method for quantifying SIB force from videotape observations in typical clinical settings. One important finding of this study was that SIB in the higher range of impact force was associated with more highly repetitive patterns of motion. This provides preliminary support for our hypothesis that SIB severity is related to patterns of SIB motion that are relatively low in dimensionality or complexity. To our knowledge, this is the first study to directly quantify the force dynamics of SIB.

As one might expect, the size of the individual plays an important role in determining the impact forces, but our analyses to date suggest that anthropometric factors are not the primary source of the SIB variance. Anthropometry seems to change the potential range of the impact forces, so individuals who have greater height and weight can have greater impact forces, but this is not necessarily always the case. Clearly, researchers need to pursue their approach using a greater number and anthropometric range of individuals to provide more grounded and refined statements.

In a follow-up analysis of various SIB types in a sample of eight adults and children with severe and profound mental retardation (Newell et al., 2000), we found a considerable between-subject variability in SIB impact force. The data are consistent with our initial finding that high impact force is related to low dimensionality of SIB motion in this limited sample. The highest impact force recorded in these participants was 1,560 N, which is considerably higher than that reported in our case study (Newell et al., 1999) outlined previously. The person that produced this impact force was not the heaviest participant in the study.

It is also important to note that in our preliminary analyses of SIB force described previously, we examined data from various ongoing protective and behavioral treatments for SIB. For example, in some instances the participants wore protective helmets as part of their management program. We were able to observe a subset of SIB actions in some of these people during prescribed periods when the helmet was removed per the program. In all video-tape segments observed of the young female patient to date (Newell et al., 1999), the highest resultant impact forces measured in each condition were 70.8 N in the no-helmet condition and 95.0 N in the helmet condition (means for the conditions were as follows: no helmet = 30.1 N, helmet = 40.4 N). Further analyses of the resultant head motion after SIB impact revealed that the helmet absorbed this increased impact force, as evidenced by less resultant motion of the head after SIB impact during the helmet-on observations. In some cases, we attempted to estimate SIB force during conditions in which the person was observed while being blocked by staff members. In these situations, we were able to record SIB attempts and measure the force of each attempt. In other situations, we had quantified ongoing staff intervention (i.e., blocking and redirecting) during the periods in which we quantified SIB force. In these cases, we saw little variation in SIB force despite the fact that the behavioral interventions were influencing the rate of SIB being produced.

CONCLUSION

It seems that a dynamical perspective on SIB may offer clinically and theoretically useful information on key features of SIB that have remained largely unexplored to date. The kinematic and kinetic techniques outlined in this chapter provide direct measurement of the impact forces of SIB and the associated limb trajectory motions. These measurements can be derived from routinely used sources of SIB data, such as videotape recordings, that can be obtained in a manner that does not interfere with the participant's behavior. This approach seems ideal for estimates of the intensity or severity of SIB. The time series and nonlinear dynamics techniques outlined in this chapter provide direct measurement of the degree of temporal organization or pattern of SIB. These measurements can be derived from routine sources of SIB data such as direct observation recordings. These measurements may offer useful insights into the reason that SIB is relatively more persistent and chronic in some cases.

The approaches outlined in this chapter could be very useful for assessing the nature of the change in SIB behavior as a function of the manipulation of other factors such as medication or behavioral treatment. Indeed, a direct estimate of impact force or temporal pattern would seem essential for differentiating the many hypotheses now available about SIB (Symons & Thompson, 1997). For example, the determination of the impact force gives a direct measure of intensity and the basis for determining the relative risk associated with no treatment and extinction-based treatment approaches. In addition, SIB seems to often manifest in a variable, waxing and waning pattern over time. Thus, time series analyses of temporal structure seem critical for determining the complete effects of treatment and whether treatment effects are maintained for clinically relevant time scales.

Several novel findings have emerged from our preliminary work on SIB dynamics. First, the temporal organization of SIB seems to often consist of a highly periodic (apparently low-dimensional) pattern that may be scale independent (i.e., invariant or nearly invariant during different time scales). This pattern is similar to the pattern of temporal organization that has been found for motor and vocal tics in people with Tourette's syndrome (Peterson & Leckman, 1998), an involuntary neurological disorder that has a frequent co-occurrence of self-injury (Trimble 1989). This finding presents the possibility that in some people, self-injury may represent a type of involuntary or partially voluntary behavior. Although purely a hypothesis at this point, such a model can be tested and may have novel treatment as well as theoretical implications.

Second, kinematic analysis of SIB has revealed that the motions involved with SIB can be highly rhythmical, repetitive, and invariant. This is intriguing in light of the fact that SIB is frequently coexpressed with stereotyped movements in people with mental retardation and autism (Bodfish et al., 1995; Lewis & Bodfish, 1998). Kinematic analysis of stereotyped behaviors has revealed a similarly rhythmic and repetitive pattern of movement organization (Newell, Bodfish, & Sprague, 1999), a finding that also indicates that SIB and stereotypy may share similar motor control features and pathophysiological mechanisms.

Finally, kinematic analyses of SIB motions revealed that the SIB of some people can involve dangerously high-impact forces and points of impact that produce oblique motions of the head and neck. This scenario carries great risk for shearing-type brain and neck injuries. Thus, for some people, SIB may present a degree of injury that is not discernable from either direct behavioral observation or resultant skin damage. Furthermore, because SIB often begins in infancy (Symons, Sperry, & Bodfish, in press), SIB of this intensity may have the potential to profoundly and deleteriously alter CNS development. These findings from our movement dynamic approach serve to further underscore the tremendous health and welfare issues that are involved in the care and treatment of people who display SIB.

IV

LESCH–NYHAN SYNDROME AS A MODEL GENETIC DISORDER OF SELF-INJURIOUS BEHAVIOR

As previously mentioned, Lesch–Nyhan syndrome has been a window for the study of self-injurious behavior (SIB) and its genetics and neurobiology since the discovery of the syndrome in 1964. It is a sex-linked, single-gene disorder of purine metabolism, in which all of the people with the syndrome exhibited severe self-biting. In fact, it was Nyhan who coined the term *behavioral phenotype* in a paper in 1972. In chapter 17, William L. Nyhan gives the syndrome's clinical features, its developmental course, and a summary of the many pharmacological and behavioral treatments that have been tried. Researchers have shown considerable interest in gene therapy for Lesch–Nyhan syndrome.

James C. Harris, Dean F. Wong, Hyder A. Jinnah, D. Schretlen, and P. Barker summarize several informative neuroimaging studies with Lesch–Nyhan cases in chapter 18. They have shown that Lesch–Nyhan syndrome has spectrum of clinical presentations, in which more moderate cases of hypoxanthine phosphoribosyltransferase (HPRT) deficiency may show the motor disorders but not self-biting. The striatum has a dopamine-related neurological deficit, but it may not be a sufficient explanation of SIB. Other neurotransmitters may also need to be examined.

In 1981 an important postmortem study of three Lesch–Nyhan cases by Lloyd et al. (1981) revealed a 60% to 90% depletion of dopamine and elevation of serotonin in striatal neurons. This finding led George R. Breese, an animal neuropharmcologist, to propose a rat model of neonatal 6-hydroxydopamine (6-OHDA) lesions as a second explanation of self-biting in those with Lesch–Nyhan syndrome (see chapter 19). He found that rats that were given 6-OHDA lesions in the corpus striatum at ages 5 to 15 days and then allowed to recover and mature tend to bite themselves severely when given the dopamine agonist L-dihydroxyphenylalanine (L-dopa). Through an extensive research program of inducing self-biting with dopamine agonists and blocking it with dopamine antagonists, he has implicated D_1 dopamine receptors as a critical link in the development of SIB in neonatally depleted rats with 6-OHDA lesions. This rat model has many far-reaching implications for the behavioral and pharmacological treatment and prevention of SIB.

Another new mouse model of Lesch–Nyhan is revealed by Suhail Kasim, Zubair Khan, and H. A. Jinnah in chapter 20. The model is based on calcium channel activation with a new drug, BayK8644, thus providings a new tool for the investigation of SIB neurobiology. The authors suggest that calcium channel antagonists may be helpful as therapeutic agents for SIB.

In chapter 21, Richard E. Tessel, Pippa S. Loupe, and Stephen R. Schroeder discuss the possibility of training-induced recovery from brain damage related to SIB. Using the Breese animal lesion model, they have been able to show that operant training replaces lost dopamine with endogenous dopamine by stimulating residual brain dopaminergic neurons in the striatum—an exciting new direction that merits further exploration.

17

LESSONS FROM
LESCH–NYHAN SYNDROME

WILLIAM L. NYHAN

Lesch–Nyhan syndrome (Lesch & Nyhan, 1964) is a unique model for the understanding of self-injurious behavior (SIB) in humans. The phenotype is highly stereotyped, and the behavioral phenotype is an integral feature. Numerous patients with Lesch–Nyhan syndrome have been recognized in a wide variety of ethnic groups throughout the world. Extensive follow-up information has now been obtained, and patients are available for observation and study in age groups ranging from infancy to young adulthood. Our oldest patients are currently in their 30s. The gene has been cloned (Jolly et al., 1982, 1983), and a substantial number of mutations has been defined (Sege-Peterson, Nyhan, & Page, 1992). The enzymatic defect has been elucidated (Seegmiller, Rosenbloom, & Kelley, 1967), and its metabolic ramifications have been extensively studied (Nyhan & Ozand, 1998). All of these accomplishments have raised the hope that the key to how such distinct biochemical abnormalities lead to such dramatic behavioral patterns will one day be found, and its elucidation will provide further insights into the chemical and genetic basis of behavior.

The inborn errors of purine metabolism have been under study since the recognition of gout by Hippocrates. Numerous disorders of purine metabolism have now been characterized on a molecular level. Exciting new relationships have been uncovered between this area of metabolism and the development of immune function in adenosine deaminase deficiency and purine nucleoside phosphorilase deficiency. The most thoroughly studied of the disorders of purine metabolism is the Lesch–Nyhan syndrome, and its recognition in 1964 ushered in the modern era of the inborn errors of purine metabolism. The gene responsible for this condition is located on the X chromosome, and the phenotype is fully a recessive X-linked characteristic. The molecular expression of the abnormal gene is in the defective activity of the enzyme hypoxanthine phosphoribosyltransferase (HPRT); E.C.2.4.2.8

(Seegmiller, Rosenbloom, & Kelley, 1967; Sweetman & Nyhan, 1972). The biological effects of this disorder are far reaching.

CLINICAL FEATURES

The cardinal clinical characteristics of Lesch–Nyhan syndrome are mental retardation, spastic cerebral palsy, choreoathetosis, and SIB (Nyhan, 1972, 1976, 1994). The patients also have hyperuricemia; crystalluria, hematuria, or renal tract stone disease may be evident even during early infancy.

Patients usually develop normally for the first 6 to 8 months of life. The onset of cerebral manifestations begins with athetosis. Infants who have been sitting and holding their heads up begin to lose these abilities. Initially, they may be hypotonic or hypertonic, but deep tendon reflexes are brisk. Later, they are all markedly hypertonic. In the established patient, the defect in motor development is of such severity that the patient can neither stand nor sit unassisted. None of our patients with the Lesch–Nyhan syndrome has walked. Most of the patients have been classified as having mental retardation, but adequate measurement is difficult because of their behavior as well as their motor defect. Most have not been successfully toilet trained. On the other hand, most speak, and it is generally agreed that cognitive behavior is superior to apparent mental development. A few of our patients have graduated from high school.

Involuntary movements of both choreic and athetoid types are prominent, and dystonic features are seen as well. Sudden opisthotonic or extensor spasms of the trunk are characteristic, and they may be incorporated into the behavior. Some aggression is directed toward other people. Scissoring of the lower extremities is a regular finding, and muscle tone and deep tendon reflexes increase. The Babinski signs are characteristically present, but reflexes of any sort are difficult to elicit in a writhing, athetoid patient. Many patients have ankle clonus.

The speech of patients with Lesch–Nyhan syndrome is characterized by athetoid dysarthria. Athetoid dysphagia is another problem. The patients have so much difficulty swallowing that they are difficult to feed, and they all vomit frequently. In a busy, crowded institution for people with mental retardation, inanition may be a major finding. In addition, patients aspirate frequently, and pneumonia develops but is not common.

Most of the patients are markedly underweight, and many are quite short. The bone age may be retarded. Convulsions are not a regular feature of the syndrome but have been observed in some patients.

Aggressive, self-mutilating behavior may be the most striking aspect of the syndrome (Christie et al., 1982; Nyhan, 1976; Nyhan & Ozand, 1998). It is an absolutely uniform feature of the classic syndrome. Self-mutilation may begin as early as the eruption of the teeth. It usually begins then or at least shortly thereafter. Most patients destructively bite both their lips and fingers. Virtually all the patients we have seen have bitten their lips destructively unless their primary teeth have been removed early, which is sometimes the case for a second or third affected patient in a kindred. In most patients the hallmark of the syndrome is loss of tissue about the lips. Partial amputations of the fingers are common, and partial amputations of the tongue have been observed. Actually, the extent of mutilation is limited only by the extent of the motor defect and the intervention of caregivers. Head banging, ear banging, and catching of the hands in wheelchair spokes or car doors have all been seen.

Sensation is intact in children with the Lesch–Nyhan syndrome. They scream in pain when they bite themselves, and it is clear that they really do not want to do what they are doing. They are only really happy when securely protected from themselves. Many of these children scream all night until their parents or guardians are taught how to restrain them securely in bed. As they grow older, these children learn to call for help. The cry of a young child with the syndrome is trying to send the same message.

Mutilation in this syndrome is a compulsive behavior. Patients also direct their aggressions against others. Effectiveness of outward aggression is limited by the extent of their motor deficiency. They bite others, and as they learn speech they become verbally aggressive, often using foul language. As mentioned, many of these patients vomit, and the act of regurgitation seems to be incorporated into the behavior in an antisocial fashion. It can interfere with activities and lead to esophagitis and life-threatening hemorrhaging.

The behavior of the patients is a striking and provocative element of the syndrome. Lesch–Nyhan syndrome is the first instance in which a stereotyped pattern of human behavior has been associated with a distinct biochemical abnormality. Aside from the behavior associated with the syndrome, the patients are outgoing, friendly, loving children, and many live at home. However, the behavior is so hard to live with for many parents that institutional life is the answer. The patients' behavior can lead to aggression against them in institutions. We have seen at least two patient victims who developed femoral fractures in institutions. In addition, depression is common among adults with the syndrome.

Numerous clinical manifestations of the Lesch–Nyhan syndrome are directly related to the accumulation of uric acid in body fluids. Patients with the syndrome have hyperuricemia from the neonatal period. They are subject to all of the clinical manifestations of gout. Acute attacks of arthritis develop only after numerous years of hyperuricemia. Three of our older patients have had acute arthritis. An affected cousin of one patient died at 21 years and was said to have had repeated episodes of arthritis in his last year.

Hematuria and crystalluria are common. During infancy, caregivers may see masses of orange crystalline material in the diapers and numerous patients have had urinary tract stones (Howard & Walzak, 1968; Nyhan,

Oliver & Lesch, 1965). Infantile colic and recurrent abdominal pains in older children may be a consequence of the presence of large amounts of insoluble material in the urine. Urinary tract infections have been common only in those with stones. Many patients develop a renal concentration defect causing them to have polyuria and polydipsia. These patients may have great difficulty satisfying their thirst in a large, busy institution; on the other hand, the dilute urine may alleviate crystalluria and obviate calculi. Urate nephropathy may lead to renal failure, which has been the most common cause of early death.

Tophaceous deposits may develop in patients who are untreated for many years. We have seen tophi in four patients. One patient had a tophus on his ear that was as large as a golf ball. Another had tophi that broke down and drained solid white urate. A third had classic periarticular deposits and tophaceous gout. The fourth had very small deposits in his ear, which had the classic appearance on biopsy.

BIOCHEMICAL FEATURES

In most patients the first evidence of metabolic abnormality is the elevated concentration of uric acid in the blood, which is usually in the range of 10 to 12 mg/dl (Christie et al. 1982), while the normal values are 2 to 5.5 mg/dl. The excretion of uric acid in the urine is always elevated. Children with Lesch–Nyhan syndrome excrete three to four times as much uric acid as do control children, often more than 600 mg/day. Adult patients with gout who have excreted this much urate have been classified as hyperexcretors. Relative to their body weight, patients with the Lesch–Nyhan syndrome excrete from 40 to 60 mg/kg. Expressed in terms of the excretion of creatinine, these patients usually excrete 3 to 4 mg of uric acid per milligram of creatinine, whereas control individuals excrete less than 1 mg.

The metabolism of purines has been studied by determining the rate at which uric acid is synthesized from glycine. This study has been done by administering isotopically labeled glycine. In our original studies the tracer glycine was labeled with ^{14}C (Lesch & Nyhan, 1964; Nyhan et al., 1967). More recently, we have explored the utility of the nonradioactive isotope of carbon—^{13}C for these studies (Sweetman et al., 1973). Uric acid was isolated from the urine and purified and its isotope content determined. In adults with overproduction gout, the cumulative percent of the isotope of administered glycine that has been converted to uric acid was about twice that of controls. In children with the Lesch–Nyhan syndrome, about 2% of the glycine administered has regularly been recovered in uric acid, representing about 20 times the control value (Nyhan, 1968). These are the highest rates of overproduction of purine ever reported.

In the presence of overproduction of purine of this magnitude, compounds other than uric acid accumulate. The patients excrete xanthine in about the quantities found in normal urine. The amounts of hypoxanthine are, however, markedly increased (Balis et al., 1967; Sweetman & Nyhan, 1967). In most individuals the molar ratio of hypoxanthine to xanthine is less than one. In the patients with Lesch–Nyhan syndrome, the ratio is considerably greater than one and may be as high as eight. When the patient is treated with allopurinol, which inhibits xanthine oxidase, urate excretion decreases, and the other oxypurines become the major products of the overproduction. The hypoxanthine:xanthine ratio decreases with small doses of allopurinol, but as the degree of the block increases, more and more purine ends up as hypoxanthine. In controls treated with allopurinol, most of the oxypurine excreted is xanthine. These observations indicate that in control individuals, most urinary urate is formed from xanthine that does not come from hypoxanthine. This is consistent with the fact that patients with a congenital absence of xanthine oxidase have xanthinuria. On the other hand, in people with the Lesch–Nyhan syndrome most of the purine usually seen as urinary urate was previously hypoxanthine.

Uric acid is not formed in the brain. The other oxypurines are the end products of purine metabolism in the central nervous system (CNS). In the cerebrospinal fluid (Sweetman, 1968), xanthine concentrations are identical to those of controls. The concentrations of hypoxanthine in patients with the Lesch–Nyhan syndrome are 4 times greater than in controls. Treatment with allopurinol increases even further the concentration of hypoxanthine in the cerebrospinal fluid of these patients.

THE ENZYME DEFECT

The primary site for the expression of the abnormal gene in the Lesch–Nyhan syndrome is the enzyme HPRT (see Figure 17.1). This enzyme converts the purine bases, hypoxanthine and guanine, to their respective nucleotides, inosinic and guanylic acids (IMP and GMP). The purine analogs, 6-mercaptopurine, 6-thioguanine, and 8-azaguanine, require the presence of this enzyme and conversion to their respective nucleotides before they can become active chemotherapeutic or cytotoxic agents.

Deficiency in the activity of HPRT in people with Lesch–Nyhan syndrome was first reported by Seegmiller, Rosenbloom, and Kelley (1967). This important observation has been amply confirmed by numerous investigators (Berman et al., 1968; Sweetman & Nyhan, 1972). The enzyme is normally present in all tissues of the body, but the greatest activity is found in the basal ganglia and in testes (Rosenbloom et al., 1967); activity is deficient in every tissue. Subcellular fractionation of brain indicated appreciable activity in synaptosomes (Gutenson & Guroff, 1972).

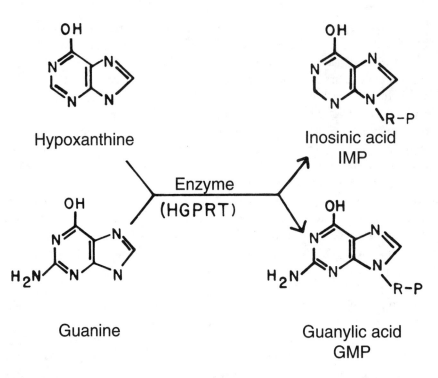

Hypoxanthine

Inosinic acid
IMP

Enzyme
(HGPRT)

Guanine

Guanylic acid
GMP

Figure 17.1. The HPRT enzyme catalyzes the conversion of hypoxanthine and guanine to nucleotides. This is the site of the defect in the Lesch–Nyhan syndrome.

HPRT is most conveniently measured in the erythrocyte. Quantitative assay of the enzyme in the erythrocyte has regularly revealed no activity in patients with the syndrome. The more precisely quantitative the determination, the more it is clear that the values obtained in patients cannot be distinguished from zero.

PATHOGENESIS

Evidence that neurotransmitter balance is involved in the genesis of the neurological or behavioral features of the disease was suggested by data on serotonin metabolites and treatment with a serotonin precursor. Even more evidence has pointed to the involvement of the dopaminergic system (Nyhan, 2000). The most compelling evidence is from the study of the brains of three patients with Lesch–Nyhan syndrome who had died (Lloyd et al., 1981). Despite the tiny series, statistically significant differences from control were found in each measure of dopaminergic function, which were depressed in the caudate putamen and nucleus accumbens. Furthermore, Silverstein et al. (1985) reported low levels of homovanillic acid in the cerebrospinal fluid of patients in a careful study that controlled for the normal age-related changes in concentration.

Imaging of the basal ganglia with ligands specific for various patterns in the basal ganglia has revealed evidence of deficiency in the dopamine transporter (Wong et al., 1996). These observations raise hope that pharmacological interventions will be devised that interrupt or reverse the abnormalities in neurotransmitter function.

GENETICS

Lesch–Nyhan syndrome is transmitted by a structural gene on the long arm of the X chromosome at position Xq26. The pattern of inheritance is that of a fully penetrant, completely recessive, X-linked disease (Nyhan et al., 1967). The syndrome is found almost exclusively in males. However, four affected females have been reported (DeGregorio et al., 2000; Ogasawara et al., 1991). The complementary deoxyribonucleic acid (cDNA) in nine exons (Jolly et al., 1982) matches the 218-amino-acid sequence that had previously been determined (Wilson et al., 1982). The transcriptional promoter region contains many copies of the sequence GGGCGG, but it lacks CAAT and TATA boxes, sequences in the promoter regions of eukaryotic genes that are critical to the rate of transcription of ribonucleic acid (RNA).

The precise nature of the mutation has now been determined in more than 50 families of patients with Lesch–Nyhan syndrome or other variants of HPRT (Chambers et al., 1992; Sege-Peterson, 1992). Most families studied have displayed a unique mutation; the same mutation has only rarely been found in unrelated pedigrees. Few patients had gross alterations in the gene. About 85% of patients produce detectable amounts of normal-size HPRT messenger RNA (mRNA) (Gordon et al., 1987; Yang et al., 1984). On the other hand, in patients with classic Lesch–Nyhan syndrome, the results of the mutation have often been major ones that essentially eliminate HPRT enzyme activity.

Some large deletions have been detectable by Southern analysis (Yang et al., 1984). Other large alterations include two duplications, one resulting from recombination of Alu sequences (repetitive sequences of human DNA) in introns (noncoding portions of DNA) 6 and 8 (Marcus et al., 1993). In other patients with Lesch–Nyhan syndrome, a single gene substitution in a nonsense mutation led to a stop mutation, which coded for a stop in transcription and created a markedly truncated protein (Sege-Peterson, Chambers, et al., 1992; Sege-Peterson, Nyhan, & Page, 1992). In some instances a point mutation—a change in a single base pair of DNA—has led to the removal of a splice site and created an abnormal mRNA and protein. Missense mutations, which change the amino acid sequence but still code for a functional protein, have generally been nonconservative—for instance, an aspartic acid for a glycine at position 16, a leucine for phenylalanine at position 74, and a tyrosine for an aspartic acid at position 201

(Arnold & Kelley, 1971; Davidson et al., 1991; Sege-Peterson, Nyhan, & Page, 1992; Tarle et al., 1991). A CpG mutational hot spot was identified at arginine 51 of the HPRT protein. A CpG sequence in which a cytosine is formed by a guanine is readily mutated because once methylated, the 5-methylcytosine is deaminated to thymine. This position has been mutated 7 times among reported patients (Davidson et al., 1991; Tarle et al., 1991).

Prenatal Diagnosis

Intrauterine diagnosis of Lesch–Nyhan syndrome is available, thus permitting control of the disease in families known to be at risk (Bakay & Francke et al., 1977; Page & Broock, 1990). Prenatal diagnosis is done by assay of the HPRT enzyme in amniotic fluid cells obtained by amniocentesis and grown in cell culture. Linkage analysis has been employed in families in whom restriction fragment length polymorphism (RFLP) has been informative (Nussbaum, 1983). When the mutation is known, this is the preferred method of prenatal diagnosis. Allele-specific oligonucleotides or polymerase chain reaction (PCR) amplification and sequencing are employed (Gibbs et al., 1990) on amniotic or chorionic villus material. These techniques permit the mother to determine whether to interrupt the pregnancy when her fetus has been diagnosed. Monitoring pregnancy in this way permits a known carrier of the gene to have normal children, because the monitoring reveals which fetuses do not have an HPRT deficiency.

Heterozygote Detection

Random inactivation of the X chromosome leads to a mosaic pattern of activity of any X-linked enzyme in two populations of cells as predicted by the Lyon hypothesis, in which one of the two X chromosomes is normally randomly inactivated. However, in carriers of the gene for the classic Lesch–Nyhan syndrome, HPRT activity in erythrocytes and leukocytes is always normal, probably reflecting selection against the HPRT-negative cells very early in embryonic development (Emmerson & Wyngaarden, 1969; Francke et al., 1976; McDonald & Kelley, 1972; Nyhan, Bakay, & Connor, 1970).

The most widely employed enzymatic method of heterozygote detection takes advantage of the fact that hair follicles are largely clonal, containing either HPRT-positive or HPRT-negative cells only (Bakay, Francke, et al., 1977; Gartler et al., 1971; Page, Bakay, & Nyhan, 1982). Enzymatic analysis is accordingly carried out on each individual hair root of a sample of sufficient size (30 hairs plucked from the head) to provide statistical reliability. When the mutation in a family is known, assay of the DNA for its presence or absence is the method of choice for heterozygote detection. This is facilitated in families in whom the mutation interferes with or creates a restriction site, permitting the development of a simplified method. Otherwise, oligonucleotides specific for regions surrounding the mutation can be synthesized and used in PCR to amplify the genomic DNA, which is then sequenced (Gibbs et al., 1990).

Discovery of the HPRT deficiency permitted the molecular exploration of the genetics of the condition. In an X-linked recessive syndrome such as Lesch–Nyhan syndrome, the father of a child with the syndrome should not have an abnormal enzyme protein; thus the fathers of children with Lesch–Nyhan syndrome have normal HPRT activity. According to the Lyon hypothesis, the mothers of children with Lesch–Nyhan syndrome are heterozygous carriers. They are mosaics in which there are two populations of cells, one completely normal and the other completely deficient. This was established by cloning single cells from cultured fibroblasts (Migeon et al., 1968; Salzman et al., 1968).

Assessment of the HPRT activity in erythrocytes or leukocytes of obligate heterozygotes for Lesch–Nyhan syndrome has always revealed normal activity. Information on this subject was obtained through the study of a key kindred in which two types of glucose-6-phosphate dehydrogenase (G6PD) were segregating as well as two types of HPRT (Nyhan et al., 1970). In this family, two sisters were heterozygous for HPRT and for the G6PD types A and B, which was proven by cloning fibroblasts that were cultured from skin. However, repeated assay of their erythrocytes and leukocytes revealed only G6PD B, as well as normal activity for HPRT. These observations indicate a clonal origin of the hematopoietic system. The data could be explained by nonrandom inactivation of the X chromosome containing the information for G6PD and for HPRT. A more likely explanation is that although there is random inactivation very early in fetal life, it is followed by selection against the HPRT-deficient cell—a phenomenon we call *hemizygous expression*. This phenomenon complicates the detection of heterozygosity in people with Lesch–Nyhan syndrome. A molecular mutational diagnosis has solved this problem and permits precise genetic counseling.

VARIANTS OF HPRT DEFICIENCY WITH PHENOTYPES DIFFERING FROM THAT OF LESCH–NYHAN SYNDROME

Patients who have defective HPRT activity but do not have the Lesch–Nyhan phenotype have been recognized. The mutant genes responsible for the HPRT defect are also on the X chromosome (Kelley et al., 1969; Kogut et al., 1970). Male patients with these enzyme variants are able to reproduce, and an absence of male-to-male transmission has been documented. Some expression has been observed in the female heterozygotes of certain families (Bakay et al., 1972). Although people with these variants do not display SIB, they are relevant because comparisons with the classic variants could provide answers to the genesis of the abnormal behavior.

Patients with HPRT-deficient variants were first found among men with clinical gout. These patients excrete large amounts of uric acid in the urine and may have renal stone disease in childhood. They may also develop urate nephropathy, which also may develop in childhood. One of our patients (Sweetman et al., 1978) presented with a syndrome of transient hematuria and oliguria following anesthesia in a pattern that suggested chronic glomerulonephritis. Acute attacks of gouty arthritis and tophaceous deposits of urate generally first appear in adult life. Many years of hyperuricemia are required before the onset of the arthritic manifestations that are ultimately the hallmark of gout. Most of these patients have no CNS or behavioral abnormalities.

On the other hand, it is becoming clear that there is a spectrum nervous system involvement, and patients with cerebral involvement tend to have neurological manifestations identical to those of Lesch–Nyhan syndrome. A patient who appears to have the Lesch–Nyhan syndrome but does not mutilate has a different HPRT deficiency variant. The same may be true of a patient who has a normal intelligence. We studied a famous case in which a patient who had both of these unusual characteristics obtained evidence that he had a unique variant (Bakay et al., 1974; Sege-Peterson et al., 1992). This 22-year-old man was among the first patients reported with hyperuricemia and CNS symptoms (Catel & Schmidt, 1959). He had choreoathetosis, spasticity, dyarthric speech, and hyperuricemia. However, his intelligence was normal, and he had no evidence of self-mutilation. He had no HPRT activity in lysates of erythrocytes and cultured fibroblasts that were analyzed in the usual manner. However, when we developed a method for the study of purine metabolism in intact cultured cells (Bakay et al., 1978), cells derived from this patient were found to metabolize 9% of 8-^{14}C-hypoxanthine, and 90% of the isotope utilized was converted to adenine and guanine nucleotides. In contrast, cells from patients with the Lesch–Nyhan syndrome were almost completely unable to convert hypoxanthine to nucleotides. The patient's fibroblasts were even more efficient in the metabolism of 8-^{14}C-guanine, which was utilized to the extent of 27%, more than 80% of which was converted to guanine and adenine nucleotides. The growth of fibroblasts in culture was intermediate in media containing hypoxanthine, aminopterin, and thymidine (HAT), whereas the growth of Lesch–Nyhan cells was inhibited, and normal cells grew normally. Similarly in 8-azaguanine, 6-thioguanine, and 8-azahypoxanthine, the growth of the patient's cells was intermediate in comparison with normal and Lesch–Nyhan cells. These observations provided further evidence for genetic heterogeneity among patients with disorders in purine metabolism involving the HPRT gene. We documented that this patient did not have the Lesch–Nyhan syndrome variant. He has often been cited as an example of the fact that patients with the Lesch–Nyhan syndrome may not have behavioral abnormalities.

Patients with these HPRT-deficient variants all have hyperuricemia and increased quantities of uric acid in the urine. Assay of the erythrocytes in some patients has revealed some HPRT activity, which has ranged from less than 5% of the normal level to 60% of normal (Sweetman, Borden, et al., 1977).

In patients with neurological abnormalities, the level of activity of the erythrocyte enzyme has usually been indistinguishable from zero. The intact cell assays of patients with *neurological variants* revealed 1.6% to 8% of control activity. Those with hyperuricemia only (and normal nervous systems) have greater activity. Thus, there has been a rough correlation between severity of clinical phenotype and activity in this assay (Page et al., 1981, 1982). A unique variant that we have called *HPRT Salamanca* had 7.5 % of residual activity in this assay and a very different neurological phenotype involving spasticity and mild mental development retardation (Page et al., 1987; Sege-Peterson et al., 1992).

In the group of patients called neurological variants, point mutations have been the rule, and the types of changes observed have been relatively conservative. In the original patient of Catel and Schmidt (1959) the mutation changed a valine to a glycine (Sege-Peterson, Chambers, et al., 1992), which is not expected to make a major difference in protein structure. Others had different changes, such as an isoleucine to a threonine. In these patients and in those with the partial or hyperuricema variants, no deletions, stop codons, or major rearrangements were observed (Sege-Peterson, Nyhan, & Page, 1992). Patients with HPRT Salamanca (Page et al., 1987) had two mutations: a thymine to guanine change at position 128 and a guanine to adenine at 130. These changes resulted in the substitution of two adjacent amino acids at position 43 and 44: methionine to arginine and aspartic acid to asparagine. The changes do not seem to be particularly nonconservative, but the phenotype was probably the mildest of the neurological variants observed. These changes may have reflected another observation, which is that the milder mutations tend to cluster at the amino-terminal end of the enzyme. Point mutations in patients with Lesch–Nyhan syndrome have been more likely to be found in areas important for substrate binding and catalytic activity.

CASE STUDIES AND APPROACHES TO TREATMENT

The renal complications of the hyperuricemia, as well as the arthritis and tophi, are effectively managed using allopurinol. The oral administration of allopurinol in a dosage of 200 to 400 mg/day causes a reduction of plasma and urinary levels of uric acid and a concomitant increase in the oxypurines hypoxanthine and xanthine (Sweetman & Nyhan, 1967). A dosage of 20 mg/kg is a good starting point. In controls and adults with gout who have normal HPRT activity, the total excretion of oxypurines (i.e., the sum of uric acid, xanthine, and hypoxanthine) is less after treatment with allopurinol than under control conditions. In patients with HPRT deficiency, this decrease in oxypurine excretion is not seen. Measurement of the concentration of oxypurines can be helpful in determining the optimal dosage of allopurinol for preventing stone formation. Probenecid and other uricosuric agents have been used in the management of this disease, but uricosuric agents are contraindicated in patients with HPRT deficiency. These individuals already process enormous amounts of renal urate; a uricosuric agent could lead to renal shutdown and death. Alkali therapy with sodium citrate or sodium bicarbonate may be helpful in a patient with acute anuria resulting from insufficient water and crystals in the tubules, but this approach is not an efficient form of chronic management.

The cornerstone of the day-to-day management of the Lesch–Nyhan syndrome is physical restraint aimed at the protection of the patients from themselves (Letts & Hobson, 1975). We have learned numerous practical procedures that facilitate the care of these patients (Nyhan, 1976). Patients do learn some control with age, so it is often possible to prevent disfigurement by the removal of primary teeth. Individualized wheelchairs that permit the patient to be up and around are very helpful adjuncts to management. The use of elbow restraints permits the patients the use of their hands without allowing them to mutilate their fingers.

Behavioral modification techniques have been employed in patients with this syndrome with provocative results. Aversive techniques, including mild shock with a prod, have been very effective in patients with mental retardation who self-mutilate such as those with de Lange syndrome. In the Lesch–Nyhan syndrome, mutilative behavior worsens when aversive behavior modification methods are used (Anderson et al., 1978). Most institutions that no longer use restraints even in short-term approaches to behavioral modification have encountered severe degrees of mutilation that were upsetting for the family and staff members. Nevertheless, successful extinction therapy has been reported in experimental programs (Anderson et al., 1978; Bull & La Vecchio, 1978; Duker, 1984; Gilbert et al., 1979). However, it has not been possible to extrapolate this form of management to the home. Behavior in patients with this syndrome, like all behavior, is clearly subject to some modification, but behavior modification is clearly not a therapy.

A similar comment could be made about pharmacological approaches. Treatment with 5-hydroxytryptophan, the serotonin precursor, combined with the peripheral decarboxylase inhibitor carbidopa led to transient modification of the behavior (Nyhan, Johnson, et al., 1980). However, tolerance developed very rapidly, and control of behavior could not be regained. These results suggested that biogenic amines may be relevant to the genesis of the behavior. Furthermore, the urinary excretion of 5-hydroxyindoleacetic acid is greater in patients with the Lesch–Nyhan syndrome than in controls, which is also suggestive of a biogenic amine imbalance (Sweetman, Borden, & Kulovich, et al., 1977).

Various therapeutic approaches have been used to modify behavior, without evident success. Most patients are treated with diazepam, which is helpful for stiffness and may be required to get patients from their beds to a chair. It may be helpful in an acute biting emergency but probably only with a largely sedative dose. We have had unsuccessful experience with naltrexone, aminoinidazolecarboxamide riboside (AICAR), fluphenazine, clonazepam, and fluoxetine (Nyhan, 1994).

Case Study: Patient Treated With Naltrexone

J.B. was an 8-year-old White boy with Lesch–Nyhan syndrome admitted for evaluation and a trial of naltrexone. In the first years of life, he displayed decreased activity and was initially diagnosed as having hypotonic cerebral palsy, despite a negative perinatal history. At age 7 months, he could not roll over, and subsequent motor development was retarded. At age 3 years, he began to bite his arms and fingers. His father imaginatively fashioned PVC piping inserts for gloves, which protected the boy from any further hand mutilation. In the past year, he had begun mutilating his lower lip, and he had destroyed a large amount of tissue. Three years previously, his mother read an article on the Lesch–Nyhan syndrome, and the diagnosis was confirmed. The level of HPRT in J.B.'s red blood cells was less than 1% of control, and his serum uric acid level was 7.6 mg/dl. He was treated with allopurinol. Although the presence of urinary crystalline material was noted at intervals until the time of diagnosis, he had not had any urinary symptoms. The mother was tested by hair-root analysis and found not to be a carrier. J.B.'s 12-year-old sister did not have the syndrome.

Physical examination revealed normal vital signs: weight, 23.5 kg; height, 131 cm; head circumference, 55 cm. J.B. had a large amount of destruction of the central lower lip. Partly because of the incompetence of the lip, he drooled continuously. His extremities were thin, and he showed signs of muscle wasting. He wore gloves with rigid inserts at the fingertips on both hands and became agitated when they were removed. His hands had no obvious signs of damage. The neurological examination was significant for athetoid and ballistic movements. His speech was somewhat dysarthric and unclear but intelligible, and he spoke in full sentences. The content of his speech was appropriate, and he demonstrated a sense of humor. When placed in his wheelchair, he could get around quite effectively.

The laboratory evaluation revealed the following: normal electrolytes; blood urea nitrogen (BUN), 17 mg/dl; creatinine, 0.8 mg/dl; normal liver function tests; uric acid, 3.1 mg/dl (indicating that the allopurinol was adequate). An intravenous pyelogram was normal. A trial of naltrexone led to no change in behavior or neurological status. J.B. received 2.13 mg/kg of the drug for 2 days followed by 24 days of 4.26 mg/kg. The initial 5 days of naltrexone administration were in hospital where he was videotaped daily for 30 min, and examined for neurological and behavioral status.

Case Study: Patient Treated With AICAR

M.S. was a 16-year-old White male with Lesch–Nyhan syndrome and a history of esophagitis, gastrointestinal bleeding, anemia, and recent weight loss. He was admitted for AICAR therapy.

The diagnosis of Lesch–Nyhan syndrome was made at age 5 years following an episode of self-mutilation while in preschool. Before this, M.S. had been diagnosed as developmentally delayed. He was treated with allopurinol. He had lived in a full-care facility since he was age 10 years. He had daily episodes of vomiting, continuously self-mutilated, and had fractured femora that appeared to be caused by one or more caregivers. He had received four blood transfusions because of macrocytic anemia. A salivary duct stone had been removed.

M.S. was constantly in restraints but despite this had an open wound on his right knee. Six of his uncles were unaffected, but his mother was a confirmed carrier. He attended special education classes; he understood the material, but his poor articulation made communication difficult. He had some experience with computers in his special education classes. He demonstrated a sense of humor.

On physical examination, M.S. weighed 22.7 kg. He was afebrile, and his vital signs were stable. His lips and tongue revealed the results of self-induced trauma. His teeth were present. M.S. had wasting of muscle mass in the lower extremities but well-preserved upper extremities. His deep tendon reflexes were very active bilaterally but were equal; no clonus was noted.

An upper gastrointestinal (GI) roentgenographic study indicated that M.S. had the ability to induce vomiting by opening his pyloric sphincter, filling his esophagus, and spilling the contents. There was no evidence of esophagitis or a duodenal ulcer. He had infrequent hematest-positive stools. The mean corpuscular volume was greater than 100 μm^3, and an RDW histogram showed a bimodal distribution of red blood cells. His B_{12} and folate levels were high-normal, and a bone marrow study revealed a paucity of erythrocyte-forming units and megaloblastic changes. Bilateral femoral fractures were noted on x-rays. The BUN and creatinine levels were normal. A renal ultrasound showed no signs of stones. Treatment with AICA riboside had no effect. However, a pharmacokinetic study revealed no evidence of intestinal absorption.

Case Study: Patient Treated With Fluphenazine and Fluoxetine

G.V. was a 6-year-old, Mexican-American boy with Lesch–Nyhan syndrome. Since birth, he had increasing problems with eating, irritability, and anxiety. He was initially diagnosed with cerebral palsy, but by age 5 years the diagnosis of Lesch–Nyhan syndrome was made clinically. The patient had developmental delays, and he self-mutilated. G.V. was currently being treated with clonazepam drops, which the mother thought had been of some benefit. Approximately 1 year before admission, he began receiving treatment with allopurinol.

At age 2 years, he began biting his lip. He had been admitted to the hospital for trauma several times after falling off chairs and hurting himself. He also hit others. His extremities were restrained, and he was unable to walk. He could say a few words, and he attended a special school.

Physical examination revealed a small boy who had multiple joint contractures. His temperature was 97.5°F, his pulse was 100, and his respiration rate was 24 breaths per minute. His blood pressure was 90/60, and his weight was 15.75 kg. G.V.'s lips were mutilated from repeated biting. His wounds were well healed and showed no evidence of infection, but his left lower lip was missing. G.V.'s extremities were stiff, and he had contractures of the wrists, knees, ankles, and hip joints. He was intermittently interactive but became aggressive at times. His sensory examination was intact. G.V.'s deep tendon reflexes were increased symmetrically in all four extremities to 3+/4+. Toes were upgoing bilaterally.

Laboratory studies showed the following: white count, $6,300/mm^3$; hematocrit, 35.3%; hemoglobin 11.8 g/dl. There were 36% segs, 6% bands, 53% lymphocytes, 5% monocytes. Uric acid concentration was measured at 3.6 mg/dl. An abnormal EEG showed bihemispheric slowing and disorganization. Following a period of noncompliance with allopurinol therapy, G.V. developed right renal calculi. Renal ultrasound showed two stones, one in the upper and one in the lower pole of the kidney with no evidence of obstruction or hydronephrosis.

G.V. was admitted for a trial of fluphenazine. While receiving this treatment, his mother felt that his behavior was considerably worse than when he was receiving clonazepam, when he displayed a calmer attitude, did not bite, slept, and ate very well. The fluphenazine trial was placebo controlled and blinded to the mother and the evaluating physicians who were not convinced of any effects of treatment. He received 0.124 mg/kg originally for 4 days. Videotapes and daily logs of his behavior were kept during his hospitalization and evaluated by observers who did not have knowledge of whether sequences represented treatment or control. They concluded that there was no effect.

At age 9 years, G.V. was admitted for a double-blind study of fluoxetine. He received 1 mg/kg/day for 3 days and a placebo for 3 days. His behavior was observed for 30 minutes each day by one of the investigators and nursing staff, and his mother also kept records of his behavior. On the third day of each phase, he was videotaped for 30 minutes. The study was completed without any complications. Analysis revealed no effect from the drug.

Treatment was initiated 2 months later with dantrolene to treat spasticity and what the mother thought were painful muscle spasms. Muscle relaxation was rewarding and associated with longer sleeping time and better morning awakening. G.V.'s biting behavior also improved. He began scratching his upper gums and lips rather than biting them. School reports were good except for one day when he purposely put his left second finger in the wheelchair, creating a laceration. Videotaping was not conducted and no blind trial was undertaken to evaluate whether these anecdotal observations represented anything but a placebo effect.

Case Study: Patient Treated With Fluphenazine

C. W. was a 22-year-old White man with Lesch–Nyhan syndrome who was admitted for treatment with fluphenazine. He had recently managed to free his left arm from its restraint and caused some abrasions. His more usual form of SIB—banging his chin on anything available to produce an injury—was treated with an elevated platform on his chair supporting multiple pillows. His self-mutilative behavior had spared much of his oral mucosa, and he had all but two of his permanent teeth. He had an essentially complete HPRT deficiency, as well as multiple flexure contractures and spasticity with scissoring. C.W. had previously had many urinary tract calculi, four of which had been surgically removed. His medications included 200 mg of allopurinol twice a day, 10 mg of diazepam at bedtime, and 2 tbsp of septra every day for chronic urinary tract infection.

Physical examination revealed athetoid quadriplegia and scars about the chin. The extremities displayed wasting and severe contractures. C.W. was alert and interactive but had garbled speech. He had increased muscle tone, symmetrically brisk deep tendon reflexes, and symmetrical scissoring. Opisthotonic behavior occurred when agitated.

Laboratory values were as follows: sodium, 142 mEq/L; potassium, 4.3 mEq/L; chloride, 107 mEq/L; bicarbonate, 21 mEg/L; calcium, 9.3 mg/dl; BUN, 11 mg/dl; creatinine, 1 mg/dl; glucose, 80 mg/dl; amylase, 109 V/L; serum glutamatic-oxaloacetic transaminase (SGOT), 22 IU; uric acid, 5.1 mg/dl.

When videotaped without restraints, C.W. was extremely agitated, thrashing, and arching. When restraints were put back on, he became more sedate. C.W. was treated with fluphenazine in a starting dosage of 1.5 mg 3 times a day (0.12 and 0.19 mg/kg) for 6 days of each dose. There were no side effects, and there were no therapeutic effects.

CONCLUSION

People with Lesch–Nyhan syndrome have the prototypical behavioral phenotype for the genetic determination of SIB. In this disorder the abnormal gene codes for an HPRT protein that is virtually devoid of enzymatic activity, which leads to massive hyperuricemia and its clinical manifestations. HPRT deficiency also leads to a stereotyped syndrome of neurological dysfunction and to SIB—the behavior is a central feature of the syndrome. Researchers hope that one day they will understand the biochemical causes of this behavior.

18

NEUROIMAGING STUDIES IN LESCH–NYHAN SYNDROME AND LESCH–NYHAN VARIANTS

JAMES C. HARRIS, DEAN F. WONG, HYDER A. JINNAH,
D. SCHRETLEN, AND P. BARKER

Lesch–Nyhan syndrome is an X-linked genetic disorder resulting from an inborn error of purine metabolism with near absence of the purine salvage enzyme, hypoxanthine phosphoribosyltransferase (HPRT; Lesch & Nyhan, 1964). Because this purine salvage pathway provides an alternative pathway to purine nucleotide synthesis de novo (i.e., continuous production without recycling), the absence of HPRT results in hyperuricemia. More importantly, affected patients have a unique behavioral phenotype that includes compulsive self-injury and aggression, neurological abnormalities, and cognitive impairment that is not accounted for by the hyperuricemia. To elucidate the basis of this neurological and behavioral phenotype, we have utilized several brain-imaging techniques alone and in combination to investigate individuals with classic Lesch–Nyhan syndrome (i.e., an HPRT level of less than 1.5%) and Lesch–Nyhan syndrome variants (i.e., an HPRT level of 1.8%–20%).

The age of onset of self-injury may be as early as 1 year of age and occasionally as late as the teens. Self-injury occurs even though all sensory modalities, including the pain sense, are intact. Self-injurious behavior (SIB) is usually expressed as self-biting; however, other patterns of SIB may emerge with time. Characteristically, the fingers, mouth, and buccal mucosa are mutilated. Self-biting is intense and causes tissue damage, often leading to amputation of fingers and loss of tissue around the lips, often requiring the extraction of primary teeth. The biting pattern is often asymmetrical in that patients preferentially mutilate the left or right side of the body and may become anxious if they perceive that one side of their body is threatened. The topography of the behavior is different from that associated with other mental retardation syndromes of self-injury, in which self-hitting and head banging are the most common initial forms. Moreover, the intensity of the SIB in people with Lesch–Nyhan syndrome generally requires that the patients be restrained.

The self-mutilation is conceptualized as a compulsive behavior that the person tries to control but generally is unable to resist. Older individuals become more skillful at finding ways to control the self-injury, including enlisting the help of others and notifying them when restraints can be removed. An older child's self-injury may progress to deliberate self-harm and compulsive aggression toward others. People with Lesch–Nyhan syndrome may injure others by pinching, grabbing, hitting, or using verbal forms of aggression. Afterward, they apologize for their behavior and say that it was out of their control. Other associated maladaptive behaviors that may occur include head or limb banging, eye poking, pulling of fingernails, and psychogenic vomiting.

We have used neuroimaging techniques to study the biological basis of Lesch–Nyhan syndrome. Our neuroimaging studies focus on understanding brain mechanisms that may be linked to SIB. Because the clinical presentation varies with the extent of the HPRT enzyme deficiency, the spectrum of clinical presentations provides an opportunity to examine the neuroanatomical and neurochemical underpinnings of phenotypic expression. The full behavioral syndrome—with dystonia, cognitive deficits, and the behavioral phenotype of compulsive self-injury and aggression—requires the virtual absence of the enzyme. Individuals who have higher levels of the HPRT enzyme (1.5%–8%) in intact cells suffer from gout and neurological symptoms but do not self-injure, whereas patients with levels higher than 8% have been reported to have only gout (Page & Nyhan, 1989). These varying degrees of HPRT deficiency (Adler & Wrabetz, 1996), in which some of the symptoms are reported to be either absent or very mild, have not been previously studied systematically. In our studies, variant cases that have the neurological features of the disorder but do not self-injure are compared to classic cases with both neurological features and self-injury. Cognitive function and specific neuropsychological features across the full spectrum of HPRT deficiency can be correlated with findings from neuroimaging studies. This approach may result in a more detailed delineation of the neurochemical basis of the disorder and aid in the understanding of SIB.

Recent refinements in magnetic resonance imaging (MRI), positron emission tomography (PET) ligand development, and multislice proton magnetic resonance spectroscopic imaging (proton MRS) make it possible to study neuroanatomy and neurochemistry in vivo. These techniques may be applied to Lesch–Nyhan syndrome and its variants. However, to make meaningful progress in understanding the neurobiological basis of the disorder, researchers need to characterize the neurological and behavioral phenotype that is associated with varying levels of HPRT deficiency. Thus, systematic assessments of HPRT levels, the dystonic movement disorder, neuropsychological function, and behavioral features (Harris et al., 1991) are needed. These findings may be correlated with measures of regional brain anatomy using MRI (Harris et al., 1998), measures of neurochemistry using proton MRS (Harris et al., 1998) and PET studies of the dopamine function (Wong et al., 1996). The sections that follow provide a summary of neuroanatomical and neurochemical studies in well-characterized classic Lesch–Nyhan syndrome and variant cases.

MRI VOLUMETRIC STUDIES

MRI studies of people with Lesch–Nyhan syndrome are uncommon because of the rarity of the disease and the technical problems in obtaining adequate images without general anesthesia. The neuroimaging studies that have been done, mainly computed tomography (CT) studies, found no consistent neuroanatomical abnormalities. More refined assessment of basal ganglia morphometry using volumetric MRI techniques is necessary to clarify whether changes are present. If present, such findings may be used to (a) establish that Lesch–Nyhan syndrome is a neurodevelopmental disorder; (b) establish a database to correlate neuroanatomical findings in the caudate and putamen and associated brain regions with neurological, behavioral, and neuropsychological measures; and (c) provide necessary data to carry out partial volume corrections for brain imaging studies involving PET (Wong et al., 1996).

Seven classic Lesch–Nyhan syndrome patients participated in volumetric MRI studies using an SPGR (Spoiled GRASS Gradient Recalled) sequence for volumetrics (Harris et al., 1998). In an eighth patient, a volumetric CT scan was performed instead of the MRI scan because of the presence of a dorsal column stimulator wire.

The volumes of the basal ganglia were measured from T1-weighted SPGR MRI scans, which used contiguous slices from just superior to the lateral ventricles through the aqueduct of Sylvius, in an oblique axial projection parallel to the AC–PC (Anterior Commissure/Posterior Commissure) line. The lateral ventricles (excluding the temporal horns), the head and body of the caudate nucleus, the putamen, and the globus pallidi were manually outlined by a trained operator. Three-dimensional volumetric images were reconstructed with standard clinical software (ISG, Mississauga, Ontario).

In comparison with seven control participants in the same age range and using the same MRI volumetric sequences, the seven Lesch–Nyhan patients demonstrated a 31% decrease in volume in the caudate ($p <$ .001) and an 11.8% decrease in the putamen. For the individuals studied, control brain volumes averaged 1163±79 cu cm and brain volumes in the classic cases averaged 964±214 cu cm. (Harris et al., 1998). Moreover, these authors found that brain size was also reduced in a separate cohort of Lesch–Nyhan variants (i.e., HPRT levels of 1.8%–20%) when compared with normal control subjects. These findings are consistent with the hypothesis that Lesch–Nyhan syndrome is a neurodevelopmental disorder.

The reduction in brain size was accompanied by thickened calvaria and increased sinus pneumatization, or sinus size. The increased thickness of the skull and increased sinus size may reflect a failure of continued brain growth. When brain growth does not continue at the normal rate throughout the developmental years, a compensatory thickening in the skull and sinuses could have occurred.

These MRI results from people with classic Lesch–Nyhan syndrome and its variants were unexpected because MRIs previously had been reported as normal by other investigators. The failure of previous studies to document abnormality in the striatum may be caused by the methodological issues related to volumetric measurements or accounted for because earlier studies utilized routine MRI or CT scans and did not carefully examine these brain regions.

Based on comparisons to MRIs of normal control participants, we propose that there is a maturational arrest of the brain in people with classic Lesch–Nyhan syndrome. The volume reduction in the caudate and putamen is not accounted for by reduction in total brain size but seems to be specific to the caudate and putamen. Moreover, the reduction in caudate volume may be correlated with cognitive dysfunction (Harris et al., 1996).

To determine correlation with cognitive functions, left and right caudate volumes were measured. (The mean [plus or minus standard deviations] volumes of the left and right caudate nuclei were 2349±257 and 2502±366 cu cm, respectively.) Analyses revealed a significant correlation ($r = .78$; $p = 0.037$, one tailed) between the left caudate volume and performance on one neuropsychological test of global cognitive functioning. Moderately strong correlations also were found between the left caudate volumes and tests of reasoning ($r = .69$; $p = 0.067$, one tailed), orientation ($r = .66$; $p = 0.077$, one tailed), and receptive vocabulary ($r = .47$). Correlations between the right caudate volume and all four cognitive measures were weak. This pattern of results is similar to a study of left versus right caudate volumes in relation to the cognitive test performance of patients with Huntington's disease.

Thus, it is proposed that brain dysfunction in HPRT deficiency involves not only the motor circuits of the basal ganglia but also the cognitive circuit (Cummings et al., 1993; Visser et al., 2000). Consistent with this proposal is the involvement of basal ganglia and prefrontal brain systems in obsessive-compulsive disorder, emotion regulation, and control of impulsive behavior.

PET makes it possible to study neurotransmitter systems in the basal ganglia in vivo. During the past 15 years, PET has been used to investigate the dopamine system in people with Lesch–Nyhan syndrome. Following the report of dopamine deficiency in postmortem studies of three patients with Lesch–Nyhan syndrome (Lloyd et al., 1981), Wong, Harris, and colleagues initiated studies of the dopamine system in vivo in classic Lesch–Nyhan syndrome (Gjedde et al., 1986). After initial investigations demonstrated the feasibility of using PET imaging to investigate the dopamine system in vivo, studies of the dopamine system in human participants were initiated, using Lesch–Nyhan syndrome as a model for SIB. Subsequently, Breese et al. (1984a, 1984b) established that rat pups given 6-hydroxydopamine (6-OHDA) in the neonatal period showed SIB when challenged with D_1 dopamine agonists as adults. The Breese rat model is consistent with a neurodevelopmental model of dopamine deficiency in Lesch–Nyhan syndrome. This model linked dopamine deficiency in early development to SIB. Moreover, Jinnah et al. (1999) demonstrated dopamine deficiency in the basal ganglia in five mutant HPRT-deficient mouse strains. In the HPRT-deficient mouse model, a failure in dopaminergic development was apparent 30 days after birth.

D_2 and D_1 Dopamine Studies

Our first PET studies, which were carried out in 1984, measured dopamine D_2-receptor density with the ligand N-methyl-spiperone before and after bone marrow transplantation in a 22-year-old man with Lesch–Nyhan syndrome. The finding of no change in D_2 density before and after transplantation was consistent with a neurodevelopmental model of dopamine deficiency. Subsequently, we hypothesized that dopaminergic denervation supersensitivity might be one mechanism involved in the neurological phenotype and behavioral phenotype (Harris et al., 1991) of self-injury in Lesch–Nyhan syndrome. Therefore, we studied postsynaptic dopamine D_2 receptor density, hypothesizing postsynaptic dopamine density would increase; studies were completed on six people with classic Lesch–Nyhan syndrome. We noted no consistent increase postsynaptic D_2 binding using the PET ligand N-methyl-spiperone when older participants were compared with age-matched control participants and younger participants age matched and compared to published postmortem D_2 receptor-binding values.

We assessed the $D_1:D_2$ ratio to evaluate the relationship of D_1 to D_2 systems in one subject. Because the D_1 system is adenylcyclase dependent, it was proposed that D_1 and D_2 dopamine systems might be differentially affected. When the D_1 receptor was implicated in the treatment of SIB with fluphenazine (Goldstein, 1985), we carried out a PET scanning procedure concurrently with a behavioral study and measured *in vivo* blockage of a D_1 PET ligand, SCH 23390, using fluphenazine. The behavioral study did not demonstrate an effect of fluphenazine on self-injury in a patient with Lesch–Nyhan syndrome. The rate of SIB did not decrease. The in vivo PET study revealed that fluphenazine, in vivo, has limited effects on blocking the D_1 receptor. This failure of fluphenazine to block the D_1 PET ligand SCH23390 may explain the lack of clinical effect.

Because significant differences in D_2 dopamine density with the PET ligand N-methyl-spiperone could not be clearly demonstrated in patients with Lesch–Nyhan syndrome, we turned to investigation of the presynaptic dopamine system, using the dopamine transporter PET ligand WIN 35,428.

Presynaptic Dopamine Transporter

We investigated possible presynaptic reduction in dopamine terminals using a ligand that binds to the dopamine transporter. The ligand chosen to evaluate the integrity of dopaminergic neurons was [¹¹C]WIN 35,428, a compound that binds to the presynaptic dopamine reuptake site (dopamine transporter). Reductions were documented in the dopamine transporter in the putamen and the caudate nuclei in patients with HPRT levels of less than 1.4%. Reductions in the dopamine transporter in the putamen with this ligand have been reported in people with Parkinson's disease.

We have studied eight people with Lesch–Nyhan syndrome and 10 people without the syndrome with the high specific activity [¹¹C]WIN compound to determine the density of the dopamine transporter. Each patient was imaged for 90 minutes following the administration of approximately 20 mCi of the radiotracer. All underwent nitrous oxide/methylhexitol anesthesia for the study, after documenting that this anesthesia protocol did not affect [¹¹C]WIN binding in a rat model. Radioarterial plasma samples were obtained along with 50 PET acquisitions, increasing in duration from 15 seconds to 6 minutes. The caudate mean for the Lesch-Nyhan syndrome group was 3.01±0.1, compared with 4.98±0.88 for controls. The putamen mean for the Lesch–Nyhan syndrome group was 1.94, compared with 5.13±0.71 for the controls. All eight of the patients studied show substantial reductions in the dopamine transporter. These findings document an in vivo abnormality in dopamine function in people with Lesch–Nyhan syndrome. Thus, our hypothesis that participants with the classic onset of Lesch–Nyhan syndrome would demonstrate significant reduction in dopamine transporter binding was confirmed. It is apparent that dopaminergic terminals are less dense in the putamen of the people with Lesch–Nyhan syndrome than in the caudate. Six of these eight individuals had classic Lesch–Nyhan syndrome with SIB; two were atypical in that neither had shown self-injury, although one was compulsively aggressive. One atypical participant had an HPRT level of 0.9% and the other a HPRT level of 1.4%.

Reductions in dopamine transporter levels of the six patients who self-injured were in the same range as those of the two participants who did not self-injure. Because the latter two participants had detectable levels of HPRT (0.9% and 1.4%), we sought to clarify the relationship between presynaptic dopamine transporter binding in the striatum and SIB in variant cases with higher levels of HPRT (Harris et al., 1999). We studied seven people who were Lesch–Nyhan variants (i.e., HPRT levels of 1.8%–20%), with an age range of 12 to 37 years. We documented the extent of dystonia on a quantitated neurological examination (Burke et al., 1985). *Dystonia* is defined as an involuntary movement disorder characterized by twisting or sustained movements. The movements scale is the sum of individual scores for each of nine body regions (speech and swallowing are considered together as a region). The individual score for each body region is the product of two factors—the provoking factor and the severity factor—each rated on a scale from 0 (the lowest) to 4 (the highest). The provoking factor quantifies the dystonia in a region by rating the circumstances in which dystonia appears.

PET imaging of two patients with HPRT levels of less than 1.5% and two patients with HPRT levels of 1.8% and 2.5% with severe movement disorder revealed no difference in WIN 35,428 dopamine transporter binding when compared with our previously reported six patients with classic Lesch–Nyhan who self-injured (Wong et al., 1996). This suggests that reductions in dopamine receptor density are not a sufficient explanation of the self-injury.

HPRT level and the extent of motor deficit are correlated with dopamine transporter binding. Dopamine transporter binding was significantly correlated with HPRT levels in whole cells (putamen k3/k4—Spearman rank correlation coefficient $[r_s]$ = .89, p = 0.001; caudate k3/k4—r_s = .66, p = 0.055). When the dystonic movement disorder was rated in the quantitated neurological examination, putamen dopamine transporter density was significantly correlated with symptom severity. These findings indicate that (a) dopamine reduction is linked to the extent of the movement disorder but is not a sufficient explanation for SIB, and (b) other neurotransmitters need to be examined.

In summary, our in vivo [^{11}C]WIN PET studies (Wong et al., 1996)—and those of Ernst et al. (1996), using ^{18}F flurodopa as the PET ligand—provide confirmation of the proposed dopaminergic abnormality in caudate and putamen in humans with HPRT deficiency. These findings are consistent with the previous autopsy study that documented dopamine reduction in three participants (Lloyd et al., 1981), the Breese rat model, and the proposal of Yeh et al. (1998) of impaired differentiation of HPRT-deficient dopaminergic neurons. However, the relationship of dopamine to self-injury remains unclear.

The relationship of dopamine to the dystonic movement disorder is better established. When both classic and variant cases were studied, those with similar neurological findings on a dystonia rating scale showed similarly severe reductions in dopamine transporter binding density on a dystonia rating scale. Thus, the extent of dopamine reduction is linked with the severity of the dystonic movement disorder.

MRS

Our PET studies are limited to regions of interest in the striatum where dopamine is found in greatest abundance. To investigate other brain regions and to further document neuronal dysfunction in the basal ganglia, we have utilized multislice MRS (Duyn et al., 1993; Harris et al., 1998; Soher et al., 1996). MRS allows for the investigation of the striatum and other regions of interest important in the functional organization of the striatum, including the thalamus and prefrontal cortex.

Developmental changes in protonated metabolic levels may be utilized to study neurodevelopmental disorders such as Lesch–Nyhan syndrome (Hashimoto et al., 1995). Three metabolites are studied—choline, creatine, and N-acetyl-L-aspartic acid (NAA). NAA has been assessed in the brains of human fetuses and children by means of high-resolution proton MRS (Kato et al., 1997). NAA has been detected in cerebral cortex and white matter of fetuses from 16 weeks onward. The metabolite increases gradually from 24 weeks' gestation but most strikingly from 40 weeks' gestation to age 1 year, with rapid changes up to age 3 years (Kato et al., 1997). As neuronal cell density decreases with neuronal maturation, changes in NAA may reflect normal or abnormal development of axons, dendrites, and synapses in addition to neuronal soma. After age 5 years, metabolic concentrations and ratios are generally stable. We studied individuals with Lesch–Nyhan syndrome ages 12 and older and age-matched control groups.

In vivo proton MRS was carried out across the full spectrum of HPRT deficiency (i.e., people with classic Lesch–Nyhan syndrome, people with Lesch–Nyhan variants, and age-matched normal control participants). We determined brain-protonated metabolite levels in the basal ganglia and in related brain regions. These regions were selected on both clinical grounds and based on our PET scan findings of reduced dopamine in the striatum.

Ten control individuals, eight individuals with classic Lesch–Nyhan syndrome, and six individuals who are HPRT variants (i.e., HPRT levels of 1.8%–8% in whole cells) participated in the MRS study (Harris et al., 2000). Multivariate analysis of variance (MANOVA) was used to assess the effects of HPRT deficiency in normal controls versus patients (combined classic Lesch–Nyhan syndrome and variants). The overall model was significant. Univariate F tests revealed significant group differences in caudate

NAA (p = 0.014), putamen NAA (p = 0.002), mesial frontal NAA (p = 0.045), caudate NAA:creatine ratio (p = 0.001), putamen NAA:creatine ratio (p = 0.002), and caudate creatine (p = 0.049). When a second MANOVA was conducted after separating the patient groups (i.e., into normal, classic Lesch–Nyhan syndrome, and variants), the F test was significant. Moreover, post hoc comparisons with Bonferroni correction revealed that Lesch–Nyhan syndrome variant cases showed significant differences from controls in the caudate, putamen, and mesial frontal regions, indicating neuronal dysfunction in patients with partial HPRT deficiency, with enzyme levels up to 8%. Additional classic Lesch–Nyhan syndrome cases are being studied to confirm the extent of NAA reduction in those with HPRT levels of less than 1%. NAA levels on the striatum were not correlated with the extent of the dystonic movement disorder.

This is the first application of quantitative MRS to both Lesch–Nyhan syndrome and its variants. Our findings of NAA reduction suggest neuronal loss or dysfunction in caudate, putamen and medial frontal cortex in HPRT deficiency. Values were also reduced in the dorsolateral prefrontal cortex but were not statistically significant. In agreement with a previous study measuring NAA in a nonquantitated single voxel in classic Lesch–Nyhan syndrome (Davanzo et al., 1998), we found NAA reduction in the prefrontal cortex in both classic and partial variant cases when using quantitated measures. However, we extended previous findings by documenting reduction in the mesial prefrontal area.

The MRS findings of neuronal dysfunction in the caudate and putamen in classic and variant cases are consistent with our PET finding of significantly reduced dopamine transporter density, a proposed marker for dendritic arborization, in caudate and putamen. The MRS studies extend our PET studies of HPRT in brain by utilizing another method to study neuronal dysfunction (Bates et al., 1996). Although our PET studies are limited to regions of interest in the striatum, MRS regions of interest included the striatum, thalamus, and prefrontal cortex. By combining imaging methods and extending our study to patients across the full spectrum of HPRT deficiency, we hope to understand better the relationship between HPRT deficiency, the dystonic movement disorder, self-control, emotion regulation, and SIB (Harris et al., 2000).

CONCLUSION

MRI, multislice proton MRS, and PET imaging may be combined to understand the neuroanatomy and neurochemistry of Lesch–Nyhan syndrome and its variants. Each imaging technique contributes to the understanding of different aspects of HPRT deficiency. Findings from imaging studies demonstrate that HPRT deficiency results in changes in brain structure and function.

Moreover, patients with classic Lesch–Nyhan syndrome and partial HPRT deficiency have both neurological and cognitive deficits that may be correlated with brain imaging results.

MRI provides information on neurodevelopment and allows correlations with neurocognitive assessment. PET scanning provides an opportunity to study specific neurotransmitter systems. PET findings of reduced dopamine transporter density in vivo demonstrate the specificity of dopamine dysfunction in the striatum in HPRT deficiency but do not allow study of extrastriate regions. These PET scan findings are consistent with a proposed abnormality in dendritic arborization of dopamine fibers in HPRT deficiency. PET findings may be correlated with the dystonic movement disorder and behavioral and neuropsychological findings. In patients with HPRT deficiency, dopamine transporter binding in the putamen is correlated with the severity of dystonic movements on a standardized movement disorder rating scale. PET studies across the full range of HPRT deficiency show no significant difference in dopamine transporter binding when participants with severe dystonia who self-injure are compared to those who do not self-injure. These findings suggest that dopamine reduction is linked to the extent of the movement disorder but is not a sufficient explanation for SIB, and other neurotransmitters need to be examined. PET studies of the dopamine system provide evidence that HPRT deficiency involves the motor circuit of the brain.

Multislice proton MRS provides a means to investigate brain dysfunction in multiple brain regions. MRS findings of reduced NAA metabolites and NAA:creatine ratio are consistent with neuronal loss or dysfunction in frontostriate systems in those with HPRT deficiency. These findings offer confirmation that Lesch–Nyhan syndrome is a disorder involving several basal ganglia circuits (Visser et al., 2000). Findings of neuronal dysfunction using MRS suggest involvement of basal ganglia cognitive and limbic circuits. These brain circuits are linked to self-control, working memory, and emotion regulation. Dysfunction in the neural circuit involved in emotion regulation (Davidson et al., 2000) may play a major role in self-injury and aggression in those with Lesch–Nyhan syndrome and its variants.

19

AGE-DEPENDENT REDUCTION OF BRAIN DOPAMINE: RELATIONSHIP TO SELF-INJURIOUS BEHAVIOR

GEORGE R. BREESE

Self-injurious behavior (SIB) associated with mental retardation is a serious affliction for which there is presently no known effective therapy. Because SIB can result in severe physical damage to the patient, this symptom associated with mental retardation dictates that patients be constantly monitored. If SIB could be ameliorated, the major costs to health systems responsible for the care of these patients could be reduced, and the quality of life for patients with mental retardation with SIB would be remarkably improved. The material reviewed in this chapter outline a strategy from basic research for providing improved therapy for patients with Lesch–Nyhan syndrome and patients with mental retardation who self-injure.

LESCH–NYHAN SYNDROME

Lesch–Nyhan syndrome (Lesch & Nyhan, 1964) is a genetically linked disorder with a deficiency of hypoxanthine phosphoribosyltransferase (HPRT; Seegmiller et al., 1967). People with Lesch–Nyhan syndrome demonstrate SIB with self-biting as the primary symptom (Nyhan, 1967, 1972). In 1981, Lloyd et al. reported that dopamine was reduced in the brains of three people with Lesch–Nyhan syndrome at autopsy. The finding that homovanillic acid, the major metabolite of dopamine, was reduced in spinal fluid from individuals with Lesch–Nyhan syndrome was consistent with dopamine loss in this disorder (Jankovic et al., 1988; Silverstein et al., 1985). This initial observation of reduced dopamine in Lesch–Nyhan syndrome was subsequently confirmed directly in living patients using PET procedures that define the integrity of dopaminergic neurons (Ernst et al., 1996; Wong et al.,

1996). Production of mice with a deletion of HPRT gene (Hooper et al., 1987; Kuehn et al., 1987) also resulted in a dopamine deficiency (Finger et al., 1988; Jinnah et al., 1994, 1998), providing further evidence for a link between the deletion of HPRT and dopamine malfunction (see review, Visser et al., 2000).

Although evidence indicated a loss of integrity of dopamine-containing neurons in people with Lesch–Nyhan syndrome just as in individuals with Parkinsonism (Hornykiewiciz, 1973), the motor symptoms (aside from the self-injury associated with Lesch–Nyhan syndrome) differed from those seen in patients with Parkinson's disease (Nyhan, 1972). In Lesch–Nyhan syndrome, motor symptoms include spasticity and choreoathetoid movements with apisthotonic posture (Nyhan, 1972). Individuals with Parkinson's disease have a stooped posture, bradykinesia, rigidity, and tremors but do not self-injure (Hornykiewicz, 1966, 1973, 1974). While allopurinol reduces the elevated uric acid levels accompanying the loss of HPRT in those individuals with Lesch–Nyhan syndrome, self-injurious behavior (SIB) and neurological symptoms are not altered (Kelley & Wyngaarden, 1983). Consequently, considerable confusion existed concerning the basis of the symptomatic differences between Lesch–Nyhan syndrome and Parkinson's disease, given that brain dopaminergic neurons were drastically reduced in people with either condition.

NEONATE AND ADULT RATS WITH 6-HYDROXYDOPAMINE LESIONS: DIFFERING BEHAVIORAL RESPONSES

Initial work in our laboratory demonstrated that intracisternal administration of the neurotoxin 6-hydroxydopamine (6-OHDA) to adult rats reduced tyrosine hydroxylase, indicative that dopamine-containing neurons were destroyed by this treatment (Breese & Traylor, 1970, 1971). Likewise, when this neurotoxin was administered to rats during development, dopaminergic neurons were drastically reduced when they had reached adulthood (Breese & Traylor, 1972; Smith et al., 1973). Evaluation of dopamine content in the striatum of rats given lesions as neonates and those given lesions as adults did not reveal a consistent difference in this measure (Breese et al., 1984a). Furthermore, regardless of the age at which dopaminergic neurons were destroyed, a greater sparing of tyrosine—hydroxylase-containing neurons was observed in medial portions of the striatum and nucleus accumbens compared to lateral portions (Simson et al., 1992).

Because there was no apparent difference in the reduction of brain dopamine after the age-dependent treatments, it was reasoned that any difference between rats that received lesions as neonates and those that received lesions as adults would be more easily observed if motor function was activated. In adult-lesioned animals believed to model Parkinson's disease, apomorphine and L-dihydroxyphenylalanine (L-dopa) induced a marked elevation in locomotor activity, presumably reflecting the therapeutic advantage of dopamine agonists in Parkinsonism (Breese et al., 1984a). In the rats that received lesions as neonates to reduce brain dopamine, apomorphine produced considerably less locomotor activation than seen in the adult-lesioned animals (Breese et al., 1984a). Furthermore, other behavioral responses differed between the rats that received lesions as adults and those that received lesions as neonates. For example, in the adult-lesioned rats, head nodding and paw treading were prominent after exposure to the dopamine agonists, behaviors seldom observed in the rats that received lesions as neonates and tested as adults (Breese et al., 1984a). Most striking of the differences after L-dopa and apomorphine administration to these age-dependent lesioned animals was the presence of self-biting that could reach the level of self-injury in the rats that received lesions as neonates without evidence of this response in the rats that received lesions as adults (Breese et al., 1984a, 1984b; Joyce et al., 1996). These data clearly exemplified the increased susceptibility of neonate-lesioned rats for SIB at adulthood. Although it remains possible that a difference in content of dopamine in a specific brain region not yet identified is responsible for the distinct behaviors in the neonate-lesioned and adult-lesioned animals, such differing damage to dopamine-containing neurons in specific brain regions has yet to be identified in these age-dependent lesioned rats. Based on the differing response patterns to L-dopa in neonate- and adult-lesioned rats, our laboratory proposed that the age at which an insult to the dopaminergic system occurred was responsible for the distinct motor dysfunction and behaviors observed between Lesch–Nyhan syndrome and Parkinsonism (Breese et al., 1984a, 1984b).

L-Dopa therapy improves most motor symptoms of Parkinsonism (Hornykiewicz, 1974). In contrast, two people with Lesch–Nyhan syndrome given L-dopa reportedly exhibited a worsening of the motor symptoms and an enhancement of compulsive self-injury (Jankovic et al., 1988). Consequently, the increased susceptibility to L-dopa-induced SIB in the neonate-lesioned rat model was predictive of the subsequent demonstration that L-dopa could worsen symptoms in individuals with Lesch–Nyhan syndrome (Jankovic et al., 1988). Consequently, with the reduced dopamine and the increased susceptibility for L-dopa-induced self injury in the rats that received lesions as neonates, the neonate-lesioned rat was proposed as a model of the dopamine reduction observed in Lesch–Nyhan syndrome, with the adult-lesioned rat emulating the characteristics of Parkinsonism (Breese & Breese, 1997; Breese et al., 1984a, 1984b, 1990a, 1994, 1995).

Relationship of Dopamine Receptor Subtypes in L-Dopa-Induced SIB in Neonate-Lesioned Rats

With the logical assumption that the L-dopa-induced behavioral response (SIB) in the neonate-lesioned rats depended on activation of dopamine receptors, research was undertaken to determine which antagonists of specific dopamine receptor subtypes would reduce the L-dopa-induced SIB in the neonate-lesioned rats. In initial work, haloperidol, a classic D_2 dopamine antagonist, had little effect on the L-dopa-induced SIB, except at extremely high doses (Breese et al., 1984a). Similarly, D_2 dopamine agonists did not induce SIB in the neonate-lesioned rats (Breese et al., 1985). In fact, the response to the D_2 dopamine agonist quinpirole was considerably less in the rats that received lesions as neonates than the responsiveness in adult-lesioned animals (Breese et al., 1985). When SCH-23390 became available, a specific antagonist for the D_1 dopamine receptors (Iorio et al., 1983), it was tested and found to block L-dopa-induced SIB in the rats that received lesions as neonates (Breese et al., 1985, 1986, 1990a). Subsequently, two additional D_1 dopamine antagonists, SCH-39166 (Chipkin et al., 1988) and NO-756 (Andersen et al., 1988), were also found to block the L-dopa-induced SIB in these neonate-lesioned animals (Criswell et al., 1992). In addition, it was observed that the D_1 dopamine agonist would produce SIB in a portion of the animals sensitive to L-dopa-induced self-injury (Breese et al., 1985, 1986). With completion of these studies, there was convincing support for the view that D_1 dopamine receptors were critically involved in the increased susceptibility for SIB observed in the neonate-lesioned rats (Breese et al., 1995).

One puzzle from data collected was that only a portion of animals positive for L-dopa-induced SIB exhibited SIB when given a D_1 dopamine agonist (Breese et al., 1985). Based on previous data demonstrating a coupling of D_1 and D_2 dopamine receptors (Breese & Mueller, 1985), specific agonists for these receptors were coadministered to emulate the action of L-dopa on both dopamine receptor subtypes (Breese et al., 1985). Combining doses of the SKF-38393 (which alone produced no SIB) with a D_2 dopamine agonist (which never produced this response), SIB could be induced (Breese et al., 1985). These latter data provided additional evidence for the physiological importance of dopamine receptor subtype coupling for an integrated responsiveness of dopaminergic function in the rats that received lesions as neonates.

Another important pharmacological difference between rats that received lesions as neonates and those that received lesions as adults was their response to D_2 dopamine antagonists. As expected, rats that received lesions as adults were extremely sensitive to the motor disrupting effects of low doses of the D_2 dopamine antagonist haloperidol (Duncan et al., 1987). In contrast, the neonate-lesioned rats seemed immune to the immobilizing effect observed in the adult-lesioned rats (Bruno et al., 1985; Duncan et al., 1987). The basis of this differing consequence of haloperidol administration to the age-dependent lesioned rats is unknown.

The neonate-lesioned rats also showed another major difference from adult-lesioned rats. In this case, they had a progressive increase in the sensitivity to a D_1 dopamine agonist with repeated dosing at 1-week intervals. This phenomenon was not observed in the adult-lesioned rats (Criswell et al., 1989a). This sensitization process has been referred to as *priming*. A link of this priming phenomenon to glutamate mechanisms was defined by MK-801, an *N*-methyl-D-aspartate (NMDA) antagonist, when this drug was found to block the consequence of repeated exposure to a D_1 dopamine agonist (Criswell et al., 1990). In addition, in animals sensitized to D_1 dopamine agonist responses, MK-801 was found to block the oral activity and mild self-biting induced by the agonist (Criswell et al., 1993). Based on this observation, neonate-lesioned rats given L-dopa were pretreated with MK-801. It was determined that MK-801, in a dose-related fashion, antagonized the L-dopa-induced SIB, with little effect on other behaviors (Criswell et al., 1993). Still, drugs in the MK-801 class (e.g., phencyclidine, ketamine) are unlikely to be useful in treating SIB because of their propensity to induce psychosis (Javitt & Zukin, 1991; Luby et al., 1959) and their potential to induce neurotoxicity in specific brain regions (Olney et al., 1989, 1991). Nonetheless, new types of agents with NMDA-blocking properties need to be tested that do not possess these undesired side effects because they may help reduce SIB. In addition, it has been observed that neonate-lesioned rats are more sensitive to the locomotor stimulation induced by NMDA antagonists, with repeated administration of these antagonists resulting in an increasing locomotor responsiveness not related to D_1 dopamine receptor activation (Criswell et al., 1990; Moy & Breese, in review). This enhanced sensitivity to NMDA antagonists may suggest that neonate-lesioned animals have reduced endogenous NMDA function.

Previous work had demonstrated that microinjection of muscimol, a γ-aminobutyric acid A (GABA [A]) agonist, into the substantia nigra reticulata (SNR) resulted in SIB in unlesioned rats (Baumeister & Frye, 1986; Scheel-Kruger et al., 1981). Other work had demonstrated that unilateral lesions to dopamine-containing neurons in adult-lesioned rats resulted in supersensitive GABA(A) receptors in the SNR (Weick et al., 1990), as reflected by an elevated density of GABA(A) receptors (Pan et al., 1983, 1985). The elevated density of these receptors was accompanied by supersensitive behavioral responses (Waddington & Cross, 1978) and enhanced electrophysiological inhibition (Waszczak & Walters, 1984) to GABA agonists. This change in GABA function was presumed to be an adaptive change to the loss of dopamine activity in the striatum. On microinjection of varying doses of muscimol into the SNR of the rats with age-dependent lesions, we found a greater sensitivity for muscimol-induced SIB in neonate-lesioned animals than in adult-lesioned rats (Breese et al., 1987b), providing further evidence for the increased susceptibility of neonate-lesioned rats to SIB.

Neurobiological Characteristics of Neonate-Lesioned Rats

Lloyd et al. (1981) reported the level of striatal serotonin to be elevated in those individuals with Lesch–Nyhan syndrome. In accordance with neonate-lesioned rats emulating characteristics of Lesch–Nyhan syndrome, striatal serotonin content was also found to be elevated in the neonate-lesioned rats (Breese et al., 1984a; Stachowiak et al., 1984; Towle et al., 1989) but not in adult-lesioned rats (Breese et al., 1984a). The elevated level of serotonin in the neonate-lesioned rats has been attributed to sprouting of serotonin-containing neurons (Snyder et al., 1986; Towle et al., 1989). Methysergide, a general serotonin antagonist, was without an effect on the SIB induced by L-dopa in the rats that received lesions as neonates (Towle et al., 1989).

In addition to SIB, D_1 dopamine agonists induce oral activity in neonate-lesioned rats, but it is uncertain whether the oral activity induced by a D_1 dopamine agonist has a direct relationship to the self-injury related to this receptor subtype in the neonate-lesioned rats. This is an important issue because studies have related the increased oral activity induced by a D_1 dopamine agonist to serotonin (Gong et al., 1992; Kostrzewa et al., 1993), with destruction of serotonergic neurons blocking the oral response mediated by the D_1 dopamine receptor in the neonate-lesioned animals (Brus et al., 1994). Given these results, future studies should give further attention to the possible involvement of serotonergic mechanisms in the various biological responses to dopamine agonists observed in neonate-lesioned rats. Because choline acetylase was reportedly reduced in those people with Lesch–Nyhan syndrome (Lloyd et al., 1981), it is surprising that release of acetylcholine was found to be enhanced after the neonatal destruction of dopamine-containing neurons (Perez-Navarro et al., 1993). This area of neurobiology in neonate-lesioned rats also warrants additional attention.

Enkephalin and tachykinin are present in high concentrations in the basal ganglia (Graybiel & Ragsdale, 1983). The striatopallidal pathway associated with D_2 dopamine receptors expresses enkephalin, and the striatonigral pathway associated with D_1 dopamine receptor function expresses tachykinins (Graybiel & Ragsdale, 1983). Lesioning of dopaminergic neurons results in adaptive changes in these peptides. Bilateral neonatal and adult lesions to dopaminergic neurons result in a constant elevation of messenger ribonucleic acid (mRNA) and protein levels of enkephalin (Cimino et al., 1991; Kurumaji et al., 1988; Sivam & Krause, 1990; Sivam et al., 1986, 1987, 1991; Soghomonian, 1994). The neonate lesion consistently decreased tachykinin peptides in the striatum, a change not seen in adult-lesioned animals (Sivam, 1989; Sivam & Krause, 1990; Sivam et al., 1987, 1991). Snyder-Keller (1991) found that neonate lesioning did not affect the patchy distribution of substance P. Finally, because neurotensin is elevated after an adult lesion of dopamine-containing neurons (Masuo et al., 1990), it would be of considerable interest to know whether neurotensin levels are affected by lesioning the dopaminergic neurons during development.

Activation of Immediate Early Genes After Neonate 6-OHDA Lesions

Immediate early genes (IEGs) are expressed transiently after activation of specific receptor subtypes (Herdegen & Leah, 1998; Hughes & Dragunow, 1995; Morgan & Curran, 1991). The observation by Robertson et al. (1989) that L-dopa increased the IEG *Fos* after an adult lesioning of dopaminergic neurons prompted our laboratory to examine whether L-dopa would induce this change in rats that received lesions as neonates. With evidence that L-dopa increased *Fos* activity in neonate-lesioned rats, we next sought to determine if activation of a specific dopamine receptor subtype was involved in this response. This effort documented that D_1 dopamine, but not D_2 dopamine, receptor agonists induce activation of *Fos* in neonate-lesioned animals (Johnson et al., 1992). Greater amounts of *Fos*-like immunoreactivity were present in the lateral portions of the striatum than in medial portions after receipt of a D_1 dopamine agonist, (Johnson et al., 1992), a finding consistent with the gradient of destruction of dopaminergic terminals in neonate-lesioned rats (Simson et al., 1992).

The uncertainty concerning the mechanism of receptor responsiveness after repeated D_1-agonist administration is related to the fact that neither the D_1 dopamine receptor number nor adenylate cyclase activated by a D_1 dopamine agonist were affected by sensitization (Breese et al., 1987a; Duncan et al., 1987, 1993; Neal-Beliveau & Joyce, 1993). Therefore, an important issue concerned whether the change in the *Fos* activity induced by a D_1 dopamine agonist reflects the increased behavioral sensitization seen with repeated D_1 dopamine agonist exposure. However, D_1 dopamine agonist administration used to sensitize neonate-lesioned rats did not induce any greater increase in *Fos* activity than did an initial dose in unprimed-lesioned animals (Johnson et al., 1992). Consequently, the search for the basis of the increased responsiveness induced by repeated exposure to D_1 dopamine agonists continues.

The Fos protein coded for by the *Fos* gene belongs to a broader family of immediate early genes that influence AP-1 sites, resulting in a change in transcription of other proteins (Beckmann & Wilce, 1997; Hughes & Dragunow, 1995; Karin et al., 1997). In addition to Fos, we have recently found that the D_1 dopamine agonist increased accumulation of the IEG Fos B in neonate-lesioned rats (Knapp et al., 1999). Because the Fos B gene can produce many protein variants (Hiroi et al., 1998), we examined FrA1, one of the variants in the striatum of neonate-lesioned rats with and without sensitization to a D_1 dopamine agonist. It was found that FRA1 levels were markedly elevated in the sensitized rats compared to those neonate-lesioned rats that had not repeatedly received the D_1 dopamine agonist (Knapp et al., 1999). Another IEG that seems to have increased activity in response to neonate lesioning of dopaminergic neurons is *JunD*, but this observation requires confirmation. Future efforts will continue to determine whether other IEGs that bind to AP1 sites are altered by priming of the D_1 dopamine agonist responsiveness. Addressing this issue will provide further understanding of the relationship of these IEG proteins to D_1 dopamine agonist sensitization and other plasticity changes that accompany neonate lesioning of dopaminergic neurons.

It must be emphasized that various other DNA binding proteins can regulate transcription, including NFκB (Gius et al., 1999; Wooten, 1999); SP1 (Zawia et al., 1998); and CREB, CREM, ICER, ATF-1&2, and SRE (Herdegen & Leah, 1998). At this time the potential involvement of these additional transcription factors in the plasticity changes in the neonate-lesioned rat after repeated exposure to a D_1 dopamine agonist has not been examined. The use of microarray-based research (Bowtell, 1999; Brown & Botstein, 1999) is a promising new approach for making an overall assessment of potential endogenous transcription factors that may have an involvement in D_1 dopamine receptor sensitization and SIB.

SIB IN LESCH–NYHAN SYNDROME AND NEONATE-LESIONED RATS AS MODELS OF SIB IN PEOPLE WITH MENTAL RETARDATION AND DEVELOPMENTAL DISABILITIES

It is well documented that SIB and an often-associated symptom, aggressive behavior, are common among people with mental retardation. Consequently, the possibility was considered that the work being addressed in the dopamine deficiency model of Lesch–Nyhan syndrome could be applicable to patients with mental retardation exhibiting SIB (Breese et al., 1987c). A literature search revealed that a drug called *SCH-12679* improved aggression and violent behavior and possibly improved SIB in a selected population of adolescent females with mental retardation (Albert et al., 1977; Itil et al., 1972). Subsequently, Elie et al. (1980) compared SCH-12679 with thioridazine, an antipsychotic, in a group of patients with mental retardation and found that SCH-12679 improved aggression and other abnormal behaviors, whereas thioridazine aggravated the symptoms. Unfortunately, the adverse effects of SCH-12679 prevented further clinical trials.

Because SCH-12679 was effective in people with mental retardation, our laboratory initiated work to examine its pharmacological properties. When SCH-12679 was administered *in vivo*, it blocked the function of D_1 dopamine receptors, but not D_2 dopamine receptors, in lesioned animals (Breese et al., 1990b). Most importantly, SCH-12679 blocked L-dopa-induced SIB in neonate-lesioned rats (Breese et al., 1990b). Collectively, clinical and preclinical data collected on SCH-12679 supported the view that D_1 dopamine antagonists not only would be potential agents for treating symptoms of Lesch–Nyhan syndrome but also could be an effective therapy for treating SIB and aggression in people with mental retardation.

In addition to those efforts already described, research has demonstrated that three drugs classified as atypical antipsychotics can effectively reduce L-dopa-induced or apomorphine-induced SIB in the neonate-lesioned rat. They are clozapine (Criswell et al., 1989b), risperidone (Allen et al., 1998), and olanzapine (Moy et al., 2001). Based upon these preclinical findings in the neonate-lesioned rats, these drugs were tested in patients with SIB. Clozapine improved SIB in three patients with mental retardation (Hammock et al., 1995). Nonetheless, researchers and practitioners should be cautious about any use of clozapine to treat SIB because some patients can develop agranulocytosis (de la Chapelle et al., 1977). Risperidone virtually eliminated SIB in one patient with Lesch–Nyhan syndrome (Allen & Rice, 1996). It is believed that a drug trial of risperidone to treat SIB in patients with mental retardation is underway. Finally, a clinical trial of olanzapine to treat SIB has been initiated in patients with mental retardation, with a report of positive results (J.W. Bodfish and B.B. Sheitman, personal communication). These clinical findings provide evidence that positive results of a drug on SIB induced in the neonate-lesioned rat model can be predictive of their clinical effectiveness to treat SIB. Given that D_1-dopamine antagonists minimize SIB in the neonate-lesioned rat, there should be a stronger impetus to initiate a clinical trial of a specific D_1-dopamine antagonist, such as SKF-39166, to treat the SIB associated with Lesch–Nyhan syndrome and mental retardation. This investigation would test directly the D_1-dopamine hypothesis of SIB in these patient populations (Breese et al., 1995; Criswell et al., 1992).

CONCLUSION

Rats lesioned as neonates are proposed to model the dopamine reduction observed in Lesch–Nyhan syndrome. When rats lesioned as neonates are administered L-dopa, SIB is induced, a response not observed in rats with dopamine-containing neurons lesioned as adults. Thus, the loss of integrity of central dopaminergic neurons in the rats lesioned as neonates results in symptoms differing from those observed in rats lesioned as adults—which serves as a model of the loss of dopaminergic neurons observed in Parkinson's disease. Drugs antagonizing D_1-dopamine receptors, but not those antagonizing D_2-dopamine receptors, block the SIB in the model of Lesch–Nyhan syndrome. This latter observation is the basis of the D_1-dopamine hypothesis of SIB. Current evidence indicates that atypical antipsychotic drugs blocking the self-injury in the neonate-lesioned rat will minimize the SIB observed in a portion of individuals with mental retardation. Future work should define the neurobiological basis of the adaptive changes responsible for the increased susceptibility for SIB that follows disruption of dopamine-containing neurons during development.

20

A NEW ANIMAL MODEL FOR LESCH–NYHAN SYNDROME: CALCIUM CHANNEL ACTIVATION WITH BAY K 8644

SUHAIL KASIM, ZUBAIR KHAN, AND H.A. JINNAH

Lesch–Nyhan syndrome is a rare genetic disorder caused by congenital deficiency of the purine salvage enzyme hypoxanthine phosphoribosyltransferase (HPRT). Affected individuals have hyperuricemia and a characteristic neurobehavioral syndrome (Jinnah & Friedmann, 2000; Lesch & Nyhan, 1964; Visser et al., 2000).

The most striking behavioral feature of Lesch–Nyhan syndrome is severe and persistent self-injurious behavior (SIB). The most common expression of SIB is biting of the lips, tongue, fingers, or hands (Anderson & Ernst, 1994). However, other forms of SIB are also common, including repetitive picking or scratching, hitting or scraping limbs against hard objects, eye poking, or head banging. The behavior is sufficiently severe that substantial tissue damage may occur. SIB generally emerges between age 2 and 4 years but may be delayed until the late teenage years. Eventually SIB develops in essentially all affected individuals. In addition to SIB, individuals with Lesch–Nyhan syndrome often display apparently aggressive behavior towards others. They occasionally bite, hit, or spit on nearby individuals (Nyhan, 1976; Visser et al., 2000). Whether this behavior reflects intended aggression or a poorly controlled compulsion remains unclear.

The neurological features of Lesch–Nyhan syndrome include cognitive disability and a severe defect in the control of voluntary movements. The most frequent and severe motor abnormality is dystonia, which is characterized by poorly controlled, slow, stiff, and twisting movements of the limbs and trunk (Jinnah & Friedmann, 2000; Visser et al., 2000). Many affected individuals also display more fluid involuntary movements or rapid flinging movements indicative of choreoathetosis or ballismus. Some also demonstrate spasticity and hyperactive reflexes. The motor impairments are sufficiently severe that affected individuals cannot walk.

Although the genetic and the biochemical bases for Lesch–Nyhan syndrome have been studied extensively, the pathophysiological components of the neurobehavioral syndrome remain poorly understood. Several animal models have therefore been developed to study the biological processes underlying the neurobehavioral syndrome (Jinnah & Breese, 1997; Jinnah et al., 1990). The present manuscript provides a brief review of some of these models, and presents a novel model based on activation of brain L-type calcium channels with Bay K 8644 (Jinnah et al., 1999, 2000). Under specific conditions, Bay K 8644 can provoke an unusual syndrome that includes SIB, aggressive behavior, and dystonia. This neurobehavioral syndrome provides a closer phenotypic resemblance to Lesch–Nyhan syndrome than other previously described animal models.

ANIMAL MODELS FOR LESCH–NYHAN SYNDROME

Psychostimulants

The acute administration of 1–5 mg/kg of amphetamine or methamphetamine to rodents typically produces motor hyperactivity with stereotyped behaviors such as repetitive sniffing, grooming, licking, or gnawing. Doses of 5–50 mg/kg cause exaggerated stereotyped behavior and often SIB, which are typically expressed by biting of the paws or abdomen (Hohn & Lasagna, 1960; Shishido et al., 2000). As described in more detail in chapter 12, pemoline provokes a similar neurobehavioral syndrome, with hyperactive motor behavior at 5–20 mg/kg and intense stereotypy with SIB at 50–200 mg/kg (Cromwell et al., 1999; Genovese et al., 1969; King et al., 1995, 1998; Mueller & Hsiao, 1980; Mueller & Nyhan, 1982; Turner et al., 1999). Although the expression of SIB typically requires relatively high doses of these psychostimulants, it may also occur with chronic delivery of smaller doses of these drugs (Brien et al., 1977; Huberman et al., 1977; King et al., 1995; Lara-Lemus et al., 1997; Mueller et al., 1986; Mueller & Nyhan, 1983; Mueller et al., 1982) or GBR-12909 (Sivam, 1995). In susceptible children, amphetamine has also been reported to precipitate extreme fingernail biting with bleeding and tissue damage (Sokol et al., 1991). It has been proposed that these psychostimulants provoke SIB by their influence on dopamine systems in the striatum.

Neonatal 6-Hydroxydopamine

As further described in chapter 19, one of the most thoroughly characterized animal models that has been developed for Lesch–Nyhan syndrome involves the administration of dopamine agonists to animals that had damage to dopamine systems during early postnatal development (Joyce et al., 1996; Moy et al., 1997). Neonatal rats given intracisternal or intrastriatal injections of the dopaminergic neurotoxin 6-hydroxydopamine (6-OHDA) during the first few days of postnatal life survive into adulthood. These animals are typically smaller than normal littermates, display mild hyperactive motor behavior, and often show extreme aggressiveness. When treated with L-dihydroxyphenylalanine (L-dopa) or other dopamine agonists, they display exaggerated stereotyped behaviors and SIB, manifested as biting of the paws or abdomen. It has been suggested that SIB results from overstimulation of supersensitized dopamine receptors in the striatum (Joyce et al., 1996; Moy et al., 1997).

Methylxanthines

Administration of the methylxanthines caffeine or theophylline in doses ranging from 5–50 mg/kg produces hyperactivity, tremor, and stereotypy in rodents. Daily administration of high doses of these drugs in the range of 50–200 mg/kg also results in the emergence of SIB in a significant proportion of animals (Ferrer et al., 1982; Lloyd & Stone, 1981; Minana & Grisolia, 1986; Minana et al., 1984; Peters, 1967). SIB is typically manifested by biting of the paws or abdomen. Unfortunately, the regimens required to induce SIB are often lethal, and the chronic use of very high doses makes interpretations of underlying neurochemical mechanisms quite difficult.

Clonidine

Clonidine at doses of 1–5 mg/kg provokes hyperactivity and aggressiveness in mice (Morpurgo, 1968; Nikulina & Klimek, 1993; Razzak et al., 1975). Much higher doses of 50–100 mg/kg produce prostration, severe tremor, and SIB (Bhattacharya et al., 1988; Katsuragi et al., 1984; Razzak et al., 1975, 1977). Animals typically bite their forepaws, and mortality is significant at the higher doses. Although clonidine is often used as an adrenergic agonist, it also binds to adenosine and imidazoline receptors (Stone & Taylor, 1978a, 1978b), and the high doses required to produce SIB make interpretations of the underlying mechanisms uncertain.

HPRT Knockout Mice

Also described in chapter 11, genetic models for Lesch–Nyhan syndrome have also been produced by knocking out (i.e., inactivating) the HPRT gene in different strains of mice (Hooper et al., 1987; Kuehn et al., 1987). These mice display several metabolic and neurochemical abnormalities analogous to those occurring in Lesch–Nyhan syndrome, such as a fourfold to fivefold increase in de novo purine synthesis and significant loss of striatal dopamine (Jinnah et al., 1993, 1994, 1999). The mice also display abnormal behavioral responses to amphetamine and related psychostimulants, though they do not display any overt neurobehavioral defects (Jinnah et al., 1991, 1992).

BAY K 8644 MODEL FOR LESCH–NYHAN SYNDROME

An L-Type Calcium Channel

Calcium channels are expressed throughout the nervous system and in other organs, where they play an important role in stimulus response coupling. Several calcium channel subtypes are currently recognized by their different pharmacological and electrophysiological properties (Catterall, 1995). The *L-type* calcium channel is voltage gated and allows a transient influx of calcium in response to cell membrane depolarization. These channels are expressed widely in the brain with particularly high levels in the striatum, cortex, and hippocampus (Hirota & Lambert, 1997). The dihydropyridine Bay K 8644 functions as an L-type calcium channel activator that increases calcium fluxes in response to depolarizing stimuli (Triggle & Janis, 1987).

SIB

Bay K 8644 was recently shown to provoke SIB in normal mice (Jinnah et al., 1999). In normal adult mice, doses in the range of 4–12 mg/kg reliably provoked self-biting that could lead to severe tissue injury in a dose-dependent manner. The behavior typically emerged 10–15 minutes after drug administration and lasted for 30–90 minutes. Biting was most commonly directed toward the forepaws, with less common targets being the rear paws, abdomen, or shoulders (Figure 20.1). Though the majority of biting was directed toward the animals' own bodies, some mice occasionally bit the bedding material or cage walls during testing. Other mice engaged in vacuous chewing movements with nothing in the mouth.

Of note, weanling mice were more susceptible to the ability of Bay K 8644 to provoke SIB than adult mice (Figure 20.2). The animals would sometimes vocalize and dart after biting, suggesting that they felt pain. The behavior did not appear to be due to drug-induced peripheral paresthesias because it could also be induced by direct injection of small amounts of the drug into the lateral ventricles.

Aggression

Unlike most other drugs capable of inducing SIB, the SIB induced by Bay K 8644 was not accompanied by an increase in stereotyped behaviors.

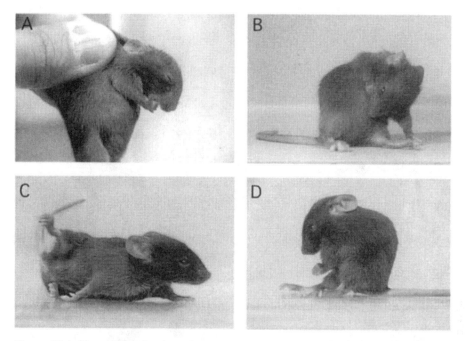

Figure 20.1. Neurobehavioral syndrome associated with Bay K 8644. *(A)*, Mouse biting paw despite being held by examiner. *(B)*, Mouse biting abdomen. *(C)*, Mouse with dystonic limb posturing. *(D)*, Mouse with dystonic trunk posturing.

However, the drug-treated animals appeared unusually aggressive, with violent biting often being directed toward any disturbing stimulus (Jinnah et al., 1999).

Motor Dysfunction

In addition to SIB and aggression, Bay K 8644 also provoked a characteristic motor syndrome (Jinnah et al., 2000). Mice treated with 2 mg/kg Bay K 8644 demonstrated reduced rearing and slowed ambulation. Animals also occasionally demonstrated ptosis, hyperreactivity to auditory or tactile stimuli, and Straub tail. At a dose of 4 mg/kg of Bay K 8644, ambulation became even slower, with more frequent episodes of hyperreactivity to sensory stimuli and Straub tail. At doses of 8–12 mg/kg of Bay K 8644, animals displayed exaggerated truncal flexion and abnormal stiff and twisting limb movements (Figure 20.1). The latter movements are best described as *generalized dystonia* (Jinnah et al., 2000), the most problematic motor abnormality in Lesch–Nyhan syndrome.

Role of Calcium Channels

Three experiments were performed to verify that the behaviors observed with Bay K 8644 were caused by activation of L-type calcium channels and

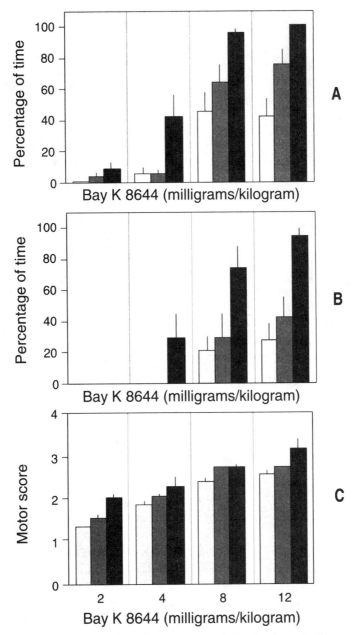

Figure 20.2. Influence of dose and age on neurobehavioral syndrome associated with Bay K 8644. Three groups of 10 mice of different ages were treated with different doses of Bay K 8644 and placed individually in clear plastic boxes. They were observed for 1 minute each for an hour, and the occurrence of self-biting *(A)* and SIB *(B)* were noted. Data for these two behaviors are expressed as the average percentage of intervals in which the behavior was observed ±SEM. The severity of motor dysfunction *(C)* was simultaneously rated with a simple 4-point scale (Jinnah et al., 2000), and data were expressed as the average motor score ±SEM. White bars represent fully adult mice (ages 6-8 weeks), gray bars represent young adult mice (age 4–5 weeks), and black bars represent weanling mice (ages 3–4 weeks).

not some nonspecific side effect. If the motor effects of Bay K 8644 are caused by calcium channel activation, then they should be provoked selectively by the (−)Bay K 8644 enantiomer, which is the active agonist of L-type calcium channels. In contrast, the (+)Bay K 8644 enantiomer, which is actually a weak antagonist, should have no effect. In fact, the entire neurobehavioral syndrome, including SIB, aggression, and dystonia was evident with (−)Bay K 8644 but absent with (+)Bay K 8644.

If the neurobehavioral effects of Bay K 8644 are caused by L-type calcium channel activation, then a structurally distinct L-type calcium channel agonist should produce similar effects. Indeed, the L-type calcium channel activator FPL 64176 (Rampe et al., 1993; Zheng et al., 1991) provoked a syndrome quite similar to that produced by Bay K 8644, except that SIB was less prominent, whereas motor dysfunction seemed worse.

If the neurobehavioral effects of Bay K 8644 are caused by L-type calcium channel activation, then calcium channel antagonists should block its effects. To verify this prediction, adult mice were pretreated with one of several calcium channel antagonists before receiving Bay K 8644. Nifedipine, nimodipine, and nitrendipine are dihydropyridine L-type calcium channel antagonists that bind to the same molecular site as Bay K 8644. Though these drugs produced no obvious behavioral effects when administered alone, each markedly attenuated the SIB and dystonia associated with Bay K 8644 (Figure 20.3).

CONCLUSION

To date, multiple animal models have been developed for Lesch–Nyhan syndrome, each with different strengths and weaknesses (Jinnah & Breese, 1997; Jinnah et al., 1990). The HPRT knockout mouse provides a powerful molecular and biochemical model of the disease but suffers from the lack of any neurobehavioral anomalies analogous to those occurring in Lesch–Nyhan syndrome. Multiple pharmacological models have been developed to reproduce the neurobehavioral syndrome, but they are unlikely to contribute to our understanding of initial genetic and biochemical events that initiate the pathogenic processes in Lesch–Nyhan syndrome. In addition, most of the pharmacological models have focused primarily on only one aspect of the neurobehavioral syndrome of Lesch–Nyhan syndrome—SIB. Each of these models is associated with changes in motor function but none that can be considered directly analogous to the motor impairments seen in Lesch–Nyhan syndrome.

The Bay K 8644 model provides several advantages over previously described models (Table 20.1). First, it induces SIB, aggressive behavior, and dystonia to provide a more complete replication of the neurobehavioral syndrome of Lesch–Nyhan syndrome than any previous model. Second, the

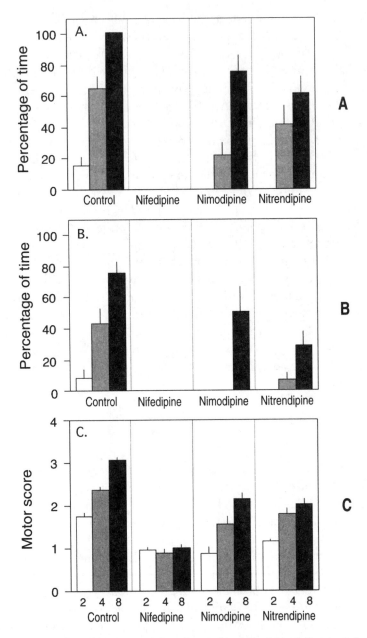

Figure 20.3. Influence of L-type calcium channel antagonists on the neurobehavioral syndrome associated with Bay K 8644. Three different groups of eight mice each were pretreated with saline or one of three calcium channel blockers 5 minutes before Bay K 8644. White bars represent 2 mg/kg, gray bars represent 4 mg/kg, and black bars represent 8 mg/kg Bay K 8644. Mice were observed for 1 minute each for an hour, and the occurrence of self-biting *(A)* and SIB *(B)* were noted. Data for these two behaviors are expressed as the average percentage of intervals in which the behavior was observed ±SEM. The severity of motor dysfunction *(C)* was simultaneously rated with a simple 4-point scale (Jinnah et al., 2000), and data were expressed as the average motor score ±SEM.

TABLE 20.1
Pharmacologic Models for LNS

Model	Temporal aspects	Motor features	Exaggerated stereotypy	Aggressiveness	Neurochemical basis
Amphetamine	Acute chronic	Hyperactivity	Yes	No	Monoamines
Methamphetamine	Acute chronic	Hyperactivity	Yes	No	Monoamines
Pemoline	Chronic	Hyperactivity	Yes	No	Monoamines
GBR-12909	Chronic	Hyperactivity	Yes	No	Dopamine
6-OHDA	Delayed	Hyperactivity	Yes	Yes	Dopamine
Methylxanthines	Chronic	Hyperactivity	Yes	No	Unknown
Clonidine	Acute	Prostration, tremor	No	Yes	Unknown
Bay K 8644	Acute	Hypoactivity, dystonia	No	Yes	Calcium channels

functions of Bay K 8644 as a specific activator of L-type calcium channels have been well characterized. In contrast, many of the other drug models provide little pharmacological specificity at the doses required to produce SIB. This lack of pharmacological specificity makes it difficult to infer potential mechanisms of action. Third, many of the other drug models are associated with extreme stereotyped behavior, leading to suggestions that SIB is an indirect consequence of automatic motor programs such as over-grooming. The administration of Bay K 8644 is not associated with any obvious increase in stereotyped behaviors, but instead appears to provoke extreme compulsive biting. Fourth, Bay K 8644 causes SIB acutely, whereas many previous models require chronic or delayed drug delivery. This difference in temporal profiles makes the Bay K 8644 model technically simpler to employ and allows for a more direct analysis of accompanying changes in brain function that might be relevant to the expression of the neurobehavioral syndrome.

To our knowledge, calcium channels have received little attention as potential mediators of SIB or motor dysfunction in Lesch–Nyhan syndrome, and calcium channel drugs have not been considered as potential therapeutic agents. The Bay K 8644 model provides a new tool for the investigation of the role of these calcium channels in the expression of the neurobehavioral syndrome. In addition, the broad availability of safe calcium channel drugs may also provide a novel treatment approach for affected individuals.

21

REPLACEMENT THERAPY FOR THE TREATMENT OF LESCH–NYHAN SYNDROME

RICHARD E. TESSEL, PIPPA S. LOUPE, AND STEPHEN R. SCHROEDER

Lesch–Nyhan syndrome is the result of a genetic abnormality caused by a deficit in hypoxanthine phosphoribosyl-transferase (HPRT; Nyhan, 1994), a purine salvage enzyme. Many Lesch–Nyhan syndrome symptoms are primarily behavioral: mental retardation, hyperaggression, choreoathetosis, dystonia, and, perhaps the most problematic, severe self-injurious behavior (SIB; Nyhan, 1994). The most common SIB topographies in people with Lesch–Nyhan syndrome are severe biting of lips and oral cavity and digit amputation. However, other SIB topographies include throwing the body against or off objects and sticking fingers in the spokes of wheelchairs (Schroeder, 1991).

LESCH–NYHAN SYNDROME: A DEVELOPMENTAL DOPAMINE DEPLETION DISORDER

In a currently unknown fashion, the genetic HPRT deficit apparently results in decreases in the following: dopamine synthesis and metabolism (Ernst et al., 1996; Jankovic et al., 1988; Lloyd et al., 1981; Silverstein et al., 1985), the number of dopaminergic nerve terminals and cell bodies (Ernst et al., 1996), dopamine concentration (Saito et al., 1999), and dopamine transporter density (Wong et al., 1996). The deficit causes increases in dopamine receptor (D_1 and D_2) immunoreactivity (Saito et al., 1999) in the Lesch–Nyhan syndrome extrapyramidal motor system. The latter findings indicate that individuals with Lesch–Nyhan syndrome have markedly reduced dopaminergic neuronal innervation of the basal ganglia and probably other brain regions (e.g., Ernst et al., 1996), perhaps causing an up-regulation of dopamine receptors in at least some affected brain areas.

299

Much preclinical evidence also supports the conclusion that the preceding innervation reduction is a major cause or predisposing factor for the behavioral abnormalities displayed by persons with Lesch–Nyhan syndrome. For example, HPRT-deficient mice have modestly reduced brain dopamine levels (Jinnah et al., 1999). However, most evidence for the importance of extrapyramidal dopamine depletion in Lesch–Nyhan syndrome behavioral abnormalities derives from the work of Breese and colleagues during the past 2 decades (e.g., Breese et al., 1995; chapter 19). These individuals have demonstrated the effects of neonatal, intracisternal treatment of postweaning rats with the catecholaminergic neurotoxin 6-hydroxydopamine (6-OHDA), which severely (i.e., by more than 90%) reduces brain dopamine. After receiving (being primed or sensitized with) repeated, intermittent systemic injections of direct dopamine agonists or of the catecholamine synthetic precursor L-dihydroxyphenylalanine (L-dopa), the rats bite through the skin of their paws and forelimbs with sufficient intensity and frequency to amputate their digits and forepaws. It might be surprising to some that L-dopa might be capable of leading to dopamine levels that are sufficient to activate postsynaptic dopamine receptors because the dopaminergic neurons have presumably been essentially eliminated by the neonatal 6-OHDA treatment. However, it is well known that the localization of L-aromatic amino acid decarboxylase (L-AAAD), the enzyme that converts L-dopa to dopamine, is not restricted to central dopaminergic neurons (Fuxe et al., 1978). Consequently, functionally significant L-dopa-derived dopamine can apparently be synthesized and released from other, nondopaminergic neurons. Other aberrant behaviors are also preferentially or selectively elicited in the 6-OHDA-treated rats by dopamine agonist administration (e.g., Breese et al., 1984a, 1984b, 1985, 1995). Moreover, the SIB induced in these rats by repeated L-dopa injection is selectively inhibited by antagonists selective for dopamine D_1 receptors, although substitution of L-dopa by coadministration of selective D_1 and D_2 agonists more effectively induces SIB than does repeated D_1 agonist administration alone.

Neonatal 6-OHDA treatment resulting in severe (i.e., >95%) dopamine depletion combined with priming by direct dopamine receptor agonists and the indirect dopamine receptor agonist L-dopa results in SIB caused primarily by activation of "functionally" supersensitive D1 receptors (e.g., Breese et al., 1995; Moy et al., 1997; Neal & Joyce, 1991; Neal-Beliveau & Joyce, 1999). How such supersensitivity occurs is unclear. However, the mechanisms involved in this supersensitivity presumably relate to the absence of endogenous dopamine (i.e., disuse supersensitivity). For example, neonatal 6-OHDA has been reported to reduce D_1 receptor binding but increase D_1 receptor messenger ribonucleic acid (mRNA; Frohna et al., 1995) and to increase the behavioral actions of selective D_1 agonists (Johnson et al., 1992). Furthermore, D_1 receptor priming in such animals seems to induce increases in postsynaptic proteins such as GFAP (Breese et al., 1994).

DOPAMINE DEPLETION IS NOT REQUIRED FOR THE PHARMACOLOGICAL INDUCTION OF SIB

SIB has also been reported to occur in *unlesioned* rats. These rats presumably possess normal dopamine receptor sensitivities after repeated systemic injections with high doses of indirect dopamine agonists such as amphetamine, the selective dopamine transporter inhibitor GBR-12909 (particularly in female rats; Sivam, 1995), pemoline (Cromwell et al., 1997), Bay K 8644, and others (see chapter 20). However, definitions for SIB may vary from laboratory to laboratory (e.g., skin present between the animals' teeth; Okamura et al., 1997; Yokoyama & Okamura, 1997). In addition, in our laboratory, repeated systemic GBR-12909 injection (20 mg/kg, one injection per day for 5 days) in otherwise untreated female rats induces repeated mouthing, nibbling, or both of the dorsal surfaces of the forepaws such that these surfaces become denuded of surface skin, an SIB topography much different from the skin punctures and amputations normally induced by repeated systemic injections with L-dopa or the mixed dopamine receptor agonist apomorphine in the neonatal 6-OHDA Lesch–Nyhan syndrome rat model (Breese et al., 1984a, 1984b, 1985, 1990; Stodgell et al., 1998)—but perhaps reminiscent of SIB manifested by persons with Rett syndrome (e.g., Phlippart, 1992; Umansky & Watson, 1998). Furthermore, as would be expected of a drug whose actions (i.e., blockade of released dopamine reuptake) are presumably absolutely dependent on dopaminergic neuronal integrity, SIB induced by GBR-12909 in rats is blocked rather than exacerbated by severe dopamine neuronal depletion by 6-OHDA (Sivam, 1995). Comparable studies with other indirect dopamine agonists (e.g., amphetamine) using Lesch–Nyhan syndrome rats do not seem to have been published, although the behavioral effects of such drugs are reduced in rats depleted of brain dopamine by 6-OHDA treatment as adults (e.g., Moore, 1977; Van Keuren et al., 1998).

The previous evidence (see chapter 19) indicates that dopaminergically mediated SIB in neonatal 6-OHDA rats can result from "excessive" receptor stimulation by exogenously administered *direct* dopamine agonists in the presence of functionally "supersensitive" D_1 receptors, and in untreated rats with normal dopamine receptor sensitivity and dopamine neuronal innervation, by high doses of *indirect* dopamine agonists. Together, these conclusions suggest that therapeutic benefit could be obtained either by reducing endogenous dopamine concentrations to minimize intermittent stimulation of supersensitive dopamine receptors or by providing sufficient continuous but modest levels of endogenous or exogenous dopamine receptor agonists to normalize the sensitivity of the receptors. The results of a small clinical study of people with Lesch–Nyhan syndrome could be taken to support the preceding treatment dichotomy. In apparently the only study to do so, Jankovic et al. (1988) attempted to examine the effects of the dopamine-depleting agent tetrabenazine, the mixed dopamine receptor antagonist fluphenazine, L-dopa (plus the standard adjunct carbidopa, a peripheral inhibitor of L-dopa metabolism), and the D_2 agonist and D_1 partial agonist, bromocriptine. Of the five patients examined, only two patients were exposed to each of these treatments. Both patients had essentially undetectable HPRT activity and subnormal cerebrospinal fluid levels of homovanillic acid concentrations. Although brain dopamine receptor function was not directly measured in the two patients exposed to each of the treatments, L-dopa reduced SIB enough in one patient (the one with the lowest homovanillic acid concentration among the patients in the study, which was perhaps reflective of too little endogenous dopamine) so that restraints were no longer required; this patient's SIB was moderately improved by bromocriptine. In contrast, the patient's SIB was worsened by both tetrabenazine and fluphenazine. In the other of these two patients (the one with the highest, although subnormal, cerebrospinal fluid homovanillic acid concentration among the study's patients, which was perhaps reflective of the presence of excessive dopamine), the opposite pattern seemed to develop: moderate improvement with tetrabenazine and either no change or worsening of SIB after fluphenazine, carbidopa-levodopa, or bromocriptine. Of the remaining three patients, only tetrabenazine induced moderate benefits, and the other treatments had no effect on SIB.

POTENTIAL SIB EXACERBATION BY ENDOGENOUS DOPAMINE

To what extent could *endogenous* dopamine contribute to the genesis or maintenance of SIB in Lesch–Nyhan syndrome? We have found that repeated intermittent exposure to sessions of electric foot shock, a stressor known to increase dopamine release within the basal ganglia and other brain regions (Finlay & Zigmond, 1997; Stodgell et al., 1998), does not itself induce SIB in adult Lesch–Nyhan syndrome rats (Stodgell et al., 1998). However, the incidence of SIB during construction of an acute cumulative apomorphine dose-effect curve was significantly increased in Lesch–Nyhan syndrome animals previously primed with either foot shock or apomorphine. These SIB incidences were doubled in Lesch–Nyhan syndrome rats that had priming histories with both foot shock and apomorphine. In addition, increases in the concentrations of the dopamine release index, 3-methoxytyramine (Wood & Altar, 1988) in the striatum (a part of the rat basal ganglia), paralleled these changes in SIB incidence. These data do not confirm that SIB was dopaminergically mediated in our study but are consistent with the possibilities that priming with stress (possibly secondary to stress-elicited dopamine release) can be a substitute for priming with an exogenous dopamine agonist, and previous stress could exacerbate the incidence of SIB in Lesch–Nyhan syndrome. Nevertheless, the suggestion that SIB results from excessive extrapyramidal D_1 receptor stimulation has led to the clinical use of dopamine receptor antagonists as a relatively standard treatment for SIB.

CONTINUOUS DOPAMINE RECEPTOR STIMULATION AS REPLACEMENT THERAPY

Pharmacological Approaches

In the previous section, the research indicates that *intermittent* dopamine receptor stimulation, induced either physiologically or pharmacologically, can induce or facilitate the occurrence of SIB in both Lesch–Nyhan syndrome and normal rats. In addition, although the efficacies of several psychotropic drug classes have been examined, when the previously indicated preclinical and clinical data concerning SIB are considered together, it becomes apparent why clinically available dopamine receptor antagonists (antipsychotic drugs) are the major pharmacological agents currently used to control the intensity and frequency of SIB (Aman & Singh, 1991; Schroeder et al., 1995). On the other hand, it is possible that *continuous* dopamine receptor stimulation has the opposite effect—that is, the induction of tolerance to SIB-eliciting stimuli even in animals with established histories of SIB. Available evidence suggests this may be possible, although we have found little effort to examine this issue in Lesch–Nyhan syndrome rats, with a few possible exceptions, which are discussed in a later section.

L-dopa as replacement therapy remains the mainstay for treating another dopamine depletion disorder that typically begins to manifest itself in late middle age—Parkinson's disease (Standaert & Young, 1996). However, the extent to which L-dopa administration to untreated rats or to the Parkinson's model exacerbates (sensitizes) or antagonizes (desensitizes, or induces tolerance to) biochemical and behavioral indices of dopamine receptor function has been less clear. For example, there are numerous variations among studies in the L-dopa dose used (typically 100 mg/kg with a peripheral L-AAAD inhibitor), as well as the length of time it is administered, the routes of drug administration (parenteral, oral, subcutaneous osmotic minipump-delivered, or in the animals' drinking water), and the interinjection interval. However, recent studies do demonstrate that the increase in D_2 binding associated with a single intraperitoneal dose of L-dopa to otherwise untreated rats is abolished by long-term moderate- to high-dose L-dopa administration (170 mg/kg/day in the drinking water for 5 weeks; Opacka-Juffry et al., 1998). Recent studies also show that doses of continuously delivered L-dopa (by osmotic minipump) higher than 100 mg/kg are much more effective in increasing extrapyramidal dopamine stores in rats (Trugman et al., 1996), and the effects of apomorphine on inducing locomotor activity are markedly reduced in mice by daily long-term (28 days of) high doses of L-dopa given in the drinking water (180–300 mg/kg/day; Tabar et al., 1989). Furthermore, using subcutaneously implanted osmotic minipumps rather than injection for drug delivery, tolerance to the actions of GBR-12909 in eliciting locomotor activity in normal rats in association with indirect indices of dopamine reuptake transporter availability has been reported (Kunko et al., 1997; Izenwasser et al., 1999). Similarly, tolerance to behavioral actions of apomorphine has been observed in patients with Parkinson's disease (a dopamine depletion disorder in which extrapyramidal dopaminergic neuronal loss occurs during adulthood; Standaert & Young, 1996), in the 6-OHDA treated rodent, and in the MPTP (N-methyl-4-phenyl-1,2,3,6-tetrahydropyridine) monkey Parkinson's models (Gancher et al., 1992, 1995, 1996; Hughes et al., 1993; Luquin et al., 1993; Montastruc et al., 1996; Winkler & Weiss, 1986). Tolerance to the stereotypy-inducing and startle-response enhancing effects of amphetamine also has been induced in rodents by minipump-delivered amphetamine (Kokkinidis, 1984; Nielsen, 1981). Continuous exposure to the D_1 agonist SKF-38393 induced tolerance to the drug's rotatory action in adult mice with unilateral lesions induced by 6-OHDA without affecting the rotatory stimulation induced by the D_2 agonist quinpirole (Winkler et al., 1988).

Surgical Approaches

Numerous studies have been performed during the last decade supporting the potential utility of injections of fetal dopaminergic cells or tissue into locations within the extrapyramidal motor system as replacement therapy for neurochemical and behavioral deficits observed in rat models of Parkinson's disease (i.e., postweaning rats treated with 6-OHDA). In general, these implants have antagonized or reversed the induction by 6-OHDA of behavioral hypersensitivity to the D_1 agonist SKF 38393, D_2 agonists (e.g., quinpirole; LY 171555), and the mixed D_1/D_2 agonist apomorphine, as well as reversed the direction of amphetamine-induced behavioral rotation normally induced in rats treated unilaterally with 6-OHDA (Blunt et al., 1992; Moukhles et al., 1994; Nikkah et al., 1994; Robertson et al., 1991; Savasta et al., 1992). Implants in adult rats treated unilaterally with 6-OHDA have also prevented behavioral sensitization induced by repeated L-dopa administration and reversed the increase in striatal D_1 and D_2 densities induced by 6-OHDA (Rioux et al., 1991a, 1991b, 1993; see also Yurek et al., 1991). In this same study, 5 weeks of L-dopa (200 mg/kg/24 hr) per se reduced D_1 receptor density in the lesioned striatum. Comparable implant-induced effects on 6-OHDA-induced dopamine receptor densities, in dopamine-agonist elicited expression of the intermediate early gene (IEG) product Fos, and changes in the behavioral actions of dopamine agonists have also been reported by many others (Dawson et al., 1991; Gagnon et al., 1991; Savasta et al., 1992).

Similar benefits from fetal tissue implantation have been observed in the few studies involving neonatal 6-OHDA-treated rats. Abrous et al.

(1993) and Mennicken et al. (1995) treated 3-day-old rats intracranially with 6-OHDA and then implanted fetal mesencephalic dopaminergic neurons into their striata very soon (5 days) afterward. From 8 to 11 months later, the behavioral hypersensitivities to apomorphine, the D_1 agonist SKF 38393, and the D_2 agonist LY 171555 were eliminated, and the behavioral hyposensitivity to amphetamine was abolished in the 6-OHDA-treated, implanted rats. However, the implant had little effect on other 6-OHDA-induced behavioral parameters (Abrous et al., 1993). Nevertheless, fetal tissue implants made similarly early after neonatal 6-OHDA administration may be capable of acting as lifelong replacement therapy. Nikkhah et al. (1995a, 1995b) also evaluated the effect of implanting fetal ventral mesencephalic dopaminergic neurons unilaterally into the substantia nigra only days after bilateral 6-OHDA treatment of 3-day-old neonatal rat pups. When examined in adulthood, the effects of amphetamine and apomorphine on striatal Fos expression in the implanted side of the brain were normalized, as were the directions of behavioral rotation induced by amphetamine and apomorphine. However, the implants induced only modest improvement in skilled forelimb use. Moreover, Bentlage, et al. (1999) has found that the beneficial effects of implantation into the substantia nigra on the behavioral actions of amphetamine, apomorphine, SKF 38393, and quinpirole in 6-month-old rats previously injected with 6-OHDA on 1 day after birth markedly depended on the number of days between 6-OHDA administration and implantation. More specifically, the effects of the dopamine agonists were appropriately altered in animals implanted 3 and 10 days after birth but were absent in animals implanted 20 days after birth. The latter findings suggest that a critical period between 6-OHDA lesion and implantation may exist, at least insofar as fetal tissue implantation is the means through which replacement therapy is provided. Moreover, although many patients with Parkinson's disease have greatly benefited from human fetal dopaminergic neuronal implantation during the last decade, it has not been universally effective. Many questions still need to be answered before these implants can be added to standard antiparkinsonism therapy (see reviews, Clarkson & Freed, 1999; Olanow et al., 1996; Tabbal et al., 1998; Widner, 1999).

Behavioral Approaches

Recent work in our laboratory supports the utility of nonsurgical and nonpharmacological dopamine replacement therapy in the treatment of SIB and other aberrant behaviors in adult humans with Lesch–Nyhan syndrome. Adult Lesch–Nyhan syndrome rats, which were severely depleted of striatal dopamine and its metabolites as neonates by intracisternal injection of 6-OHDA, underwent prolonged exposure (i.e., 90 30-minutes daily training sessions, five sessions per week) to a conditional discrimination procedure involving the learning of progressively more difficult fixed-ratio discrimination training (FRDT). The FRDT markedly antagonized or completely reversed the neonatal 6-OHDA-induced depletions (Stodgell et al., 1996; Tessel et al., 1995) for at least 2 months following cessation of training. Furthermore, four prolonged, massed FRDT sessions significantly increased extracellular, microdialysis-assessed, dopamine concentrations in Lesch–Nyhan syndrome rats, whereas these concentrations slightly decreased in untrained Lesch–Nyhan syndrome rats (Loupe et al., unpublished observations). The effects of 6-OHDA treatment on striatal dopamine and metabolite content had heretofore been thought to be irreversible.

The extent to which such training may function as replacement therapy for the treatment of SIB has not yet been directly tested. However, we are in the process of examining this possibility. Nevertheless, we (Van Keuren et al., 1998) have demonstrated that like fetal dopaminergic neuronal implantation (see previous discussion), fixed-ratio discrimination training markedly or completely reverses the behavioral supersensitivity to some behavioral effects of the mixed dopamine agonist apomorphine in rats treated postweaning with 6-OHDA (a rat model of Parkinson's disease). This normalization presumably occurred because of training-induced dopamine receptor sensitivity normalization secondary to training-elicited dopamine release. However, despite comparable magnitudes of 6-OHDA-induced striatal dopamine depletions in both studies (96%–97%; Stodgell et al., 1996; Van Keuren et al., 1998), Parkinson's disease rats were quantitatively resistant to FRDT-induced increases in striatal tissue dopamine (and homovanillic acid) concentrations. The reasons for this quantitative discrepancy are unclear. Nevertheless, it is recognized that extracellular striatal dopamine concentrations are much less affected by prior 6-OHDA treatment in Parkinson's disease rats than are striatal tissue dopamine measures (e.g., Schwarting & Huston, 1996; Zigmond & Hastings, 1998). Consequently, it is still possible that FRDT may have had significantly increased extracellular dopamine release within the striatum (or other functionally important dopaminergically innervated tissues whose tissue dopamine and metabolite concentrations were not assessed in our study; e.g., nucleus accumbens).

POTENTIAL MECHANISMS OF TRAINING-INDUCED
RECOVERY FROM 6-OHDA-INDUCED
DOPAMINERGIC NEURONAL DEPLETION

In Lesch–Nyhan syndrome and Parkinson's disease, the loss of dopamine neurons derived from the substantia nigra pars compacta (SNpc) seems to be significantly responsible for symptomatology (e.g., Frohna et al.,

1997; Penit-Soria et al., 1997; Rodriguez et al., 1998). Brown et al. (1999) have described a basal ganglia pathway in primates that they propose relates conditioned and primary rewarding stimuli to the induction of "burst" firing of SNpc. According to these authors, information about conditioned rewarding stimuli derived from the prefrontal cortex and information about primary rewarding stimuli both first inform the ventral striatum (i.e., nucleus accumbens), which, in turn, activates successive excitatory pathways (i.e., ventral pallidum, then the pedunculopontine tegmental nucleus) to induce burst firing of the SNpc and consequent striatal dopamine synthesis and release (see also Lokwan et al., 1999). In addition, nigrostriatal neurons are activated by unpredicted appetitive rewards, such as those occurring during the learning of a task, but this activation is eliminated on completion of the learning (see Schultz et al., 2000; Suri & Schultz, 1999). However, after this completion the dopamine neurons can be activated if reinforcement occurs earlier or later than predicted, but dopaminergic firing is depressed when a predicted reward is omitted. Furthermore, dopamine neurons are activated by novel stimuli and physically salient stimuli (e.g., stress).

The importance of the previously described pathways and temporal alterations in food reinforcement presentation to the reversal of the 6-OHDA treatment effects in the Lesch–Nyhan syndrome or Parkinson's disease rats (e.g., Stodgell et al., 1996; Tessel et al., 1995; Van Keuren et al. 1998) has not been directly tested. However, our FRDT program involved learning progressively more difficult FRDs, led to progressive increases in discrimination errors, and thus presumably led to gradual decreases in the predictablity of reinforcement over time. We found it interesting that by "pruning" dopaminergic neurons and reducing their density, 6-OHDA treatment may have actually facilitated the extent to which FRDT could increase the synthesis and release of striatal dopamine and its detectability (see Zigmond & Hastings, 1998). In addition, we compared the effects of our progressively more difficulty FRDT in one group of Lesch–Nyhan syndrome rats with those in Lesch–Nyhan syndrome animals that were only required to learn and continuously perform a single, rapidly acquired FRD (FR1 vs. FR16). The training-associated recovery of striatal dopamine and its metabolites was much larger in the former than in the latter Lesch–Nyhan syndrome animals (Stodgell et al., 1996). These findings appear consistent with the results of Brown et al. (1999), Lokwan et al. (1999), Suri and Schultz (1999), and Schultz et al. (2000) in animals and of Elliott et al. (2000) in humans, and suggests mechanisms through which FRDT-induced increases in endogenous striatal dopamine (i.e., of replacement therapy using endogenous dopamine) could occur in Lesch–Nyhan syndrome and possibly Parkinson's disease. They also suggest that the approaches should be assessed in the clinical setting to examine whether FRDT or related behavioral training exert therapeutic efficacy.

CONCLUSION

The preceding evidence strongly supports the conclusion that the SIB associated with Lesch–Nyhan syndrome results from "excessive" but intermittent activation of dopamine-depletion-produced, functionally supersensitive D_1 receptors by dopamine or exogenous dopamimetics. However, it is clear that SIB can be induced in otherwise untreated animals by sufficiently high doses of dopamimetics. It therefore seems to us and is implied by the data presented by Jankovic et al. (1988) that the excessive D_1 stimulation in some circumstances (even in people with Lesch–Nyhan syndrome) may be caused by (a) the presence of overly large amounts of extracellular dopamimetics interacting with D_1 receptors of relatively normal sensitivity or (b) reduced amounts of these dopamimetics interacting with functionally supersensitive D_1 receptors. We also propose that continuous administration of exogenous chemicals or use of behavioral procedures that increase the availability of endogenous dopamine to induce the central availability of direct dopamine receptor agonists (e.g., L-dopa, dopamine) may be clinically helpful in at least some people with Lesch–Nyhan syndrome, particularly those who have not benefited by treatment with dopamine receptor antagonists.

The veracity of our proposed treatment approach must still be examined in either humans with Lesch–Nyhan syndrome or in the 6-OHDA Lesch–Nyhan syndrome model. However, we have obtained clinically positive results in Parkinson's disease rats (van Keuren et al., 1998). In collaboration with Drs. Richard and Muriel Saunders, we will soon begin to examine the efficacy of conditional discrimination training on neurological and neuropsychological symptoms manifested in people with Parkinson's disease. Demonstration of the clinical efficacy of relevant training procedures in both preclinical and clinical situations would contribute significantly to the introduction of a novel, noninvasive method that alone or in conjunction with more standard therapies may enhance the quality of life for people with Parkinson's disease and people with Lesch–Nyhan syndrome.

REFERENCES

Abbott Laboratories. (1975). Cylert (Pemoline) Drug Monograph. North Chicago, IL: Abbott Laboratories.

Abrous, D. N., Choulli, K., Rouge-Pont, F., Simon, H., Le Moal, M., & Herman, J. P. (1993). Effects of intracerebral dopaminergic grafts on behavioural deficits induced by neonatal 6-hydroxydopamine lesions of the mesotelencephalic dopaminergic pathway. *Neuroscience, 54*, 499–511.

Adler C. H., & Wrabetz, L. (1996). Lesch–Nyhan variant: dystonia, ataxia, near-normal intelligence, and no self-mutilation. *Movement Disorders, 11*, 583–584.

Adler, C, M., Elman, I., Weisenfeld, N., Kestler, L., Pickar, D., & Brier, A. (2000). Effects of acute metabolic stress on striatal dopamine release in healthy volunteers. *Neuropsychopharmacology, 22*, 545–550.

Albert, J.-M., Elie, R., Cooper, S. F., Clermont, A., & Langlois, Y. (1977). Efficacy of SCH-12679 in the management of aggressive mental retardates. *Current Therapeutic Research, 21*, 786–795.

Alexander, G. E., Delong, M. R., & Strick, P. L. (1986). Parallel organization of functionally segregated circuits linking basal ganglia and cortex. *Annual Review of Neuroscience, 9*, 357–381.

Allen, S. M., Freeman, J. N., & Davis, W. M. (1998). Evaluation of risperidone in the neonatal 6-hydroxydopamine model of Lesch–Nyhan syndrome. *Pharmacology, Biochemistry, and Behavior, 59*, 327–330.

Allen, S. M., & Rice, S. N. (1996). Risperidone antagonism of self-mutilation in a Lesch–Nyhan patient. *Progress in Neuro-Psychopharmacology & Biological Psychiatry, 20*, 793–800.

Aman, M. G. (1993). Efficacy of psychotropic drugs for reducing self-injurious behavior in the developmental disabilities. *Annals of Clinical Psychiatry, 5*, 171–188.

Aman, M. G. (1997). Recent studies in psychopharmacology in mental retardation. In N. N. Bray (Ed.), *International review of research in mental retardation* (pp. 113–146). New York: Academic Press.

Aman, M. G., & Madrid, A. (1999). Atypical antipsychotics in persons with developmental disabilities. *Mental Retardation and Developmental Disabilities Research Reviews, 5*, 253–263.

Aman, M. G., & Singh, N. N. Pharmacological Intervention. (1991). In J. L. Matson, & J. A. Mulick (Eds.), *Handbook of mental retardation* (pp. 347–372). Pergamon Press: New York.

Aman, M. G., White, A. J., & Field, C. (1984). Chlorpromazine effects on stereotypic and conditioned behaviour of severely retarded patients: A pilot study. *Journal of Mental Deficiency Research, 28*, 253–260.

Ames, D., Cummings, J. L., Wirshing, W. C., Quinn, B., & Mahler, M. (1994). Repetitive and compulsive behavior in frontal lobe degenerations. *The Journal of Neuropsychiatry and Clinical Neuroscience, 6*, 100–113.

Andersen, P. H., Groenvald, F. C., Hohlweg, R., Hansen, L. B., Guddal, E., & Braestrup, E. (1988). NO-112, NO-0756-New dopamine D_1 selective antagonists. *Society of Neuroscience Abstracts, 14,* 935.

Anderson, L., Dancis, J., & Alpert, M. (1978). Behavioral contingencies and self-mutilation in Lesch–Nyhan disease. *Journal of Consulting⁰ ⁰ Clinical Psychology, 46,* 529–536.

Anderson, L. T., & Ernst, M. (1994). Self-injury in Lesch–Nyhan disease. *Journal of Autism and Developmental Disorders, 24,* 67–81.

Ando, H., & Yoshimura, I. (1978). Prevalence of maladaptive behavior in retarded children as a function of IQ and age. *Journal of Abnormal Child Psychology, 6,* 345–349.

Angulo, J. A., & McEwen, B. S. (1994). Molecular aspects of neuropeptide regulation and function in the corpus striatum and nucleus accumbens. *Brain Research Reviews, 19,* 1–28.

Arnold, W. J., & Kelley, W. N. (1971). Molecular basis of hypoxanthine-guanine phospho-ribosyl transferase and subunit structure. *Journal of Biological Chemistry, 246,* 7398–7404.

Axelrod, S. (1987). Functional and structural analyses of behavior: Approaches leading to reduced use of punishment procedures? *Research in Developmental Disabilities, 8,* 165–178.

Azrin, N. H., Gottlieb, L., Hughart, L., Wesolowski, M. D., & Rahn, T. (1975). Eliminating self-injurious behavior by educative procedures. *Behaviour Research and Therapy, 13,* 101–111.

Bachman, J. A. (1972). Self-injurious behavior: A behavioral analysis. *Journal of Abnormal Psychology, 80,* 211–224.

Bacopoulos, N. G., Hattox, S. E., & Roth, R. H. (1979). 3,4-Dihydroxyphenylacetic acid and homovanillic acid in rat plasma: Possible indicators of central dopaminergic activity. *European Journal of Pharmacology, 56,* 225.

Bacopoulos, N. G., Heninger, G. K., & Roth, R. H. (1978). Effects of haloperidol and probenecid on plasma and CSF dopamine metabolites in the rhesus monkey (*Maccaca mulatta*). *Life Sciences, 23,* 1805–1814.

Bacopoulos, N. G., Redmond, D. E., Baulu, J., & Roth, R. H. (1980). Chronic haloperidol or fluphenazine: Effects on dopamine metabolism in brain, cerebrospinal fluid, and plasma of *Cercopithecus aethiops* (vervet monkey). *Journal of Pharmacology and Experimental Therapeutics, 212,* 1–5.

Baer, D. M., Wolf, M. M., & Risley, T. R. (1968). Some current dimensions of applied behavior analysis. *Journal of Applied Behavior Analysis, 1,* 91–97.

Bailey, J. S., & Pyles, D. A. (1989). Behavioral diagnostics. In E. Cipani (Ed.), *The treatment of severe behavior disorders* (pp. 85–107). Washington, DC: Monographs of the American Association on Mental Retardation, 12.

Bakay, B., Francke, U., Nyhan, W. L., & Seegmiller, J. E. (1977). Experience with detection of heterozygous carriers and prenatal diagnosis of Lesch–Nyhan disease. In M. M. Muller, E. Kaiser, & J. E. Seegmiller (Eds.), *Purine metabolism in man II: Regulation of pathways and enzyme defects* (pp. 351–358). New York: Plenum Press.

Bakay, B., Nissinen, E., & Sweetman, L. (1978). Analysis of radioactive and non-radioactive purine bases, nucleosides, nucleotides by high-speed chromatography on a single column. *Annals of Biochemistry, 86*, 65–77.

Bakay, B., Nissinen, E., Sweetman, L., Francke, U., & Nyhan, W. L. (1979). Utilization of purines by an HPRT variant in an intelligent, nonmutilative patient with features of the Lesch–Nyhan syndrome. *Pediatric Research, 13*, 1365–1370.

Bakay, B., Nissinen, E. A., Sweetman, L., & Nyhan, W. L. (1978). Analysis of radioactive and nonradioactive purine bases, purine nucleosides and purine nucleotides by high-speed chromatography on a single column. *Monographs of Human Genetics, 9*, 127–134. Karger, Basel.

Bakay, B., Nyhan, W. L., Fawcett, N., & Kogut, M. D. (1972). Isoenzymes of hypoxanthine-guanine phospho-ribosyl transferase in a family with partial deficiency of the enzyme. *Biochemical Genetics, 7*, 73–85.

Bakeman, R., & Gottman, J. M. (1986). *Observing interaction: An introduction to sequential analysis.* Cambridge: Cambridge University Press.

Balis, M. E., Krakoff, I. H., Berman, P. H., & Dancis, J. (1967). Urinary metabolites in congenital hyperuricosuria. *Science, 156*, 1122–1123.

Ballinger, B. R. (1971). Minor self-injury. *British Journal of Psychiatry, 118*, 535–538.

Bardo, M. T., & Neisewander, J. L. (1987). Chronic naltrexone supersensitizes the reinforcing and locomotor-activating effects of morphine. *Pharmocology, Biochemistry, and Behavior, 28*, 267–273.

Barker, R., Duncan, J., & Lees, A. (1989). Subcutaneous apomorphine as a diagnostic test for dopaminergic responsiveness in Parkinsonian syndromes. *Lancet, 25*, 675.

Barrera, F. J., Teodoro, J. M., Selmeci, T., & Madappuli, A., (1994). Self-injury, pain, and the endorphin theory. *Journal of Developmental and Physical Disabilities, 6*, 169–192.

Barrett, R. P., Feinstein, C., & Hole, W. T. (1989). Effects of naloxone and naltrexone on self-injury: A double blind, placebo-controlled analysis. *American Journal of Mental Retardation, 93*, 644–651.

Barron, J. L., & Sandman, C. A. (1983). Relationship of sedative-hypnotic response to self-injurious behavior and stereotypy in mentally retarded clients. *American Journal of Mental Retardation, 88*, 177–186.

Barron, J., & Sandman, C. A. (1984). Self-injurious behavior and stereotypy in an institutionalized mentally retarded population. *Applied Research in Mental Retardation, 5*, 499–511.

Barron, J. L., & Sandman, C. A. (1985). Paradoxical excitement to sedative–hypnotics in mentally retarded clients. *American Journal on Mental Deficiency, 90*, 124–129.

Bartak, L., & Rutter, M. (1976). Differences between mentally retarded and normally intelligent autistic children. *Journal of Autism and Childhood Schizophrenia, 6*, 109–120.

Bartlett, L. B., Rooney, V., & Spedding, S. (1985). Nocturnal difficulties in a population of mentally handicapped children. *British Journal of Mental Subnormality, 31*, 54–59.

Bassingthwaighte, J. B., Liebovitch, L. S., & West, B. J. (1994). *Fractal physiology*. New York: Oxford University Press.

Bates, T. E., Strangward, M., Keelan, J., Davey, G. P., Munro, P. M., & Clark, J. B. (1996). Inhibition of N-acetylaspartate production: Implications for ^{1}H MRS studies in vivo. *Neuroreport, 7*, 1397–1400.

Baumeister, A. A., & Forehand, R. (1973). Stereotyped acts. In N. R. Ellis (Ed.), *International review of research in mental retardation*, (Vol. 6) (pp. 55–96). New York: Academic Press.

Baumeister, A. A., & Frye, G. D. (1984). Self-injurious behavior in rats produced by intranigral microinjection of GABA agonists. *Pharmacology, Biochemistry, and Behavior, 21*, 89–95.

Baumeister, A. A., & Frye, G. D (1986). Involvement of the midbrain reticular formation in self-injurious behavior, stereotyped behavior, and analgesia induced by intranigral microinjection of muscimol. *Brain Research, 369*, 231–242.

Baumeister, A. A., Frye, G. D., & Schroeder, S. R. (1984). Neurochemical correlates of self-injurious behavior. In J. A. Mulick, & B. L. Mallory (Eds.), *Transitions in mental retardation: Advocacy, technology, and science*. Norwood, NJ: Ablex Publishing.

Baumeister, A. A., & Rollings, J. P. (1976). Self-injurious behaviors. In N. R. Ellis (Ed.), *International review of research in mental retardation*, (Vol. 8) (pp. 1–34). New York: Academic Press.

Baumeister, A. A., & Sevin, J. A. (1990). Pharmacologic control of aberrant behavior in the mentally retarded: Toward a more rational approach. *Neuroscience and Biobehavioral Reviews, 14*, 253–262.

Baumeister, A. A., Sevin, J. A., & King, B. H. (1998). Neuroleptics. In S. Reiss, & M. G. Aman (Eds.), *Psychotropic medications and developmental disabilities: The international consensus handbook* (pp. 133–150). Columbus, OH: The Ohio State University Nisonger Center.

Baumeister, A. A., Sevin, J. A., & Todd, M. E. (1993). Efficacy and specificity of pharmacological therapies for behavioral disorders in persons with mental retardation. *Clinical Neuropharmacology, 16*, 271–294.

Beckmann, A. M., & Wilce, P. A. (1997). Egr transcription factors in the nervous system. *Neurochemistry International, 31*, 477–510.

Bellanca, R. U., & Crockett, C. M. (2000). Factors predicting increased incidence of abnormal behavior in male pigtailed macaques. *American Journal of Primatology, 50*, 27–32.

Bellanca, R. U., Heffernan, K. S., Grabber, J. E., & Crockett, C. M. (1999). Behavior profiles of laboratory monkeys referred to a regional primate research center's psychological well-being program. *American Journal of Primatology, 49*, 33.

Belluzzi, J. D., & Stein, L. (1977). Enkephaline may mediate euphoria and drive-reduction reward. *Nature, 266*, 556–558.

Bentladge, C., Nikkah, G., Cunningham, M. G., & Bjorklund, A. (1999). Reformation of the nigrostriatal pathway by fetal dopaminergic micrografts into the substantia nigra is critically dependent on the age of the host. *Experimental Neurology, 159*, 177–190.

Berkson, G. (1967). Abnormal stereotyped motor acts. In J. Zubin, & G. A. Jervis (Eds.), *Psychopathology of mental development* (pp. 76–94). New York: Grune and Stratton.

Berkson, G. (1983). Repetitive stereotyped behaviors. *American Journal of Mental Deficiency, 88,* 239–246.

Berkson, G., & Davenport, R. K. (1962). Stereotyped movements of mental defectives: Initial survey. *American Journal of Mental Deficiency, 66,* 849–852.

Berkson, G., & Mason, W. A. (1963). Stereotyped movements of mental defectives: III. Situation effects. *American Journal of Mental Deficiency, 68,* 409–412.

Berkson, G., & Mason, W. A. (1965). Stereotyped movements of mental defectives: IV. The effects of toys and the character of the acts. *American Journal of Mental Deficiency, 70,* 511–524.

Berkson, G., McQuiston, S., Jacobson, J. W., Eyman, R., & Borthwick, S. (1985). The relationship between age and stereotyped behaviors. *Mental Retardation, 23,* 31–33.

Berkson, G., Rafaeli-Mor, N., & Tarnovsky, S. (1999). Body-rocking and other habits of college students and persons with mental retardation. *American Journal of Mental Retardation, 104,* 107–116.

Berkson, G., & Tupa, M. (2000). Early development of stereotyped and self-injurious behaviors. *Journal of Early Intervention, 23,* 1–19.

Berkson, G., & Tupa, M. (2000). Studies of the development of stereotyped and self-injurious behaviors in young children. In S. Schroeder, M. L. Oster-Granite, & T. Thompson (Eds.), *Self-injurious behavior: Gene-brain-behavior relationships.* Washington, DC: American Psychological Association.

Berman, P. H., Balis, M. E., & Dancis, J. (1968). Diagnostic test for hyperuricemia with central nervous system dysfunction. *Journal of Laboratory and Clinical Medicine, 71,* 247–253.

Bernard, C. (1949). *An introduction to the study of medicine.* New York: Henry Schuman, Inc.

Berney, T. P., Ireland, M., & Burn, J. (1999). Behavioral phenotype of Cornelia de Lange syndrome. *Archives of Disease in Childhood, 81,* 333–336.

Bernstein, D. J., & Ebbesen, E. B. (1978). Reinforcement and substitution in humans: A multi-response analysis. *Journal of the Experimental Analysis of Behavior, 30,* 243–253.

Bettelheim, B. (1973). *A home for the heart.* New York: Knopf.

Bhatia, K. P., & Marsden, C. D. (1994). The behavioral and motor consequences of focal lesions of the basal ganglia in man. *Brain, 117,* 859–876.

Bhattacharya, S. K., Jaiswal, A. K., Mukhopadhyay, M., & Datla, K. P. (1988). Clonidine-induced automutilation in mice as a laboratory model for clinical self-injurious behavior. *Journal of Psychiatric Research, 22,* 43–50.

Biersdorff, K. K. (1994). Incidence of significantly altered pain experience among individuals with developmental disabilities. *American Journal on Mental Retardation, 98,* 619–631.

Bijou, S., & Baer, D. M. (1961). *Child development: Vol. I. A systematic and empirical theory*. New York: Appleton-Century-Crofts.

Bijou, S., Peterson, R. F., & Ault, M. H. (1968). A method to integrate descriptive and experimental field studies at the level of data and empirical concepts. *Journal of Applied Behavior Analysis, 1*, 175–191.

Blunt, S. B., Jenner, P., & Marsden, C. D. (1992). Autoradiography study of striatal D_1 and D_2 dopamine receptors in 6-OHDA-lesioned rats receiving fetal ventral mesencephalic grafts and chronic treatment with L-dopa and carbidopa. *Brain Research, 582*, 299–311.

Bodfish, J. W., Crawford, T. W., Powell, S. B., Parker, D. E., Golden, R. N., & Lewis, M. H. (1995). Compulsions in adults with mental retardation: Prevalence, phenomonology and co-morbidity with stereotypy and self-injury. *American Journal on Mental Retardation, 100*, 183–192.

Bodfish, J. W., & Lewis, M. H. (1997). *Co-occurrence of tics, stereotypy, and self-injury in adults with mental retardation*. Proceedings of the 30th Annual Gatlinburg Conference on Research & Theory in Mental Retardation.

Bodfish, J. W., Newell, K. M., Sprague, R. L., Harper, V. N., & Lewis, M. H. (1996). Dyskinetic movement disorder among adults with mental retardation: Phenomology and co-occurrence with stereotypy. *American Journal on Mental Retardation, 101*, 118–129.

Bodfish, J. W., Newell, K. M., Sprague, R. L., Harper, V. N., & Lewis, M. H. (1997). Akathisia in adults with mental retardation: Development of the Akathisia Ratings of Movement Scale (ARMS). *American Journal on Mental Retardation, 101*, 413–423.

Bodfish, J. W., Powell, S. B., Golden, R. N., & Lewis, M. H. (1995). Blink rate as an index of dopamine function in adults with mental retardation and repetitive behavior disorders. *American Journal on Mental Retardation, 99*, 335–344.

Bodfish, J. W., Symons, F. J., & Lewis, M. H. (1999). *Dynamic measures of self-injury*. Paper presented at the Gatlinburg Conference on Research and Theory in Mental Retardation and Developmental Disabilities.

Bodfish, J. W., Symons, F. J., Parker, D. E., & Lewis, M. H. (2000). Varieties in repetitive behavior in autism: Comparisons to mental retardation. *Journal of Autism and Developmental Disorders, 30*, 237–243.

Bohmer, C. M. J. (1996). *Gastro-esophageal reflux disease in intellectually disabled individuals*. Amsterdam: VU University Press.

Bonthala, C. M., & West, A. (1983). Pemoline-induced chorea and Gilles de la Tourette's syndrome. *British Journal of Psychiatry, 143*, 300–302

Bornstein, R. A. (1991). Neuropsychological correlates of obsessive characteristics in Tourette's syndrome. *Journal of Neuropsychiatry and Clinical Neuroscience, 3*, 157–162.

Borthwick, S. A., Meyers, C. E., & Eyman, R. K. (1981). Comparative adaptive and maladaptive behavior of mentally retarded clients of five residential settings in three western states. In R. H. Bruininks, C. E. Meyers, B. B. Sigford, & K. C. Lakin (Eds.), *Deinstitutionalization and community adjustment of mentally retarded people, monograph 4*, (pp. 351–359). Washington, DC: American Association on Mental Deficiency.

Borthwick-Duffy, S. A. (1994). Prevalence of destructive behaviors: A study of aggression, self-injury, and property destruction. In T. Thompson, & D. B. Gray (Eds.), *Destructive behavior in developmental disabilities: Diagnosis and treatment* (pp. 3–23). Thousand Oaks, CA: Sage Publishing.

Borthwick-Duffy, S. A., Eyman, R. K., & White, J. F. (1987). Client characteristics and residential placement pattern. *American Journal on Mental Deficiency, 92*, 24–30.

Bosch, J., Van Dyke, D. C., Smith, S. M., & Poulton, S. (1997). Role of medical conditions in the exacerbation of self-injurious behavior: An exploratory study. *Mental Retardation, 35*, 124–130.

Bouvard, M. P., Leboyer, M., Launay, J. M., Recasens, C., Plumet, M. H., Waller-Perotte, D., et al. (1995). Low-dose naltrexone effects on plasma chemistries and clinical symptoms in autism: A double-blind, placebo-controlled study. *Psychiatry Research, 58*, 191–201.

Bowtell, D. D. L. (1999). Options available—from start to finish—for obtaining expression data by microarray. *Nature Genetics, 21*(Suppl.), 25–32.

Boyd, E. M., Dolman, M., Knight, M., & Sheppard, E. P. (1965). The chronic oral toxicity of caffeine. *Canadian Journal of Physiology, 43*, 955–1005.

Brandt, B. R., & Rosen, I. (1998). Impaired peripheral somatosensory function in children with Prader–Willi syndrome. *Neuropediatrics, 29*, 124–126.

Braun, A. R., Jaskiw, G. E., Vladar, K., Sexton, R. H., Kolachana, B. S., & Weinberger, D. R. (1993). Effects of ibotenic acid lesion of the medial prefrontal cortex on dopamine agonist-related behaviors in the rat. *Pharmacology, Biochemistry, and Behavior, 46*, 51–60.

Breese, C. R., & Breese, C. R. (1997). Use of neurotoxins to destroy cetecholamine-containing neurons in neonatal and adult animals to model clinical disorders: Approach for defining adaptive neural mechanisms and role of neurotrophic factors in brain. In R. M. Kostrewa (Ed.), *Highly selective neurotoxins: Basic and clinical applications* (pp. 19–73). Totowa, NJ: Humana Press.

Breese, G. R., Baumeister, A. A., McCown, T. J., Emerick, S. G., Frye, G. D., & Mueller, R. A. (1984). Neonatal-6-hydroxydopamine: Model of susceptibility for self-mutilation in the Lesch–Nyhan syndrome. *Pharmacology, Biochemistry, and Behavior, 21*, 459–461.

Breese, G. R., Baumeister, A. A., McCowen, T. J., Emerick, S. G., Frye, G. D., Crotty, K., et al. (1984a). Behavioral differences between neonatal- and adult-6-hydroxydopamine-treated rats to dopamine agonists: Relevance to neurological symptoms in clinical syndromes with reduced brain dopamine. *Journal of Pharmacology and Experimental Therapeutics, 234*, 447–455.

Breese, G. R., Baumeister, A. A., McCown, T. J., Emerick, S. G., Frye, G. D., & Mueller, R. A. (1984b). Behavioral differences between neonatal and adult 6-hydroxydopamine-treated rats. Relevance to neurological symptoms in clinical syndromes with reduced dopamine. *Journal of Pharmacology and Experimental Therapeutics, 231*, 343–354.

Breese, G. R., Baumeister, A. A., Napier, T. C., Frye, G. D., & Mueller, R. A. (1985). Evidence that D_1-dopamine receptors contribute to super-sensitive behavioral responses induced by L-dihydroxyphenylalanine in rats treated neonatally with 6-hydroxydopamine. *Journal of Pharmacology and Experimental Therapeutics, 235,* 287–295.

Breese, G. R., Criswell, H. E., Duncan, G. E., Moy, S. S., Johnson, K. B., Wong, D. F., et al. (1995). Model for reduced brain dopamine in Lesch–Nyhan syndrome and the mentally retarded: Neurobiology of neonatal-6-hydroxydopamine-lesioned rats. *Mental Retardation and Developmental Disabilities Research Reviews, 1,* 111–119.

Breese, G. R., Criswell, H. E., Duncan, G. E., & Mueller, R. A. (1990a). A dopamine deficiency model of Lesch–Nyhan disease—the neonatal-6-OHDA-lesioned rat. *Brain Research Bulletin, 25,* 477–484.

Breese, G. R., Criswell, H. E., Johnson, K. B., O'Callaghan, J. P., Duncan, G. E., Jensen, K. F., et al. (1994). Neonatal destruction of dopaminergic neurons. *Neurotoxicology, 15,* 149–160.

Breese, G. R., Criswell, H. E., McQuade, R. J., Mueller, R. A., Iorio, L. C., & Barnett, A. (1990b). Pharmacological evaluation of SCH-12679: Evidence for in vivo antagonism of D-dopamine receptors. *Journal of Pharmacology and Experimental Therapeutics, 252,* 558–567.

Breese, G. R., Duncan, G., Napier, T. C., Bondy, S. C., Emerick, S., Iorio, L. C., et al. (1987a). 6-Hydroxydopamine treatments enhance behavioral responses to intracerebral microinjection of D_1 and D_2 dopamine agonists into nucleus accumbens and striatum without changing dopamine antagonist binding. *Journal of Pharmacology and Experimental Therapeutics, 240,* 167–176.

Breese, G. R., Hulebak, K. L., Napier, T. C., Baumeister, A. A., Frye, G. D., & Mueller, R. A. (1987b). Enhanced muscimol-induced behavioral responses after 6-OHDA lesions: Relevance to susceptibility for self-mutilation behavior in neonatally lesioned rats. *Psychopharmacology, 91,* 356–362.

Breese, G. R., & Mueller, R. A. (1985). SCH-23390 antagonism of a D_2 dopamine agonist depends upon catecholaminergic neurons. *European Journal of Pharmacology, 113,* 109–114.

Breese, G. R., Mueller, R. A., Napier, T. C., & Duncan, G. E. (1986). Neurobiology of D_1 dopamine receptors after neonatal-6-OHDA treatment: Relevance to Lesch–Nyhan disease. *Advances in Experimental Medicine and Biology, 204,* 197–215.

Breese, G. R., Mueller, R. A., & Schroeder, S. R. (1987c). Studies of the neurochemical basis of symptoms in the Lesch–Nyhan syndrome: Relationship to central symptoms in other developmental disorders. In E. Schopler, & G. B. Meslbov (Eds.), *Neurobiological issues in autism* (pp. 145–160). New York: Plenum Press.

Breese, G. R., & Traylor, T. D. (1970). Effects of 6-hydroxydopamine on brain norepinephrine and dopamine: Evidence for selective degeneration of catecholamine neurons. *Journal of Pharmacology and Experimental Therapeutics, 174,* 413–420.

Breese, G. R., & Traylor, T. D. (1971). Depletion of brain noradrenaline and dopamine by 6-hydroxydopamine. *British Journal of Pharmacology, 42,* 88–99.

Breese, G. R., & Traylor, T. D. (1972). Developmental characteristics of brain catecholamines and tyrosine hydroxylase in the rat: Effects of 6-hydroxy-dopamine. *British Journal of Pharmacology, 44*, 210–222.

Breier, A. (1989). Experimental approaches to human stress research: Assessment of neurobiological mechanisms of stress in volunteers and psychiatric patients. *Biological Psychiatry, 26*, 438–462.

Brien, J. F., Peachy, J. E., Rogers, B. J., & Kitney, J. C. (1977). Amphetamine-induced stereotyped behaviour and brain concentrations of amphetamine and its hydrox-ylated metabolites in mice. *Journal of Pharmacy and Pharmacology, 29*, 49–50.

Brown, J., Bullock, D., & Grossberg, S. (1999). How the basal ganglia use parallel excitatory and inhibitory learning pathways to selectively respond to unex-pected rewarding cues. *Journal of Neuroscience, 19*, 10502–10511.

Brown, P. O., & Botstein, D. (1999). Exploring the new world of the genome with DNA microarrays. *Nature Genetics, 21*(Suppl.), 33–37.

Brown, R. L., Genel, M., & Riggs, J. A. (2000). Use of seclusion and restraint in children and adolescents. *Archives of Pediatrics and Adolescent Medicine, 154*, 653–656.

Brucke, T., Sofic, E., Killian, W., Rett, A., & Riederer, P. (1987). Reduced concen-trations and increased metabolism of biogenic amines in a single case of Rett syndrome: A postmortem brain study. *Journal of Neural Transmission, 68*, 315–324.

Brunello, N., Volterra, A., DiGiulio, A. M., Cuomo, V., & Racagni, G. (1984). Mod-ulation of opioid system in C57 mice after repeated treatment with morphine and naloxone: Biochemical and behavioral correlates. *Life Sciences, 34*, 1669–1678.

Bruno, J. P., Striker, E. M., & Zigmond, M. J. (1985). Rats given dopamine-depleting brain lesions as neonates are subsensitive to dopaminergic antagonists as adults. *Behavioral Neuroscience, 99*, 771–775.

Brus, R., Kostrzewa, M., Perry, K. W., & Fuller, R. W. Supersensitivity of the oral response to SKF 38393 in neonate 6-hydroxydopamine-lesioned rats is elimi-nated by neonatal 5,7-dihydroxytryptamine treatment. (1994). *Journal of Phar-macology and Experimental Therapeutics, 268*, 231–237.

Brusca, R. M., Nieminen, G. S., Carter, R., & Repp, A. C. (1989). The relationship of staff contact and activity to the stereotypy of children with multiple disabil-ities. *Journal of the Association for Persons with Severe Handicaps, 14*(2), 127–136.

Bucher, B., & Lovaas, O. I. (1968). Use of aversive stimulation in behavior modifi-cation. In M. R. Jones (Ed.), *Miami symposium on the prediction of behavior, 1967: Aversive stimulation.* Coral Gables, FL: University of Miami Press.

Buitelaar, R. M. (1993). Self-injurious behavior in retarded children: Clinical phe-nomena and biological mechanisms. *Acta Peadopsychiatrica, 56*, 105–111.

Bull, M., & LaVecchio, F. (1978). Behavior therapy for a child with Lesch–Nyhan syndrome. *Developmental Medicine and Child Neurology, 20*, 368–374.

Burd, L., Kauffman, D. W., & Kerbeshian, J. (1992). Tourette's syndrome and learn-ing disabilities. *Journal of Learning Disabilities, 25*, 598–604.

Burke, R. E., Fann, S., Marsden, C. D., Bressman, S. B., Moskowitz, C., & Friedman, J. (1985). Validity and reliability of a rating scale for the primary torsion dystonias. *Neurology, 35*, 73–77.

Busbaur, A. I. (1974). Effects of central lesion on disorders produced by dorsal rhizotomy in rats. *Experimental Neurology, 42*, 490–501.

Butler, I. J., Koslow, S. H., Seifer, W. E., Caprioli, R. M., & Singer, S. S. (1979). Biogenic amine metabolism in Tourette's syndrome. *Annals of Neurology, 6*, 37–39.

Cacioppo, J. T., & Petty, R. E. (1982a). A biosocial model of attitude change. In J. T. Cacioppo & R. E. Petty (Eds.), *Perspectives in cardiovascular psychophysiology* (pp. 151–188). New York: Guilford Press.

Cacioppo, J. T., & Petty, R. E. (1982b). Editor's overview. In J. T. Cacioppo, & R. E. Petty (Eds.), *Perspectives in cardiovascular psychophysiology* (pp. 1–2). New York: Guilford Press.

Calabrese, J. R., & Woyshville, M. J. (1995). A medication algorithm for treatment of bipolar rapid cycling? *Journal of Clinical Psychiatry, 56*, 11–18.

Campbell, D. T., & Stanley, J. C. (1963). *Experimental and quasi-experimental designs for research.* Chicago: Rand McNally.

Campbell, M., Anderson, L., Meier, M., Cohen, I. L., Small, A. M., Sarnit, C., et al. (1978). A comparison of haloperidol and behavior therapy and their interaction in autistic children. *Journal of the American Academy of Child and Adolescent Psychiatry, 17*, 640–655.

Campbell, M., Anderson, L., Small, A., Perry, R., Green, W., & Caplan, R. (1982). The effects of haloperidol on learning and behavior in autistic children. *Journal of Autism and Developmental Disorders, 12*, 167–175.

Canales, J. J., Gilmour, G., Iversen, & Iversen, S. D. (2000). The role of nigral and thalamic output pathways in the expression of oral stereotypies induced by amphetamine injections into the striatum. *Brain Research, 856*, 176–183.

Canales, J. J., & Graybiel, A. M. (2000). A measure of striatal function predicts motor stereotypy. *Nature Neuroscience, 3*(4), 377–383.

Capitanio, J. P. (1986). Behavioral pathology. In G. Mitchell, & J. Erwin (Eds.), *Comparative primate biology, Vol. 2. Part A: Behavior, conservation, and ecology* (pp. 411–454). New York: Alan R. Liss, Inc.

Carlson, N. R. (1988). *Foundations of physiological psychology.* Boston: Allyn & Bacon.

Carr, E. G. (1977). The motivation of self-injurious behavior: A review of some hypotheses. *Psychological Bulletin, 84*, 800–816.

Carr, E. G. (1994). Emerging themes in the functional analysis of problem behavior. *Journal of Applied Behavior Analysis, 27*, 393–399.

Carr, E. G., & Carlson, J. I. (1993). Reduction of severe behavior problems in the community using a multicomponent treatment approach. *Journal of Applied Behavior Analysis, 26*, 157–172.

Carr, E. G., & Durand, V. M. (1985). Reducing behavior problems through functional communication training. *Journal of Applied Behavior Analysis, 18*, 111–126.

Carr, E. G., Levin, L., McConnachie, G., Carlson, J. I., Kemp, D. C., & Smith, C. E. (1994). *Communication-based intervention for problem behavior: A user's guide for producing positive change.* Baltimore: Paul H. Brookes Publishing.

Carr, E. G., Newsom, C. D., & Binkoff, J. A. (1976). Stimulus control of self-destructive behavior in a psychotic child. *Journal of Abnormal Child Psychology, 4,* 139–153.

Carr, E. G., Newsom, C. D., & Binkoff, J. A. (1980). Escape as a factor in the aggressive behavior of two retarded children. *Journal of Applied Behavior Analysis, 13,* 101–117.

Carr, E. G., Reeve, C. E., & Magito-McLaughlin, D. (1996). Contextual influences on problem behavior in people with developmental disabilities. In L. K. Koegel, R. L. Koegel, & G. Dunlap (Eds.), *Positive behavioral support: Including people with difficult behavior in the community* (pp. 403–423). Baltimore: Paul H. Brookes Publishing.

Carr, E. G., Schreibman, L., & Lovaas, O. I. (1975). Control of echolalic speech in psychotic children. *Journal of Abnormal Child Psychology, 3,* 331–351.

Carr, E. G., Yarbrough, S. C., & Langdon, N. A. (1997). Effects of idiosyncratic stimulus variables on functional analysis outcomes. *Journal of Applied Behavior Analysis, 30,* 673–686.

Carr, K. D. (1984). The physiology of opiate hedonic effects and the role of opioids in motivated behavior. *Advances in Alcohol and Substance Abuse, 3,* 5–18.

Carter, C. J., & Pycock, C. J. (1981). The role of 5-hydroxytryptamine in dopamine-dependent stereotyped behaviour. *Neuropharmacology, 20,* 261–265.

Casdagli, M. C., Iasemidis, L. D., Savit, R. S., Gilmore, R. L., Roper, S. N., & Sackellares, C. (1997). Non-linearity in invasive EEG recordings from patients with temporal lobe epilepsy. *Electroencephalography and Clinical Neurophysiology, 102,* 98–105.

Casner, J. A., Weinheimer, B., & Gualtieri, C. T. (1996). Naltrexone and self-injurious behavior: A retrospective population study. *Journal of Clinical Psychopharmacology, 16,* 389–394.

Cassidy, S. B. (1984). Prader–Willi syndrome. *Current Problems in Pediatrics, 14,* 1–55.

Castells, S., Chakrabarti, C., Winsberg, B. G., Hurwic, M., Perel, J. J., & Nyhan, W. (1979). Effects of L-5-hydroxytryptophan on monoamine and amino acid turnover in the Lesch–Nyhan syndrome. *Journal of Autism and Developmental Disorders, 9,* 95–103.

Cataldo, M. F., & DeLeon, I. G. (in press). Treatment: Current standards of care and their research implications. In S. Schroeder, M. L. Oster-Granite, & T. Thompson (Eds.), *Self-injurious behavior: Gene-brain-behavior relationships.* Washington, DC: American Psychological Association.

Cataldo, M. F., & Harris, J. (1982). The biological basis for self-injury in the mentally retarded. *Analysis and Intervention in Developmental Disabilities, 2,* 21–39.

Catania, A. C. (1966). Concurrent operants. In W. K. Honig (Ed.), *Operant behavior: Areas of research and application.* Englewood, NJ: Prentice Hall.

Catania, A. C. (1991). The phylogeny and ontogeny of behavior. In N. A. Krasnegor (Ed.), *Biobehavioral determinants of language development*. Hillsdale, NJ: Erlbaum.

Catania, A. C. (1992). *Learning* (3rd ed.). Englewood Cliffs, NJ: Prentice Hall.

Catania, A. C., & Keller, K. J. (1981). Contingency, contiguity, correlation, and the concept of causation. In P. Harzem, & M. D. Zeiler (Eds.), *Predictability, correlation, and contiguity*. New York: Wiley.

Catel, V. W., Schmidt, J. (1959). Uber familiar gichtische diathese in verbinding mit zerebralen und renalen symptomen bei einem kleinkind. *Deutsche Medizinische Wochenschrift, 84*, 2145–2147.

Catterall, W. A. (1995). Structure and function of voltage-gated ion channels. *Annual Review of Biochemistry, 64*, 493–531.

Cautela, J. P., & Baron, M. G. (1973). Multifaceted behavior therapy of self-injurious behavior. *Journal of Behavior Therapy and Experimental Psychiatry, 4*, 125–131.

Cautela, J. P., & Groden, J. (1978). *Relaxation: a comprehensive manual for adults, children, and children with special needs*. Champaign, IL: Research Press.

Cazzullo, A. G., Musetti, M. C., Musetti, L., Bajo, S., Sacerdote, P., & Panerai, A. (1999). β-Endorphin levels in peripheral blood mononuclear cells and long-term naltrexone treatment in autistic children. *European Neuropsycholopharmacology, 9*, 361–363.

Chandler, M., Gualtieri, C. T., & Fahs, J. J. (1988). Other psychotropic drugs: Stimulants, anti-depressants, anxiolytics, and lithium carbonate. In M. G. Aman, & N. N. Singh (Eds.), *Psychopharmacology of the developmental disabilities*. New York: Springer-Verlag.

Chase, W. K., Marius, L. M., Jorgensen, M. J., Rassmussen, K. L., Suomi, S. J, & Novak, M. A. (1999). Heart rate patterns in rhesus monkeys with self-injurious behavior (SIB): Are these monkeys high reactors? *American Journal of Primatology, 49*, 42–43.

Chipkin, R. E., Iorio, L. C., Coffin, V. L., McQuade, R. D., Berger, J. G., & Barnett A. (1988). Pharmacological profile of SCH-39166: A dopamine D_1 selective benzonaphthazepine with potential antipsychotic activity. *Journal of Pharmacology and Experimental Therapeutics, 247*, 1093–1102.

Chiron, C., Bulteau, C., Loc'h, C., Raynaud, C., Garreau, B., Syrota, A., et al. (1993). Dopaminergic D_2 receptor SPECT imaging in Rett syndrome: Increase of specific binding in striatum. *Journal of Nuclear Medicine, 34*, 1717–1721.

Christie, R., Bay, C., Kaufman, I., Bakay, B., Border, M., & Nyhan, W. (1982). Lesch–Nyhan disease: Clinical experience with 19 patients. *Developmental Medicine and Child Neurology, 24*, 293–306.

Cimino, M., Zoli, M., & Weiss, B. (1991). Differential ontogenetic expression and regulation of proenkephalin and preprosomatostatin mRNAs in rat caudate-putamen as studied by in situ hybridization histochemisty. *Brain Research Developmental Brain Research, 60*, 115–122.

Clark, F. C. (1962). Some observations on the adventitious reinforcement of drinking under food reinforcement. *Journal of the Experimental Analysis of Behavior, 5*, 61–63.

Clarke, D. J. (1998). Psychopharmacology of severe self-injury associated with learning disabilities. *British Journal of Psychiatry, 172*, 389–394.

Clarkson, E. D., & Freed, C. R. (1999). Development of fetal neural transplantation as a treatment for Parkinson's disease. *Life Sciences, 65,* 2427–2437.

Clements, J., Wing, L., & Dunn, G. (1986). Sleep problems in handicapped children: A preliminary study. *Journal of Child Psychology and Psychiatry, 27,* 399–407.

Coccaro, E., Sivier, L., Klar, H., Maurer, G., Cochrane, K., Cooper, T., et al. (1989). Serotonergic studies in patients with affective and personality disorders: Correlates with suicidal and impulsive aggressive behavior. *Archives of General Psychiatry, 46,* 587–599.

Coderre, T. J., & Melzack, R. (1986). Procedures which increase acute pain sensitivity also increase autotomy. *Experimental Neurology, 92,* 713–722.

Cohen, D. J., Shaywitz, B. A., Caparulo, B. K., Young, J. G., & Bowers, M. B., Jr. (1978). Chronic, multiple tics of Gilles de la Tourette's disease: CSF acid monoamine metabolites after probenecid administration. *Archives of General Psychiatry, 35,* 245–250.

Coid, J., Allolio, B., & Rees, L. H. (1983). Raised plasma metenkephalin in patients who habitually mutilate themselves. *Lancet, 1,* 545–546.

Collacott, R. A., Cooper, S. A., Branford, D., & McGrother, C. (1998). Epidemiology of self-injurious behaviour in adults with learning disabilities. *British Journal of Psychiatry, 173,* 428–432.

Colpaert, F., & Balster, R. L. (1988). *Transduction mechanisms of drug stimuli.* Berlin: Springer-Verlag.

Cook, E. H., Courchesne, R., Lord, C., Cox, N. J., Yan, S., Lincoln, A., et al., (1997). Evidence of linkage between the serotonin transporter and autistic disorder. *Molecular Psychiatry, 2,* 247–250.

Cook, L., & Catania, A. C. (1964). Effects of drugs on avoidance and escape behavior. *Federation Proceedings, 23,* 818–835.

Corbett, J. A., & Campbell, H. J. (1981). Causes of severe self-injurious behavior. In P. Mittler (Ed.), *Frontiers of knowledge in mental retardation,* (Vol. 2), 285–292. Baltimore: University Park Press.

Corte, H. E., Wolf, M. M., & Locke, B. J. (1971). A comparison of procedures for eliminating self-injurious behavior of retarded adolescents. *Journal of Applied Behavior Analysis, 4,* 201–213.

Cowdery, G. E., Iwata, B. A., & Pace, G. M. (1990). Effects and side effects of DRO as treatment for self-injurious behavior. *Journal of Applied Behavior Analysis, 23,* 497–506.

Crain, S. M., & Shen, K. F. (1995). Ultra-low concentrations of naloxone selectively antagonize excitatory effects of morphine on sensory neurons, thereby increasing its antinociceptive potency and attenuating tolerance/dependence during chronic cotreatment. *Proceedings of the National Academy of Sciences, USA, 92,* 10540–10544.

Creese, I., & Iversen, S. D. (1973). Blockage of amphetamine-induced motor stimulation and stereotypy in the adult rat following neonatal treatment with 6-hydroxydopamine. *Brain Research, 55,* 369–382.

Crews, W. D., Jr., Bonaventura, S., Rowe, F. B., & Bonsie, D. (1993). Cessation of long-term naltrexone therapy and self-injury: A case study. *Research in Developmental Disabilities, 14*, 331–340.

Criswell, H. E., Breese, G. R., & Mueller, R. A. (1989b). Priming of D_1-dopamine receptor responses: Long lasting supersensitivity to D_1-dopamine agonist following repeated administration to neonatal 6-hydroxydopamine-lesioned rats. *Journal of Neuroscience, 9*, 125–133.

Criswell, H. E., Breese, G. R., & Mueller, R. A. (1992). Pharmacological evaluation of SCH-39166, A-69024 and NO-756 in neonatal-6-OHDA-lesioned rats: Further evidence that self-mutilatory behavior induced by L-dopa is related to D_1-dopamine receptors. *Neuropsychopharmacology, 7*, 95–103.

Criswell, H. E., Johnson, K. B., Mueller, R. A., & Breese, G. R. (1993). Evidence for involvement of brain dopamine and other mechanisms in the behavioral action of the N-methyl-D-aspartic acid antagonist MK-801 in control and 6-hydroxydopamine-lesioned rats. *Journal of Pharmacology and Experimental Therapeutics, 265*, 1001–1010.

Criswell, H. E., Mueller, R. A., & Breese, G. R. (1989a). Clozapine antagonism of D_1- and D_2-dopamine receptor mediated behaviors. *European Journal of Pharmacology, 159*, 141–147.

Criswell, H. E., Mueller, R. A., & Breese, G. R. (1990). Long-term D_1-dopamine receptor sensitization in neonatal-6-OHDA-lesioned rats is blocked by an NMDA antagonist. *Brain Research, 512*, 284–290.

Critchley, M. (1934). Some aspects of pain. *British Medical Journal, II*, 891–896.

Cromwell, H. C., King, B. H., & Levine, M. S. (1997). Pemoline alters dopamine modulation of synaptic responses of neostriatal neurons in vitro. *Developmental Neuroscience, 19*, 497–504.

Cromwell, H. C., Levine, M. S., & King, B. H. (1999). Cortical damage enhances pemoline-induced self-injurious behavior in prepubertal rats. *Pharmacology, Biochemistry, and Behavior, 62*, 223–227.

Cromwell, H. C., Witte, E. A., Crawford, C. A., Ly, H. T., Maidmen, N. T., & King, B. H. (1996). Pemoline produces ipsilateral turning behavior in unilateral 6-OHDA-lesioned rats. *Progress in Neuro-Psychopharmacology and Biological Psychiatry, 20*, 503–514.

Cummings, J. L. (1993). Frontal-subcortical circuits and human behavior. *Archives of Neurology, 50*, 873–880.

Curzon, G. (1990). Stereotyped and other motor responses to 5-hydroxytryptamine receptor activation. In S. J. Cooper, & C. T. Dourish (Eds.), *Neurobiology of stereotyped behaviour*. Oxford: Oxford University Press.

Czeisler, C. A., Richardson, G. S., Coleman, R. M., Zimmerman, J. C., Moore-Ede, M. C., Dement, W. C., et al. (1981). Chronotherapy: Resetting the circadian clocks of patients with delayed sleep phase insomnia. *Sleep, 4*, 1–21.

Dahlin, P. A., Van Buskirk, N. E., Novotny, R. W., Hollis, I. R., & George, J. (1985). Self-biting with multiple finger amputations following spinal cord injury. *Paraplegia, 23*, 306–318.

Danford, D. E., & Huber, A. M. (1982). Pica among mentally retarded adults. *American Journal of Mental Deficiency, 87*(2), 141–146.

Dantzer, R. (1986). Behavioral, physiological and functional aspects of stereotyped behavior: A review and re-interpretation. *Journal of Animal Science, 62,* 1776–1786.

Davanzo, P., Ke, Y., Thomas, A., Anderson, C., King, B., Belin, T., et al. (1998). Proton MR spectroscopy in Lesch–Nyhan disease. *American Journal of Neuro-radiology, 19,* 672–674.

Davenport, R. K., & Menzel, E. W. (1963). Stereotyped behavior of the infant chimpanzee. *Archives of General Psychiatry, 8,* 99–104.

Davidson, B. L., Tarle, S. A., Antwerp, M. V., Gibbs, D. A., Watts, R. W. E., Kelley, W. N., et al. (1991). Identification of 17 independent mutations responsible for human hypoxanthine-guanine phosphoribosyltransferase (HPRT) deficiency. *American Journal of Human Genetics, 48,* 951–958.

Davidson, P. W., Kleene, B. M., Carroll, M., & Rockowitz, R. J. (1983). Effects of naloxone on self-injurious behavior: A case study. *Applied Research in Mental Retardation, 4,* 1.

Davidson, R. J., Putnam, K. M., & Larson, C. L. (2000). Dysfunction in the neural circuitry of emotion regulation: A possible prelude to violence. *Science, 289,* 591–594.

Dawson, T. M., Dawson, V. L., Gage, F. H., Fisher, L. J., Hunt, M. A., & Wamsley, J. K. (1991). Functional recovery of supersensitive dopamine receptors after intrastriatal grafts on fetal substantia nigra. *Experimental Neurology, 111,* 282–292.

Day, M. H., Horner, R. H., & O'Neill, R. E. (1994). Multiple functions or problem behaviors: Assessment and intervention. *Journal of Applied Behavior Analysis, 27,* 279–289.

De Gregorio, L., Nyhan, W. L., Serafin, E., & Chamoles, N. A. (2000). An unexpected affected female patient in a classical Lesch–Nyhan family. *Molecular Genetics and Metabolism, 69,* 263–268.

Dehen, H., Willer, J. C., Boureau, F., & Cambier, J. (1977). Congenital insensitivity to pain and endogenous morphine-like substances. *Lancet, 2,* 293–294.

De Kloet, E. R., Korte, S. M., Rots, N. Y., & Kruk, M. R. (1996). Stress hormones, genotype, and brain organization. Implications for aggression. *Annals of the New York Academy of Sciences, 794,* 179–191.

De La Chapelle, A., Kari, C., Nurminen, M., & Hernberg, S. (1977). Clozapine-induced agranulocytosis. A genetic and epidemiologic study. *Human Genetics, 37,* 183–194.

DeLeon, I. G., Anders, B. M., Rodriguez-Catter, V., & Neidert, P. L. (2000). The effects of single versus multiple stimuli on self-injury during environmental enrichment. *Journal of Applied Behavior Analysis, 33,* 623–626.

Delfs, J. M., & Kelley, A. E. (1990). The role of D_1 and D_2 dopamine receptors in oral stereotypy induced by dopaminergic stimulation of the ventrolateral striatum. *Neuroscience, 39,* 59–67.

Delini-Stula, A., & Vassout, A. (1979). Modulation of dopamine-mediated behavioral responses by antidepressants: Effects of single and repeated treatment. *European Journal of Pharmacology, 58,* 443–451.

DeLissovoy, V. (1963). Head banging in early childhood: A suggested cause. *Journal of Genetic Psychology, 102,* 109–114.

Demchak, M. A., & Halle, J. (1985). Motivational assessment: A potential means of enhancing treatment success of self-injurious individuals. *Education and Training of the Mentally Retarded, 20*(1), 25–38.

Derby, K. M., Fisher, W. W., & Piazza, C. C. (1996). The effects of contingent and noncontingent attention on self-injury and self-restraint. *Journal of Applied Behavior Analysis, 29*(1), 107–110.

Derby, K. M., Wacker, D. P., Berg, W., DeRaad, A., Ulrich, S., Asmus, J., et al. (1997). The long-term effects of functional communication training in home settings. *Journal of Applied Behavior Analysis, 30,* 507–531.

Derby, K. M., Wacker, D. P., Sasso, G., Steege, M., Northrup, J., Cigrand, K., et al. (1992). Brief functional assessment techniques to evaluate aberrant behavior in an outpatient clinic: A summary of 79 cases. *Journal of Applied Behavior Analysis, 25,* 713–721.

Desrochers, M. N., Hile, M. G., & Williams-Moseley, T. L. (1997). Survey of functional assessment procedures used with individuals who display mental retardation and severe problem behaviors. *American Journal on Mental Retardation, 101,* 535–546.

Deutsch, S. I. (1986). Rationale for the administration of opiate antagonists in treating infantile autism. *American Journal of Mental Retardation, 90,* 631–635.

Dimitropoulos, A., Feurer, I., Butler, M., & Thompson, T. (in press). Emergence of compulsive behavior and tantrums in children with Prader–Willi syndrome. *American Journal on Mental Retardation.*

Dix, D. (1843). *Memorial to the legislature of Massachusetts.* Boston: Monroe and Francis.

Dren, A. T., & Janicki, R. S. (1977). Pemoline. In M. E. Goldberg (Ed.), *Pharmacological and biochemical properties of drug substances.* Washington, DC: American Pharmaceutical Association, Academy of Pharmaceutical Sciences.

Duker, P. (1975). Behaviour control of self-biting in a Lesch–Nyhan patient. *Journal of Mental Deficiency Research, 19,* 11–19.

Duker, P. C., & Seys, D. M. (1997). An inventory method for assessing the degree of restraint imposed by others. *Journal of Behavior Therapy and Experimental Psychiatry, 28,* 113–121.

Duncan, G., Criswell, H., McCown, T. J., Paul, I., Mueller, R. A., & Breese, G. R. (1987). Behavioral and neurochemical response to haloperidol and SCH-23390 in rats treated neonatally or as adults with 6-hydroxydopamine. *Journal of Pharmacology and Experimental Therapeutics, 243,* 1027–1034.

Duncan, G. E., Breese, G. R., Criswell, H. E., Johnson, K. B., Schambra, U. B., Mueller, R. A., et al. (1993). D_1 dopamine receptor binding and mRNA levels are not altered after neonatal 6-hydroxydopamine treatment: Evidence against dopamine-mediated induction of D_1 dopamine receptors during postnatal development. *Journal of Neurochemistry, 61,* 1255–1262.

Dunger, D. B., Leonard, J. V., Wolff, O. H., & Preece, A. (1980). Effect of naloxone in a previously undescribed hypothalamic syndrome. *Lancet, 1,* 1277–1281.

Durand, V. M. (1990). *Severe behavior problems: A functional communication training approach*. New York, NY: The Guilford Press.

Durand, V. M. (1993). Functional communication training using assistive devices: Effects on challenging behavior and affect. *Augmentative and Alternative Communication, 9*, 168–176.

Durand, V. M. (1999). Functional communication training using assistive devices: Recruiting natural communities of reinforcement. *Journal of Applied Behavior Analysis, 32*, 247–267.

Durand, V. M., & Carr, E. G. (1982). *Differential reinforcement of communicative behavior (DRC): An intervention for the disruptive behaviors of developmentally disabled children*. Paper presented at the meeting of the Berkshire Association for Behavior Analysis and Therapy, Amherst, Massachusetts.

Durand, V. M., & Carr, E. G. (1983). *Differential reinforcement of communicative behavior: Classroom intervention and maintenance*. Paper presented at the meeting of the Berkshire Association for Behavior Analysis and Therapy, Amherst, Massachusetts.

Durand, V. M., & Carr, E. G. (1985). Self-injurious behavior: Motivating conditions and guidelines for treatment. *School Psychology Review, 14*, 171–176.

Durand, V. M., & Carr, E. G. (1987). Social influences on self-stimulatory behavior: Analysis and treatment application. *Journal of Applied Behavior Analysis, 20*, 119–132.

Durand, V. M., & Carr, E. G. (1991). Functional communication training to reduce challenging behavior: Maintenance and application in new settings. *Journal of Applied Behavior Analysis, 24*, 251–264.

Durand, V. M., & Carr, E. G. (1992). An analysis of maintenance following functional communication training. *Journal of Applied Behavior Analysis, 25*, 777–794.

Durand, V. M., & Crimmins, D. B. (1988). Identifying the variables maintaining self-injury. *Journal of Autism and Developmental Disorders, 18*, 99–117.

Durand, V. M., & Kishi, G. (1987). Reducing severe behavior problems among persons with dual sensory impairments: An evaluation of a technical assistance model. *Journal of the Association for Persons with Severe Handicaps, 12*, 2–10.

Duyn, J. H., Gillen, J., Sobering, G., van Zijl, P. C. M., & Moonen, C. T. W. (1993), Multislice proton MR spectroscopic imaging of the brain. *Radiology, 188*, 277–282.

Dykens, E. M., Hodapp, R. M., Walsh, K., & Nash, L. J. (1992). Profiles, correlates and trajectories of intelligence in Prader–Willi syndrome. *Journal of the American Academy of Child and Adolescent Psychiatry, 31*, 1125–1130.

Dykens, E. M., & Kasari C. (1997). Maladaptive behavior in children with Prader–Willi syndrome, Down syndrome, and nonspecific mental retardation. *American Journal of Mental Retardation, 102*(3), 228–237.

Dykens, E. M., Leckman, M. D., & Cassidy, S. B. (1996). Obsessions and compulsions in Prader–Willi syndrome. *Journal of Child Psychology and Psychiatry and Allied Disciplines, 37*, 995–1002.

Ebert, M. H., Schmidt, D. E., Thompson, T., & Butler, M. G. (1997). Elevated plasma γ-amino butyric acid (GABA) levels in individuals with Prader–Willi or Angelman syndromes. *Journal of Neuropsychiatry and Clinical Neuroscience, 9*, 75–80.

Ehlers, C., Havstad, J., Garfinkel, A., & Kupfer, D. (1991). Nonlinear analysis of sleep states. *Neuropsychopharmacology, 5*, 167–176.

Eichler, A. J., Antelman, S. M., & Black, C. A. (1980). Amphetamine stereotypy is not a homogeneous phenomenon: Sniffing and licking show distinct profiles of sensitization and tolerance. *Psychopharmacology 68*, 287–290.

Ekman, P., & Friesen, W. (1978). *Investigator's guide to the facial action coding system.* Palo Alto, CA: Consulting Psychologists Press.

Elie, R., Langlois, Y., Cooper, S. F., Gravel, G., & Albert, J. M. (1980). Comparison of SCH-12679 and thioridazine in aggressive mental retardates. *Canadian Journal of Psychiatry, 25*, 484–491.

Elliott, R., Friston, K. J., & Dolan, R. J. (2000). Dissociable neural responses in human reward systems. *Journal of Neuroscience, 20*, 6159–6165.

Elsworth, J. D., Lawrence, M. S., Roth, R. H., Taylor, J. R., Mailman, R. B. Nichols, D. E., et al. (1991). D_1 and D_2 dopamine receptors independently regulate spontaneous blink rate in the vervet monkey. *Journal of Pharmacology and Experimental Therapeutics, 259*, 595–600.

Emberson, J., & Walker, E. (1990). Self-injurious behaviour in people with a mental handicap. *Nursing Times, 86*, 43–46.

Emerson, E., Reeves, D., Thompson, S., Henderson, D., Robertson, J., & Howard, D. (1996). Time-based lag sequential analysis and the functional assessment of challenging behavior. *Journal of Intellectual Disability Research, 40*, 260–274.

Emmerson, B. T., & Wyngaarden, J. B. (1969). Purine metabolism in heterozygous carriers of hypoxanthine-guanine phosphoribosyltransferase deficiency. *Science, 166*, 1533–1535.

Erinoff, L., Kelly, P. H., Basura, M., & Snodgrass, S. R. (1984). 6-Hydroxy-dopamine-induced hyperactivity: Neither sex differences nor caffeine stimulation are found. *Pharmacology, Biochemistry, and Behavior, 20*, 707–713.

Ernst, M., Devi, L., Silva, R. R., Gonzalez, N. M., Small, A. M., Malone, R. P., et al. (1993). Plasma β-endorphin levels, naltrexone, and haloperidol in autistic children. *Psychopharmacology Bulletin, 29*, 221–227.

Ernst, M., Zametkin, A. J., Matochik, J. A., Pascualvaca, D., Jons, P. H., Hardy, K., et al. (1996). Presynaptic dopaminergic deficits in Lesch–Nyhan disease. *New England Journal of Medicine, 334*(24), 1568–1572.

Evans, C., & Lacey, J. (1992). Multiple self-damaging behavior among alcoholic women: A prevalence study. *British Journal of Psychiatry, 161*, 643–647.

Everett, G. M. (1975). A unique dopamimetic, Pemoline (abstract). *Pharmacologist, 17*, 227.

Eyman, R. K., & Call, T. (1977). Maladaptive behavior and community placement of mentally retarded persons. *American Journal of Mental Deficiency, 82*(2), 137–144.

Farber, J. M. (1987). Psychopharmacology of self-injurious behavior in the mentally retarded. *Journal of the American Academy of Child and Adolescent Psychiatry, 26*, 296–302.

Favaro, A., & Santonastoso, P. (1998). Impulsive and compulsive self-injurious behavior in bulimia nervosa: Prevalence and psychological correlates. *The Journal of Nervous and Mental Disease, 186*, 157–165.

Favazza, A. R. (1987). *Bodies under siege: Self-mutilation in culture and psychiatry.* Baltimore: Johns Hopkins University Press.

Favazza, A. (1998). The coming of age of self-mutilation. *The Journal of Nervous and Mental Disease, 186*, 259–268.

Favazza, A. R., & Conterio, K. (1989). Female habitual self-mutilators. *Acta Psychiatrica Scandinavia, 79*, 283–289.

Favazza, A., DeRosear, L., & Conterio, K. (1989). Self-mutilation and eating disorders. *Suicide Life-Threatening Behaviors, 19*, 352–361.

Favazza, A., & Rosenthal, R. (1990). Varieties of pathological self-mutilation. *Behavioral Neurology, 3*, 77–85.

Favell, J. E., McGimsey, J. F., & Jones, M. L. (1978). The use of physical restraint in the treatment of self-injury and as a positive reinforcement. *Journal of Applied Behavior Analysis, 11*, 225–241.

Favell, J. E., McGimsey, J. F., Jones, M. L., & Cannon, P. R. (1981). Physical restraint as positive reinforcement. *American Journal of Mental Deficiency, 85*, 425–432.

Favell, J. E., McGimsey, J. F., & Schell, R. M. (1982). Treatment of self-injury by providing alternate sensory activities. *Analysis and Intervention in Developmental Disabilities, 2*, 83–104.

Feifel, D. (1999). Neurotransmitters and neuromodulators in frontal-subcortical circuits. In B. L. Miller and J. L. Cummings (Eds.), *The human frontal lobes: Function and disorders* (pp. 174–176). New York: The Guilford Press.

Feldman, M. D. (1988). The challenge of self-mutilation: A review. *Comprehensive Psychiatry, 3*, 252–269.

Ferrari, M., Matthews, W. S., & Barabas, G. (1984). Children with Tourette's syndrome: Results of psychological tests. *Journal of Developmental and Behavioral Pediatrics, 5*, 116–119.

Ferre, S., Von Euler, G., Johansson, B., Fredholm, B., & Fuxe, K. (1991). Stimulation of high affinity adenosine A_2 receptors decreases the affinity of dopamine D_2 receptors in rat striatal membranes. *Proceedings of the National Academy of Sciences, USA, 88*, 7238–7241.

Ferrer, I., Costell, M., & Grisolia, S. (1982). Lesch–Nyhan syndrome-like behavior in rats from caffeine ingestion. *FEBS Letters, 141*, 275–278.

Feurer, I. D., Dimitropoulos, A., Stone, W. L., Roof, E., Butler, M. G., & Thompson, T. (1998). The latent variable structure of the Compulsive Behaviour Checklist in people with Prader–Willi syndrome. *Journal of Intellectual Disability Research, 42*, 472–80.

Fielding, S., & Lal, H. (1978). Behavioral actions of neuroleptics. In L. L. Iverson, S. D. Iversen, & S. H. Snyder (Eds.), *Handbook of psychopharmacology: Neuroleptics and schizophrenia*, (Vol. 10) (pp. 91–128). New York: Plenum Press.

Finger, S., Heavens, R. P., Sirinathsinghji, D. J., & Kuehn, M. R. (1988). Behavioral and neurochemical evaluation of a transgenic mouse model of Lesch–Nyhan syndrome. *Journal of Neurological Science, 86,* 203–213.

Finlay, J. M., & Zigmond, M. J. (1997). The effects of stress on central dopaminergic neurons: possible clinical implications. *Neurochemical Research, 22,* 1387–1394.

Fisher, W. W., Grace, N. C., & Murphy, C. (1996). Further analysis of the relationship between self-injury and self-restraint. *Journal of Applied Behavior Analysis, 29,* 103–106.

Fisher, W. W., & Iwata, B. A. (1996). On the function of self-restraint and its relationship to self-injury. *Journal of Applied Behavior Analysis, 29,* 93–98.

Fisher, W., Piazza, C. C., Bowman, L. G., Hagopian, L. P., & Langdon, N. A. (1994). Empirically derived consequences: A data-based method for prescribing treatments for destructive behavior. *Research in Developmental Disabilities, 15,* 133–149.

Fisher, W., Piazza, C. C., Bowman, L. G., Hagopian, L. P., Owens, J. C., & Slevin, I. (1992). A comparison of two approaches for identifying reinforcers for persons with severe and profound disabilities. *Journal of Applied Behavior Analysis, 25,* 491–498.

Fisher, W. W., Piazza, C. C., Bowman, L. G., Hanley, G. P., & Adelinis, J. D. (1997). Direct and collateral effects of restraints and restraint fading. *Journal of Applied Behavior Analysis, 30,* 105–120.

Fisher, W., Piazza, C., Cataldo, M., Harrell, R., Jefferson, G., & Conner, R. (1993). Functional communication training with and without extinction and punishment. *Journal of Applied Behavior Analysis, 26,* 23–36.

Fisher, W. W., Piazza, C. C., & Page, T. (1989). Assessing independent and interactive effects of behavioral and pharmacologic interventions for a client with dual diagnoses. *Journal of Behavior Therapy and Experimental Psychiatry, 20,* 241–250.

Fisher, W., Thompson, R. H., Hagopian, L. P., Bowman, L. G., & Krug, A. (2000). Facilitating tolerance of delayed reinforcement during functional communication training. *Behavior Modification, 24,* 3–29.

Folstein, S., & Rutter, M. (1977). Infantile autism: A genetic study of 21 twin pairs. *Journal of Child Psychology and Psychiatry, 18,* 297–321.

Forman, L. J., Cavalieri, R., Estilow, S., & Tatarian, G. T. (1990). The elevation of immunoreactive β-endorphin in old male rats is related to alterations in dopamine and serotonin. *Neurobiology of Aging, 11,* 223–227.

Fovel, J. T., Lash, P. S., Barron, D. A., & Roberts, M. S. (1989). A survey of self-restraint, self-injury, and other maladaptive behaviors in an institutionalized retarded population. *Research in Developmental Disabilities, 10,* 377–382.

Fowles, D. C. (1982). Heart rate as an index of anxiety: Failure of a hypothesis. In J. T. Cacioppo, & R. E. Petty (Eds.), *Perspectives in cardiovascular psychophysiology* (pp. 93–126). New York: Guilford Press.

Fox, R. M., & Dufrense, D. (1984). "Harry": The use of physical restraint as a reinforcer, timeout from restraint, and fading restraint in treating a self-injurious man. *Analysis and Intervention in Developmental Disabilities, 4*, 1–13.

Francezon, J., Visier, J. P., & Mennesson, J. F. (1981). Circannual fluctuation of a stereotype behaviour with possible self-mutilation in a mentally deficient adolescent. *International Journal of Chronobiology, 7*(3), 129–140.

Francke, U., Felsenstein, J., Gartler, S. M., Migeon, B. R., Dancis, J., Seegmiller, et al. (1976). The occurrence of new mutants in the X-linked recessive Lesch–Nyhan disease. *American Journal of Human Genetics, 28*, 123–137.

Frankel, F., & Simmons, J. Q. (1976). Self-injurious behavior in schizophrenic and retarded children. *American Journal of Mental Deficiency, 80*, 512–522.

Freeman, R., Horner, R., & Reichle, J. (1999). Relation between heart rate and problem behaviors. *American Journal on Mental Retardation, 104*(4), 330–345.

Frohna, P. A., Neal-Beliveau, B. S., & Joyce, J. N. (1995). Neonatal 6-hydroxydopamine lesions lead to opposing changes in the levels of dopamine receptors and their messenger RNAs. *Neuroscience, 68*, 505–518, 1995.

Frohna, P. A., Neal-Beliveau, B. S., & Joyce, J. N. (1997). Delayed plasticity of the mesolimbic dopamine system following neonatal 6-OHDA lesions. *Synapse, 25*, 293–305.

Fuxe, K., Hokfelt, T., Agnati, L. F., Johansson, O., Goldstein, M., Perez de la Mora, M., et al. (1978). Mapping out central catecholamine neurons: Immunohistochemical studies on catecholamine-synthesizing enzymes. In M. A. Lipton, A. DiMascio, & K. F. Killam (Eds.), *Psychopharmacology: A generation of progress* (pp. 67–94), New York: Raven Press.

Gagnon, C., Bedard, P. J., Rioux, L., Gaudin, D., Martinoli, M. G., Pelletier, G., et al. (1991). Regional changes of striatal dopamine receptors following denervation by 6-hydroxydopamine and fetal mesencephalic grafts in the rat. *Brain Research, 558*, 251–263.

Gancher, S., Crabbe, J., Garland, A., Lea, E., & Woodward, E. (1995). Dose- and duration-dependent tolerance to rotational effects of apomorphine in a rat model of Parkinsonism. *Journal of Pharmacology and Experimental Therapeutics, 272*, 275–281.

Gancher, S. T., Nutt, J. G., & Woodward, W. R. (1992). Time course of tolerance to apomorphine in Parkinsonism. *Clinical Pharmacology and Therapeutics, 52*, 504–510.

Gancher, S. T., Woodward, W. R., & Nutt, J. G. (1996). Apomorphine tolerance in Parkinson's disease: Lack of a dose effect. *Clinical Neuropharmacology, 19*, 59–64, 1996.

Garber, H. J., Ananth, J. V., Chui, L. C., Griswold, V. J., & Oldendorf, W. H. (1989). Nuclear magnetic resonance study of obsessive-compulsive disorder. *American Journal of Psychiatry, 146*, 1001–1005.

Garber, H. J., McGonigle, J. J., Slomka, G. T., & Monteverde, E. (1992). Clomipramine treatment of stereotypic behaviors and self-injury in patients with developmental disabilties. *Journal of the American Academy of Child and Adolescent Psychiatry, 31*, 1157–1160.

Garcia, D., & Smith, R. G. (1999). Using analog baselines to assess the effects of naltrexone on self-injurious behavior. *Research in Developmental Disabilities, 20*, 1–21.

Gardner, A. R., & Gardner, A. J. (1975). Self-mutilation, obsessionality, and narcisism. *British Journal of Psychiatry, 127*, 127–132.

Garfinkel, A., Spano, M. L., Ditto, W. L., & Weiss, J. N. (1992). Controlling cardiac chaos. *Science, 257*, 1230–1235.

Gartler, S. M., Scott, R. C., Goldstein, J. L., & Campbell, B. (1971). Lesch–Nyhan syndrome: Rapid detection of heterozygotes by the use of hair follicles. *Science, 172*, 572–574.

Gatti, R. A., Robinson, W. A., Deinare, A. S., Nesbit, M., McCullogh, J. J., Ballow, M., et al. (1973). Cyclic leukocytosis in chronic myelogenous leukemia. *Blood, 41*, 771–782.

Gedye, A. (1989). Extreme self-injury attributed to frontal lobe seizures. *American Journal on Mental Retardation, 94*, 20–26.

Gedye, A. (1992). Anatomy of self-injurious movements. *Journal of Clinical Psychology, 48*, 766–778.

Genovese, E., Napoli, P. A., & Bolego-Zonta, N. (1969). Self-aggressiveness: A new type of behavioral change induced by pemoline. *Life Sciences, 8*, 513–515.

George, M. S., Trimble, M. R., Ring, H., Sallee, F. R., & Robertson, M. M. (1993). Obsessions in obsessive-compulsive disorder with and without Tourette's syndrome. *American Journal of Psychiatry, 150*, 93–97.

Gibbs, R. A., Nguyen, P., Edwards, A., Civitello, A. B., & Caskey, C. T. (1990). Multiplex DNA deletion detection and exon sequencing of the hypoxanthine phosphoribosyltransferase gene in Lesch–Nyhan families. *Genomics, 7*, 235–244.

Gibson, A. K., Hetrick, W. P., Taylor, D. V., Sandman, C. A., & Touchette, P. (1995). Relating the efficacy of naltrexone in treating self-injurious behavior to the Motivation Assessment Scale. *Journal of Developmental and Physical Disabilities, 7*, 215–220.

Gilbert, S., Spellacy, E., & Watts, R. W. E. (1979). Problems in the behavioral treatment of self-injury in the Lesch–Nyhan syndrome. *Developmental Medicine and Child Neurology, 21*, 795–800.

Gillberg, C. (1995). Endogenous opioids and opiate antagonists in autism: Brief review of empirical findings and implications for clinicians. *Developmental and Medical Child Neurology, 37*, 239–245.

Gillberg, C., Terenius, L. G., Hagberg, B., Witt-Engerstom, I., & Eriksson, I. (1990). CSF β-endorphins in childhood neuropsychiatric disorders. *Brain and Development, 12*, 88–92.

Gillberg, C., Terenius, L. G., & Lonnerhom, G. (1985). Endorphin activity in childhood psychosis. *Archives of General Psychiatry, 42*, 780–783.

Giuffre, K. A., Udelsman, R., Listwak, S., & Chrousos, G. P. (1988). Effects of immune neutralization of corticotropin-releasing hormone, adrenocorticotropin, and β-endorphin in the surgically stressed rat. *Endocrinology, 122,* 306–310.

Gius, D., Botero, A., Shah, S., & Curry, H. A. (1999). Intracellular oxidation/reduction status in the transcription factors NF-kappaB and AP1. *Toxicology Letters, 106,* 93–106.

Gjedde, A., Wong, D. F., Harris, J., Dannals, R. F., Ravert, H. T., et al. (1986). Quantification of D_1 and D_2 dopamine receptors in Lesch–Nyhan syndrome as measured by positron tomography. *Society for Neuroscience Abstracts, 12,* 486.

Glass, L., & Mackey, M. C. (1988). *From clocks to chaos: The rhythms of life.* Princeton, NJ: Princeton University Press.

Gluck, J. P., & Sackett, G. P. (1974). Frustration and self-aggression in social isolate rhesus monkeys. *Journal of Abnormal Psychology, 83,* 331–334.

Goldberger, A. L. (1997). Fractal variability versus pathologic periodicity: Complexity loss and stereotypy in disease. *Perspectives in Biology and Medicine, 40,* 543–561.

Goldberger, A. L., Shabetai, R., Bhargava V., West B. J., & Mandell, A. J. (1984). Nonlinear dynamics, electrical alternans, and pericardial tamponade. *The American Heart Journal, 107*(6), 1297–1299.

Goldstein, M., Anderson, L. T., Reuben, R., & Dancis, J. (1985). Self-mutilation in Lesch–Nyhan disease is caused by dopaminergic denervation. *Lancet, 1,* 338–339.

Goldstein, M., Kuga, S., Kusano, N., Meller, E., Dancis, J., & Schwarcz, R. (1986). Dopamine agonist induced self-mutilative biting behavior in monkeys with unilateral ventral medial tegmental lesions of the brain stem: Possible pharmacological model for Lesch–Nyhan syndrome. *Brain Research, 3676,* 114–120.

Gong, L., Kostrzewa, R. M., Fuller, R. W., & Perry, K. W. (1992). Supersensitization of the oral response to SKF-38393 in neonatal 6-OHDA-lesioned rats is mediated through a serotonin system. *Journal of Pharmacology and Experimental Therapeutics, 261,* 1000–1007.

Gonzalez, J. P., & Brogden, R. N. (1988). Naltrexone: A review of its pharmacodynamic and pharmacokinetic properties and therapeutic efficacy in the management of opioid dependence. *Drugs, 35,* 192–213.

Gordon, R. B., Emmerson, B. I., Stout, J. T., & Caskey, C. T. (1987). Molecular studies of hypoxanthine-guanine phosphoribosyltransferase mutations in six Australian families. *Australian and New Zealand Journal of Medicine, 17,* 424–429.

Gorman-Smith, D., & Matson, J. L. (1985). A review of treatment for self-injurious and stereotyped responding. *Journal of Mental Deficiency Research, 29,* 295–308.

Gottman, J. M. (1981). *Time-series analysis: A comprehensive introduction for social scientists.* New York: Cambridge University Press.

Gottman, J. M., & Roy, A. K. (1990). *Sequential analysis.* New York: Cambridge University Press.

Gottschalk, A., Bauer, M. S., & Whybrow, P. C. (1995). Evidence of chaotic mood variation in bipolar disorder. *Archives of General Psychiatry, 52,* 947–959.

Grabowski, J. (1984). *Cocaine: Pharmacology, effects, and treatment of abuse.* Washington, DC: National Institute on Drug Abuse.

Grandin, T. (1996). *Thinking in pictures: And other reports from my life with autism.* New York: Vintage Books/Random House Publishers.

Graybiel, A. M. (1990). Neurotransmitters and neuromodulators in the basal ganglia. *Trends in Neuroscience, 13,* 244–254.

Graybiel, A. M., & Ragsdale, C. W., Jr. (1983). Biochemical anatomy of the striatum. In P. C. Emson (Ed.), *Chemical neuroanatomy,* (pp. 427–504). New York: Raven Press.

Greendyke, R. M., Kanter, D. R., Schuster, D. B., Verstreate, S., & Wooten, J. (1986). Propranolol treatment of assaultive patients with organic brain disease. *Journal of Nervous and Mental Disease, 174,* 290–294.

Greenswag, L. R. (1987). Adults with Prader–Willi syndrome: A survey of 232 cases. *Developmental Medicine and Child Neurology, 29,* 145–152.

Grevert, P., & Goldstein, A. (1977). Effect of naloxone experimentally induced ischemic pain on mood in human subjects. *Proceedings of the National Academy of Sciences, USA, 74,* 1291–1294.

Griffin, J. C., Ricketts, R. W., Williams, D. E., Locke, B. J., Altmeyer, B. K., & Stark, M. T. (1987). A community survey of self-injurious behavior among developmentally disabled children and adolescents. *Hospital and Community Psychiatry, 38*(9), 959–963.

Griffin, J. C., Williams, D. E., Stark, M. T., Altmeyer, B. K., & Mason, M. (1986). Self-injurious behaviour: A state-wide prevalence survey of the extent and circumstances. *Applied Research in Mental Retardation, 7,* 105–116.

Groden, G., & Baron, M. G. (Eds.), (1991). *Autism: Strategies for change—A comprehensive approach to the education and treatment of children with autism and related disorders.* New York: Gardner Press.

Grunau, R. V. E., & Craig, K. D. (1987). Pain expression in neonates: Facial action and crying. *Pain, 28,* 395–410.

Grunau, R. V. E., & Craig, K. D. (1990). Facial activity as a measure of neonatal pain expression. In D. C. Tyler, & E. J. Crane (Eds.), *Advances in pain research and therapy,* (Vol. 15) (pp. 147–156). New York: Raven Press.

Gualtieri, C. T., & Schroeder, S. R. (1989). Pharmacotherapy of self-injurious behavior: Preliminary tests of the D_1 hypothesis. *Psychopharmacology Bulletin, 25,* 364–371.

Guess, D., & Carr, E. (1991). Emergence and maintenance of stereotypy and self-injury. *American Journal of Mental Retardation, 96,* 335–344.

Gunsett, R. P., Mulick, J. A., Fernald, W. B., & Martin, J. L. (1989). Brief report: Indications for medical screening prior to behavioral programming for severely and profoundly mentally retarded clients. *Journal of Autism and Developmental Disorders, 19,* 1989.

Gutenson, W., & Guroff, G. (1972). Hypoxanthine-guanine phosphoribosyltransferase from rat brain (purification kinetic properties, development, and distribution). *Journal of Neurochemistry, 19,* 2139–2150.

Hagopian, L. P., Fisher, W. W., & Legacy, S. M. (1994). Schedule effects of non-contingent reinforcement on attention-maintained destructive behavior in identical quadruplets. *Journal of Applied Behavior Analysis, 27,* 317–325.

Hammock, R. G., Levine, W. R., & Schroeder, S. R. (2001) Effects of clozapine on self-injurious behavior of two risperidone non-responders with mental retardation. *Journal of Autism and Developmental Disorders, 41,* 109–113.

Hammock, R. G., Schroeder, S. R., & Levine, W. R. (1995). The effect of clozapine on self-injurious behavior. *Journal of Autism and Developmental Disorders, 25,* 611–626.

Harkness, J. E., & Wagner, J. E. (1975). Self-mutilation in mice associated with otitis media. *Laboratory Animal Science, 25,* 315–318.

Harlow, H., & Harlow, C. M. (1979). *The human model: Primate perspectives.* Washington: V. H. Winston.

Harlow, H. F., & Harlow, M. K. (1965). The affectional systems. In A. M. Schrier, H. F. Harlow, & F. Stollnitz (Eds.), *Behavior of nonhuman primates* (pp. 287–334). New York: Academic Press.

Harlow, H. F., & Harlow, M. K. (1969). Effects of various mother-infant relationships on rhesus monkey behaviors. In B. M. Foss (Ed.), *Determinants of infant behaviour IV* (pp. 15–36). London: Methuen.

Harris, J. C. (1995). Destructive behavior: Aggression and self-injury. In J. C. Harris (Ed.), *Developmental neuropsychiatry: Assessment, diagnosis, and treatment of developmental disorders* (pp. 463–484). New York: Oxford University Press.

Harris, J. C., Barker, P., Jinnah, H. A., Schretlen, D., Wong, D. F., & Yokoi, F. Combining proton MRS and PET imaging of dopamine transporters to establish neuronal dsyfunction in Lesch–Nyhan disease and its variants. *Abstracts, Genetics and Neuroscience,* Terni, Italy, 2000.

Harris, J., Lee, R. R., Jinnah, H. A., Wong, D. F., Yaster, M., & Bryon, R. N. (1998). Craniocerebral magnetic resonance imaging measurement and findings in Lesch–Nyhan syndrome. *Archives of Neurology, 55*(4), 547–553.

Harris J. C., Schretlen D., Bryan N., & Wong D. F. (1996). Magnetic resonance imaging in Lesch–Nyhan disease: Correlation of caudate nucleus volume and cognitive functioning. *Society for Neuroscience Abstracts, 22,* 265.

Harris, J., Wang, P., Jinnah, H., & Barker, P. (1998). *Quantitative proton MR spectroscopic imaging in Lesch–Nyhan disease.* Abstracts. 5th International Meeting of the Society for the Study of Behavioural Phenotypes. Johns Hopkins University, Baltimore.

Harris, J. C., Wong, D. F., Jinnah, H. A., Schretlen, D., Yokoi, F., Stephane, M., et al. (1999). Dopamine Transporter Binding of WIN 35,428 Correlates With HPRT Level And Extent of Movement Disorder But Not With Self Injurious Behavior [Abstracts]. Society for Neuroscience, Annual Meeting (No. 855.9). Miami, FL.

Harris, J., Wong, D., Wagner, H., Rett, A., Naidu, S., Dannals, R., et al. (1986). Positron emission tomographic study of D_2 dopamine receptor binding and CSF biogenic amine metabolites in Rett syndrome. *American Journal of Medical Genetics, 24,* 201–210.

Harris, J., Wong, D. F., Yaster, M., Dannals, R., Nyhan, W., Hyman, S., et al. (1991). Clinical investigation of the dopamine hypothesis of self-injurious behavior in the Lesch–Nyhan syndrome. *Society for Neuroscience Abstracts, 17*(266.13), 678.

Hartgraves, S. L., & Randall, P. K. (1986). Dopamine agonist-induced stereotypic grooming and self-mutilation following striatal dopamine depletion. *Psychopharmacology 90*, 358–363.

Hashimoto, T., Tayama, M., Miyazaki, M., Fujii, E., Harada, M., Miyoshi, H., et al. (1995). Developmental brain changes investigated with proton magnetic resonance spectroscopy. *Developmental Medicine and Child Neurology, 37*, 398–405.

Hassett, J., & Danforth, D. (1982). An introduction to the cardiovascular system. In J. T. Cacioppo, & R. E. Petty (Eds.), *Perspectives in cardiovascular psychophysiology* (pp. 4–18). New York: Guilford Press.

Heinz, A., Knable, M. B., Wolf, S. S., Jones, D. W., Gorey, J. G., Hyde, T. M., et al. (1998). Tourette's syndrome: [I-123]beta-CIT SPECT correlates of vocal tic severity. *Neurology, 51*, 1069–1074.

Heise, G. A., & Boff, E. (1962). Continuous avoidance as a base-line for measuring behavioral effects of drugs. *Psychopharmacologia, 3*, 264–282.

Hellings, J. A., & Warnock, J. K. (1994). Self-injurious behavior and serotonin in Prader–Willi syndrome. *Psychopharmacology Bulletin, 30*, 245–250.

Hellings, J., Schroeder, S., Zarcone, J., Reese, M., & Crandall, K. (1999). *A double blind, placebo-controlled evaluation of risperidone in the treatment of severe behavior disorder.* Paper presented at the Gatlinburg Conference on Research and Theory in Mental Retardation and Developmental Disabilities, San Diego, CA.

Herdegen, T., & Leah, J. D. (1998). Inducible and constitutive transcription factors in the mammalian nervous system: Control of gene expression by Jun, Fos, and Krox, and CREB/ATF proteins. *Brain Research Review, 28*, 370–490.

Herman, B. H., Hammock, M. K., Arthur-Smith, A., Egan, J., Chatoor, I., Werner, A., et al. (1987). Naltrexone decreases self-injurious behavior. *Annals of Neurology, 22*, 550–552.

Herman, B. H., Hammock, M. K., Egan, J., Arthur-Smith, A., Chatoor, I., & Werner, A. (1989). Role of opioid peptides in self-injurious behavior: Dissociation from autonomic nervous system functioning. *Developmental Pharmacology and Therapeutics, 12*, 81–89.

Herpertz, S. (1995). Self-injurious behavior: Psychopathological and nosological characteristics in subtypes of self-injurers. *Acta Psychiatrica Scandinavica, 91*, 57–68.

Herrnstein, R. J. (1970). On the law of effect. *Journal of the Experimental Analysis of Behavior, 13*, 243–266.

Hetrick, W. P., Isenhart, R. C., Taylor, D. V., & Sandman, C. A. (1991). ODAP: A stand-alone program for observational data acquisition. *Behavior Research Methods, Instruments, and Computers, 23*, 66–71.

Hilborn, R. C. (1994). *Chaos and nonlinear dynamics.* New York: Oxford University Press.

Hill, B. K., & Bruininks, R. H. (1984). Maladaptive behavior of mentally retarded individuals in residential facilities. *American Journal of Mental Deficiency, 88,* 380–387.

Hillery, J., & Mulcahy, M. (1997). Self-injurious behaviour in persons with a mental handicap: An epidemiological study in an Irish population. *Irish Journal of Psychiatric Medicine, 14,* 12–15.

Hiroi, N., Marek, G. J., Brown, J. R., Ye, H., Saudou, F., Vaidya, V. A., et al. (1998). Essential role of the *fosB* gene in molecular, cellular, and behavioral actions of chronic electroconvulsive seizures. *Journal of Neuroscience, 18,* 6952–6962.

Hirota, K., & Lambert, D. G. (1997). A comparative study of L-type voltage sensitive Ca^{2+} channels in rat brain regions and cultured neuronal cells. *Neuroscience Letters, 223,* 169–172.

Hohn, R., & Lasagna, L. (1960). Effects of aggregation and temperature on amphetamine toxicity in mice. *Psychopharmacology, 1,* 210–220.

Holson, R. R., Scallet, A. C., Ali, S. F., Sullivan, P., & Gough, B. (1988). Adrenocortical, β-endorphin and behavioral responses to graded stressors in differentially reared rats. *Physiology and Behavor, 42,* 125–130.

Hooper, M., Hardy, K., Handyside, A., Hunter, S., & Monk, M. (1987). HPRT-deficient (Lesch–Nyhan) mouse embryos derived from germline colonization by cultured cells. *Nature, 326,* 292–295.

Horner, R. H. (1994). Functional assessment: Contribution and future directions. *Journal of Applied Behavior Analysis, 27,* 401–404.

Horner, R. H., & Carr, E. G. (1997). Behavioral support for students with severe disabilities: Functional assessment and comprehensive intervention. *The Journal of Special Education, 31,* 88–104.

Horner, R. H., Day, H. M., & Day, J. R. (1997). Using neutralizing routines to reduce problem behaviors. *Journal of Applied Behavior Analysis, 30,* 601–614.

Horner, R. H., Vaughn, B. J., Day, H. M., & Ard, W. R. (1996). The relationship between setting events and problem behavior: Expanding out understanding of behavioral support. In L. K. Koegel, R. L. Koegel, & G. Dunlap (Eds.), *Positive behavioral support: Including people with difficult behavior in the community* (pp. 381–402). Baltimore: Paul H. Brookes Publishing.

Hornykiewicz, O. (1966). Metabolism of brain dopamine in human Parkinsonism: Neurochemical and clinical aspects. In E. Costa, L. J. Cote, & M. D. Yahr (Eds.), *Biochemistry and Pharmacology of the Basal Ganglia* (pp. 171–181). New York: Raven Press.

Hornykiewicz, O. (1973). Parkinson's Disease: From homogenate to treatment. *Federation Proceedings, 32,* 183–190.

Hornykiewicz, O. (1974). The mechanisms of action of L-dopa in Parkinson's disease. *Life Sciences, 15,* 1249–1259.

Howard, R. S., & Walzak, M. P. (1968). A new cause for uric acid stones in childhood. *Journal of Urology, 98,* 639–642.

Hsiao, J. K., Agren, H., Bartko, J. J., Rudorfer, M. V., Linnoila, M., & Potter, W. Z. (1987). Monoamine neurotransmitter interactions and the prediction of anti-depressant response. *Archives of General Psychiatry, 44,* 1078–1083.

Huberman, H. S., Eison, M. S., Bryan, K. S., & Ellison, G. (1977). A slow-release silicone pellet for chronic amphetamine administration. *European Journal of Pharmacology, 45,* 237–242.

Hughes, A., Lees, A., & Stern, G. (1990). Apomorphine test to predict dopamin-ergic responsiveness in Parkinsonian syndromes. *Lancet, 336,* 32–34.

Hughes, A. J., Bishop, S., Kleedorfer, B., Turjanski, N., Fernandez, W., Lees, A. J., et al. (1993). Subcutaneous apomorphine in Parkinson's disease: Response to chronic administration for up to 5 years. *Movement Disorders, 8,* 165–170.

Hughes, P., & Dragunow, M. (1995). Induction of immediate-early genes and the control of neurotransmitter-regulated gene expression within the nervous system. *Pharmacological Reviews 47,* 133–178.

Hutt, C., & Hutt, S. J. (1970). Stereotypes and their relation to arousal: A study of autistic children. In S. J. Hutt, & C. Hutt (Eds.), *Behavior studies in psychiatry* (pp. 175–204). New York: Pergammon Press.

Hyman, S. L., Fisher, W. W., Mercugliano, M., & Cataldo, M. F. (1990). Children with self-injurious behavior. *Pediatrics, 85,* 437–441.

Hyson, R. L., Aschcraft, L. J., Drugan, R. C., Grau, J. W., & Maier, S. F. (1982). Extent and control of shock affects naltrexone sensitivity of stress-induced analgesia and reactivity to morphine. *Pharmacology, Biochemistry, and Behavior, 17,* 1019–1025.

Individuals With Disabilities Education Act of 1997, P. L. 105-17, 105th Cong. (1997). 1st session.

Iorio, L. C., Barnett, A., Leitz, F. H., Houser, V. P., & Korduba, C. A. (1983). SCH-23390, a potential benzazepine antipsychotic with unique interactions on dopaminergic systems. *Journal of Pharmacology and Experimental Therapeutics, 226,* 462–468.

Isley, E. M., Kartsonis, C., McCurley, C. M., Weisz, D. E., & Roberts, M. S. (1991). Self-restraint: A review of etiology and applications in mentally retarded adults with self-injury. *Research in Developmental Disabilities, 12,* 87–95.

Itil, T. M., Stock, M. J., Duffy, A. D., Esquenazi, A., Saleuty, B., & Han, T. H. (1972). Therapeutic trials and EEG investigations with SCH-12679 in behaviorally disturbed adolescents. *Current Therapeutic Research, 14,* 136–150.

Iversen, S. D. (1971). The effect of surgical lesions to frontal cortex and substantia nigra on amphetamine responses in rats. *Brain Research, 31,* 295–311.

Iwamoto, E. T., & Way, E. L. (1977). Circling behavior and stereotypy induced by intranigral opiate microinjection. *Journal of Pharmacology and Experimental Therapeutics, 20,* 347–359.

Iwata, B. A. (1988). The development and adoption of controversial default technologies. *The Behavior Analyst, 11,* 149–157.

Iwata, B. A. (1994). Functional analysis methodology: Some closing comments. *Journal of Applied Behavior Analysis, 27*, 413–418.

Iwata, B. A., Dorsey, M. F., Slifer, K. J., Bauman, K. E., & Richman, G. S. (1982). Toward a functional analysis of self-injury. *Analysis and Intervention in Developmental Disabilities, 2*, 3–20.

Iwata, B. A., Dorsey, M. F., Slifer, K. J., Bauman, K. E., & Richman, G. S. (1994). Toward a functional analysis of self-injury. *Journal of Applied Behavior Analysis, 27*, 197–209. (Reprinted from *Analysis and Intervention in Developmental Disabilities, 2*, 3–20, 1982).

Iwata, B. A., Kahng, S., Wallace, M. D., & Lindberg, J. S. (in press). The functional analysis model of behavioral assessment. In J. Austin, & J. E. Carr (Eds.), *Handbook of applied behavior analysis*. Reno, NV: Context Press.

Iwata, B. A., Pace, G. M., Cowdery, G. E., & Miltenberger, R. G. (1994). What makes extinction work: An analysis of procedural form and function. *Journal of Applied Behavior Analysis, 27*, 131–144.

Iwata, B. A., Pace, G. M., Dorsey, M. F., Zarcone, J. R., Vollmer, T. R., Smith, R. G., et al. (1994). The functions of self-injurious behavior: An experimental-epidemiological analysis. *Journal of Applied Behavior Analysis, 27*, 215–240.

Iwata, B. A., Pace, G. M., Kalsher, M. J., Cowdery, G. E., & Cataldo, M. F. (1990). Experimental analysis and extinction of self-injurious escape behavior. *Journal of Applied Behavior Analysis, 23*, 11–27.

Iwata, B. A., Pace, G. M., Kissel, R. C., Nau, P. A., & Farber, J. M. (1990). The self-injury trauma (SIT) scale: A method for quantifying surface tissue damage caused by self-injurious behavior. *Journal of Applied Behavior Analysis, 23*, 99–110.

Iwata, B. A., Roscoe, E. M., Zarcone, J. R., & Richman, D. M. (in press). Environmental determinants. In S. Schroeder, M. L. Oster-Granite, & T. Thompson (Eds.), *Self-injurious behavior: Gene-brain-behavior relationships*. Washington, DC: American Psychological Association.

Iwata, B. A., Vollmer, T. R., & Zarcone, J. R. (1990). The experimental (functional) analysis of behavior disorders: Methodology, applications, and limitations. In A. C. Repp, & N. N. Singh (Eds.), *Perspectives on the use of nonaversive and aversive interventions for persons with developmental disabilities* (pp. 301–330). Sycamore, IL: Sycamore.

Izard, C. E., Huebner, R. R., Risser, D., McGinnes, G. C., & Dougherty, L. M. (1980). The young infant's ability to produce discrete emotional expressions. *Developmental Psychology, 16*, 132–140.

Izenwasser, S., French, D., Carroll, F. I., & Kunko, P. M. (1999). Continuous infusion of selective dopamine reuptake inhibitors or cocaine produces time-dependent changes in rat locomotor activity. *Behavioural Brain Research, 99*, 201–208.

Jacobs, B. L., & Cohen, A. (1976). Differential behavioral effects of lesions of the median or dorsal raphe nuclei in rats: Open field and pain-elicited aggression. *Journal of Comparative Physiology and Psychology, 90*, 102–108.

Jacobson, J. W. (1982). Problem behavior and psychiatric impairment within a developmentally disabled population I: Behavior frequency. *Applied Research in Mental Retardation, 3,* 121–139.

James, A. L., & Barry, R. J. (1980). A review of psychophysiology in early onset psychosis. *Schizophrenia Bulletin, 6,* 506–525.

Jankovic, J. (1988). Orofacial and other self-mutilations. In J. Jankovic, & E. Tolosa (Eds.), *Advances in Neurology, 49,* 365–381. Raven Press: New York.

Jankovic, J., Caskey, T. C., Stout, J. T., & Butler, I. J. (1988). Lesch–Nyhan syndrome: A study of motor behavior and cerebrospinal fluid neurotransmitters. *Annals of Neurology 23,* 466–469.

Javitt, D. C., & Zukin, S. R. (1991). Recent advances in the phencyclidine model of schizophrenia. *American Journal of Psychiatry, 148,* 1301–1308.

Jinnah, H. A., & Breese, G. R. (1997). Animal models for Lesch–Nyhan disease. In P. M. Iannocconne, & D. G. Scarpelli. *Biological aspects of disease: Contributions from animal models* (pp. 93–143). Amsterdam: Harwood Academic Publishers.

Jinnah, H. A., & Friedmann, T. (2000). Lesch–Nyhan disease and its variants. In C. R. Scriver, A. L. Beaudet, W. S. Sly, & D. Valle (Eds.), *The metabolic and molecular bases of inherited disease,* (8th ed.). New York: McGraw-Hill.

Jinnah, H. A., Gage, F. H., & Friedmann, T. (1990). Animal models of LNS. *Brain Research Bulletins, 25,* 467–475.

Jinnah, H. A., Jones, M. D., Wojcik, B. E., Rothstein, J. D., Hess, E. J., Friedman, T., et al. (1999). The influence of age and strain on striatal dopamine loss in a genetic mouse model of Lesch–Nyhan disease. *Journal of Neurochemistry, 72,* 225–229.

Jinnah, H. D., Langlais, P. J., & Friedmann, T. (1992). Functional analysis of brain dopamine systems in a genetic mouse model of Lesch–Nyhan syndrome. *Journal of Pharmacology and Experimental Therapeutics, 263,* 596–607.

Jinnah, H. A., Page, T., & Friedmann, T. (1993). Brain purines in a genetic mouse model of Lesch–Nyhan disease. *Journal of Neurochemistry, 60,* 2036–2045.

Jinnah, H. A., Sepkuty, J., Ho, T., Drew, T., Kim, B., & Rothstein, J. D. (2000). Calcium channel agonists and dystonia in the mouse. *Movement Disorders, 15,* 542–551.

Jinnah, H. D., Yitta, S., Drew, T., Kim, B. S., Visser, J. E., & Rothstein, J. D. (1999). Calcium channel activation and self-biting in mice. *Proceedings of the National Academy of Sciences, USA, 96,* 15228–15232.

Jinnah, H. A., Wojckik, B. E., & Hunt, M. (1994). Dopamine deficiency in a genetic mouse model of Lesch–Nyhan syndrome. *Journal of Pharmacology and Experimental Theraputics, 263,* 596–607.

Jinnah, H. A., Wojcik, B. E., Hunt, M., Narang, N., Lee, K. Y., Goldstein, M., et al. (1994). Dopamine deficiency in a genetic mouse model of Lesch–Nyhan disease. *Journal of Neuroscience, 14,* 1164–1175.

Johnson, K. (1999). Reliability and comorbidity of measures of repetitive movement disorders in children and adolescents with severe mental retardation. *Dissertation Abstracts International, 59* (9-B), 5066.

Johnson, K. B., Criswell, H. E., Jensen, K. F., Simson, P. E., Mueller, R. A., & Breese, G. R. (1992). Comparison of the D$_1$-dopamine agonists SKF-38393 and A-68930 in neonatal 6-OHDA-lesioned rats: Behavioral effects and induction of c-fos immunoreactivity. *Journal of Pharmacology and Experimental Therapeutics, 262,* 855–865.

Johnson, W. L., & Baumeister, A. A. (1978). Self-injurious behavior: A review and analysis of methodological details of published studies. *Behavior Modification, 2,* 465–487.

Johnson, W. L., & Day, R. M. (1992). The incidence and prevalence of self-injurious behavior. In J. K. Luiselli, J. L. Matson, & N. N. Singh (1992). *Self-injurious behavior—Analysis, assessment, and treatment* (pp. 21–56). New York: Springer.

Johnson, W. L., Day, R. M., & Hassanian, R. E. S. (1988). *Prevalence of self-injurious behaviors within public school special education program.* Paper presented at the 112th annual Meeting of the American Association on Mental Retardation, Washington, DC.

Jolly, D. H., Esty, A. C., Bernard, H. U., & Friedmann, T. (1982). Isolation of a genomic clone encoding human hypoxanthine guanine phosphoribosyl transferase. *Proceedings of the National Academy of Sciences, USA, 79,* 5038–5041.

Jolly, D. J., Okayama, H., Berg, P., Esty, A. C., Filpula, D., Bohlen, G. G., et al. (1983). Isolation and characterization of a full-length, expressible cDNA for human hypoxanthine guanine phosphoribosyl transferase. *Proceedings of the National Academy of Sciences, USA, 80,* 477–479.

Jones, I. H., & Barraclough, B. M. (1978). Auto-mutilation in animals and its relevance to self-injury in man. *Acta Psychiatrica Scandinavica, 58,* 40–47.

Joyce, J. N., Frohna, P. A., & Neal-Beliveau, B. S. (1996). Functional and molecular differentiation of the dopamine system induced by neonatal denervation. *Neuroscience and Biobehavioral Reviews, 20,* 453–486.

Kalachnik, J. E., Hanzel, T. E., Harder, S. R., Bauernfeind, J. D., & Engstrom, E. A. (1995). Antiepileptic drug behavioral side effects in individuals with mental retardation and the use of behavioral measurement techniques. *Mental Retardation, 33,* 374–382.

Kalin, N. H. (1999). Primate models and aggression. *Journal of Clinical Psychiatry Monograph Series, 17,* 22–24.

Kanner, L. (1943). Autistic disturbances of affective contact. *Nervous Child, 2,* 217–250.

Kantor, J. R. (1959). *Interbehavioral psychology.* Granville, OH: Principia Press.

Karin, M., Liu, Z., & Zandi, E. (1997). AP-1 function and regulation. *Current Opinions in Cell Biology, 9,* 240–246.

Karler, R., Calder, L. D., Thai, D. K., & Bedingfield, J. B. (1998). The role of dopamine and GABA in the frontal cortex of mice in modulating a motor-stimulant effect of amphetamine and cocaine. *Pharmacology, Biochemistry, and Behavior, 60*(1), 237–244.

Karson, C. N. (1983). Spontaneous eye-blink rates and dopaminergic systems. *Brain, 106,* 643–653.

Karson, C. N., Burns, R. S., Le Witt, P. A., Foster, N. L., & Newman, R. P. (1984). Blink rates and disorders of movement. *Neurology, 34,* 677–678.

Karson, C. N., Staub, R. A., Kleinman, J. E., & Wyatt, R. J. (1981). Drug effect on blink rates in rhesus monkeys: Preliminary studies. *Biological Psychiatry, 16,* 249–254.

Kato, T., Nishina, M., Matsushita, K., Hori, E., Mito, T., & Takashima, S. (1997). Neuronal maturation and N-acetyl-L-aspartic acid development in human fetal and child brains. *Brain Development, 19,* 131–133.

Katsuragi, T., Ushijima, I., & Furukawa, T. (1984). The clonidine-induced self-injurious behavior of mice involves purinergic mechanisms. *Pharmacology, Biochemistry, and Behavior, 20,* 943–946.

Kazdin, A. E. (1982). *Single-case research designs: Methods for clinical and applied settings.* New York: Oxford University Press.

Kebbon, L., & Windahl, S-I. (1985, March). Self-injurious behavior: Results of a nationwide survey among mentally retarded persons in Sweden. Paper presented at the 7th World Congress of the International Association for the Scientific Study of Mental Deficiency, New Delhi.

Kelley, A. E., Lang, C. G., & Gauthier, A. M. (1988). Induction of oral stereotypy following amphetamine microinjection into a discrete subregion of the striatum. *Psychopharmacology, 95,* 556–559.

Kelley, W. L., Greene, M. L., Rosenbloom, F. M., Henderson, J. F., & Seegmiller, J. E. (1969). Hypoxanthine-guanine phosphoribosyltransferase deficiency in gout: A review. *Annals of Internal Medicine, 70,* 155–206.

Kelley, W. N., & Wyngaarden J. B. (1983). Clinical syndromes associated with hypoxanthine-guanine phosphoribosyltransferase deficiency. In J. B. Stanbury (Ed.), *The metabolic basis of inherited disease,* (5th ed.) (pp. 1115–1143). New York: McGraw Hill.

Kemp, D. C., & Carr, E. G. (1995). Reduction of severe problem behavior in community employment using a hypothesis-driven multicomponent intervention approach. *Journal of the Association for Persons with Severe Handicaps, 20,* 229–247.

Kemperman, I., Russ, M. J., & Shearin, E. (1997). Self-injurious behavior and mood regulation in borderline patients. *Journal of Personality Disorders, 11,* 146–157.

Kendler, K. S., Heninger, G. R., & Roth, R. H. (1981). Brain contribution to the haloperidol-induced increase in plasma homovanillic acid. *European Journal of Pharmacology, 71,* 321–326.

Kendler, K. S., Hsieh, J. Y-K., & Davis, K. L. (1982). Studies of plasma homovanillic acid as an index of brain dopamine function. *Psychopharmacology Bulletin, 18,* 152–155.

Kennedy, C. H. (1994). Automatic reinforcement: Oxymoron or hypothetical construct? *Journal of Behavioral Education, 4,* 387–396.

Kennedy, C. H., & Meyer, K. A. (1996). Sleep deprivation, allergy symptoms, and negatively reinforced problem behavior. *Journal of Applied Behavior Analysis, 29,* 133–135.

Kennedy, C. H., & Meyer, K. A. (1998). Establishing operations and the motivation of challenging behavior. In J. K. Luiselli, & M. J. Cameron (Eds.),

Antecedent control: Innovative approaches to behavioral support (pp. 329–346). Baltimore: Paul H. Brookes Publishing.

Kennedy, C. H., Meyer, K. A., Knowles, T., & Shukla, S. (2000). Analyzing the multiple functions of stereotypical behavior for students with autism: Implications for assessment and treatment. *Journal of Applied Behavior Analysis, 33,* 559–571.

Kennedy, C. H., Tang, J-C, Koppekin, A., & Caruso, M. (2000). *Experimental analysis and intervention for stereotypical behavior negatively reinforced by reductions in auditory stimulation.* Manuscript submitted for publication.

Kennedy, C. H., & Thompson, T. (2000). Health conditions contributing to problem behavior among people with mental retardation and developmental disabilities. In M. L. Wehmeyer, & J. R. Patton (Eds.), *Mental Retardation in the 21st Century* (pp. 211–231). Austin, TX: Pro-Ed Inc.

Kern, L., Carberry, N., & Haidara, C. (1997). Analysis and intervention with two topographies of challenging behavior exhibited by a young woman with autism. *Research in Developmental Disabilities, 18,* 275–287.

Kiley, M., & Lubin, R. (1983). Epidemiological methods. In J. L. Matson, & J. A. Mulick (Eds.), *Handbook of Mental Retardation* (pp. 541–556). New York: Pergamon.

King, B. H. (1991). Fluoxetine reduced self-injurious behavior in an adolescent with mental retardation. *Journal of Clinical and Adolescent Psychopharmacology, 1*(5), 321–329.

King, B. H. (1993). Self-injury by people with mental retardation: A compulsive behavior hypothesis. *American Journal on Mental Retardation, 98,* 93–112.

King, B. H., Au, D., & Poland, R. E. (1993). Low-dose naltrexone inhibits pemoline-induced self-biting behavior in prepubertal rats. *Journal of Child and Adolescent Pharmacology, 3,* 71–79.

King, B. H., Au, D., & Poland, R. E. (1995). Pretreatment with MK-801 inhibits pemoline-induced self-biting in prepubertal rats. *Developmental Neuroscience, 17,* 47–52.

King, R., Barchas, J. D., & Huberman, B. A. (1984). Chaotic behavior in dopamine neurodynamics. *Proceedings of the National Academy of Sciences, USA, 81*(4), 1244–1247.

King, B. H., Cromwell, H. C., Lee, H. T., Behrsteck, S. P., Schmanke, T., & Maidment, N. T. (1998). Dopaminergic and glutamatergic interactions in the expression of self-injurious behavior. *Developmental Neuroscience, 20,* 180–187.

King, B. H., Turman, J., Cromwell, H. C., Davanzo, P. A., & Poland, R. E. (1994). Pharmacological and neuroanatomical substrates of pemoline-mediated self-injurious behavior in prepubertal rats. *International Journal of Developmental Neuroscience, 12,* 58.

Kirman, B. H., & Bicknell, J. (1968). Congenital insensitivity to pain in an imbecile boy. *Developmental Medicine and Child Neurology, 10,* 57–63.

Knapp, D. J., Moy, S. S., & Breese, G. R. (1999). Neonatal 6-OHDA lesions persistently activate *Fos B, COX2,* and *JunD* in the adult rat striatum. *ACNP Abstracts,* 190.

Knigge, U., Matzen, S., Bach, F., Bang, P., & Warberg, J. (1989). Involvement of histaminergic neurons in the stress-induced release of pro-opiomelanocortin-derived peptides in rats. *Acta Endocrinology (Copenhagen)*, 120, 533–539.

Koegel, L. K., Koegel, R. L., & Dunlap, G. (1996). *Positive behavior support: Including people with difficult behavior in the community.* Baltimore: Paul H. Brookes Publishing.

Kogut, M. D., Donnell, G. N., Nyhan, W. L., & Sweetman, L. (1970). Disorder of purine metabolism due to partial deficiency of hypoxanthine-guanine phosphoribosyltransferase. *American Journal of Medicine*, 48, 148–161.

Kokkinidis, L. (1984). Effects of chronic intermittent and continuous amphetamine administration on acoustic startle. *Pharmacology, Biochemistry, and Behavior*, 20, 367–371.

Konopka Lukas, Z. M., Cooper, R., & Crayton, J. (1996). Serotonin-induced increases in platelet cytosolic calcium concentration in depressed, schizophrenic, and substance abuse patients. *Biological Psychiatry*, 39, 708–713.

Korsgaard, S., Gerlach, J., & Christensson, E. (1985). Behavioral aspects of serotonin-dopamine interaction in the monkey. *European Journal of Pharmacology*, 118, 245–252.

Koslow, S. H., & Cross, C. K. (1982). Cerebrospinal fluid monoamine metabolites in Tourette's syndrome and their neuroendocrine implications. *Advances in Neurology*, 35, 185–197.

Kostrzewa, R. M., Brus, R., Perry, K. W., & Fuller, R. W. (1993). Age-dependence of a 6-hydroxydopamine lesion on SKF-38393- and m-chlorophenylpiperazine-induced oral activity responses of rats. *Developmental Brain Research*, 76, 87–93.

Kraemer, G. W., Schmidt, D. E., & Ebert, M. H. (1997). The behavioral neurobiology of self-injurious behavior in rhesus monkeys–Current concepts and relations to impulsive behavior in humans. *Annals of the New York Academy of Sciences*, 836, 12–38.

Kravitz, H., & Boehm, J. J. (1971). Rhythmic habit patterns in infancy: Their sequence, age of onset, and frequency. *Child Development*, 42, 399–413.

Kravitz, H., Rosenthal, V., Teplitz, Z., Murphy, J. B., & Lesser, R. E. (1960). A study of head banging in infants and children. *Diseases of the Nervous System*, 21, 3–8.

Krude, H., Biebermann, H., Luck, W., Horn, R., Brabant, G., & Gruters, A. (1998). Severe early-onset obesity, adrenal insufficiency, and red hair pigmentation caused by POMC mutations in humans. *Nature Genetics*, 19, 155–157.

Kuehn, M. R., Bradley, A., Robertson, E. J., & Evans, M. J. (1987). A potential animal model for Lesch–Nyhan syndrome through introduction of HPRT mutations into mice. *Nature*, 326, 295–298.

Kuhn, D., Piazza, C. C., Thompson, R., Fisher, W. W., Hanley, G., & Contrucci, S. (1996). *On the relationship between sleep and self-injurious behavior.* Poster presented at the 22nd Annual Convention of the Association for Behavior Analysis, San Francisco.

Kulik, A. V., & Wilbur, R. (1982). Delirium and stereotypy from anticholinergic antiparkinson drugs. *Progress in Neuropsychopharmacology and Biological Psychiatry, 6*, 75–82.

Kunko, P. M., Loeloff, R. J., & Izenwasser, S. (1997). Chronic administration of the selective dopamine reuptake inhibitor GBR 12909, but not cocaine, produces marked decreases in dopamine transporter density. *Naunyn-Schmiedeberg's Archives of Pharmacology, 356*, 562–569.

Kurumaji, A., Takashima, M., Watanabe, S., & Takahashi, K. (1988). An increase in striatal metenkephalin-like immunoreactivity in neonatally dopamine-depleted rats. *Neuroscience Letters, 87*, 109–113.

LaChapelle, D. L., Hadjistavropoulos, T., & Craig, K. D. (1999). Pain measurement in persons with intellectual disabilities. *The Clinical Journal of Pain, 15*, 13–23.

Lader, M. (1988). α-Adrenergic antagonists in neuropsychology: An update. *Journal of Clinical Psychiatry, 49*, 213–223.

Lal, H. (1975). Narcotic dependence, narcotic action, and dopamine receptors. *Life Sciences, 17*, 483–496.

Lalli, J. S., & Goh, H. L. (1993). Naturalistic observations in community settings. In J. Reichle, & D. P. Wacker (Eds.), *Communicative alternatives to challenging behavior: Integrating functional assessment and intervention strategies*, (Vol. 3). Baltimore: Paul H Brooks Publishing.

Lalli, J. S., Casey, S., & Kates, K. (1995). Reducing escape behavior and increasing task completion with functional communication training, extinction, and response chaining. *Journal of Applied Behavior Analysis, 28*, 261–268.

Lane, H. (1976). *The wild boy of Aveyron*. Cambridge, MA: Harvard University Press.

Lara-Lemus, A., Mora, M. P., Mendez-Franco, J., Palomero-Rivero, M., & Drucker-Colin, R. (1997). Effects of REM sleep deprivation on the d-amphetamine-induced self-mutilating behavior. *Brain Research, 770*, 60–64.

Lattal, K. A., & Perone, M. (1998). *Handbook of research methods in human operant behavior*. New York: Plenum Press.

Lautenbacher, S., & Krieg, J.-C. (1994). Pain perception in psychiatric disorders: A review of the literature. *Journal of Psychiatric Research, 28*, 109–122.

Leboyer, M., Bouvard, M. P., Recasens, C., Philippe, A., Guilloud-Bataille, M., Bondoux, D., et al. (1994). Difference between plasma N- and C-terminally directed β-endorphin immunoreactivity in infantile autism. *American Journal of Psychiatry, 151*, 1797–1801.

Leboyer, M., Philippe, A., Bouvard, M., Guilloud-Bataille, M., Bondoux, D., Tabuteau, F., et al. (1999). Whole blood serotonin and plasma β-endorphin in autistic probands and their first-degree relatives. *Society of Biological Psychiatry, 45*, 58–163.

Leckman, J. F., Walkup, J. T., Riddle, M. A., Towbin, K. E., & Cohen, D. J. (1987). Tic disorders. In H. Y. Meltzer (Ed.), *Psychopharmacology: The third generation of progress*, (Vol. 2) (p. 1241). Raven Press: New York.

Lennox, D. B., Miltenberger, R. G., Spengler, P., & Erfanian, N. (1988). Decelerative treatment practices with persons who have mental retardation: A review of 5 years of the literature. *American Journal on Mental Retardation, 92,* 492–501.

Leonard, H. L., Lenane, M. C., Swedo, S. E., Rettew, D. C., Gershon, E. S., & Rapoport, J. L. (1992). Tics and Tourette's disorder: A 2- to 7-year follow-up of 54 obsessive-compulsive children. *American Journal of Psychiatry, 149,* 1244–1251.

Lerman, D. C., & Iwata, B. A. (1993). Descriptive and experimental analyses of variables maintaining self-injurious behavior. *Journal of Applied Behavior Analysis, 26,* 293–319.

Lerman, D. C., & Iwata, B. A. (1996). A methodology for distinguishing between extinction and punishment effects associated with response blocking. *Journal of Applied Behavior Analysis, 29,* 231–233.

Lerman, D. C., Iwata, B. A., Smith, R. G., & Vollmer, T. R. (1994). Restraint fading and the development of alternative behavior in the treatment of self-restraint and self-injury. *Journal of Intellectual Disability Research, 38,* 135–148.

Lerman, D. C., Iwata, B. A., Smith, R. G., Zarcone, J. R., & Vollmer, T. R. (1994). Transfer of behavioral function as a contributing factor in treatment relapse. *Journal of Applied Behavior Analysis, 27,* 357–370.

Lesch, M., & Nyhan, W. L. (1964). A familial disorder of uric acid metabolism and central nervous system function. *American Journal of Medicine, 36,* 561–70.

Lester, D. (1972). Self-mutilating behavior. *Psychological Bulletin, 78,* 119–128.

Letts, R. M., & Hobson, D. A. (1975). Special devices as in aids in the management of child self-mutilation in the Lesch–Nyhan syndrome. *Pediatrics, 55,* 853–855.

Levine, I. M., Estes, J. W., & Looney, J. M. (1968). Hereditary neurological disease with acanthocytosis. *Archives of Neurology, 19,* 403–409.

Lewis, M. H., & Baumeister, A. A. (1982). Stereotyped mannerisms in mentally retarded persons: Animal models and theoretical analyses. In N. R. Ellis (Ed.), *International review of research in mental retardation,* (Vol. 12). New York: Academic Press.

Lewis, M. H., Baumeister, A. A., & Mailman, R. B. (1987). A neurobiological alternative to the perceptual reinforcement hypothesis of stereotyped behavior: A commentary on "self-stimulatory behavior and perceptual reinforcement." *Journal of Applied Behavior Analysis, 20,* 253–258.

Lewis, M. H., & Bodfish, J. W. (1998). Repetitive behavior disorders in autism. Special Issue: "Autism." *Mental Retardation Development Disabilities Research Review, 4,* 80–89.

Lewis, M. H., Bodfish, J. B., Powell, S. B., & Golden, R. N. (1995). Clomipramine treatment for stereotypy and related repetitive movement disorders associated with mental retardation. *American Journal on Mental Retardation, 100,* 299–312.

Lewis, M. H., Bodfish, J. B., Powell, S. B., & Parker, D. E. (1996). Clomipramine treatment for self-injurious behavior of individuals with mental retardation: A double-blind comparison with placebo. *American Journal on Mental Retardation, 100,* 654–665.

Lewis, M. H., Bodfish, J. W., Powell, S. B., West, K., Darling, M., & Golden, R. N. (1996). Plasma HVA in adults with mental retardation and stereotyped behavior: Biochemical evidence for a dopamine deficiency model. *American Journal on Mental Retardation, 100,* 413–427.

Lewis, M. H., Gluck, J. P., Beauchamp, A. J., Keresztury, M. F., & Mailman, R. B. (1990). Long-term effects of early social isolation in *Macaca mulatta:* In vivo evidence for changes in dopamine receptor function. *Brain Research, 513,* 67–73.

Lewis, M. H., Gluck, J. P., Bodfish, J. W., Beauchamp, A. J., & Mailman, R. B. (1996). Neurobiological basis of stereotyped movement disorder in animals and humans. In R. L. Sprague, & K. M. Newell (Eds.), *Stereotypy: Brain-behavior relationships.* Washington, DC: American Psychological Association.

Lewis, M. H., MacLean, W. E., Johnson, W. L., & Baumeister, A. A. (1981). Ultradian rhythms in stereotyped and self-injurious behavior. *American Journal of Mental Deficiency, 85*(6), 601–610.

Lewis, M. H., Silva, J. R., & Gray-Silva, S. (1995). Cyclicity of aggression and self-injurious behavior in individuals with mental retardation. *American Journal on Mental Retardation, 99,* 436–444.

Lichstein, L., & Sackett, G. P. (1971). Reactions of differentially raised rhesus monkeys to noxious stimulation. *Developmental Psychobiology, 4,* 339–352.

Light, K. C., & Obrist, P. A. (1980). Cardiovascular response to stress: Effects of opportunity to avoid shock experience, and performance feedback. *Psychophysiology, 17*(3), 243–252.

Lindauer, S. E., DeLeon, I. G., & Fisher, W. W. (1999). Decreasing signs of negative affect and correlated self-injury in an individual with mental retardation and mood disturbances. *Journal of Applied Behavior Analysis, 32,* 103–106.

Lindberg, J. S., Iwata, B. A., & Kahng, S. K. (1999). On the relation between object manipulation and stereotypic self-injurious behavior. *Journal of Applied Behavior Analysis, 32,* 51–62.

Linscheid, T. R., Pejeau, C., Cohen, S., & Footo-Lenz, M. (1994). Positive side effects in the treatment of SIB using the self-injurious behavior inhibiting system (SIBIS): Implications for operant and biochemical explanations of SIB. *Research in Developmental Disabilities, 15*(1), 81–90.

Lloyd, H. G. E., & Stone, T. W. (1981). Chronic methylxanthine treatment in rats: A comparison of Wistar and Fisher 344 strains. *Pharmacology, Biochemistry, and Behavior, 14,* 827–830.

Lloyd, K. G., Hornykiewicz, O., Davidson, L., Shannak, K., Farley, I., Goldstein, M., et al. (1981). Biomedical evidence of dysfunction of brain neurotransmitters in the Lesch–Nyhan syndrome. *New England Journal of Medicine, 305,* 1106–1111.

Lokwan, S. J. A., Overton, P. G., Berry, M. S., & Clark, D. (1999). Stimulation of the pedunculopontine tegmental nucleus in the rat produces burst firing in A9 dopaminergic neurons. *Neuroscience, 92,* 245–254.

Lott, R. S., Kerrick, M. J., & Cohen, S. A. (1996). Clinical and economic aspects of risperidone treatment in adults with mental retardation and behavioral disturbance. *Psychopharmacology Bulletin, 32,* 721–729.

Lourie, R. S. (1949). The role of rhythmic patterns in childhood. *American Journal of Psychiatry, 105,* 653–660.

Lovaas, O. I. (1987). Behavioral treatment and normal educational and intellectual functioning in young autistic children. *Journal of Consulting and Clinical Psychology, 55,* 309.

Lovaas, O. I., Freitag, G., Gold, V. J., & Kassorla, I. C. (1965). Experimental studies in childhood schizophrenia: Analysis of self-destructive behavior. *Journal of Experimental Child Psychology, 2,* 67–84.

Lovaas, I., Newsom, C., & Hickman, C. (1987). Self-stimulatory behavior and perceptual reinforcement. *Journal of Applied Behavior Analysis, 20,* 45–68.

Lovaas, O. I., & Simmons, J. Q. (1969). Manipulation of self-destruction in three retarded children. *Journal of Applied Behavior Analysis, 2,* 143–157.

Luby, E. D., Cohen, B. D., Rosenbaum, G., Gottlieb, J. S., & Kelley, R. (1959). Study of a new schizophrenomimetic drug—sernyl. *AMA Archives of Neurology and Psychiatry, 81,* 363–369.

Luiselli, J. K. (1991). Functional assessment and treatment of self-injury in a pediatric, nursing-care resident. *Behavioral Residential Treatment, 6,* 311–319.

Luiselli, J. K. (1993). Treatment of self-restraining behavior in persons displaying self-injury. *The Habilitative Mental Healthcare Newsletter, 12*(3), 39–41.

Luiselli, J. K., Matson, J. L., & Singh, N. N. (Eds.). (1992). *Self-injurious behavior: Analysis, assessment, and treatment.* New York: Springer-Verlag.

Lundervold, D., & Bourland, G. (1988). Quantitative analysis of treatment of aggression, self-injury, and property destruction. *Behavior Modification, 12,* 590–617.

Luquin, M. R., Laguna, J., Herro, M. T., & Obeso, J. A. (1993). Behavioral tolerance to repeated apomorphine administration in parkinsonian monkeys. *Journal of Neurological Science, 114,* 40–44.

Lutz, C. K., Chase, W. K., & Novak, M. A. (2000). Abnormal behavior in singly housed *Macaca mulatta*: Prevalence and risk factors. *American Journal of Primatology, 51,* 71.

Mace, F. C. (1994). The significance and future of functional analysis methodologies. *Journal of Applied Behavior Analysis, 27,* 385–392.

Mace, F. C., & Belfiore, P. (1990). Behavioral momentum in the treatment of escape-motivated stereotypy. *Journal of Applied Behavior Analysis, 23,* 507–514.

Mace, F. C., & Lalli, J. S. (1991). Linking descriptive and experimental analyses in the treatment of bizarre speech. *Journal of Applied Behavior Analysis, 24,* 553–562.

Mace, F. C., Lalli, J. S., & Lalli, E. P. (1991). Functional analysis and treatment of aberrant behavior. *Research in Developmental Disabilities, 12,* 155–180.

Mace, F. C., Lalli, J. S., Lalli, E. P., & Shea, M. C. (1993). Functional analysis and treatment of aberrant behavior. In R. VanHouten, & S. Axelrod (Eds.), *Behavior analysis and treatment* (pp. 75–99). New York: Plenum Press.

Mace, F. C., Lalli, J. S., & Shea, M. C. (1992). Functional analysis and treatment of self-injury. In J. K. Luiselli, J. L. Matson, & N. N. Singh (Eds.), *Self-injurious behavior: Analysis, assessment, and treatment* (pp. 122–152). New York: Springer-Verlag.

Mace, F. C., & Mauk, J. E. (1995). Bio-behavioral diagnosis and treatment of self-injury. *Mental Retardation and Developmental Disabilities Research Reviews, 2,* 104–110.

Mace, F. C., & Mauk, J. E. (1999). Bio-behavioral diagnosis and treatment of self-injury. In A. C. Repp, & R. H. Horner (Eds.), *Functional analysis of problem behaviors: From effective assessment to effective support* (pp. 78–97). Pacific Grove, CA: Brooks/Cole.

MacKay, D., McDonald, G., & Morrissey, M. (1974). Self-mutilation in the mentally subnormal. *Journal of Psychological Research in Mental Subnormality, 1,* 25–31.

MacLean, Jr., W. E., Ellis, D. N., Galbreath, H. N., Halpern, L. F., & Baumeister, A. A. (1991). Rhythmic motor behavior of preambulatory motor impaired, Down syndrome, and nondisabled children: A comparative analysis. *Journal of Abnormal Child Psychology, 19,* 319–330.

MacLean, W. E., Lewis, M. H., Bryson-Brockman, W. A., Ellis, D. N., Arendt, R. E., & Baumeister, A. A. (1985). Blink rate and stereotyped behavior: Evidence for dopamine involvement? *Biological Psychiatry, 20,* 1321–1325.

Madden, J. I., Akil, H., Patrick, R. L., & Barchas, J. D. (1977). Stress-induced parallel changes in central opioid levels and pain responsiveness in the rat. *Nature, 265,* 358–360.

Maestrini, E., Lai, C., Marlow, A., Matthews, N., Wallace, S., Bailey, A., et al. (1999). Serotonin transporter (5-HTT) and γ-aminobutyric acid receptor subunit B (GABRB3) gene polymorphisms are not associated with autism in IMGSA families. *American Journal of Medical Genetics (Neuropsychiatric Genetics), 88,* 492–496.

Mailis, A. (1996). Compulsive targeted self-injurious behaviour in humans with neuropathic pain: A counterpart of animal autotomy? Four case reports and literature review. *Pain, 64,* 569–578.

Maisto, C. R., Baumeister, A. A., & Maisto, A. A. (1978). An analysis of variables related to self-injurious behavior among institutionalized retarded persons. *Journal of Mental Deficiency Research, 22,* 27–36.

Marcus, S., Hellgren, D., Lambert, B., et al. (1993). Duplication in the hypoxanthine phosphoribosyl-transferase gene caused by Alu-Alu recombination in a patient with Lesch–Nyhan syndrome. *Human Genetics, 90,* 477–482.

Markowitz, P. I. (1992). Effect of fluoxetine on self-injurious behavior in the developmentally disabled: A preliminary study. *Journal of Clinical Psychopharmacology, 12,* 27–31.

Marley, R. J., Shimosato, K., Gewiss, M., Thorndike, E., Goldberg, S. R., & Schindler, C. W. (1995). Long-term sensitization to the behavioral effects of naltrexone is associated with regionally specific changes in the number of Mu and Delta opioid receptors in rat brain. *Life Sciences, 56,* 767–774.

Marsden, C. D. (1994). Parkinson's disease. *Journal of Neurology, Neurosurgery, and Psychiatry, 57,* 672–681.

Marshall, F. J., & Shoulson, I. (1997). Clinical features and treatment of Huntington's disease. In R. Watts, & W. Keller (Eds.), *Movement disorders: Principles and practice* (pp. 491–502). McGraw Hill: New York.

Marshall, J. F., & Ungerstedt, U. (1977). Supersensitivity to apomorphine follow-ing destruction of the ascending dopamine neurons: Quantification using the rotational model. *European Journal of Pharmacology, 41*, 361–367.

Martin, G., & Pear, J. (1988). *Behavior modification: What it is and how to do it*, (3rd ed.). Englewood Cliffs, NJ: Prentice Hall.

Martin, L., Spicer, D. M., Lewis, M. H., Gluck, J. P., & Cork, L. C. (1991). Social deprivation of infant rhesus monkeys alters the chemoarchitecture of the brain: I. Subcortical regions. *Journal of Neuroscience, 11*, 3344–3358.

Mason, S. T., Sanberg, P. R., & Fibiger, H. C. (1978). Kainic acid lesions of the striatum dissociate amphetamine and apomorophine stereotypy: Similarities to Huntington's chorea. *Science, 201*, 352–355.

Masuo, Y., Pelaprat, D., Montagne, M. N., Scherman, D., & Rostene, W. (1990). Regulation of neurotensin-containing neurons in the rat striatum and substan-tia nigra: Effects of unilateral nigral lesion with 6-hydroxydopamine on neu-rotensin content and its binding site density. *Brain Research, 510*, 203–210.

Mathur, A., Shandarin, A., LaViolette, S. R., Parker, J., & Yeomans, J. S. (1997). Locomotion and stereotypy induced by scopolamine: Contributions of mus-carinic receptors near the pedunculopontine tegmental nucleus. *Brain Research, 775*, 144–155.

Matson, J. L., Bamburg, J. W., Mayville, E. A., Pinkston, J., Bielecki, J., Kuhn, D., et al. (2000). Psychopharmacology and mental retardation: A 10 year review (1990–1999). *Research in Developmental Disabilities, 21*, 263–296.

Matson, J. L., & Keyes, J. B. (1990). A comparison of DRO to movement suppres-sion time-out and DRO with two self-injurious and aggressive mentally retarded adults. *Research in Developmental Disabilities, 11*, 111–120.

Matson, J. L., & Taras, M. E. (1989). A 20-year review of punishment and alterna-tive methods to treat problem behaviors in developmentally delayed persons. *Research in Developmental Disabilities, 10*, 85–104.

Maurice, P., & Trudel, G. (1982). Self-injurious behavior prevalence and relationship to environmental events. In J. H. Hollis, & C. E. Meyers (Eds.), *Life-threatening behavior* (pp. 81–103). Washington, DC: American Association on Mental Deficiency.

Mazaleski, J. L., Iwata, B. A., Vollmer, T. R., Zarcone, J. R., & Smith, R. G. (1993). Analysis of the reinforcement and extinction components in DRO contingen-cies with self-injury. *Journal of Applied Behavior Analysis, 26*, 143–156.

McCleary, R., Ly, J., & Bruinsma, Y. (1997). *A probability model for analysis of self-injurious behavior*. Poster session presented at the 30th annual Gatlinberg Con-ference, Riverside, CA.

McDonald, J. A., & Kelley, W. N. (1972). Lesch–Nyhan syndrome: Absence of the mutant enzyme in erythrocytes of a heterozygote for both normal and mutant hypoxanthineguanine phosphoribosyltransferase. *Biochemical Genet-ics, 6*, 21–26.

McDougle, C. J., Holmes, J. P., & Bronson, M. (1997). Risperidone treatment of children and adolescents with pervasive developmental disorders: A prospective open-label study. *Journal of the American Academy of Child and Adolescent Psychiatry, 36,* 685–693.

McDougle, C. J., Holmes, J. P., Carlson, D. C., Pelton, G. H., Cohen, D. J., & Price, L. H. (1998). A double-blind, placebo-controlled study of risperidone in adults with autistic disorder and other pervasive developmental disorders. *Archives in General Psychiatry, 55,* 633–641.

McDougle, C. J., Naylor, S. T., Cohen, D. J., Aghajanian, G. K., Heninger, G. R., & Price, L. H. (1996). Effects of tryptophan depletion in drug-free adults with autistic disorder. *Archives of General Psychiatry, 53*(11), 993–1000.

McDougle, C. J., Price, L. H., Volkmar, F. R., Goodman, W. K., Ward-O'Brien, D., Nielsen, J., et al. (1992). Clomipramine in autism: Preliminary evidence of efficacy. *Journal of the American Academy of Child and Adolescent Psychiatry, 31,* 746–750.

McKerracher, D. W., Loughnane, T., & Watson, R. A. (1968). Self-mutilation in female psychopaths. *British Journal of Psychiatry, 114,* 829–832.

McNeil, J. R. (1979). Accidental ingestion of pemoline. *Clinical Pediatrics, 18*(12), 761–762.

Mennicken, F., Savasta, M., Chritin, M., Feuerstein, C., La Moal, M., Herman, J. P., et al. (1995). The neonatal lesion of the meso-telencephalic dopaminergic pathway increases intrastriatal D_2 receptor levels and synthesis and this effect is reversed by neonatal dopaminergic-rich graft. *Brain Research Molecular Brain Research, 28,* 211–221.

Menninger, K. A. (1935). A psychoanalytic study of the significance of self-mutilation. *Psychoanalytic Quarterly, 4,* 408–466.

Menninger, K. A. (1938). *Man against himself.* New York: Harcourt Brace.

Michael, J. (1982). Distinguishing between discriminative and motivational functions of stimuli. *Journal of the Experimental Analysis of Behavior, 37,* 149–155.

Michael, J. (1993). Establishing operations. *The Behavior Analyst, 16,* 191–206.

Michael, J. (2000). Implications and refinements of the establishing operation concept. *Journal of Applied Behavior Analysis, 33,* 401–410.

Migeon, B. R., DerKaloustian, V. M., Nyhan, W. L., Young, W. J., & Childs, B. (1968). X-linked hypoxanthine-guanine phosphoribosyl transferase deficiency: Heterozygote has two clonal populations. *Science, 160,* 425–427.

Miguel, E. C., Coffey, B. J., Baer, L., Savage, C. R., Ranch, S. L., & Jenike, M. A. (1995). Phenomenology of intentional repetitive behaviors in obsessive-compulsive disorder and Tourette's disorder. *Journal of Clinical Psychiatry, 56,* 246–255.

Mileson, B. E., Lewis, M. H., & Mailman, R. B. (1991). Dopamine receptor supersensitivity occurring without receptor up-regulation. *Brain Research, 561,* 1–10.

Miller, M., Canen, E., Roebel, A., & MacLean, W. (2000). *Prevalence of behavior problems in people with mental retardation.* Poster session presented at the 108th annual convention of the American Psychological Association, Washington, DC.

Miller, N. E. (1959). Liberalization of basic S-R concepts: Extensions to conflict behavior, motivation, and social learning. In S. Koch (Ed.), *Psychology: A study of a science,* (Vol. 2) (pp. 196–293). New York: McGraw-Hill.

Miller, R. E., Caul, W. F., & Mirsky, I. A. (1971). Patterns of eating and drinking in socially isolated rhesus monkeys. *Physiology and Behavior, 7,* 127–134.

Minana, M. D., & Grisolia, S. (1986). Caffeine ingestion by rats increases noradrenaline turnover and results in self-biting. *Journal of Neurochemistry, 47,* 728–732.

Minana, M. D., Portoles, M., Jorda, A., & Grisolia, S. (1984). Lesch–Nyhan syndrome, caffeine model: Increase of purine and pyrimidine enzymes in rat brain. *Journal of Neurochemistry, 43,* 1556–1560.

Mitchell, G. (1968). Persistent behavior pathology in rhesus monkeys following early social isolation. *Folia Primatologica, 8,* 132–147.

Mitchell, G. (1979). *Behavioral sex differences in nonhuman primates.* New York: Van Nostrand Reinhold.

Modell, J., Mountz, J., Curtis, G., & Greden, J. (1989). Neurophysiologic dysfunction in basal ganglia/limbic striatal and thalamocortical circuits as a pathogenetic mechanism of obsessive–compulsive disorder. *Journal of Neuropsychiatry and Clinical Neuroscience, 1*(1), 27–36.

Molina, V. A., & Orsingher, O. A. (1981). Effects of Mg-pemoline on the central catecholaminergic system. *Archives of International Pharmacodynamics, 251,* 66–79.

Montastruc, J. L., Llau, M. E., Senard, J. M., Tran, M. A., Rascol., O., & Montastruc, P. (1996). A study of tolerance to apomorphine. *British Journal of Pharmacology, 117,* 781–786.

Moodley, M. (1993). Treatment of Rett syndrome with bromocriptine. *South African Medical Journal, 83,* 138.

Moody, C. A., & Spear, L. P. (1992). Effects of acute dopamine depletion on responsiveness to D_1 and D_2 receptor agonists in infant and weanling rat pups. *Psychopharmacology, 107,* 39–49.

Moore, K. E. (1977). The actions of amphetamine on neurotransmitters: A brief review. *Biological Psychiatry, 12,* 451–462.

Morgan, J. I., & Curran, T. (1991). Stimulus-transcription coupling in the nervous system: Involvement of the inducible proto-oncogenes *fos* and *jun. Annual Review of Neuroscience 14,* 421–451.

Morpurgo, C. (1968). Aggressive behavior induced by large doses of 2-(2,6-dichlorphenylamino)-2-imidazoline hydrochloride (ST 155) in mice. *European Journal of Pharmacology, 3,* 374–377.

Moukhles, H., Forni, C., Nieoullon, A., & Daszuta, A. (1994). Regulation of dopamine levels in intrastriatal grafts of fetal mesencephalic cell suspension: An in vivo voltammetric approach. *Experimental Brain Research, 102,* 10–20.

Moy, S. S., & Breese, G. R. (in review) Phencylidine sensitization in rates with neonatal dopamine loss: Model of NMDA hypofunction. *Psychopharmacology.*

Moy, S. S., Criswell, H. E., & Breese, G. R. (1997). Differential effects of bilateral dopamine depletion in neonatal and adult rats. *Neuroscience and Biobehavioral Reviews, 21,* 425–435.

Moy, S. S., Knapp, D. J., & Breese, G. R. (2001). Effect of Olanzapine on functional responses from sensitized D$_1$-dopamine receptors in rats lesioned with 6-hydroxydopamine as neonates. *Neuropsychopharmacology, 25,* 224–233.

Mudford, O. C., Boundy, K., & Murray, A. D. (1995). Therapeutic shock device (TSD): Clinical evaluation with self-injurious behaviors. *Research in Developmental Disabilities, 16*(4), 253–267.

Mueller, K., Hollingsworth, E., & Petit, H. (1986). Repeated pemoline produces self-injurious behavior in adult and weanling rats. *Pharmacology, Biochemistry, and Behavior, 25,* 933–938.

Mueller, K., & Hsiao, S. (1980). Pemoline-induced self-biting in rats and self-mutilation in the de Lange syndrome. *Pharmacology, Biochemistry, and Behavior, 13,* 627–631.

Mueller, K., & Nyhan, W. L. (1982). Pharmacologic control of pemoline-induced self-injurious behavior in rats. *Pharmacology, Biochemistry, and Behavior, 16,* 957–963.

Mueller, K., & Nyhan, W. L. (1983). Clonidine potentiates drug induced self-injurious behavior in rats. *Pharmacology, Biochemistry, and Behavior, 18,* 891–894.

Mueller, K., Saboda, S., Palmour, R., & Nyhan, W. L. (1982). Self-injurious behavior produced in rats by daily caffeine and continuous amphetamine. *Pharmacology, Biochemistry, and Behavior, 17,* 613–617.

Mueller-Vahl, K. R., Berding, G., Brucke, T., Kolbe, H., Meyer, G. J., Hundeshagen, H., et al. (2000). Dopamine transporter binding in Gilles de la Tourette's syndrome. *Journal of Neurology, 247,* 514–520.

Mulick, J. A., Dura, J. R., Rasnake, L. K., & Callahan, C. (1986). *Prevalence of SIB in institutionalized nonambulatory profoundly retarded people.* Poster session presented at the 94th annual convention of the American Psychological Association, Washington, DC.

Murphy, G., Hall, S., Oliver, C., & Kissi-Debra, R. (1999). Identification of early self-injurious behaviour in young children with intellectual disability. *Journal of Intellectual Disability Research, 43*(3), 149–163.

Mutti, A., Ferroni, C., Vescovi, P. P., Bottazzi, R., Selis, L., Gerra, G., et al. (1989). Endocrine effects of psychosocial stress associated with neurobehavioral performance testing. *Life Science, 44,* 1831–1836.

Myrianthopoulos, N. C. (1981). Gilles de la Tourette's syndrome. In P. J. Vinken, & G. W. Bruyn (Eds.), *Handbook of Clinical Neurology, 42,* 221–222). Amsterdam: North Holland Publishing Company.

National Institutes of Health (1989). *NIH consensus development conference on the treatment of destructive behaviors in persons with developmental disabilities.* Bethesda, MD: Author.

National Institutes of Health (1991). National Institutes of Health Consensus Development Conference Statement. In *Treatment of destructive behaviors in persons with developmental disabilities* (NIH Publication No. 91-2410, pp. 6–8). Washington, DC: U. S. Department of Health and Human Services.

National Research Council. (1998). *The psychological well-being of nonhuman primates.* Washington, DC, National Academy Press.

Nausieda, P. A., Koller, W. C., Weiner, W. J., & Klawans, H. L. (1981). Pemoline-induced chorea. *Neurology, 31,* 356–360.

Naylor, G. J., Reid, A. H., Dick, D. A., & Dick, E. G. (1976). A biochemical study of short-cycle manic-depressive psychosis in mental defectives. *British Journal of Psychiatry, 128,* 169–180.

Neal, B. S., & Joyce, J. N. (1991). Dopamine D_1 receptor behavioral responsivity following selective lesions of the striatal patch compartment during development. *Brain Research Developmental Brain Research, 60,* 105–113.

Neal-Beliveau, B. S., & Joyce, J. N. (1993). D_1 and D_2 dopamine receptors do not up-regulate in response to neonatal intrastriatal 6-hydroxydopamine lesions. *Neuroscience Letters, 160,* 77–80.

Neal-Beliveau, B. S., & Joyce, J. N. (1999). Timing: A critical determinant of the functional consequences of neonatal 6-OHDA lesions. *Neurotoxicology and Teratology, 21,* 129–140.

Newell, K. M. (1996a). Motor skills and mental retardation. In W. MacLean (Ed.), *Handbook of mental deficiency,* (Vol. 3) (pp. 275–308). Hillsdale, NJ: Lawrence Erlbaum Associates.

Newell, K. M. (1996b). The dynamics of stereotypic behaviors. In R. L. Sprague, & K. M. Newell (Eds.), *Stereotypies: Brain-behavior relationships* (pp. 115–138). Washington, DC: American Psychological Association.

Newell, K. (in press). Temporal and force dynamics of self-injury. In S. Schroeder, M. L. Oster-Granite, & T. Thompson (Eds.), *Self-injurious behavior: Gene-brain-behavior relationships.* Washington, DC: American Psychological Association.

Newell, K. M., Bodfish, J. W., & Sprague, R. (1999). The variability of stereotyped body rocking in adults with mental retardation. *American Journal of Mental Retardation, 104,* 279–288.

Newell, K. M., Challis, J. H., Boros, R., & Bodfish, J. W. (2000). Further evidence on the dynamics of self-injurious behavior. Manuscript under review.

Newell, K. M., & Corcos, D. M. (1993). *Variability and motor control.* Champaign, IL: Human Kinetics.

Newell, K. M., Gao, F., & Sprague, R. L. (1995). The dynamics of finger tremor in tardive dyskinesia. *Chaos, 5,* 43–47.

Newell, K. M., Incledon, T., Bodfish, J. W., & Sprague, R. L. (in press). The variability of stereotypic body rocking in adults with mental retardation. *American Journal on Mental Retardation.*

Newell, K. M., & Molenaar, P. C. M. (Eds.), (1998). *Applications of nonlinear dynamics to developmental process modeling.* Mahwah, NJ: Lawrence Erlbaum Associates.

Newell, K. M., & Slifkin, A. B. (1998). The nature of movement variability. In J. P. Piek (Ed.), *Motor behavior and human skill: A multidisciplinary approach* (pp. 143–160). Champaign, IL: Human Kinetics.

Newell, K. M., Sprague, R. L., Pain, M. T., Deutsch, K. M., & Meinhold, P. (1999). Dynamics of self-injurious behaviors. *American Journal on Mental Retardation, 104,* 11–21.

Newell, K. M., van Emmerik, R. E. A., & Sprague, R. L. (1993). Stereotypy and variability. In Newell, K. M., & Corcos, D. M. (Eds.), *Variability and motor control*. Champaign, IL: Human Kinetics.

Newsom, C. D., Carr, E. G., & Lovaas, O. I. (1977). The experimental analysis and modification of autistic behavior. In R. S. Davidson (Ed.), *Modification of pathological behavior* (pp. 109–187). Thousand Oaks, CA: Sage.

Nielsen, E. B. (1981). Rapid decline of stereotyped behavior in rats during constant 1-week administration of amphetamine via implanted ALZET osmotic minipumps. *Pharmacology, Biochemistry, and Behavior, 15*, 161–165.

Nikkhah, G., Bentlage, C., Cunningham, M. G., & Bjorklund, A. (1994). Intranigral fetal dopamine grafts induce behavioral compensation in the rat Parkinson model. *Journal of Neuroscience, 14*, 3449–3461.

Nikkah, G., Cunningham, M. G., Cenci, M. A., McKay, R. D., & Bjorklund, A. (1995a). Dopaminergic microtransplants into the substantia nigra of neonatal rats with bilateral 6-OHDA lesions. I. Evidence for anatomical reconstruction of the nigrostriatal pathway. *Journal of Neuroscience, 15*, 3548–3561.

Nikkah, G., Cunningham, M. G., McKay, R., & Bjorklund, A. (1995b). Dopaminergic microtransplants into the substantia nigra of neonatal rats with bilateral 6-OHDA lesions. II. Transplant-induced behavioral recovery. *Journal of Neuroscience, 15*, 3562–3570.

Nikulina, E. M., & Klimek. V. (1993). Strain differences in clonidine-induced aggressiveness in mice and its interaction with the dopamine system. *Pharmacology, Biochemistry, and Behavior, 44*, 821–825.

Nomura, Y., & Segawa., M. (1990). Characteristics of motor disturbances of the Rett syndrome. *Brain Development, 12*, 27–30.

Northup, J., Fusilier, I., Swanson, V., Roane, H., & Borrero, J. (1997). An evaluation of methylphenidate as a potential establishing operation for some common classroom reinforcers. *Journal of Applied Behavior Analysis, 30*(4), 615–625.

Northup, J., Wacker, D., Sasso, G., Steege, M., Cigrand, K., Cook, J. et al. (1991). A brief functional analysis of aggressive and alternative behavior in an out-clinic setting. *Journal of Applied Behavior Analysis, 24*, 509–522.

Novak, M. A. (1979). Social recovery of monkeys isolated for the first year of life: 2. Long-term assessment. *Developmental Psychology, 15*, 50–61.

Novak, M. A., & Harlow, H. F. (1975). Social recovery of monkeys isolated for the first year of life: 1. Rehabilitation and Therapy. *Developmental Psychology, 11*, 453–465.

Novak, M. A., Jorgensen, M. J., Chase, W. K., Rasmussen, K. L., & Suomi, S. J. (2000). *Archives of General Psychiatry*. Manuscript submitted for publication.

Novak, M. A., Kinsey, J. H., Jorgensen, M. J., & Hazen, T. J. (1998). Effects of puzzle feeders on pathological behavior in individually housed rhesus monkeys. *American Journal of Primatology, 46*, 213–227.

Novak, M. A., Lutz, C. K., Marius, L. M., Jorgensen, M. J., & Kinsey, J. Self-injurious behavior in rhesus monkeys: Risk factors and behavioral styles. *Laboratory Animal Science*. Manuscript submitted for publication.

Novak, M. A., & Petto, A. J. (1991). *Through the looking glass: Issues of psychological well-being in captive nonhuman primates*. Washington, DC: American Psychological Association.

Novak, M. A., & Suomi, S. J. (1988). Psychological well-being of primates in captivity. *American Psychologist, 43*, 765–773.

Nussbaum, R. L., Crowder, W. E., Nyhan, W. L., & Caskey, C. T. (1983). A three-allele restriction fragment length polymorphism at the hypoxanthine phosphoribosyl-transferase locus in men. *Proceedings of the National Academy of Sciences, USA, 80*, 4035–4039.

Nyhan, W. L. (1967). The Lesch–Nyhan syndrome: Self-destructive biting, mental retardation, neurological disorder, and hyperuricemia. *Developmental Medicine and Child Neurology, 9*, 563–572.

Nyhan, W. L. (1968). Seminars on the Lesch–Nyhan syndrome, Introduction, *Federation Proceedings, 27*, 1027–1033.

Nyhan, W. L. (1972). Behavioral phenotypes in organic genetic disease. Presidential address to Society of Pediatric Research, May 1, 1971. *Pediatric Research, 6*, 1–9.

Nyhan, W. L. (1972). Clinical features of the Lesch–Nyhan syndrome. *Archives of Internal Medicine, 130*, 186–192.

Nyhan, W. L. (1976). Behavior in the Lesch–Nyhan syndrome. *Journal of Autism and Childhood Schizophrenia, 6*, 235–252.

Nyhan, W. L. (1994). The Lesch–Nyhan disease. In T. Thompson, & D. B. Gray (Eds.), *Destructive behavior in developmental disabilities, diagnosis, and treatment* (pp. 181–197). Thousand Oaks, CA: Sage Productions.

Nyhan, W. L. (2000). Dopamine function in Lesch–Nyhan disease. *Environmental Health Perspectives, National Institutes of Health, 108*, 409–411.

Nyhan, W. L., Bakay, B., Connor, J. D., Marks, J. F., & Keele, D. K. (1970). Hemizygous expression of glucose-6-phosphate dehydrogenase in erythrocytes of heterozygotes for the Lesch–Nyhan syndrome. *Proceedings of the National Academy of Sciences, USA, 65*, 214–218.

Nyhan, W. L., Johnson, H. G., Kaufman, I. A., & Jones, K. L. (1980). Serotonergic approaches to the modification of behavior in the Lesch–Nyhan syndrome. *Applied Research in Mental Retardation, 1*, 25–40.

Nyhan, W. L., Oliver, W. J., & Lesch, M. (1965). A familial disorder of uric acid metabolism and central nervous system function: II. *Journal of Pediatrics, 67*, 257–262.

Nyhan, W. L., & Ozand, P. T. (1998). Lesch–Nyhan disease. In *Atlas of metabolic diseases* (pp. 376–388). London: Chapman & Hall.

Nyhan, W. L., Pesek, J., Sweetman, L., Carpenter, D. G., & Carter, C. H. (1967). Genetics of an X-linked disorder of uric acid metabolism and cerebral function. *Pediatric Research, 1*, 5–13.

Oberlander, T. F., Gilbert, C. A., Chambers, C. T., O'Donnell, M. E., & Craig, K. D. (in press). Biobehavioral responses to acute pain in adolescents with a significant neurologic impairment. *The Clinical Journal of Pain*.

Obrist, P. A. (1976). The cardiovascular-behavioral interaction—as it appears today. *Psychophysiology, 13*(2), 95–107.

Obrist, P. A. (1982). Cardiac-behavioral interactions: A critical appraisal. In J. T. Cacioppo, & R. E. Petty (Eds.), *Perspectives in cardiovascular psychophysiology* (pp. 265–295). New York: Guilford Press.

Obrist, P. A., Webb, R. A., Sutterer, J. R., & Howard, J. L. (1970). The cardiac–somatic relationship: Some reformulations. *Psychophysiology, 6*(5), 569–587.

O'Donoghue, E. G. (1915). *The story of Bethlehem Hospital from its foundation in 1247* (p. 246). New York: E. P. Dutton & Company.

Ogasawara, N., Yamada, Y., & Goto, H. (1991). HPRT gene mutations. *Advanced Experimental Medical Biology, 309B*, 261–264.

Okamura, H., Murakami, T., Yokoyama, C., Nakamura, T., & Ibata, Y. (1997). Self-injurious behavior and dopaminergic neuron system in neonatal 6-hydroxy-dopamine-lesioned rat: 2. Intracerebral microinjection of dopamine agonists and antagonists. *Journal of Pharmacology and Experimental Therapeutics, 280*, 1031–1037.

Olanow, C. W., Kordower, J. H., & Freeman, T. B. (1996). Fetal nigral transplantation as a therapy for Parkinson's disease. *Trends in the Neurosciences, 19*, 102–109.

Oliver, C., Hall, S., Hales, J., Murphy, G., & Watts, D. (1998). The treatment of severe self-injurious behavior by the systematic fading of restraints: Effects on self-injury, self-restraint, adaptive behavior, and behavioral correlates of affect. *Research in Developmental Disabilities, 19*, 143–165.

Oliver, C., & Head, D. (1990). Self-injurious behaviour in people with learning disabilities: Determinants and interventions. *International Review of Psychiatry, 2*, 99–114.

Oliver, C., Murphy, G. H., & Corbett, J. A. (1987). Self-injurious behavior in people with mental handicap: A total population study. *Journal of Mental Deficiency Research, 31*, 147–162.

Oliver, C., Murphy, G., Crayton, L., & Corbett, J. (1993). Self-injurious behavior in Rett syndrome: Interactions between features of Rett syndrome and operant conditioning. *Journal of Autism and Developmental Disorders, 23*(1), 91–109.

Olney, J. W., Labruyere, J., & Price, M. T. (1989). Pathological changes induced in cerebrocortical neurons by phencyclidine and related drugs. *Science, 244*, 360–1362.

Olney, J. W., Labruyere, J., Wang, G., Wozniak, D. F., Price, M. T., & Sesma, M. A. (1991). NMDA antagonist neurotoxicity: Mechanism and prevention. *Science, 254*, 1515–1518.

Olson, L., & Houlihan, D. (2000). A review of behavioral treatments used for Lesch–Nyhan syndrome. *Behavior Modification, 24*, 202–222.

Oltras, C. M., Mora, F., & Vives, F. (1987). β-Endorphin and ACTH in plasma: Effects of physical and psychological stress. *Life Science, 40*, 1683–1686.

Ommaya, A. K., Fisch, F. J., Mahone, R. M., Corrao, P., & Letcher, R. (1993). Comparative tolerances for cerebral concussion by head impact and whiplash injury in primates. In S. H. Backaitis (Ed.), *Biomechanics of impact injury and injury tol-*

erance of the head-neck complex (pp. 265–274). Warrendale, PA: Society of Automotive Engineers.

Ommaya, A. K., Yarnell, P., Hirsch, A. E., & Harris, E. H. (1967). *Scaling of experimental data on cerebral concussion in sub-human primates to concussion threshold in man.* Proceedings of the 11th Strapp Car Crash Conference. Anaheim, CA.

Opacka-Juffry, J., Ashworth, S., Ahier, R. G., & Hume, S. P. (1998). Modulatory effects of L-dopa on D_2 dopamine receptors in rat striatum, measured using in vivo microdialysis and PET. *Journal of Neural Transmission, 105,* 349–364.

O'Reilly, M. F. (1995). Functional analysis and treatment of escape-maintained aggression correlated with sleep deprivation. *Journal of Applied Behavior Analysis, 28,* 225–226.

O'Reilly, M. F. (1997). Functional analysis of episodic self-injury correlated with recurrent otitis media. *Journal of Applied Behavior Analysis, 30,* 165–167.

Ornitz, E. M. (1976). The modulation of sensory input and motor output in autistic children. In E. Schopler, & R. J. Reichler (Eds.), *Psychopathology and child development* (pp. 115–133). New York: Plenum Press.

Osborne, J. G., Baggs, A. W., Darvish, R., Blakelock, H., Peine, H., & Jenson, W. R. (1992). Cyclical self-injurious behavior, contingent water mist treatment, and the possibility of rapid-cycling bipolar disorder. *Journal of Behavior Therapy and Experimental Psychiatry, 23,* 325–334.

Pace, G. M., Ivancic, M. T., Edwards, G. L., Iwata, B. A., & Page, T. J. (1985). Assessment of stimulus preference and reinforcer value with profoundly retarded individuals. *Journal of Applied Behavior Analysis, 18,* 249–255.

Pace, G. M., Iwata, B. A., Edwards, G. L., & McCosh, K. C. (1986). Stimulus fading and transfer in the treatment of self-restraint and self-injurious behavior. *Journal of Applied Behavior Analysis, 19,* 381–389.

Page, T., Bakay, B., Nissinen, E., & Nyhan, W. L. (1981). Hypoxanthine-guanine phosphoribosyltransferase variants: Correlation of clinical phenotype with enzyme activity. *Journal of Inherited Metabolic Disease, 4,* 203–206.

Page, T., Bakay, B., & Nyhan, W. L. (1982). Kinetic studies of normal and variant hypoxanthine phospho-ribosyltransferases in intact fibroblasts. *Annals of Biochemistry, 122,* 144–147.

Page, T., Bakay, B., & Nyhan, W. L. (1982). An improved procedure for detection of hypoxanthine-guanine phosphoribosyltransferase heterozygotes. *Clinical Chemistry, 28,* 1181–1184.

Page, T., & Broock, R. L. (1990). A pitfall in the prenatal diagnosis of Lesch–Nyhan syndrome by chorionic villus sampling. *Prenatal Diagnosis, 10,* 153–157.

Page, T., & Nyhan W. L. (1989). The spectrum of HPRT deficiency: An update. *Advances in Experimental Medicine and Biology, 253,* 129–132.

Page, T., Nyhan, W. L., & Morena de Vega, V. (1987). Syndrome of mild mental retardation, spastic gait, and skeletal malformation in a family with partial deficiency of hypoxanthine-guanine phosphoribosyltransferase. *Pediatrics, 79,* 713–717.

Pan, H. S., Frey, K. A., Young, A. B., & Penney, J. B., Jr. (1983). Changes in [³H]muscimol binding in substantia nigra, entopeduncular nucleus, globus pallidus, and thalamus after striatal lesions as demonstrated by quantitative receptor autoradiography. *Journal of Neuroscience, 3,* 1189–1198.

Pan, H. S., Penney, J. B., & Young, A. B. (1985). γ-Aminobutyric acid and benzodiazepine receptor changes induced by unilateral 6-hydroxydopamine lesions of the medial forebrain bundle. *Journal of Neurochemistry, 45,* 1396–1404.

Panksepp, J., & Lensing, P. (1991). Brief report: A synopsis of an open-trial of naltrexone treatment of autism with four children. *Journal of Autism and Developmental Disorders, 21,* 243–249.

Partington, M. W., & Hennen, B. K. (1967). The Lesch–Nyhan syndrome: Self-destructive biting, mental retardation, neurological disorder, and hyperuricemia. *Developmental Medicine and Child Neurology, 9,* 563–572.

Paul, A. (1997). Epilepsy or stereotypy? Diagnostic issues in learning disabilities. *Seizure, 6,* 111–120.

Pelios, L., Morren, J., Tesch, D., & Axelrod, S. (1999). The impact of functional analysis methodology on treatment choice for self-injurious and aggressive behavior. *Journal of Applied Behavior Analysis, 32,* 185–195.

Penit-Soria, J., Durand, C., Herve, D., & Besson, M. J. (1997). Morphological and biochemical adaptations to unilateral dopamine denervation of the neostriatum in newborn rats. *Neuroscience, 77,* 753–766.

Perez-Navarro, E., Alberch, J., & Marsal, J. (1993). Postnatal development of functional dopamine, opioid, and tachykinin receptors that regulate acetylcholine release from rat neostriatal slices. Effect of 6-hydroxydopamine lesion. *International Journal of Developmental Neuroscience, 11,* 701–708.

Perry, T., Dunn, H., Ho, H., & Crichton, J. (1988). Cerebrospinal fluid values for monoamine metabolites, g-aminobutyric acid, and other amino compounds in Rett syndrome. *Journal of Pediatrics, 112,* 234–238.

Pert, C. B., & Synder, S. H. (1973). Opiate receptor: Demonstration in nervous tissue. *Science, 179,* 1011–1014.

Peters, J. M. (1967). Caffeine-induced hemorrhagic automutilation. *Archives of International Pharmacodynamics, 169,* 139–146.

Peterson, B., Riddle, M. A., Cohen, D. J., Katz, L. D., Smith, J. C., Hardin, M. T., et al. (1993). Reduced basal ganglia volumes in Tourette's syndrome using three-dimensional reconstruction techniques from magnetic resonance images. *Neurology, 43,* 941.

Peterson, B. S., & Leckman, J. F. (1998). The temporal dynamics of Gilles de la Tourette's syndrome. *Biological Psychiatry, 44,* 1337–1348.

Philippart, M. (1992). Handwringing in Rett syndrome: A normal developmental stage. *Pediatric Neurology, 8,* 197–199.

Piazza, C. C., Adelinis, J. D., Hanley, G. P., Goh, H., & Delia, M. D. (2000). An evaluation of the effects of matched stimuli on behaviors maintained by automatic reinforcement. *Journal of Applied Behavior Analysis, 33,* 13–27.

Piazza, C. C., & Fisher, W. W. (1991). A faded bedtime with response cost protocol for treatment of multiple sleep problems in children. *Journal of Applied Behavior Analysis, 24*, 129–140.

Piazza, C. C., Fisher, W. W., Hyman, S. L., Fleishell, J., Lou, K. K., & Cataldo, M. F. (1994). Evaluation of pharmacologic treatment of destructive behaviors: Aggregated results from single-case, experimental studies. *Journal of Developmental and Physical Disabilities, 6*, 149–168.

Piazza, C. C., Fisher, W. W., & Kahng, S. W. (1996). Sleep patterns in children and young adults with mental retardation and severe behavior disorders. *Developmental Medicine and Child Neurology, 38*, 335–344.

Piazza, C. C., Fisher, W. W., & Sherer, M. (1997). Treating multiple sleep problems in children with developmental disabilities: Faded bedtime with response cost versus bedtime scheduling. *Developmental Medicine and Child Neurology, 39*, 414–418.

Piazza, C. C., Hagopian L. P., Hughes, C. R., & Fisher, W. W. (1998). Using chronotherapy to treat the severe sleep problems in a child with mental retardation. *American Journal on Mental Retardation, 102*, 358–366.

Pies, R. W., & Popli, A. P. (1995). Self-injurious behavior: Pathophysiology and implications for treatment. *Journal of Clinical Psychiatry, 56*, 580–588.

Pinsky, L., & Digeorge, A. M. (1966). Congenital familial sensory neuropathy with anhidrosis. *Journal of Pediatrics, 68*, 1–13.

Piven, J., Chase, G. A., Landa, R., Wzorek, M., Gayle, J., Cloud, D., et al. (1991). Psychiatric disorders in the parents of autistic individuals. *Journal of the American Academy of Child and Adolescent Psychiatry, 30*, 471–478.

Pomeranz, B. (1987). Scientific basis of acupuncture. In G. Stux, & B. Pomeranz (Eds.), *Acupuncture: textbook and atlas* (pp. 1–34). New York: Springer-Verlag.

Poon, C., & Merrill, C. K. (1997). Decrease of cardiac chaos in congestive heart failure. *Nature, 389*, 492–495.

Porter, F. (1993). Pain assessment in children: Infants. In N. L. Schechter, C. B. Berde, & M. Yaster (Eds.), *Pain in infants, children, and adolescents* (pp. 87–96). Baltimore: Williams & Wilkins.

Potenza, M. N., Holmes, J. P., Kanes, S. J., & McDougle, C. J. (1999). Olanzapine treatment of children, adolescents, and adults with pervasive developmental disorders: An open-label pilot study. *Journal of Clinical Psychopharmacology, 19*(1), 37–44.

Powell, S., Bodfish, J., Parker, D., Crawford, T., & Lewis, M. (1996). Self-restraint and self-injury: Occurrence and motivational significance. *American Journal of Mental Retardation, 101*, 41–48.

Prasad, B. M., Sorg, B. A., Ulibarri, C., & Kalivas, P. W. (1995). Sensitization to stress and psychostimulants: Involvement of dopamine transmission versus the HPA axis. *Annals of the New York Academy of Sciences, 771*, 617–625.

Premack, D. (1971). Catching up with common sense or two sides of a generalization: Reinforcement and punishment. In R. Glaser (Ed.), *The nature of reinforcement*. New York: Academic Press.

Price, M. T. C., Fibiger, H. C. (1974). Apomorphine and amphetamine stereotypy after 6-hydroxydopamine lesions of the substantia nigra. *European Journal of Pharmacology, 29*, 249–252.

Prizant, B. M., & Wetherby, A. M. (1989). Enhancing language and communication in autism: From theory to practice. In G. Dawson (Ed.), *Autism: Nature, diagnosis, and treatment* (pp. 282–309). New York: Guilford Press.

Procacci, P., & Maresca, M. (1990). Autotomy. *Pain, 43*, 394.

Purcell, R., Maruff, P., Kyrios, M., & Pantelis, C. (1998). Neuropsychological deficits in obsessive-compulsive disorder. *Archives of General Psychiatry, 55*, 415–423.

Purdon S. E., Lit W., Labelle A., & Jones, B. D. (1994). Risperidone in the treatment of pervasive developmental disorder. *Canadian Journal of Psychiatry, 39*(7), 400–405.

Qureshi, H., & Alborz, A. (1992). Epidemiology of challenging behaviour. *Mental Handicap Research, 5*, 130–145.

Racusin, R., Kovner-Kline K., & King, B. H. (1999). Selective serotonin reuptake inhibitors in intellectual disability. *Mental Retardation and Developmental Disabilities Research Reviews, 5*, 264–269.

Rampe, D., Anderson, B., Rapien-Pryor, V., Li, T., & Dage, R. C. (1993). Comparison of the in vitro and in vivo cardiovascular effects of two structurally distinct Ca^{++} channel activators, Bay K 8644, and FPL 64176. *Journal of Pharmacology and Experimental Therapeutics, 265*, 1125–1130.

Randall, L. O., Schallek, W., Heise, G. A., Keith, E. F., & Bagdon, R. E. (1960). The psychosedative properties of methaminodiazepoxide. *Journal of Pharmacology and Experimental Therapeutics, 129*, 163–171.

Randrup, A., & Munkvad, I. (1968). Behavioral stereotypies induced by pharmacological agents. *Pharmakosychiatry Neuro-Psychopharmacology 1*, 18–26.

Rapoport, J. L. (1988). The neurobiology of obsessive–compulsive disorder [Clinical conference], *Journal of the American Medical Association, 260*, 2888–2890.

Rapoport, J. (1991). Basal ganglia dysfunction as a proposed cause of obsessive–compulsive disorder. In B. Carroll, & J. Barrett (Eds) *Psychopathology and the brain* (pp. 77–95). New York: Raven Press.

Rasmussen, P. (1996). The congenital insensitivity-to-pain syndrome (analgesia congenita): Report of a case. *International Journal of Paediatric Dentistry, 6*, 117–122.

Ratey, J. J., Sorgi, P., O'Driscoll, G. A., Sands, S. K., Dachler, M. L., Fletcher, et al. (1992). Nadolol to treat aggression and pscyhiatric symptomatology in chronic psychiatric patients: A double blind-placebo controlled study. *Journal of Clinical Psychiatry, 53*, 41–46.

Rauch, S. L., & Savage, C. R. (1997). Neuroimaging and neuropsychology of the striatum. In E. C. Miguel, S. L. Rauch, & M. A. Jenike (Eds.), *Psychiatry Clinics of North America, 20*(4), 741–768.

Razzak, A., Fujiwara, M., Oishi, R., & Ueki, S. (1977). Possible involvement of a central noradrenergic system in automutilation induced by clonidine in mice. *Japanese Journal of Pharmacology, 27*, 145–152.

Razzak, A., Fujiwara, M., & Ueki, S. (1975). Automutilation induced by clonidine in mice. *European Journal of Pharmacology, 30,* 356–359.

Recher, H., Willis, G. L., Smit, G. C., & Copolov, D. L. (1988). β-Endorphin, corticosterone, cholesterol, and triglyceride concentrations in rat plasma after stress, cingulotomy, or both. *Pharmacology and Biochemistry of Behavior, 31,* 75–79.

Reid, A. H. (1972). Psychoses in adult mental defectives: I. Manic depressive psychosis. *British Journal of Psychiatry, 120,* 205–212.

Reid, A. H., Ballinger, B. R., Heather, B. B., & Melvin, S. J. (1984). The natural history of behavioural symptoms among severely and profoundly mentally retarded patients. *British Journal of Psychiatry, 145,* 289–293.

Reisine, T., & Pasternak, G. (1996). Opioid analgesics and antagonists. In J. G. Hardman, L. E. Limbird, P. B. Molinoff, R. W. Ruddon, & A. G. Gilman (Eds.), *The pharmacological basis of therapeutics* (pp. 521–556). New York: McGraw-Hill.

Repp, A. C., Felce, D., & Barton, L. E. (1988). Basing the treatment of stereotypic and self-injurious behaviors on hypotheses of their causes. *Journal of Applied Behavior Analysis, 21,* 281–289.

Repp, A. C., & Karsh, K. G. (1994). Hypothesis-based interventions for tantrum behaviors of persons with developmental disabilities in school settings. *Journal of Applied Behavior Analysis, 27,* 21–31.

Repp, A. C., Karsh, K. G., Deitz, D. E., & Singh, N. N. (1992). A study of the homeostatic level of stereotypy and other motor movements of persons with mental handicaps. *Journal of Intellectual Disability Research, 36,* 61–75.

Ressman, A. C., & Butterworth, T. (1952). Localized acquired hypertrichosis. *Archives of Dermatology and Syphilis, 65,* 418–423.

Richardson, J. S., & Zaleski, W. A. (1983). Naloxone and self-mutilation. *Biological Psychiatry, 18,* 99–101.

Ridley, R. M. (1994). The psychology of perseverative and stereotyped behaviour. *Progress in Neurobiology, 44,* 221–231.

Riederer, P., Brucke, T., Sofic, E., Kienzl, E., Schnecker, K., Schay, V., et al. (1985). Neurochemical aspects of the Rett syndrome. *Brain Development, 7*(3), 351–360.

Rincover, A., Cook, R., Peoples, A., & Packard, D. (1979). Sensory extinction and sensory reinforcement principles for programming multiple adaptive behavior change. *Journal of Applied Behavior Analysis, 12,* 221–233.

Rincover, A., & Devany, J. (1982). The application of sensory extinction procedures to self-injury. *Analysis and Intervention in Developmental Disabilities, 2,* 67–81.

Rincover, A., & Koegel, R. L. (1975). Setting generality and stimulus control in autistic children. *Journal of Applied Behavior Analysis, 8,* 235–246.

Rioux, L., Gagnon, C., Gaudin, D. P., Di Paolo, T., & Bedard, P. J. (1993). A fetal nigral graft prevents behavioral supersensitivity associated with repeated injections of L-dopa in 6-OHDA rats. Correlation with D_1 and D_2 receptors. *Neuroscience, 56,* 45–51.

Rioux, L., Gaudin, D. P., Bui, L. K., Gregoire, L., DiPaolo, T., & Bednard, B. (1991b). Correlation of functional recovery after a 6-hydroxydopamine lesion with survival of grafted fetal neurons and release of dopamine in the striatum of the rat. *Neuroscience, 40,* 123–131.

Rioux, L., Gaudin, D. P., Gagnon, C., Di Paolo, T., & Bednard, P. J. (1991a). Decrease of behavioral and biochemical denervation supersensitivity of rat striatum by nigral transplants. *Neuroscience, 44,* 75–83.

Roach, E. S., Abramson, J. S., & Lawless, M. R., (1985). Self-injurious behavior in acquired sensory neuropathy. *Neuropediatrics, 16,* 159–161.

Robertson, G. S., Fine, A., & Robertson, H. A. (1991). Dopaminergic grafts in the striatum reduce D_1 and D_2 receptor-mediated rotation in 6-OHDA-lesioned rats. *Brain Research, 539,* 304–311.

Robertson, G. S., Herrera, D. G., Dragunow, M., & Robertson, H. A. (1989). L-dopa activates *c-fos* in the striatum ipsilateral to a 6-hydroxydopamine lesion of the substantia nigra. *European Journal of Pharmacology, 159,* 99–100.

Robertson, M. M., Trimble, M. R., & Lees, A. J. (1989). Self-injurious behavior and the Gilles de la Tourette's syndrome: A clinical study and review of the literature. *Psychological Medicine, 19,* 611–625.

Rodriguez, M. C., Obeso, J. A., & Olanow, C. W. (1998). Subthalamic nucleus-mediated excitotoxicity in Parkinson's disease: A target for neuroprotection. *Annals of Neurology, 44,* S175–S188.

Rogers, D. (1992). *Motor disorder in psychiatry: Towards a neurological psychiatry.* John Wiley and Sons: New York.

Rojahn, J. (1984). Self-injurious behavior in institutionalized severely/profoundly retarded adults—prevalence data and staff agreement. *Journal of Behavioral Assessment, 6,* 13–27.

Rojahn, J. (1986). Self-injurious and stereotypic behavior of noninstitutionalized mentally retarded people: Prevalence and classification. *American Journal of Mental Deficiency, 91,* 268–276.

Rojahn, J. (1994). Epidemiology and topographic taxonomy is self-injurious behavior. In T. Thompson, & D. B. Gray (Eds.), *Destructive behavior in developmental disabilities: Diagnosis and treatment* (pp. 49–67). Thousand Oaks, CA: Sage Publications.

Rojahn, J., Borthwick-Duffy, S. A., & Jacobson, J. W. (1993). The association between psychiatric diagnoses and severe behavior problems in mental retardation. *Annals of Clinical Psychiatry, 5,* 163–170.

Rojahn, J., Matson, J. L., Lott, D., Esbensen, A. J., & Smalls, Y. (1999). *Epidemiology and topographic assessment of SIB.* Invited address, Workshop on Self-Injurious Behavior, Rockville, MD.

Rojahn, J., Matson, J. L., Lott, D., Esbensen, A. J., & Smalls, Y. (in press). *The revised Behavior Problems Inventory (BPI-R) for mental retardation: Psychometric Properties.*

Rollings, J. P., Baumeister, A. A., & Baumeister, A. A. (1977). The use of overcorrection procedures to eliminate the stereotypical behaviors of retarded individuals: An analysis of collateral behaviors and generalization of suppressive effects. *Behavior Modification, 1,* 29–46.

Romanczyk, R. G. (1977). *Treatment of self-injurious behavior and self-stimulatory behavior: The contrast between treatment and follow-up.* Paper presented at the 24th annual meeting of the American Association on Mental Deficiency, Pittsfield, MA.

Romanczyk, R. G. (1987). *Aversive conditioning as a component of comprehensive treatment: The impact of etiological factors on clinical decision making.* Paper presented at Rutgers Symposium on Applied Psychology, New Brunswick, NJ.

Romanczyk, R. G., Gordon, W. C., Crimmins, D. B., Wenzel, A. M., & Kistner, J. A. (1980). Childhood psychosis and 24-hour rhythms: A behavioral and psychophysiological analysis. *Chronobiologia, 7,* 1–14.

Romanczyk, R. G., & Goren, E. R. (1975). Severe self-injurious behavior: The problem of clinical control. *Journal of Consulting and Clinical Psychology, 43,* 730–739.

Romanczyk, R. G., Lockshin, S., & O'Conner, J. O. (1992). Psycho-physiology and issues of anxiety and arousal. In J. K. Luiselli, J. L. Matson, & N. N. Singh (Eds.), *Self-injurious behavior: Analysis, assessment and treatment* (pp. 93–121). New York: Springer.

Romanczyk, R. G., & Mathews, A. L. (1998). Physiological state as antecedent: Utilization in functional analyses. In J. K. Luiselli, & M. J. Cameron (Eds.), *Antecedent control: Innovative approaches to behavioral support* (115–138). Baltimore: Brookes.

Roscoe, E. M., Iwata, B. A., & Goh, H. (1998). A comparison of noncontingent reinforcement and sensory extinction as treatments for self-injurious behavior. *Journal of Applied Behavior Analysis, 31,* 635–646.

Rosenbloom, F. M., Kelley, W. N., Miller, J., et al. (1967). Inherited disorder of purine metabolism: Correlation between central nervous system dysfunction and biochemical defects. *Journal of the American Medical Association, 202,* 195–197.

Rosenquist, P. B., Bodfish, J. W., & Thompson, R. (1997). Tourette's syndrome associated with mental retardation: A single-subject treatment study with haloperidol. *American Journal of Mental Retardation, 101,* 497–504.

Ross, R. T. (1972). Behavioral correlates of levels of intelligence. *American Journal of Mental Deficiency, 76,* 545–549.

Ross, D. L., Klykylo, W. M., & Hitzemann, R. (1987). Reduction of elevated CSF β-endorphin by fenfluramine in infantile autism. *Pediatric Neurology, 3,* 83–86.

Roy, A., & Simon, G. B. (1987). Intestinal obstruction as a cause of death in the mentally handicapped. *Journal of Mental Deficiency Research, 31,* 193–197.

Ruppenthal, G. C., Arling, G. L., Harlow, H. F., Sackett, G. P., & Suomi, S. J. (1976). A 10-year perspective of motherless-mother monkey behavior. *Journal of Abnormal Psychology, 85,* 341–349.

Russ, M. J., Roth, S. D., Kakuma, T., Harrison, K., & Hull, J. W., (1994). Pain perception in self-injurious borderline patients: Naloxone effects. *Biological Psychiatry, 35,* 207–209.

Russ, M. J., Roth, S. D., Lerman, A., Kakuma, T., Harrison, K., Shindledecker, R. D., et al. (1992). Pain perception in self-injurious patients with borderline personality disorder. *Biological Psychiatry, 32*, 501–511.

Rutter, M. (1997). Child psychiatric disorder: Measures, causal mechanisms, and interventions. *Archives of General Psychiatry, 54*, 785–789.

Sackett, G. P. (1972a). Isolation rearing in monkeys: Diffuse and specific effects on later behavior. In R. Chauvin (Ed.), *Animal models of human behavior*, (pp. 61–110). Paris: Colloques Internationaux du C. N. R. S.

Sackett, G. P. (1972b). Exploratory behavior of rhesus monkeys as a function of rearing experience and sex. *Developmental Psychology, 6*, 260–270.

Sackett, G. P., Ruppenthal, G. C., Fajrenbruch, C. E., Holm, R. A., & Greenough, W. T. (1981). Social isolation rearing effects in monkeys vary with genotype. *Developmental Psychology, 17*, 313–318.

Saito, Y., Ito, M., Hanaoka, S., Ohama, E., Akaboshi, S., & Takashima, S. (1999). Dopamine receptor upregulation in Lesch–Nyhan syndrome: A postmortem study. *Neuropediatrics, 30*, 66–71.

Sallustro, F., & Atwell, C. W. (1978). Body-rocking, head-banging, and head-rolling in normal children. *Journal of Pediatrics, 93*, 704–708.

Sallee, F. R., Stiller, R. L., Perel, J. M., & Everett, G. (1989). Pemoline-induced abnormal involuntary movements. *Journal of Clinical Psychopharmacology, 9*, 125–129.

Salzman, J., DeMars, R., & Benke, P. (1968). Single-allele expression at an X-linked hyperuricemia locus in heterozygous human cells. *Proceedings of the National Academy of Sciences, USA, 60*, 545–552.

Sandler, J. (1964). Reinforcement combinations and masochistic behavior: A preliminary report. *Psychological Reports, 11*, 110.

Sandman, C. A. (1988). β-endorphin disregulation in autistic and self-injurious behavior: A neurodevelopmental hypothesis. *Synapse, 2*, 193–199.

Sandman, C. A. (1990–1991). The opiate hypothesis in autism and self-injury. *Journal of Child and Adolescent Psychopharmacology, 1*, 235–246.

Sandman, C. A., Barron, J. L., Chicz-DeMet, A., & DeMet, E. M. (1990). Plasma β-endorphin levels in patients with self-injurious behavior and stereotypy. *American Journal on Mental Retardation, 95*, 84–92.

Sandman, C. A., Barron, J. L., Chicz-DeMet, A., & DeMet, E. (1991). Brief report: Plasma β-endorphin and cortisol levels in autistic patients. *Journal of Autism and Developmental Disorders, 21*, 83–87.

Sandman, C. A., Barron, J. L., & Colman, H. (1990). An orally administered opiate blocker, naltrexone, attenuates self-injurious behavior. *American Journal on Mental Retardation, 95*, 93–102.

Sandman, C. A., Datta, P., Barron, J. L, Hoehler, E., Williams, C., & Swanson, J. (1983). Naloxone attenuates self-abusive behavior in developmentally disabled subjects. *Applied Research in Mental Retardation, 4*, 5–11.

Sandman, C. A., & Hetrick, W. P. (1995). Opiate mechanisms in self-injury. *Mental Retardation and Developmental Disabilities Research Reviews, 1*, 130–136.

Sandman, C. A., Hetrick, W. P., Taylor, D. V., Barron, J. L., Touchette, P., Lott, I., et al. (1993). Naltrexone reduces self-injury and improves learning. *Experimental and Clinical Psychopharmacology, 1*, 242–258.

Sandman, C. A., Hetrick, W. P., Taylor, D. V., & Chicz-Demet, A. (1997). Dissociation of POMC peptides after self-injury predicts responses to centrally acting opiate blockers. *American Journal on Mental Retardation, 102*, 182–199.

Sandman, C. A., Hetrick, W., Taylor, D. V., Marion, S., & Chicz-DeMet, A. (2000). Uncoupling of proopiomelancortin (POMC) fragments is related to self-injury. *Peptides, 21*, 785–791.

Sandman, C. A., Hetrick, W. P., Taylor, D. V., Marion, S. D., Touchette, P., Barron, J. L., et al. (2000). Long-term effects of naltrexone on self-injurious behavior. *American Journal on Mental Retardation, 105*, 103–117.

Sandman, C., Spence, M. A., & Smith, M. (1999). Proopiomelanocortin (POMC) disregulation and response to opiate blockers. *Mental Retardation and Developmental Disabilities Research Review, 5*, 314–321.

Sandman, C. A., Thompson, T., Barrett, R. P., Verhoeven, W. M. A., McCubbin, J. A., Schroeder, S. R., et al. (1998). Opiate blockers. In M. Aman, & S. Reiss (Eds.), *Consensus handbook on psychopharmacology* (pp. 291–302). Columbus, OH: Ohio State University.

Sandman, C., Touchette, P., Ly, J., DeBoard-Marion, S., & Bruinsma, Y. (2000). Computerized-assessment of treatment effects among individuals with developmental disabilities. In T. Thompson, D. Felces, & F. Symons (Eds.), *Behavioral observations: Technology and applications in developmental disabilities* (pp. 271–293). Baltimore: Paul H. Brookes Publishing.

Sandyk, R. (1987). Opioid neuronal denervation in Gilles de la Tourette's syndrome. *International Journal of Neuroscience, 35*(1–2), 95–98.

Sansom, D., Krishnan, V. H., & Corbett, J. (1993). Emotional and behavioral aspects of Rett syndrome. *Developmental Medicine and Child Neurology, 35*, 340–345.

Savasta, M., Menniken, F., Chritin, M., Abrous, D. N., Feuerstein, C., Le Moal, M., et al. (1992). Intrastriatal dopamine-rich implants reverse the changes in dopamine D_2 receptor densities caused by 6-hydroxydopamine lesion of the nigrostriatal pathway in rats: An autoradiographic study. *Neuroscience, 46*, 729–738.

Schaal, D. W., & Hackenberg, T. (1994). Toward a functional analysis of drug treatment for behavior problems of people with developmental disabilities. *American Journal on Mental Retardation, 99*, 123–140.

Scheel-Kruger, J., Arnt, J., Braestrup, C., Christensen, A. V., Cools, A. R., & Maglund, G. (1978). GABA-dopamine interactions in substantia nigra and nucleus accumbens: Relevance to behavioral stimulation and stereotyped behavior. In P. J. Roberts, G. N. Woodruff, & L. L. Iversen (Eds.), *Advances in Biochemical Pharmacology* (Vol. 19), New York: Raven Press.

Scheel-Kruger, J., Arnt, J., Magelund, G., Olianas, M., Przewlocka, B., & Christensen, A. V. (1980). Behavioral functions of GABA in basal ganglia and limbic system. *Brain Research Bulletin*, 5, 261–267.

Scheel-Kruger, J., Magelund, G., & Olianas, M. C. (1981). Role of GABA in the striatal output system: Globus pallidus, nucleus entopeduncularis, substantia nigra, and nucleus subthalamicus. *Advances in Biochemical Psychopharmacology*, 30, 165–186.

Schindler, S. D., Stamencovic, M., Asenbaum, S., Neumeister, A., Willinger, U., de Zwaan, M., et al. (1999). *No change in dopamine reuptake site density in drug naïve and drug free patients with Gilles de la Tourette-syndrome (GTS): A [^{123}I]-bCIT SPECT-study*. Poster abstract, 3rd International Scientific Symposium on Tourette's Syndrome, New York.

Schorstein, J. (1943). Erosion of the ala nasi following trigeminal denervation. *Journal of Neuropsychiatry*, 6, 46–51.

Schroeder, S. R. Self-injury and stereotypy. (1991). In J. L. Matson, & J. A. Mulick (Eds.), *Handbook of Mental Retardation* (pp. 382–396). Pergamon Press, New York.

Schroeder, S. R., Hammock, R. G., Mulick, J. A., Rojahn, J., Walson, P., Fernald, W., et al. (1995). Clinical trails of D$_1$ and D$_2$ dopamine modulating drugs and self-injury in mental retardation and developmental disability. *Mental Retardation and Developmental Disabilities Research Reviews*, 1, 120–129.

Schroeder, S., R., & Luiselli, J. K. (1992). Self-restraint. In J. K. Luiselli, J. L. Matson, & N. N. Singh, (Eds.), *Self-injurious behavior: Analysis, assessment, and treatment* (pp. 293–306). New York: Springer-Verlag.

Schroeder, S. R., Mulick, J. A., & Rojahn, J. (1980). The definition, taxonomy, epidemiology, and ecology of self-injurious behavior. *Journal of Autism and Developmental Disorder*, 10, 417–432.

Schroeder, S. R., Oster-Granite, M., Berkson, G., Bodfish, J. W., Breese, G. R., Cataldo, M. F., et al. (2001). Self-injurioius behavior: Gene-brain-behavior relationships. *Mental retardation and developmental Disabilities Research Reviews*, 7, 3–12.

Schroeder, S. R., Peterson, C., Solomon, L. J., & Artley, J. J. (1977). EMG feedback and the contingent restraint of self-injurious behavior among the severely retarded: Two case illustrations. *Behavior Therapy*, 8, 738–741.

Schroeder, S. R., Reese, R. M., Hellings, J., Loupe, J., & Tessel, R. E. (1999). The causes of self-injurious behavior and their implications. In N. A. Wieseler, & R. Hanson (Eds.), *Challenging behavior with mental health disorders and severe developmental disabilities* (pp. 65–87). Washington, DC: AAMR Monograph Series.

Schroeder, S. R., Rojahn, J., & Oldenquist, A. (1991). Treatment of destructive behaviors among people with mental retardation and developmental disabilities: Overview of the problem. In *Treatment of destructive behaviors in persons with developmental disabilities* (NIH Publication No. 91-2410, pp. 173–230). Washington, DC: U. S. Department of Health and Human Services.

Schroeder, S. R., Schroeder, C. S., Smith, B., & Dalldorf, J. (1978). Prevalence of self-injurious behaviors in a large state facility for the retarded: A three-year follow-up study. *Journal of Autism and Childhood Schizophrenia*, 8(3), 261–269.

Schultz, W., Tremblay, L., & Hollerman, J. R. (2000). Reward processing in primate orbitofrontal cortex and basal ganglia. *Cerebral Cortex, 10*, 272–383.

Schwarting, R. K. W., & Huston, J. P. (1996). Unilateral 6-hydroxydopamine lesions of mesostriatal neurons and their physiological sequelae. *Progress in Neurobiology, 49*, 215–266.

Schwartz, B. (1989). *Psychology of learning and behavior* (3rd ed.). New York: Norton.

Scifo, R., Cioni, M., Nicolosi, A., Batticane, N., Tirolo, C., Testa, N., et al. (1996). Opioid-immune interactions in autism: Behavioural and immunological assessment during a double-blind treatment with naltrexone. *Annali dell Instituto Superiore di Sanita, 32*, 351–359.

Seegmiller, J. E., Rosenbloom, F. M., & Kelley, W. N. (1967). Enzyme defect associated with sex-linked human neurological disorder and excessive purine synthesis. *Science, 155*, 1682–1684.

Sege-Peterson, K., Chambers, J., Page, T., Jones, O. W., & Nyhan, W. L. (1992). Characterization of mutations in phenotypic variants of hypoxanthine-guanine phosphoribosyltransferase deficiency. *Human Molecular Genetics, 1*, 427–432.

Sege-Peterson, K., Nyhan, W. L., & Page, T. (1992). Lesch–Nyhan disease and HPRT deficiency. In R. N. Rosenberg, S. B. Prusiner, S. DiMauro, R. L. Barchi, & L. M. Kunkel (Eds.) *The molecular and Genetic Basis of Neurological Disease* (pp. 241–259). Stoneham, MA: Butterworth-Heinemann.

Shapiro, D., & Reeves, J. L. (1982). Modification of physiological and subjective responses to stress through heart rate and biofeedback. In J. T. Cacioppo, & R. E. Petty (Eds.), *Perspectives in cardiovascular psychophysiology* (pp. 127–150). New York: Guilford Press.

Shearer, S. L. (1994). Phenomenology of self-injury among inpatient women with borderline personality disorder. *The Journal of Nervous and Mental Disease, 182*, 524–526.

Shearer, S. L., Peter, C. P., Quaytman, M. S., & Wadman, B. E. (1988). Intent and lethality of suicide attempts among female borderline in-patients. *American Journal of Psychiatry, 145*, 1424–1427.

Shen, K., & Crain, S. M. (1992). Chronic selective activation of excitatory opioid receptor functions in sensory neurons results in opioid "dependence" without tolerance. *Brain Research, 597*, 74–83.

Sherman, B. R. (1988). Predictors of the decision to place developmentally disabled members in residential care. *American Journal on Mental Retardation, 92*, 344–351.

Shirley, M. J., Iwata, B. A., Kahng, S., Mazaleski, J. L., & Lerman, D. C. (1997). Does functional communication training compete with ongoing contingencies of reinforcement? An analysis during response acquisition and maintenance. *Journal of Applied Behavior Analysis, 30*, 93–104.

Shishido, T., Watanabe, Y., Kato, K., Horikoshi, R., & Niwa, S. (2000). Effects of dopamine, NMDA, opiate, and serotonin-related agents on acute methamphetamine-induced self-injurious behavior in mice. *Pharmacology, Biochemistry, and Behavior, 66*(3), 579–583.

Shutt, D. A., Smith, A. I., Wallace, C. A., Connell, R., & Fell, L. R. (1988). Effect of myiasis and acute restraint stress on plasma levels of immunoreactive β-endorphin, adrenocorticotrophin (ACTH) and cortisol in the sheep. *Australian Journal of Biological Sciences, 41*, 297–301.

Sidman, M. (1958). Some notes on "bursts" in free-operant avoidance experiments. *Journal of the Experimental Analysis of Behavior, 1*, 167–172.

Sidman, M. (1960). Normal sources of pathological behavior. *Science, 132*, 61–68.

Sidman, M. (1960). *Tactics of scientific research: Evaluating experimental data in psychology.* New York: Basic Books.

Sigafoos, J., & Meikle, B. (1996). Functional communication training for the treatment of multiply determined challenging behavior in two boys with autism. *Behavior Modification, 20*, 60–84.

Silverman, K., Watanbe, K., Marshall, A. M., & Baer, D. M. (1984). Reducing self-injury and corresponding self-restraint through the strategic use of protective clothing. *Journal of Applied Behavior Analysis, 17*, 545–552.

Silverstein, F. S., Johnston, M. V., Hutchinson, R. J., & Edwards, N. L. (1985). Lesch–Nyhan syndrome: CSF neurotransmitter abnormalities. *Neurology, 35*, 907–911.

Simeon, D., Cohen, L. J., Stein, D. J., Schmeidler, J., Spadaccini, E., & Hollonder, E. (1997). Comorbid self-injurious behaviors in 71 female hair-pullers: A survey study. *The Journal of Nervous and Mental Disease, 185*, 117–119.

Simeon, D., Stanley, B., Frances, A., Mann, J. J., Wichel, R., & Stanley, M. (1992). Self-mutilation in personality disorders: Psychological and biological correlates. *American Journal of Psychiatry, 148*, 1665–1671.

Simeon, D., Stein, D., & Hollander, E. (1995). Self-injurious behavior. *Journal of Clinical Psychiatry, 56*, 36–39.

Simon-Soret, C., & Borenstein, P. (1987). Essai de la bromocriptine dans le traitement de l'autisme infantile. *La Presse Medicale, 16*, 1286.

Simson, P. E., Johnson, K. B., Jurevics, H. A., Criswell, H. E., Napier, T. C., Duncan, G. E., et al. (1992). Augmented sensitivity of D_1-dopamine receptors in lateral but not medial striatum following 6-hydroxydopamine-induced lesions in the neonatal rat. *Journal of Pharmacology and Experimental Therapeutics, 263*, 1454–1463.

Singer, H. S., Hahn, I. H., & Moran, T. H. (1991). Abnormal dopamine uptake sites in postmortem striatum from patients with Tourette's syndrome. *Annals of Neurology, 30*, 558–562.

Singer, H. S., Reiss, A. L., Brown, J. E., Aylward, E. H., Shih, B., Chee, E., et al. (1993). Volumetric MRI changes in basal ganglia of children with Tourette's syndrome. *Neurology, 43*, 950.

Singh, B. K., Singh, A., & Chusid, E. (1983). Chorea in long-term use of pemoline [Letter]. *Annals of Neurology, 13*, 218

Singh, N. N. (1977). Prevalence of self-injury in institutionalized retarded children. *New Zealand Medical Journal, 86,* 325–327.

Singh, N., & Aman, M. (1981). Effects of thioridazine dosage on the behavior of severely retarded persons. *American Journal on Mental Deficiency, 85,* 580–587.

Singh, N. N., & Pullman, R. M. (1979). Self-injury in the de Lange syndrome. *Journal of Mental Deficiency Research, 23,* 79–84.

Sivam, S. P. (1995). GBR-12909-induced self-injurious behavior: Role of dopamine. *Brain Research, 690,* 259–263.

Sivam, S. P. (1996). Dopamine, serotonin, and tachykinin in self-injurious behavior. *Life Sciences, 24,* 2367–2375.

Sivam, S. P., Breese, G. R., Krause, J. E., Napier, T. C., Mueller, R. A., & Hong, J. S. (1987). Neonatal and adult-6-hydroxydopamine-induced lesions differentially alter tachykinin and enkephalin gene expression. *Journal of Neurochemistry, 49,* 1623–1633.

Sivam, S. P., Breese, G. R., Napier, T. C., Mueller, R. A., & Hong, J. S. (1986). Dopaminergic regulation of prenkephalin-A gene expression in the basal ganglia. *NIDA Research Monographs, 75,* 389–392.

Sivam, S. P., & Krause, J. E. (1990). The adaptation of enkephalin, tachykinin, and monoamine neurons of the basal ganglia following neonatal dopaminergic denervation is dependent on the extent of dopamine depletion. *Brain Research, 536,* 169–175.

Sivam, S. P., Krause, J. E., Breese, G. R., & Hong, J. S. (1991). Dopamine-dependent postnatal development of enkephalin and tachykinin neurons of rat basal ganglia, *Journal of Neurochemistry, 56,* 1499–1508.

Skinner, B. F. (1938). *The behavior of organisms.* New York: Appleton-Century-Crofts.

Skinner, B. F. (1953). *Science and human behavior.* New York: McMillan.

Skinner, B. F. (1966). The phylogeny and ontogeny of behavior. *Science, 153,* 1204–2113.

Slifkin, A. B., & Newell, K. M. (1999). Is variability in human performance a reflection of system noise? *Current Directions in Psychological Science, 7,* 170–176.

Smalley, S. L., McCracken, J., & Tanguay, P. (1995). Autism, affective disorders, and social phobia. *American Journal of Medical Genetics, 60,* 19–26.

Smart, D., & Lambert, D. G. (1996). The stimulatory effects of opioids and their possible role in the development of tolerance. *Trends in Pharmacological Sciences, 17,* 264–269.

Smeets, P. M. (1971). Some characteristics of mental defectives displaying self-mutilative behaviors. *Training School Bulletin, 68,* 131–135.

Smith, A. C., Dykens, E., & Greenberg, F. (1998). Behavioral phenotype of Smith-Magenis syndrome. *American Journal of Medical Genetics, 81,* 179–185.

Smith, R. D., Cooper, B. R., & Breese, G. R. (1973). Growth and behavioral changes in developing rats treated intracisternally with 6-hydroxydopamine: Evidence for involvement of brain dopamine. *Journal of Pharmacology and Experimental Therapeutics, 185,* 609–619.

Smith, S. G., Gupta, K. K., & Smith, S. H. (1995). Effects of naltrexone on self-injury, stereotypy, and social behavior of adults with developmental disabilities. *Journal of Developmental and Physical Disabilities, 35*, 283–323.

Smith, R. G., Iwata, B. A., Goh, H., & Shore, B. A. (1995). Analysis of establishing operations for self-injury maintained by escape. *Journal of Applied Behavior Analysis, 28*, 515–535.

Smith, R. G., Iwata, B. A., Vollmer, T. R., & Pace, G. M. (1992). On the relationship between self-injurious behavior and self-restraint. *Journal of Applied Behavior Analysis, 25*, 433–445.

Smith, R. G., Lerman, D. C., & Iwata, B. A. (1996). Self-restraint as positive reinforcement for self-injurious behavior. *Journal of Applied Behavior Analysis, 29*, 99–102.

Smith, R. G., Russo, L., & Le, D. D. (1999). Distinguishing between extinction and punishment effects of response blocking: A replication. *Journal of Applied Behavior Analysis, 32*, 367–370.

Snyder, A. M., Zigmond, M. J., & Lund, R. D. (1986). Sprouting of serotoninergic afferents into striatum after dopamine-depleting lesions in infant rats: A retrograde transport and immunocytochemical study. *Journal of Comparative Neurology, 245*, 274–281.

Snyder, R. G., Schneider, L. W., Owings, C. L., Reynolds, H. M., Golomb, D. H., & Shork, M. A. (1977). *Anthropometry of infants, children, and youths to age 18 for product safety design.* Warrendale, PA: Society for Automotive Engineers.

Snyder-Keller, A. M. (1991). Developmental striatal compartmentalization following pre- and post-natal dopamine depletion. *Journal of Neuroscience, 11*, 810–821.

Soghomonian, J. J. (1994). Differential regulation of glutamate decarboxylase and pre-proenkephalin mRNA levels in the rat striatum. *Brain Research, 640*, 146–154.

Soher, B. J., van Zijl, P. C. M., Duyn, J. H., & Barker, P. B. (1996). Quantitative proton spectroscopic imaging of the human brain. *Magnetic Resonance Medicine, 35*, 356–363.

Sokol, M. S., Campbell, M., Goldstein, M., & Kriechman, A. M. (1991). Attention deficit disorder with hyperactvity and the dopamine hypothesis: Case presentations with theoretical background. *Journal of the American Academy of Child and Adolescent Psychiatry, 26*, 428–433.

Soule, B., & O'Brien, D. (1974). Self-injurious behavior in a state center for the retarded: Incidence. *Research and the Retarded*, Spring, 1–8.

Spitz, M. C., Jankovic, J., & Killian, J. M. (1985). Familial tic disorder, Parkinsonism, motor neuron disease, and acanthocytosis: A new syndrome. *Neurology, 35*, 366–370.

Sprague, J. R., & Horner, R. H. (1994). Covariation within functional response classes: Implications for treatment of severe problem behavior. In. T. Thompson, & D. B. Gray (Eds.), *Destructive behavior in developmental disabilities: Diagnosis and treatment* (pp. 213–242). Thousand Oaks, CA: Sage.

Sprague, R. L., & Newell, K. M. (Eds.). (1996). *Stereotyped movements: Brain and behavior relationships.* Washington, DC: American Psychological Association.

Stachowiak, M. K., Bruno, J. P., Snyder, A. M., Stricker, E. M., & Zigmond, M. J. (1984). Apparent sprouting of striatal serotonergic terminals after dopamine-depleting brain lesions in neonatal rats. *Brain Research, 291,* 164–167.

Standaert, D. G., & Young, A. B. (1996). Treatment of central nervous system degenerative disorders. In J. G. Hardman, L. E., Limbird, P. B., Molinoff, R. W. Ruddon, & A. G. Gilman (Eds.), *Goodman and Gilman's The pharmacological basis of therapeutics* (pp. 503–519), New York: McGraw-Hill.

Steege, M. W., Wacker, D. P., Berg, W. K., Cigrand, K. K., & Cooper, L. J. (1989). The use of behavioral assessment to prescribe and evaluate treatments for severely handicapped children. *Journal of Applied Behavior Analysis, 22,* 23–33.

Steen, P. L., & Zuriff, G. E. (1977). The use of relaxation in the treatment of self-injurious behavior. *Journal of Behavior Therapy and Experimental Psychiatry, 8,* 447–448.

Stein, D. J., Shoulberg, N., Helton, K., & Hollander, E. (1992). The neuroethological approach to obessive–compulsive disorder. *Comprehensive Psychiatry, 33,* 274–281.

Sternberg, L., Taylor, R. L., & Babkie, A. (1994). Correlates of interventions with self-injurious behaviour. *Journal of Intellectual Disability Research, 38,* 475–485.

Stewart, J. (1984). Reinstatement of heroin and cocaine self-administration behavior in the rat by intracerebral application of morphine in the ventral tegmental area. *Pharmacology Biochemistry and Behavior, 20,* 917–923.

Stewart, J., & Wise, R. A. (1992). Reinstatement of heroin self-administration habits: Morphine prompts and naltrexone discourages renewed responding after extinction. *Psychopharmacology, 108,* 79–84.

Stodgell, C. J., Loupe, P. S., Schroeder, S. R., & Tessel, R. E. (1998). Cross-sensitization between foot shock stress and apomorphine on self-injurious behavior and striatal catecholamines in a rat model of Lesch–Nyhan syndrome. *Brain Research, 783,* 10–18.

Stodgell, C. J., Schroeder, S. R., & Tessel, R. E. (1996). FR discrimination training reverses 6-hydroxydopamine-induced striatal dopamine depletion in a rat model of Lesch–Nyhan syndrome. *Brain Research, 713,* 246–252.

Stone, T. W., & Taylor, D. A. (1978a). Antagonism by clonidine of neuronal depressant responses to adenosine and adenosine-5'-monophosphate and adenosine triphosphate. *British Journal of Pharmacology, 64,* 369–374.

Stone, T. W., & Taylor, D. A. (1978b). Clonidine as an adenosine antagonist. *Journal of Pharmacy and Pharmacology, 30,* 792–793.

Stores, G. (1998). Sleep studies in children with mental handicap. *Journal of Child Psychology and Psychiatry and Allied Disciplines, 33,* 1303–1317.

Sturmey, P. (1994). Assessing the functions of aberrant behaviors: A review of psychometric instruments. *Journal of Autism and Developmental Disorders, 24,* 293–304.

Sturmey, P. (1995). Diagnostic-based pharmacological treatment of behavior disorders in persons with developmental disabilities: A review and decision-making typology. *Research in Developmental Disabilities, 16,* 235–252.

Sturmey, P. (1997). Introductory remarks: Long-term follow-up of behavioral interventions for challenging behaviors in persons with developmental disabilities. *Behavioral Interventions, 4*, 157–162.

Suomi, S. J., & Harlow, H. F. (1971). Abnormal social behavior in young monkeys. In J. Hellmuth (Ed.), *The Exceptional Infant*, (Vol. 2). New York: Bruner-Mazel.

Suomi, S. J., Harlow, H. F., & Novak, M. A. (1974). Reversal of social deficits produced by isolation rearing in monkeys. *Journal of Human Evolution, 3*, 527–534.

Suri, R. E., & Schultz, W. A. (1999). A neural network model with dopamine-like reinforcement signal that learns a spatial delayed response task. *Neuroscience, 91*, 871–890.

Surwillo, W. W. (1990). *Psychophysiology for clinical psychologists*. Norwood, NJ: Ablex.

Sweet, W. H. (1981). Animal models of chronic pain: Their possible validation from human experience with posterior rhizotomy and congenital analgesia. *Pain, 10*, 275–295.

Sweetman, L. (1968). Urinary and cerebrospinal fluid oxypurine levels and allopurinol metabolism in the Lesch–Nyhan syndrome. *Federation Proceedings, 27*, 1055–1059.

Sweetman, L., Borden, M., Kulovich, S., Kaufman, I., & Nyhan, W. L. (1977). Altered excretion of 5-hydroxyindoleacetic acid and glycine in patients with the Lesch–Nyhan disease. In M. M. Muller, E. Kaiser, & J. E. Seegmiller (Eds.), *Purine metabolism in man II: Regulation of pathways and enzyme defects* (pp. 398–404). New York: Plenum Publishing.

Sweetman, L., Borden, M., Lesh, P., Bakay, B., & Becker, M. A. (1977). Diminished affinity for purine substrates as a basis for gout with mild deficiency of hypoxanthine guanine phosphoribosyl transferase. In M. M. Muller, E. Kaiser, & J. E. Seegmiller (Eds.), *Purine metabolism in man II: Regulation of pathways and enzyme defects* (pp. 325–329). New York: Plenum Publishing.

Sweetman, L., Hoch, M. A., Bakay, B., Borden, M., Lesh, P., & Nyhan, W. L. (1978). A distinct human variant of hypoxanthine-guanine phosphoribosyltransferase. *Journal of Pediatrics, 92*, 385–389.

Sweetman, L., & Nyhan, W. L. (1967). Excretion of hypoxanthine and xanthine in a genetic disease of purine metabolism. *Nature, 215*, 859–860.

Sweetman, L., & Nyhan, W. L. (1972). Further studies of the enzyme composition of mutant cells in X-linked uric aciduria. *Archives of Internal Medicine, 130*, 214–220.

Sweetman, L., Nyhan, W. L., Klein, P. D., & Szczepanik, P. A. (1973). Glycine 1,2-^{13}C in the investigation of children with inborn errors of metabolism. In P. D. Klein, & S. V. Peterson (Eds.), *Proceedings of the First International Conference on Stable Isotopes in Chemistry, Biology, and Medicine, U. S. Atomic Energy Commission, National Technical Information Service, U. S. Department of Commerce* (pp. 404–409). Argonne, IL: Argonne National Laboratory.

Swoboda, K. J., Engle, E. C., Scheindlin, B., Anthony, D. C., & Jones, H. R. (1998). Mutilating hand syndrome in an infant with familial carpal tunnel syndrome. *Muscle and Nerve, 21*, 104–111.

Symons, F. J., Butler, M. G., Sanders, M. D., Feurer, I. D., & Thompson, T. (1999). Self-injurious behavior and Prader–Willi syndrome: Behavioral forms and body locations. *American Journal on Mental Retardation, 104*, 260–269.

Symons, F. J., Clark, R. D., Roberts, J. P., & Bailey, D. B. (in press). Classroom behavior of elementary school-aged boys with fragile X syndrome. *The Journal of Special Education.*

Symons, F. J., Davis, M. L., & Thompson, T. (2000). Self-injurious behavior and sleep disturbance in adults with developmental disabilities. *Research in Developmental Disabilities, 21*, 115–123.

Symons, F. J., Fox, N. D., & Thompson, T. (1998). Functional communication training and naltrexone treatment of self-injurious behavior: An experimental case report. *Journal of Applied Research and Intellectual Disabilities, 3*, 273–292.

Symons, F., & MacLean, W. E., Jr. (2000). Analyzing and treating severe behavior problems in people with developmental disabilities: Observational methods using computer assisted technology. In T. Thompson, D. Felce, & F. J. Symons (Eds.), *Behavior observation: Technology and applications in developmental disabilities* (pp. 143–157). Baltimore: Paul H. Brookes Publishing.

Symons, F. J., Sperry, L., & Bodfish, J. W. (in press). The early development of stereotypy and self-injury. *Mental Retardation.*

Symons, F. J., Sutton, K. A., & Bodfish, J. W. (2001). A preliminary study of altered skin temperature at body sites associated with self-injury in adults with developmental disabilities. *American Journal on Mental Retardation, 106*, 336–343.

Symons, F. J., & Thompson, T. (1997). Self-injurious behavior and body site preference. *Journal of Intellectual Disability Research, 6*, 456–468.

Symons, F., Thompson, T., Sanders, M., Feurer, I., & Butler, M. (1999). Skin picking by people with Prader–Willi syndrome: Behavioral forms and body locations. *American Journal on Mental Retardation, 104*, 260–269.

Tabar, J., Hashizume, M., Cook, C. J., Beart, P. M., & Jackson, D. M. (1989). The effects on central dopamine function of chronic L-dopa (methylester hydrochloride) treatment of mice. *Pharmacology, Biochemistry, and Behavior, 33*, 139–146.

Tabbal, S., Fahn, S., & Frucht, S. (1998). Fetal tissue transplantation in Parkinson's disease. *Current Opinions in Neurology, 11*, 341–349.

Tarle, S. A., Davidson, B. L., Wu, V. C., Zidar, F. J., Seegmiller, J. E., Kelly, W. N., & Pelella, T. D. (1991). Determination of the mutations responsible for the Lesch–Nyhan syndrome in 17 subjects. *Genomics, 10*, 499–501.

Tate, B. G., & Baroff, G. S. (1966). Aversive control of self-injurious behavior in a psychotic boy. *Behavior Research and Therapy, 4*, 281–287.

Taylor, D. V., Rush, D., Hetrick, W. P., & Sandman, C. A. (1993). Self-injurious behavior within the menstrual cycle of women with mental retardation. *American Journal on Mental Retardation, 97*, 659–664.

Teixeira, N. A., Pereira, D. G., & Hermini, A. H. (1997). Effects of naltrexone and cross-tolerance to morphine in a learned helplessness paradigm. *Brazilian Journal of Medical and Biological Research, 30*, 775–782.

Tessel, R. E., Schroeder, S. R., Loupe, P. S., & Stodgell, C. J. (1995). Reversal of 6HD-induced brain catecholamine depletion after operant training. *Pharmacology, Biochemistry, and Behavior, 51*, 861–867.

Thelen, E. (1981). Rhythmical behavior in infancy: An ethological perspective. *Developmental Psychology, 17*, 237–257.

Thompson, T., Egli, M., Symons, F., & Delaney, D. (1994). Neurobehavioral mechanisms of drug action in developmental disabilities. In T. Thompson, & D. B. Gray (Eds.), *Destructive behavior in developmental disabilities: Diagnosis and treatment* (pp. 133–179). Thousand Oaks, CA: Sage Publications.

Thompson, T., Felces, D., & Symons, F. (2000). *Behavioral observations: Technology and applications in Developmental Disabilities*. Baltimore: Paul H. Brookes Publishing.

Thompson, T., & Gray, D. B. (1994). *Destructive behavior in developmental disabilities: Diagnosis and treatment*. Thousand Oaks, CA: Sage.

Thompson, T., Hackenberg, T., Cerutti, D., Baker, D., & Axtell, S. (1994). Opioid antagonist effects on self-injury in adults with mental retardation: Response form and location as determinants of medication effects. *American Journal on Mental Retardation, 99*, 85–102.

Thompson, T., Hackenberg, T. D., & Schaal, D. W. (1991). Pharmacological treatments for behavior problems in developmental disabilities. In *Treatment of Destructive Behaviors in Persons with Developmental Disabilities* (NIH Publication No. 91-2410, pp. 343–440). Washington, DC: U. S. Department of Health and Human Services.

Thompson, T., & Schroeder, S. R. (Eds.). (1995). Self-injury in developmental disabilities: Neurobiological and environmental mechanisms. *Mental Retardation and Developmental Disabilities Research Reviews, 1*(2).

Thompson, T., & Symons, F. (1999). Neurobehavioral mechanisms of drug action. In N. A. Wieseler, & R. H. Hanson (Eds.), *Challenging Behavior of Persons with Mental Health Disorders and Server Developmental Disabilities* (pp. 125–150). Washington, DC: American Association on Mental Retardation.

Thompson, T., Symons, F., Delaney, D., & England, C. (1995). Self-injurious behavior as endogenous neurochemical self administration. *Mental Retardation and Developmental Disabilities Research Reviews, 1*, 137–148.

Thoren, P., Asberg, M., Bertilsson, L., Mellstrom, B., Sjoqvist, F., & Traskman, L. (1980). Clomipramine treatment of obsessive–compulsive disorder: II. Biochemical aspects. *Archives of General Psychiatry, 37*, 1289–1294.

Tiefenbacher, S., Novak, M. A., Jorgensen, M. J., & Meyer, J. S. (2000). Physiological correlates of self-injurious behavior in captive, socially reared, rhesus monkeys. *Psychoneuroimmunology, 25*, 799–817.

Todorov, C., Freeston, M. H., & Borgeat, F. (2000). On the pharmacotherapy of obsessive–compulsive disorder: Is a consensus possible? *Canadian Journal of Psychiatry, 45*, 257–262.

Toke, L. A. (1909/1999). Flagellants (D. J. Potter, Trans.). *The Catholic encyclopedia* (Vol. 6), Robert Appleton Company. Online edition (1999), K. Knight, N. Obstat.

Touchette, P. E., MacDonald, R. F., & Langer, S. N. (1985). A scatter plot for identifying stimulus control of problem behavior. *Journal of Applied Behavior Analysis, 18*, 343–351.

Towle, A. C., Maynard, E. H., Criswell, H. E., Lauder, J. M., Joh, T. H., Mueller, R. A., et al. (1989). Serotonergic innervation of the rat caudate following a neonatal-6-hydroxydopamine lesion: An anatomical, biochemical and pharmacological study. *Pharmacology, Biochemistry, and Behavior, 34*, 367–374.

Triggle, D. J., & Janis, R. A. (1987). Calcium channel ligands. *Annals Review of Pharmacology and Toxicology, 27*, 347–369.

Trimble M. (1989). Psychopathology and movement disorders: A new perspective on the Gilles de la Tourette's syndrome. *Journal of Neurology, Neurosurgery, and Psychiatry, 17*, 90–95.

Trugman, J. M., Hubbard, C. A., & Bennett, J. P., Jr. (1996). Dose-related effects of continuous levodopa infusion in rats with unilateral lesions of the substantia nigra. *Brain Research, 725*, 177–183.

Turner, C., Panksepp, J., Bekkedal, M., Borkowski, C., & Burgdorf, J. (1999). Paradoxical effects of serotonin and opioids in pemoline-induced self-injurious behavior. *Pharmacology, Biochemistry, and Behavior, 63*(3), 361–366.

Turner, J. R. (1994). *Cardiovascular reactivity and stress: Patterns of physiological response.* New York: Plenum Press.

Turpin, G., & Clements, K. (1993). Electrodermal activity and psychopathology: The development of the palmar sweat index (PSI) as an applied measure for use in clinical settings. In J. Roy, W. Boucsein, D. C. Fowles, & J. H. Gruzelier (Eds.), *Progress in electrodermal research* (pp. 49–59). New York: Plenum.

Tursky, B., & Jamner, L. D. (1982). Measurement of cardiovascular functioning. In J. T. Cacioppo, & R. E. Petty (Eds.), *Perspectives in cardiovascular psychophysiology* (pp. 19–92). New York: Guilford Press.

Umansky, R., & Watson, J. S. (1998). Influence of eye movements on Rett stereotypies: Evidence suggesting a stage-specific regression. *Journal of Child Neurology, 13*, 158–162.

Ungerstedt, U. (1968). 6-Hydroxydopamine induced degeneration of central monoamine neurons. *European Journal of Pharmacology, 5*, 107–110.

Ungerstedt, U. (1971). Postsynaptic supersensitivity after 6-hydroxydopamine induced degeneration of the nigro-striatal dopamine system. *Acta Physiologica Scandanavica, 367*, 1–48.

Van der Kolk, B. A. (1997). The psychobiology of posttraumatic stress disorder. *Journal of Clinical Psychiatry, 58*, 16–24.

van Emmerik, R. E. A., Sprague, R. L., & Newell, K. M. (1993). Assessment of postural dynamics in tardive dyskinesia and developmental disability: Sway profile orientation and stereotypy. *Movement Disorders, 8*, 305–314.

Van Keuren, K. R., Stodgell, C. J., Schroeder, S. R., & Tessel, R. E. (1998). Fixed-ratio discrimination training as replacement therapy in Parkinson's disease: Studies in a 6-hydroxydopamine-treated rat model. *Brain Research, 780*, 56–66.

Vaughan, M. E., & Michael, J. (1982). Automatic reinforcement: An important but ignored concept. *Behaviorism, 10*, 217–227.

Verhoeven, W. M. A., & Tuinier, S. (1999). The psychopharmacology of challenging behaviours in developmental disabilities. In N. Bouras (Ed.), *Psychiatric and behavioural disorders in developmental disabilities and mental retardation*. New York: Cambridge University Press.

Verhoeven, W. M. A., Tuinier, S., van den Berg, Y. W. M. M., Coppus, M. W., Fekkes, D., Pepplinkhuizen, L., et al. (1999). Stress and self-injurious behavior: Hormonal and serotonergic parameters in mentally retarded subjects. *Pharmacopsychiatry, 32*, 13–20.

Visser, J. E., Bar, P. R., & Jinnah, H. A. (2000). Lesch–Nyhan disease and the basal ganglia. *Brain Research Reviews, 32*, 449–475.

Vollmer, T. R., Iwata, B. A., Zarcone, J. R., Smith, R. G., & Mazaleski, J. L. (1993). The role of attention in the treatment of attention-maintained self-injurious behavior: Noncontingent reinforcement and differential reinforcement of other behavior. *Journal of Applied Behavior Analysis, 26*, 9–21.

Vollmer, T. R., Marcus, B. A., & LeBlanc, L. (1994). Treatment of self-injury and hand mouthing following inconclusive functional analyses. *Journal of Applied Behavior Analysis, 27*, 331–344.

Vollmer, T. R., Marcus, B. A., & Ringdahl, J. E. (1995). Noncontingent escape as treatment for self-injurious behavior maintained by negative reinforcement. *Journal of Applied Behavior Analysis, 28*, 15–26.

Vollmer, T. R., Marcus, B. A., Ringdahl, J. E., & Roane, H. S. (1995). Progressing from brief assessments to extended experimental analyses in the evaluation of aberrant behavior. *Journal of Applied Behavior Analysis, 28*, 561–576.

Vollmer, T. R., & Vorndran, C. M. (1998). Assessment of self-injurious behavior maintained by access to self-restraint materials. *Journal of Applied Behavior Analysis, 31*, 647–650.

Wacker, D. P., Berg, W. K., Harding, J., & Asmus, J. (1996). A functional approach to dealing with severe challenging behavior. In S. B. Stainback, & W. C. Stainback (Eds.), *Inclusion: A guide for educators* (pp. 327–342). Baltimore: Paul H. Brookes Publishing.

Waddington, J. L., & Cross, A. J. (1978). Denervation supersensitivity in the striatonigral GABA pathway. *Nature, 276*, 618–620.

Wagstaff, J., Knoll, J. H. M., Fleming, J., Kirkness, E. F., Martin-Gallardo, A., Greenberg, F., et al. (1991). Localization of the gene encoding the GABA(A) receptor beta-3 subunit to the Angelman/Prader–Willi region of human chromosome 15. *American Journal of Human Genetics, 49*, 330–337.

Wahler, R. G., & Graves, M. B. (1983). Setting events in social networks: Ally or enemy in child behavior therapy. *Behavior Therapy, 14*, 19–36.

Walker, B. B., & Sandman, C. A. (1979). Influences of an analog of the neuropeptide ACTH 4-9 on mentally retarded adults. *American Journal of Mental Deficiency, 83*, 346–352.

Wall, P. D., & Melzack, R. (Eds.). (1994). *Textbook of pain* (3rd ed.). New York: Churchill Livingstone.

Walsh, B. W., & Rosen, P. M. (1988). *Self-mutilation: Theory, research, and treatment.* New York: Guilford Press.

Walter, A. S., Barrett, R. P., Feinstein, A. M., Mercurio, A., & Hole, W. T. (1990). A case report of naltrexone treatment of self-injury and social withdrawal in autism. *Journal of Autism and Developmental Disorders, 20,*169–176.

Waszczak, B. L., & Walters, J. R. (1984). A physiological role for dopamine as modulator of GABA effects in substantia nigra: Supersensitivity in 6-OHDA-lesioned rats. *European Journal of Pharmacology, 105,* 369–373.

Wehmeyer, M. L. (1991). Typical and atypical repetitive motor behaviors of young children at risk for severe mental retardation. *American Journal on Mental Retardation, 96,* 53–62.

Wei, E., & Loh, H. (1976). Physical dependence of opiate-like peptides. *Science, 193,* 1242–1243.

Weick, B. G., Engber, T. M., Susel, Z., Chase, T. N., & Walters J. R. (1990). Responses of substantia nigra pars reticulata neurons to GABA and SKF 38393 in 6-hydroxydopamine-lesioned rats are differentially affected by continuous and intermittent levodopa administration. *Brain Research, 523,* 16–22.

Weiner, W. J., Goetz, C., & Klawans, H. L. (1975). Serotonergic and antiserotonergic influences on apomorphine-induced stereotyped behavior. *Acta Pharmacologica Toxicologica, 36,* 155.

Weizman, R., Weitman, A., Tyano, S., Szekely, B. A., & Sarne, Y. H. (1984). Humoral-endorphin blood levels in autistic, schizophrenic, and healthy subjects. *Psychopharmacology, 82,* 368–370.

Weld, K. P., Mench, J. A., Woodward, R. A., Bolesta, M. S., Suomi, S. J., & Higley, J. D. (1998). Effect of tryptophan treatment on self-biting and central nervous system serotonin metabolism in rhesus monkeys (*Macaca mulatta*). *Neuropsychopharmacology, 19,* 314–321.

Whitehurst, G. J., Fischel, J. E., DeBaryshe, B., Caulfield, M. B., & Falco, F. L. (1986). Analyzing sequential relations in observational data: A practical guide. *Journal of Psychopathology and Behavioral Assessment, 8*(2), 129–148.

Whitman, B. Y., & Accardo, P. (1987). Emotional symptoms in Prader–Willi syndrome. *American Journal of Medical Genetics, 28,* 897–905.

Whitney, L. R. (1966). The effects of operant conditioning on the self-destructive behavior of retarded children. In *Exploring Progress in Maternal and Child Health Nursing Practice,* American Nursing Association, 1965 Regional Conference #3. New York: Appleton-Century-Crofts.

Widner, H. (1999). The case for neural tissue transplantation as a treatment for Parkinson's disease. *Advances in Neurology, 80,* 641–649.

Wieseler, N. A., Campbell, G. J., & Sonis, W. (1988). Ongoing use of an affective rating scale in the treatment of a mentally retarded individual with a rapid-cycling bipolar affective disorder. *Research in Developmental Disabilities, 9,* 47–53.

Wiethoff, L., Yoo, H., Napolitano, D., Jack, S., Peyton, R., Stewart, K., et al. (2000). *Interaction of risperidone and environment on aberrant behavior in persons with developmental disabilities.* 33rd Gatlinburg Conference Proceedings, San Diego, CA.

Wilhelm, S., Keuthen, N. J., Deckersbach, T., Engelhard, I. M., Fortes, A. E., Baer, L., et al. (1999). Self-injurious skin-picking: Clinical characteristics and comorbidity. *Journal of Clinical Psychiatry, 60,* 454–459.

Willemsen-Swinkels, S. H. N., Buitelaar, J. K., Nijhof, G. J., & van Engeland, H. (1995). Failure of naltrexone to reduce self-injurious and autistic behavior in mentally retarded adults. *Archives of General Psychiatry, 52,* 766–773.

Willemsen-Swinkels, S. H. N, Buitelaar, J. K., van Berchelaer-Onnes, I., & van Engeland, H. (1999), Brief report: Six months continuation treatment in naltrexone-responsive children with autism: An open-label case-control design. *Journal of Autism and Developmental Disabilities, 29,* 167–169.

Williamson, P. D. (1995). Frontal lobe epilepsy: Some clinical characteristics. In H. Jasper, S. Riggio, & P. Goldman-Rakic (Eds.), *Epilepsy and the functional anatomy of the frontal lobe* (pp. 127–152). New York: Raven Press.

Williamson, P. D., Spencer, D. D., Spencer, S. S., Novelly, R. A., & Mattson, R. H. (1985). Complex partial seizures of frontal lobe orgin. *Annals of Neurology, 18,* 492–504.

Wilson, J. M., Tarr, G. E., Mahoney, W. C., & Kelley, W. N. (1982). Human hypoxanthine-guanine phosphoribosyl-transferase. Complete amino acid sequence of the erythrocyte enzyme. *Journal of Biological Chemistry, 257,* 10978–10985.

Winchel, R. M., & Stanley, M. (1991). Self-injurious behavior: A review of the behavior and biology of self-mutilation. *American Journal of Psychiatry, 148,* 306–317.

Winkler, J. D., Callison, K., Cass, S. A., & Weiss, B. (1988). Selective down-regulation of D_1 dopamine mediated rotational supersensitive mice. *Neuropharmacology, 27,* 439–442.

Winkler, J. D., & Weiss, B. (1986). Reversal of supersensitive apomorphine-induced rotational behavior by continuous exposure to apomorphine. *Journal of Pharmacology and Experimental Therapeutics, 238,* 242–247.

Winter, D. A. (1979). *Biomechanics of human movement.* New York: Wiley.

Wise, S. P., & Rapoport, J. L. (1989). Obsessive–compulsive disorder: Is it a basal ganglia dysfunction? In J. L. Rapoport (Ed.), *Obsessive–compulsive disorder in children and adolescents.* Washington, DC: American Psychiatric Press.

Wong, D. C., Harris, J. C., Naidu, S., Yokoi, F., Marenco, S., Dannals, R. F., et al. (1996). Dopamine transporters are markedly reduced in Lesch–Nyhan disease in vivo. *Proceedings of the National Academy of Sciences, USA, 93,* 5539–5543.

Wong, D. F., Singer, H. S., Brandt, J., Shaya, E., Chen, C., Brown, J., et al. (1997). D_2-like dopamine receptor density in Tourette's syndrome measured by PET. *Journal of Nuclear Medicine, 38,* 1243–1247.

Wong, D. C., Singer, H., Marenco, S., Brown, J., Yung, B., Yokoi, F., et al. (1994). Dopamine transporter reuptake sites measured by [C11]WIN 35:428 PET imaging are elevated in Tourette's syndrome [Abstract]. *Journal of Nuclear Medicine, 35,* 130.

Wood, P. L., & Altar, C. A. (1988). Dopamine release in vivo from nigrostriatal, mesolimbic, and mesocortical neurons: Utility of 3-methoxytyramine measurements. *Pharmacological Reviews, 40,* 163–187.

Wooten, M. W. (1999). Function for NFkB in neuronal survival: Regulation of atypical protein kinase. *Canadian Journal of Neuroscience Research, 58,* 607–611.

Wright, M., & Hewlett, W. (1994). Neurobiology of obsessive compulsive disorder. *Comprehenive Therapy, 20,* 95–100.

Yang, T. P., Patel, P. I., Chinault, A. C., Stout, J. T., Jackson, L. G., Hildebrand, B. M., et al. (1984). Molecular evidence for new mutation at the HPRT locus in Lesch–Nyhan patients. *Nature, 310,* 412–414.

Yeh, J., Zheng, S., Howard, B. D. (1998). Impaired differentiation of HPRT-deficient dopaminergic neurons: A possible mechanism underlying neuronal dysfunction in Lesch–Nyhan syndrome. *Journal of Neuroscience Research, 53,* 78–85.

Yoder, P. J., & Fuerer, I. D. (2000). Qualifying the magnitude of sequential association between events or behaviors. In T. Thompson, D. Felces, & F. Symons (Eds.), *Behavioral observations: Technology and applications in developmental disabilities* (pp. 317–333). Baltimore: Paul H. Brookes Publishing.

Yokoyama, C., & Okamura, H. (1997). Self-injurious behavior and dopaminergic neuron syusem in neonatal 6-hydroxydopamine-lesioned rat: 1. Dopaminergic neurons and receptors. *Journal of Pharmacology and Experimental Therapeutics 280,* 1016–1030.

Yurek, D. M., Steece-Collier, K., Collier, T. J., & Sladek, J. R., Jr. (1991). Chronic levodopa impairs the recovery of dopamine agonist-induced rotational behavior following neural grafting. *Experimental Brain Research, 86,* 97–107.

Zaczek, R., Battaglia, G., Contrera, J. F., Culp, S., & De Souza, E. B. (1989). Methylphenidate and pemoline do not cause depletion of rat brain monoamine markers similar to that observed with methamphetamine. *Toxicology and Applied Pharmacology, 100,* 227–233.

Zammarchi, E., Savelli, A., Donati, M. A., & Pasquini, E. (1994). Self-mutilation in a patient with mucolipidosis III. *Pediatric Neurology, 11,* 68–70.

Zappella, M., & Genazzani, A. (1986). Girls with Rett syndrome treated with bromocriptine. *Wiener klinische Wochenschrift, 98,* 22.

Zarcone, J., Hellings, J., Crandall, K., Reese, R. M., Marquis, J., Fleming, K., et al. (2001). Effects of risperidone on aberrant behavior of persons with developmental disabilities: I. A double-blind crossover study using multiple measures. *American Journal on Mental Retardation, 106,* 525–538.

Zarcone, J. R., Iwata, B. A., Smith, R. G., Mazaleski, J. L., & Lerman, D. C. (1994). Reemergence and extinction of self-injurious escape behavior during stimulus (instructional) fading. *Journal of Applied Behavior Analysis, 27,* 307–316.

Zarcone, J. R., Rodgers, T. A., Iwata, B. A., Rourke, D. A., & Dorsey, M. F. (1991). Reliability analysis of the Motivation Assessment Scale: A failure to replicate. *Research in Developmental Disabilities, 12,* 349–362.

Zatsiorsky, V. M. (1997). *Kinematics of human motion*. Champaign, IL: Human Kinetics.

Zawia, N. H., Sharan, R., Brydie, M., Oyama, T., & Crumpton, T. (1998). Sp1 as a target site for metal-induced perturbations of transcriptional regulation of developmental brain gene expression. *Brain Research Developmental Brain Research, 107*, 292–298.

Zheng, W., Rampe, D., & Triggle, D. J. (1991). Pharmacological, radioligand binding, and electrophysiological characteristics of FPL 64176, a novel nondihydrophyridine Ca2+ channel activator, in cardiac and vascular preparations. *Molecular Pharmacology, 40*, 734–741.

Zigmond, M. J., & Hastings, T. G. (1998). Neurochemical responses to lesions of dopaminergic neuron: Implications for compensation and neuropathology. *Advances in Pharmacology, 42*, 788–792.

Zlotnick, C., Mattia, J. I., & Zimmerman, M. (1999). Clinical correlates of self-mutilation in a sample of general psychiatric patients. *The Journal of Nervous and Mental Disease, 187*, 296–301.

Zoghbi, H., Percy, A., Glaze, D., Butler, I., & Riccardi, V. (1985). Reduction of biogenic amine levels in the Rett syndrome. *New England Journal of Medicine, 313*, 921–924.

Zohar, A. H., Pauls, D. L., Ratzoni, G., Apter, A., Dycian, A., Binder, M., et al. (1997). Obsessive–compulsive disorder with and without tics in an epidemiological sample of adolescents. *American Journal of Psychiatry, 154*, 274–276.

Zukin, R. S., Sugarman, J. R., Fitz-Syage, G., Gardner, E. L., Zurkin, S. R., & Gintzler, A. R. (1982). Naltrexone-induced opiate receptor supersensitivity. *Brain Research, 245*, 285–292.

AUTHOR INDEX

Gilbert, S., 262
Gillberg, C., 174, 196
Giuffre, K. A., 196
Gius, D., 286
Gjedde, A., 273
Glass, L., 239, 240
Gluck, J. P., 19, 160
Goh, H., 13, 84, 99, 100
Gold, V. J., 79, 93–94, 119
Goldberg, S. R., 201
Goldberger, A. L., 238, 239, 240
Golden, R. N., 26
Goldstein, A., 192
Goldstein, M., 7, 172, 274
Golomb, D. H., 242
Gong, L., 284
Gonzalez, J. P., 201
Gordon, R. B., 257
Gordon, W. C., 117
Goren, E. R., 19, 82, 109, 191
Gorman-Smith, D., 120
Gottlieb, L., 82
Gottman, J. M., 115
Gottschalk, A., 239, 240
Gough, B., 196
Grabber, J. E., 155
Grabowski, J., 7
Grace, N. C., 106
Grandin, T., 17
Grau, J. W., 233
Graves, M. B., 113
Graybiel, A. M., 175, 177, 284
Gray-Silva, S., 210
Greenberg, F., 33
Greendyke, R. M., 116
Greenough, W. T., 152
Greenswag, L. R., 9
Grevert, P., 192
Griffin, J. C., 18, 150
Grisolia, S., 291
Groden, G., 116
Grunau, R. V. E., 230
Gruters, A., 203
Gualtieri, C. T., 8, 116
Guess, D., 106, 107, 117, 118, 134, 137
Gunsett, R. P., 229
Gupta, K. K., 201
Guroff, G., 255
Gutenson, W., 255

Hackenberg, T., 8, 87, 101, 199
Hagberg, B., 196

Hagopian, L. P., 15, 84, 96, 209
Haidara, C., 83
Hales, J., 84
Hall, S., 69
Halle, J., 106, 107
Hammock, R. G., 170, 287
Hanley, G., 84, 99
Hanzel, T. E., 86
Harder, S. R., 86
Harding, J., 7, 12, 13
Harlow, H. F., 5, 151, 152, 153, 172
Harlow, M. K., 5, 151, 153
Harper, V. N., 28, 241
Harris, J., 8, 79, 86, 87, 90, 166, 167, 191,
     196, 225, 249, 269–278
Hartgraves, S. L., 186
Hashimoto, T., 276
Hassett, J., 114
Hastings, T. G., 306, 307
Head, D., 118
Heffernan, K. S., 155
Heinz, A., 169
Heise, G. A., 107
Hellings, J., 5, 8, 10, 77, 107
Helton, K., 38
Herdegen, T., 285, 286
Herman, B. H., 8, 87, 199
Hermini, A. H., 233
Herpertz, S., 226, 227
Herrnstein, R. J., 141
Hetrick, W. P., 19, 87–88, 94, 102, 191,
     192, 196, 199, 210, 229, 233
Hewlett, W., 176
Hickman, C., 94, 135
Hile, M. G., 120
Hill, B. K., 69, 75
Hiroi, N., 285
Hirota, K., 292
Hitzemann, R., 196
Hobson, D. A., 262
Hoehler, E., 191
Hohn, R., 290
Hole, W. T., 200
Hollander, E., 27, 31, 32, 38
Hollis, I. R., 225
Holm, R. A., 152
Holson, R. R., 196
Hooper, M., 280, 291
Horn, R., 203
Horner, R. H., 7, 13, 15, 17, 20, 79,
     105–118, 142, 207
Hornykiewicz, O., 280, 281

Houlihan, D., 84
Howard, J. L., 114
Howard, R. S., 253
Hsiao, S., 182, 290
Huberman, B. A., 239
Huberman, H. S., 290
Huebner, R. R., 230
Hughart, L., 82
Hughes, A. J., 178, 304
Hughes, C. R., 209
Huston, J. P., 306
Hutt, C., 107
Hutt, S. J., 107
Hyson, R. L., 233

Incledon, T., 240
Iorio, L. C., 282
Ireland, M., 10
Isenhart, R. C., 199
Isley, E. M., 105, 108, 110, 117
Itil, T. M., 286
Ivanic, M. T., 83
Iversen, S. D., 172, 187
Iwamoto, E. T., 174
Iwata, B. A., 12, 13, 83, 84, 93–103, 105,
        106, 108, 109, 110, 117, 118–131,
        133, 191, 209, 231, 234, 235, 236
Izard, C. E., 230
Izenwasser, S., 304

Jacobs, B. L., 228
Jacobson, J. W., 69, 70, 135
James, A. L., 115
Jamner, L. D., 114
Janicki, R. S., 184
Janis, R. A., 292
Jankovic, J., 30, 34, 279, 281, 299, 301
Javitt, D. C., 283
Jenson, W. R., 210
Jinnah, H. A., 33, 36, 172, 249, 250,
        269–278, 280, 289–298, 300
Johnson, H. G., 262
Johnson, K., 26
Johnson, K. B., 285, 300
Johnson, W. L., 42, 85, 117, 120, 128
Jolly, D. H., 251, 257
Jones, H. R., 224–225
Jones, I. H., 182, 225
Jones, M. L., 110
Jorgensen, M. J., 155, 159
Joyce, J. N., 186, 281, 285, 291, 300

Kahng, S., 84, 95, 99, 100, 119–131, 205
Kalachnik, J. E., 86
Kalin, N. H., 160
Kalsher, M. J., 84, 94
Kanner, L., 5
Kanter, D. R., 116
Kantor, J. R., 113
Karin, M., 285
Karsh, K. G., 98, 135
Karson, C. N., 16, 166–167
Karsonis, C., 105
Kasim, S., 250, 289–298
Kassorla, I. C., 79, 93–94, 119
Kates, K., 15, 83
Kato, T., 276
Katsuragi, T., 291
Kauffman, D. W., 29
Kebbon, L., 69
Keith, E. F., 107
Keller, K. J., 137
Kelley, A. E., 187
Kelley, W. L., 259
Kelley, W. N., 251, 252, 255, 258, 280
Kelly, W. N., 185
Kemp, D. C., 14–15
Kemperman, I., 226, 227
Kendler, K. S., 167
Kennedy, C. H., 17, 18, 79, 133–143
Kerbeshian, J., 29
Kern, L., 83
Keyes, J. B., 191
Khan, Z., 250, 289–298
Kiley, M., 71
Killian, J. M., 30
King, B. H., 15–16, 38, 116, 163, 168–169,
        171, 176, 181–189, 231, 290
King, R., 239
Kinsey, J. H., 155
Kirman, B. H., 224
Kishi, G., 120
Kissi-Debra, R., 69
Kistner, J. A., 117
Kleene, B. M., 191
Klimek, V., 291
Klyklyo, W. M., 196
Knapp, D. J., 285
Knigge, U., 196
Knowles, T., 134
Koegel, L. K., 7
Koegel, R. L., 7, 191
Kogut, M. D., 259

Kokkinidis, L., 304
Konopka Lukas, Z. M., 228
Koppekin, A., 140
Korsgaard, S., 174
Koslow, S. H., 169
Kostrzewa, R. M., 284
Kovner-Kline, K., 38
Kraemer, G. W., 160
Krause, J. E., 284
Kravitz, H., 42, 145
Krieg, J-C., 223, 227
Krude, H., 203
Krug, A., 15
Kuehn, M. R., 280, 291
Kuhn, D., 206
Kulik, A. V., 175
Kulovich, S., 263
Kunko, P. M., 304
Kurumaji, A., 284
Kyrios, M., 33

Lacey, J., 226
LaChapelle, D. L., 230
Lader, M., 116
Lal, H., 87, 192
Lalli, E. P., 119, 231
Lalli, J. S., 13, 15. 83, 96, 98, 106, 119, 231
Lambert, D. G., 292
Lane, H., 4
Langdon, N. A., 14, 84
Langer, S. N., 14, 130
Lara-Lemus, A., 290
Lasagna, L., 290
Lash, P. S., 105
Lattal, K. A., 134
Lautenbacher, S., 223, 227
LaVecchio, F., 262
Lawless, M. R., 224, 225
Le, D. D., 100, 122
Leah, J. D., 285, 286
LeBlanc, L., 106
Leboyer, M., 196, 197, 204
Leckman, J. F., 16, 240, 246
Leckman, M. D., 34
Lees, A., 16, 27, 29, 225
Legacy, S. M., 96
Lennox, D. B., 124–125, 126
Lensing, P., 200
Leonard, H. L., 29
Leonard, J. V., 192

Lerman, D. C., 84, 98, 100, 105, 110, 120, 122
Lesch, M., 79, 251, 254, 269, 279, 289
Letts, R. M., 262
Levine, I. M., 29–30
Levine, M. S., 188
Lewin, A. B., 119–131
Lewis, M. H., 1, 6, 16, 21, 23–39, 71, 105, 106, 117, 160, 165–179, 210, 238, 241, 247
Lichstein, L., 138
Liebovitch, L. S., 239
Light, K. C., 114
Lindauer, S. E., 231
Lindberg, J. S., 95, 100
Linscheid, T. R., 105, 118
Listwak, S., 196
Lloyd, H. G. E., 249, 256, 273, 275, 291
Lloyd, K. G., 165–166, 283, 284, 299
Locke, B. J., 82
Lockshin, S., 109
Loh, H., 192
Lokwan, S. J. A., 307
Lonnerhom, G., 196
Looney, J. M., 29–30
Lott, D., 69
Lott, R. S., 170
Loughnane, T., 31
Loupe, J., 5, 77, 107
Loupe, P. S., 250, 299–308
Lourie, R. S., 6, 145
Lovaas, O. I., 6, 20, 79, 82, 93–94, 100, 109, 119, 135, 137, 140, 191, 231
Lubin, R., 71
Luby, E. D., 283
Luck, W., 203
Luiselli, J. K., 84, 105, 108, 110, 237
Lundervold, D., 85, 125, 126
Luquin, M. R., 304
Ly, J., 192, 193

Mace, F. C., 13, 14, 83, 88, 96, 97–98, 101, 106, 107, 116, 117, 119, 120, 135, 140
Mackey, M. C., 239, 240
MacLean, W. E., 16, 17, 167
MacLean, W. E., Jr., 13, 145
Madappuli, A., 223
Madden, J. I., 192
Madrid, A., 38, 170

Maestrini, E., 16
Magito-McLaughlin, D., 17
Mahler, M., 33
Maier, S. F., 233
Mailis, A., 225, 226
Mailman, R. B., 106, 169
Marcus, B. A., 99, 106
Marcus, S., 257
Maresca, M., 225
Marion, S., 192, 196
Marius, L. M., 159
Markowitz, P. I., 116
Marley, R. J., 201
Marsden, C. D., 36
Marshall, A. M., 109
Marshall, F. J., 36
Marshall, J. F., 185
Martin, G., 110, 118
Martin, J. L., 229
Martin, L., 160, 172
Maruff, P., 33
Mason, S. T., 183
Mason, W. A., 94, 138
Masuo, Y., 284
Mathews, A. L., 20, 29, 110, 112, 113, 115, 116
Mathur, A., 187
Matson, J. L., 69, 86, 120, 191, 237
Mattia, J. I., 31, 227
Mattson, R. H., 30
Matzen, S., 196
Mauk, J. E., 88, 101, 107, 116, 117
Maurice, P., 8
Mazaleski, J. L., 84, 99, 100
McCleary, R., 193
McCosh, K. C., 110
McCurley, C. M., 105
McDonald, G., 14, 130, 258
McDougle, C. J., 170, 173
McEwen, B. S., 174
McGimsey, J. F., 84, 100, 110
McGinnes, G. C., 230
McGrother, C., 27
McKerracher, D. W., 31
McNeil, J. R., 184
McQuiston, S., 135
Meikle, B., 15
Meinhold, P., 241
Melzack, R., 225, 226, 230
Mennesson, J. F., 117
Mennicken, F., 305
Menninger, K. A., 4, 5

Menzel, E. W., 19
Merrill, C. K., 239
Meyer, J. S., 159
Meyer, K. A., 17, 18, 134
Meyers, C. E., 5, 69
Michael, J., 94, 99
Migeon, B. R., 259
Miguel, E. C., 29
Mileson, B. E., 172
Miller, N. E., 108
Miller, R. E., 158
Miltenberger, R. G., 84, 125
Minana, M. D., 291
Mirsky, I. A., 158
Mitchell, G., 153
Modell, J., 176
Molenaar, P. C. M., 236
Molina, V. A., 184
Montastruc, P., 304
Moodley, M., 167
Moody, C. A., 186
Moore, K. E., 301
Mora, F., 196
Morgan, J. I., 285
Morpurgo, C., 291
Morren, J., 84, 120
Moukhles, H., 304
Moy, S. S., 283; 287, 291, 300
Mudford, O. C., 105
Mueller, K., 171, 182, 183, 184, 186, 188, 290
Mueller, R. A., 282
Mueller-Vahl, K. R., 169
Mulick, J. A., 229, 238
Munkvad, I., 181
Murphy, C., 106
Murphy, G., 69, 71, 72, 84, 145
Murray, A. D., 105
Musetti, L., 196
Musetti, M. C., 196
Mutti, A., 196
Myrianthopoulos, N. C., 5

Nausieda, P. A., 184
Naylor, G. J., 210
Neal, B. S., 300
Neal-Beliveau, B. S., 186, 285, 300
Newell, K. M., 28, 139, 163, 235–247
Newsom, C., 94, 106, 109, 135, 231
Niedert, P. L., 85
Nielsen, E. B., 304

Schuster, D. B., 116
Schwarting, R. K. W., 306
Schwartz, B., 109, 110, 118
Seegmiller, J. E., 251, 252, 255, 279
Segawa, M., 11
Sege-Peterson, K., 251, 257, 258, 260, 261
Selmeci, T., 223
Sevin, J. A., 86
Seys, D. M., 235
Shapiro, D., 114, 115, 116
Shea, M. C., 106, 231
Shearer, S. L., 31, 208, 227
Shearin, E., 226
Sheitman, B. B., 287
Shen, K., 201
Sherman, B. R., 5
Shimosato, K., 201
Shirley, M. J., 84
Shishido, T., 171, 290
Shore, A. B., 99
Shork, M. A., 242
Shoulberg, N., 38
Shouldon, I., 36
Shukla, S., 134
Shutt, D. A., 196
Sidman, M., 133–134, 136, 237
Sigafoos, I., 15
Silva, J. R., 210, 238
Silva-Gray, S., 238
Silverman, K., 109
Silverstein, F. S., 256, 279, 299
Simeon, D., 27, 31, 32
Simmons, J. Q., 6, 20, 82, 94, 100, 109, 191
Simon, G. B., 229
Simon-Soret, C., 167
Simson, P. E., 280, 285
Singer, H. S., 169
Singh, B. K., 184
Singh, N. N., 5, 135, 170, 237, 303
Sivam, S. P., 171, 184, 188, 189, 284, 290, 301
Skinner, B. F., 19, 95, 138, 139, 237
Slifer, K. J., 7, 83, 95, 122, 191, 235
Slifkin, A. B., 236
Smalley, S. L., 17
Smalls, Y., 69
Smit, G. C., 196
Smith, A. C., 33
Smith, A. I., 196
Smith, M., 191, 196, 203
Smith, R. D., 280

Smith, R. G., 84, 99, 100, 102, 105, 106, 108, 109, 110, 120, 122
Smith, S. G., 200, 201
Smith, S. H., 201
Smith, S. M., 94, 229
Snodgrass, S. R., 185
Snyder, A. M., 284
Snyder, R. G., 242
Snyder-Keller, A. M., 284
Soghomonian, J. J., 284
Soher, B. J., 276
Sokol, M. S., 290
Solomon, L. J., 110
Sonis, W., 210
Spear, L. P., 186
Spence, M. A., 191, 196, 203
Spencer, D. D., 30
Spencer, S. S., 30
Spengler, P., 124–125
Sperry, L., 247
Spicer, D. M., 160
Spitz, M. C., 30
Sprague, J. R., 142
Sprague, R., 28, 240, 241, 247
Stachowiak, M. K., 284
Standaert, D. G., 303, 304
Stanley, J. C., 76
Stanley, M., 86
Steege, M., 100
Steen, P. L., 116
Stein, D., 27, 31, 32
Stein, D. J., 38
Stein, L., 192
Sternberg, L., 120
Stewart, J., 20
Stewart, K., 20
Stodgell, C. J., 301, 302, 306, 307
Stone, T. W., 291
Stores, G., 18
Strick, P. L., 33–34
Sturmey, P., 85, 87, 88, 98
Sullivan, P., 196
Suomi, S. J., 152, 153, 154, 159, 172
Suri, R. E., 307
Surwillo, W. W., 112
Sutterer, J. R., 114
Sutton, K. A., 234
Swanson, J., 191
Swanson, V., 107
Sweet, W. H., 225
Sweetman, L., 252, 254, 255, 260, 261, 263
Swoboda, K. J., 224, 225

SUBJECT INDEX

5-Hydroxy-L-tryptophan, 171
5-Hydroxytryptophan, in Lesch–Nyhan
    syndrome, 262
Flagellants, 3
Fluoxetine, in physiological arousal, 116
Fluphenazine, in Lesch–Nyhan syndrome,
    265, 266, 274
Fragile X syndrome, 33, 34
Frontal cortex, self-biting behavior and, 187
Frontal-lobe seizures, SIB in, 30
Functional analysis, 79, 102–103
Functional assessment, 106, 117
    impact of, 119–131
    social negative reinforcement and, 126
Functional assessment procedures, 119
    classification of, 121–122
    endorsement of, 119–120
    for evaluation of treatment, 120
    functional analysis in, 130
    interobserver agreement on, 123
    literature search of, 124–126
    search methodology and, 121–123
    selection of treatment and, 120
Functional communication training, 14–15

GABA, dopaminergic and serotonergic
    neurons and, 16
γ-Aminobutyric acid, 173
Gastroesophageal reflux disease, self-
    injury associated with, 18
GBR-12909, 171, 188
    and pemoline, 184–185
Genetic disorders, self-injury and comor-
    bid behaviors in, 23–39
    SIB in, 33–34

Haloperidol, 182, 183
    in study of L-dopa-induced SIB, 282
Head, impact forces and, 247
    injuries to, SIB as cause of, 241–242, 247
Head hitting, 25, 26
Health conditions, contributing to SIB,
    17–19
Heart rate, increased, self-injury follow-
    ing, 20
    measurement of, in problem behavior,
    114–115
    reactivity of, individual patterns of, 115
Hematuria, in Lesch–Nyhan syndrome, 253
Heterozygotes, detection of, in
    Lesch–Nyhan syndrome, 258–259

Hogarth, William, 3
HPRT enzyme, deficiency of, in
    Lesch–Nyhan syndrome, 270, 279
    genetic deficit of, results of, 299
    in Lesch–Nyhan syndrome, 255, 259–260
    variants of, 259–260, 261
HPRT knockout mouse, 172
    as model for Lesch–Nyhan syndrome,
    291–292
HPRT Salamanca, 261
Huntington's disease, 36
Hypoxanthine phosphoribosyl-transferase.
    See HPRT.

Impact force(s), body weight and, 245
    head and, 247
Interdisciplinary research, need for, 118
Intervention strategies, environmental
    mechanisms and, 79–161
Interventions, based on physiological
    data, 116–117
    multicomponent approach to, 116
IQ, and SIB, 28–29
Isolation syndrome, 152

Knockout mouse, HPRT, 172
    as model for Lesch–Nyhan syndrome,
    291–292

L-Dopa, 172
    in Lesch–Nyhan syndrome, 281
    in Parkinson's disease, 281
    replacement therapy, in Parkinson's
    disease, 303
Learned behavior, extinction of, 99–100
Learning, respondent, 109
Lesch–Nyhan syndrome, 5, 28, 33, 34, 39,
    79, 84, 86, 175–176, 249–308
    aggressive self-mutilating behavior in,
    252–253, 270
    animals models of, 290–292
    BAY K 8644 model for, 291–292, 293
    behavioral abnormalities in, 299, 300
    behavioral management of, 305–306
    biochemical features of, 254–255
    calcium channels in, 292, 298
    case studies of, 261–266
    clinical characteristics of, 252–254
    computed tomography in, 271
    disorder of purine metabolism in, 251,
    254, 269

Methylxanthines, 173
in Lesch–Nyhan syndrome, 291
Missense mutations, in Lesch–Nyhan syndrome, 257–258
MK-801, 188, 189
Monkeys, captive, colonies, abnormal behavior in, 154–159
individually housed, SIB in, 172
Macaque. *See* Macaque monkeys.
Motor abnormalities, in Lesch–Nyhan syndrome, 269–278, 289–290
Movement disorders, 32
Muscimol, 187
in study of SIB in rats, 283

Naloxone, 102, 163, 174, 198, 201
Naltrexone, 10, 11–12, 102, 198–201
autism and, 199
effects of, on SIB following SIB, 202–203
in Lesch–Nyhan syndrome, 263–264
Negative-reinforcement hypothesis, 108–109
Neuroacanthocytosis, 30
Neurochemical dysregulation, in SIB, 15–16
Neuroimaging studies, in Lesch–Nyhan syndrome, 269–278
Neuroleptics, 87
Neurological disorders, SIB in, 29–30
Neurological features, for Lesch–Nyhan syndrome, 289, 290
Neuropathy, acquired, 224
sensory, congenital, patterns of SIB in, 224–225
Neurotransmitters, in Lesch–Nyhan syndrome, 256–257
New England Regional Primate Research Center (NERPRC), studies of macaque monkeys at, 154, 155–156, 159

Obsessive–compulsive disorder, 15–16, 25, 26, 29, 32
Obsessive–compulsive spectrum disorders, 168–169, 176
Olanzapine, 170–171, 237
Onychophagia, 27, 32, 168
Operant and respondent conditioning, 109
Operant functions, of SIB, 235
Operant learning approaches, in autism, 6
Opiate antagonists, in SIB, 102
treatment using, 231, 234
Opiate blockers, response to, endogenous opioid levels and, 201–203

SIB and, 198–201
Opiates, endogenous, 8
Opioid levels, endogenous, and response to opiate blockers, 201–203
Opioid peptides, 174
Opioid system, endogenous, SIB and, 195–204
Opioids, and maintenance of self-injurious behavior, 191–204
Otitis media, self-injury in, 17–18

Pain, aberrant experience of, disorders displaying, 223
definition of, 230
dysesthesia and, 226
elevated threshold of, SIB and, 191
insensitivity to, SIB in, 225
menstrual, escape-motivated self-injury in, 19
perception of, in psychiatric disorders, 227
reduced sensitivity to, in developmental disorders, 230
self-injury and, 223–234
Panic attack, 20
Parkinson's disease, 16, 36
dopaminergic function in, 178
dopaminergic neuronal depletion in, training-induced recovery from, 306–307
L-dopa in, 281
L-dopa replacement therapy in, 303
and Lesch–Nyhan syndrome, 280
pharmacological approaches to, 303–304
surgical approaches to, 304–305
Paroxetine, 171, 188
p-Chloroamphetamine, 182–183
p-Chlorophenylaline, 182–183
Pemoline, 171, 181
GBR-12909, 184–185
mechanism of action of, 184
self-biting behavior induced by, 181, 183, 185
pharmacology of, 182, 188–189
Perceptual reinforcement hypothesis, 137–138
of stereotypy, 135
Personality disorder, borderline, 31
SIB in, 227
Pharmacological treatment, prescriptive models in, hypothesis-driven, 86

Treatment(s), efficacy of, 122–123, 128–130
    selection for, 127–128
    types of, 122
Trichotillomania, 27, 31, 32, 168, 169

Ventrolateral striatum, of rat, stereotypy
    and, 187

Washington Regional Primate Research
    Center (WaRPRC), studies of
    macaque monkeys at, 154,
    156–157, 158
Weight, body, impact force and, 245

ABOUT THE EDITORS

Stephen R. Schroeder is Emeritus Professor and Director of the Schiefelbusch Institute for Life Span Studies at the University of Kansas. Currently he directs the KU Center for Excellence in Developmental Disabilities there. Dr. Schroeder received his PhD from the University of Pittsburgh in 1967. He is a fellow of the American Psychological Association, and he is past editor of the *American Journal on Mental Retardation* and co-editor of *Research in Developmental Disabilities* and of *Mental Retardation and Developmental Disabilities Research Reviews*. He has also served on numerous review panels at NICHD, NIEHS, EPA, and NIDRR. Dr. Schroeder's primary research interests are in biobehavioral interactions in development across the life span, with a focus on developmental neurobehavioral pharmacology and developmental neurobehavioral toxicology related to disabilities. He currently holds an NICHD-funded program project on severe aberrant behavior among people with mental retardation that explores the causes and remedies for aggression, stereotyped behavior, and self-injurious behavior. He has been involved with animal models and human studies of self-injury for over 30 years.

Travis Thompson is Director of the Institute for Child Development and Smith Professor of Psychiatry at the University of Kansas Medical Center. He was previously Director of the John F. Kennedy Center for Research on Human Development at Vanderbilt University, where he was recipient of the Earl Sutherland Prize of Vanderbilt University (1999), the highest recognition Vanderbilt provides for research scholarship. Dr. Thompson received his PhD in psychology (1961) from the University of Minnesota and held visiting positions at the University of Maryland (1961–1963), Cambridge University (UK) (1968–1969), and the National Institute on Drug Abuse (1978–1979). He is a Licensed Psychologist in Minnesota and Tennessee.

Mary Lou Oster-Granite received her PhD from Johns Hopkins University. She held faculty appointments at the University of Maryland School of Medicine and at the Johns Hopkins University School of Medicine in Baltimore, MD, before becoming a Professor of Biomedical Science at the University of California, Riverside. She is currently a Health Scientist Administrator for the Mental Retardation and Developmental Disabilities Branch of the Center for Research for Mothers and Children at the National Institute of Child Health and Human Development at the National Institutes of Health in Bethesda, MD. Dr. Oster-Granite is a developmental neurobiologist and neurovirologist with a long-standing interest in mental retardation and developmental disabilities. She has published extensively on neurobiological studies of animal models for various conditions such as Down syndrome, Alzheimer disease, cerebellar disorders, and inborn errors of urea metabolism.